RICHARD BENTLEY

Erotic Art

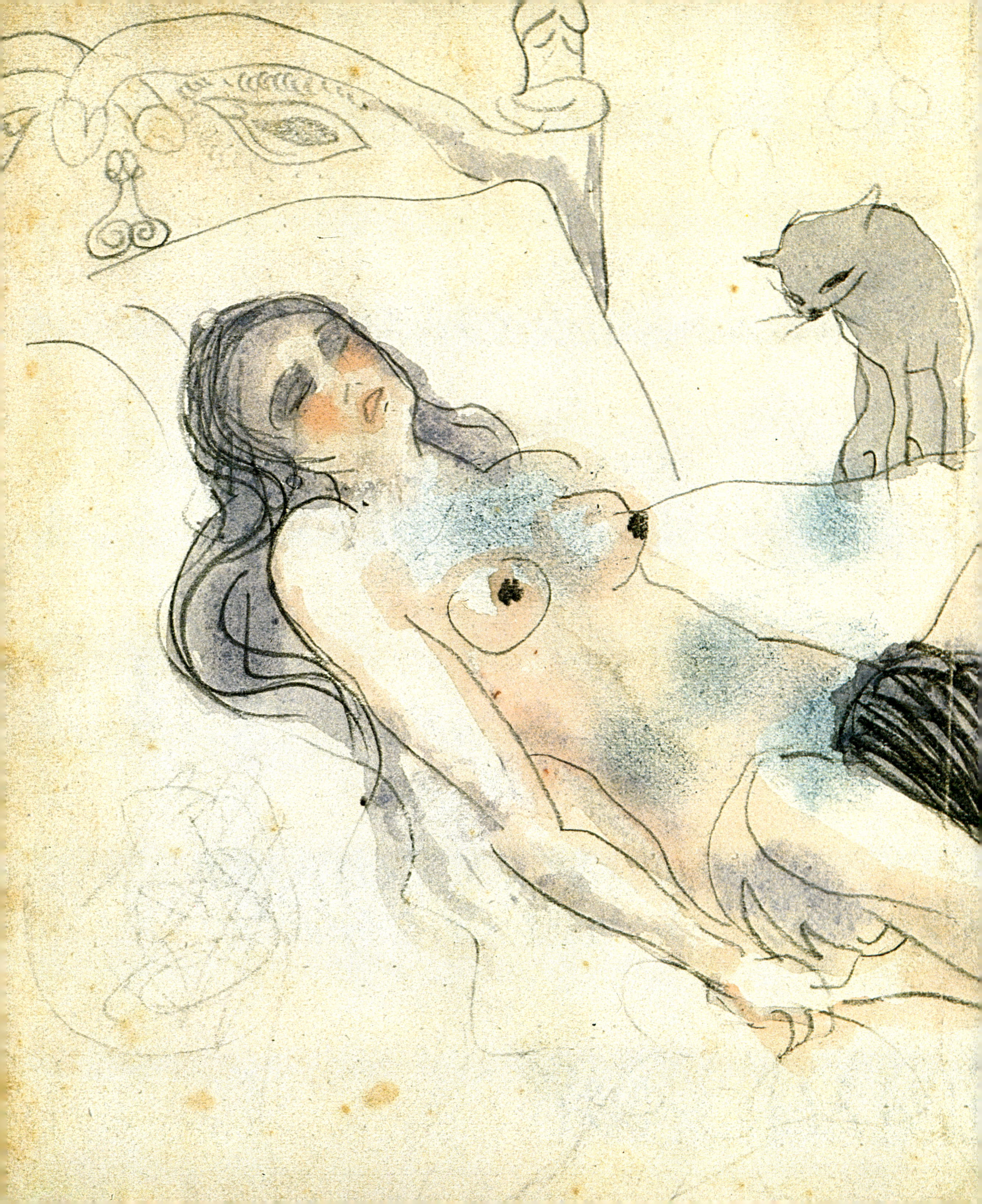

RICHARD BENTLEY

Erotic Art

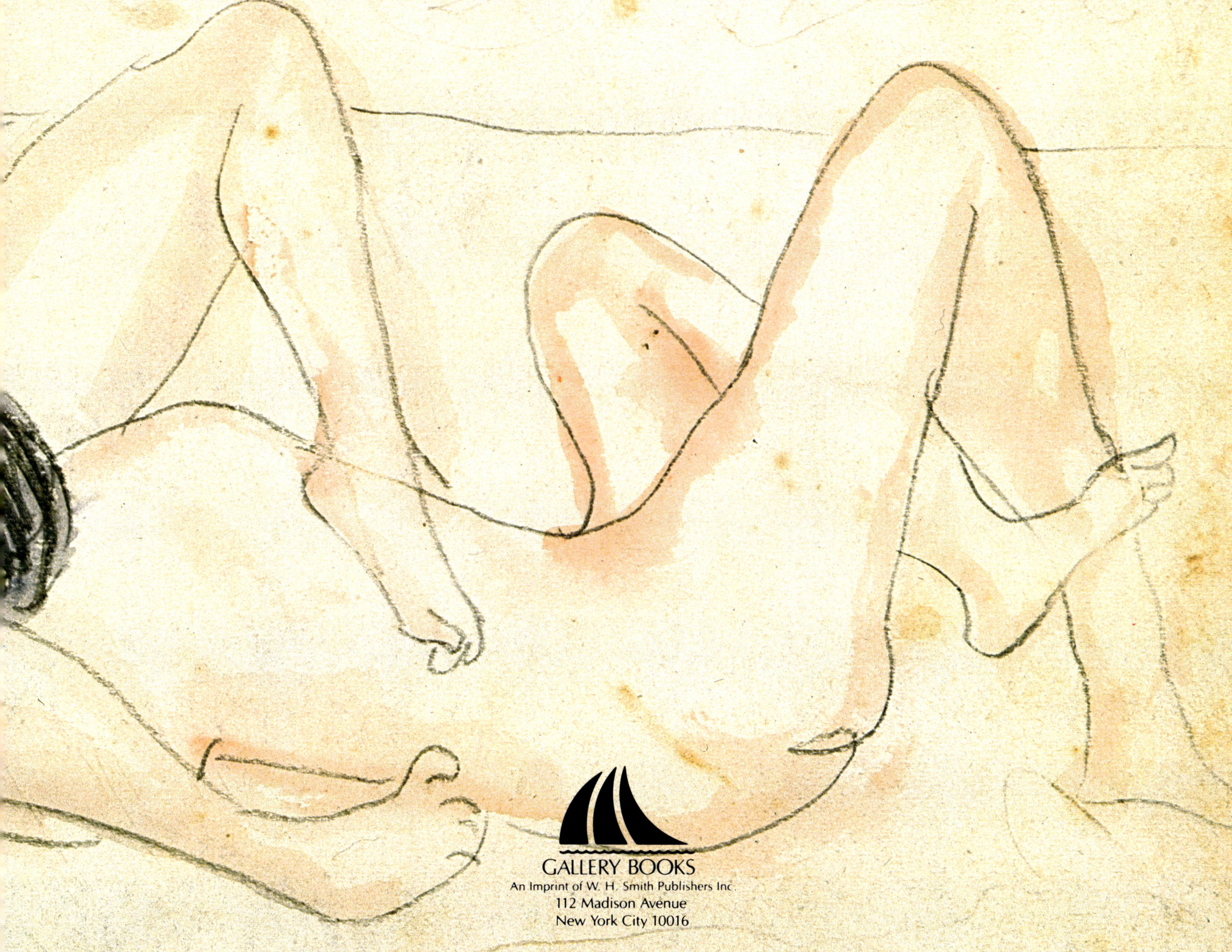

GALLERY BOOKS
An Imprint of W. H. Smith Publishers Inc.
112 Madison Avenue
New York City 10016

1 *(Title-page)* Pablo Picasso: *The Lovers and the Cat*. Pen and wash, 1902

Published by Gallery Books
An imprint of W.H. Smith Publishers Inc.
112 Madison Avenue
New York, New York 10016

This book was designed and produced by
John Calmann and Cooper Ltd, London

ISBN 0-8317-9403-8

Typeset by Black Box Graphics, Maidenhead, Berkshire

Printed in Hong Kong by Mandarin Offset Ltd

Contents

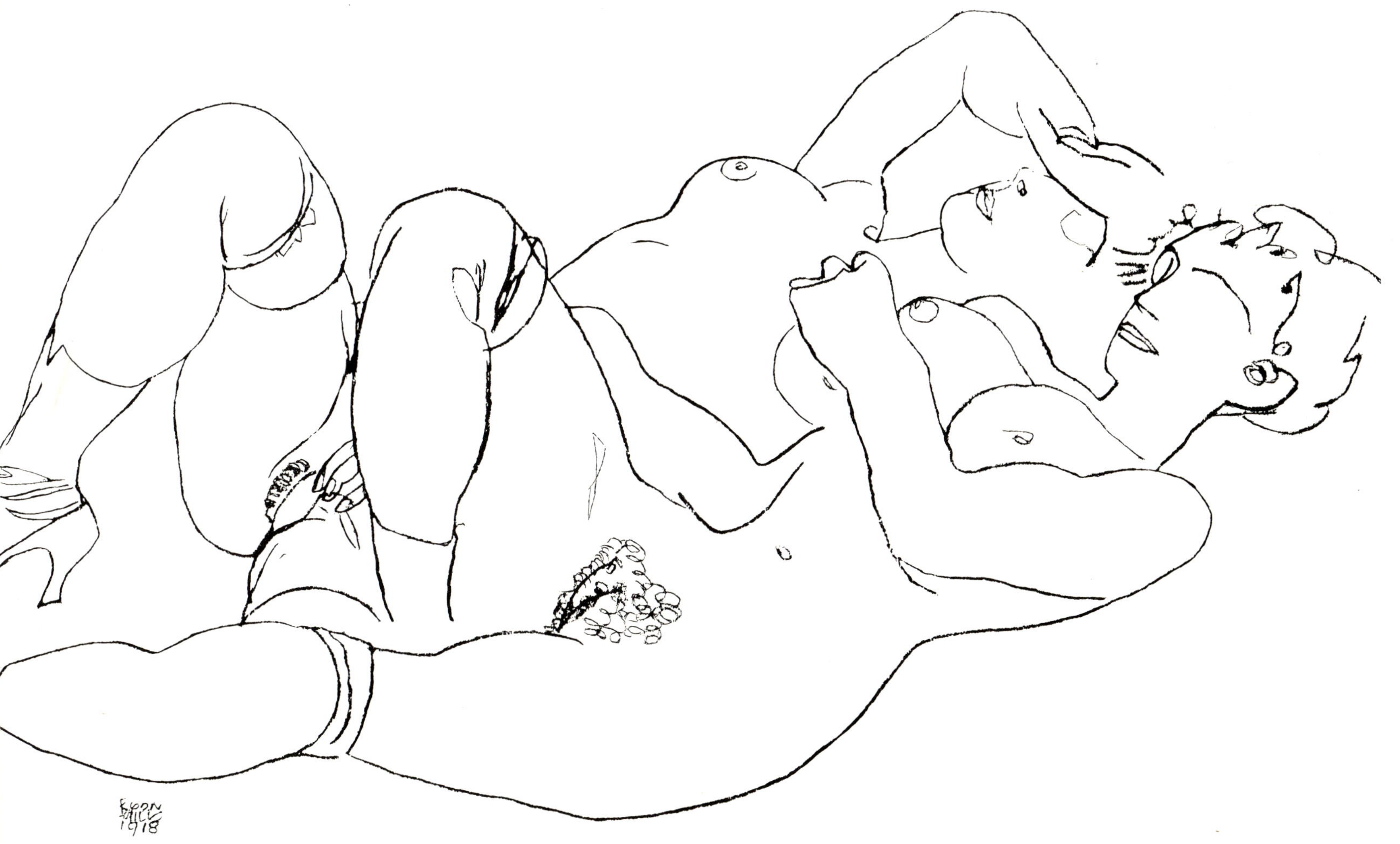

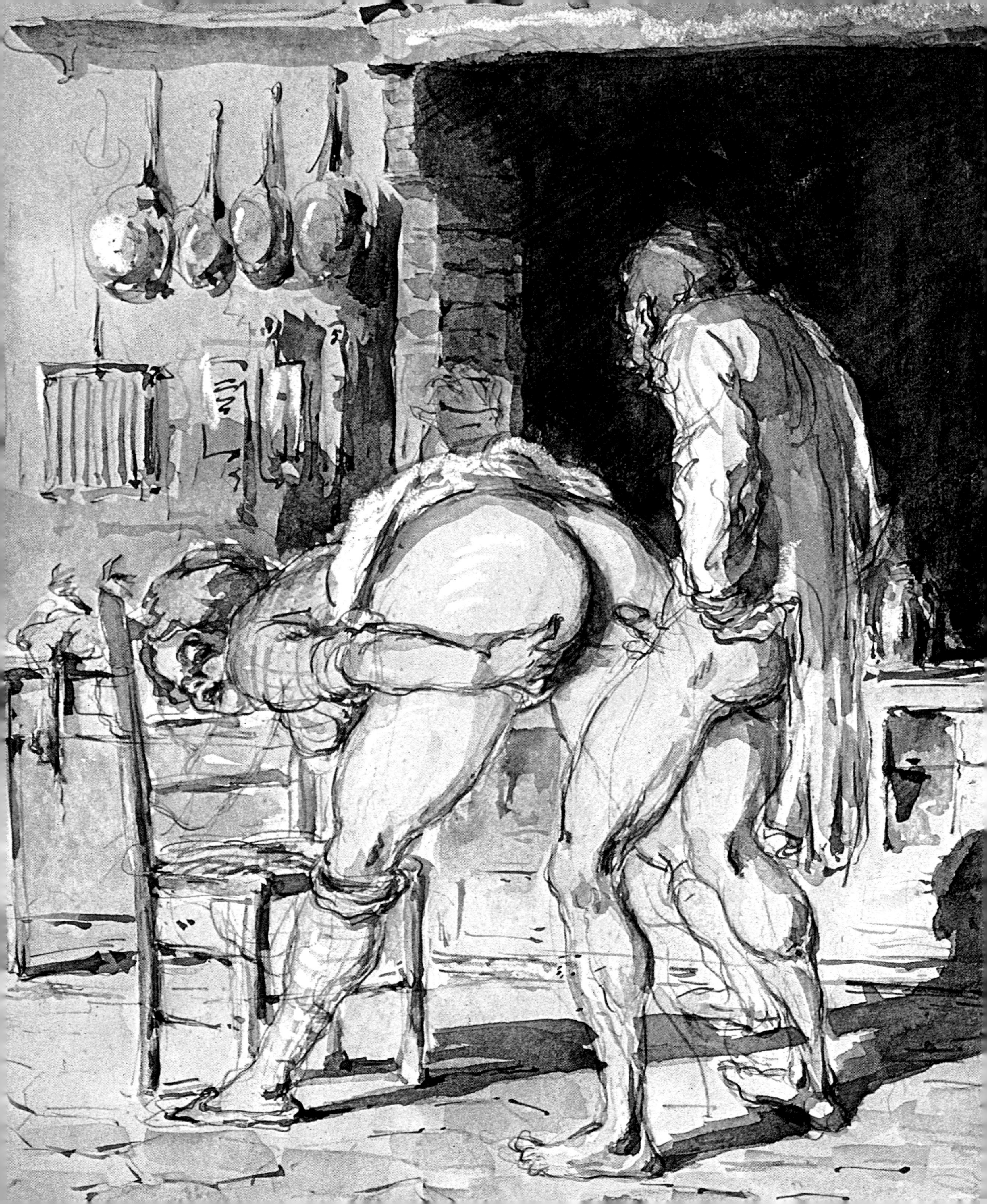

Preface

In every culture there has been a belief that at some time, far back in history, there was a 'Golden Age' when men and women, living in peace and prosperity, could give themselves up to the pursuit of pleasure, including the enjoyment of sex. In fact such times were rare, and most early men and women lived short, hard, brutish lives, while their powerful instinct to procreate filled them with strong emotions mixed with fear and awe. These evoked superstitions and a belief that the whole well-being of the community, particularly its fertility and that of its animals and crops, was dependent on its sexual conduct. In consequence sexual expression was strictly controlled. In these early days the work of the artist was more or less confined to producing phallic symbols, which frequently had a religious or magic significance.

With the dawn of civilization there was a change. Prosperity increased and, in an age with no inhibitions about sex, artists began to depict all forms of sexual pleasure. In the great days of Greece and Rome these themes were modified by a belief in the supreme beauty of the human body. The result was a period of increasingly skilful erotic art and of masterpieces of nude sculpture. When these civilizations were overthrown by the Barbarian invasions artistic skill declined, and the increasing power and influence of the Christian Church, with its belief in the sinfulness of sexual pleasure, inhibited artistic vision for hundreds of years. The forces which produced the Renaissance, together with the Reformation, liberalized thought and rekindled artistic interest in sexual subjects. From then until the present day artists all over Europe have included elements of eroticism in many of their masterpieces and a wide variety of these, some of which are very erotic indeed, are shown throughout this book.

2 Honoré Daumier: *In the Kitchen*. Watercolour, 1863. Lawrence E. Gichner, Washington DC

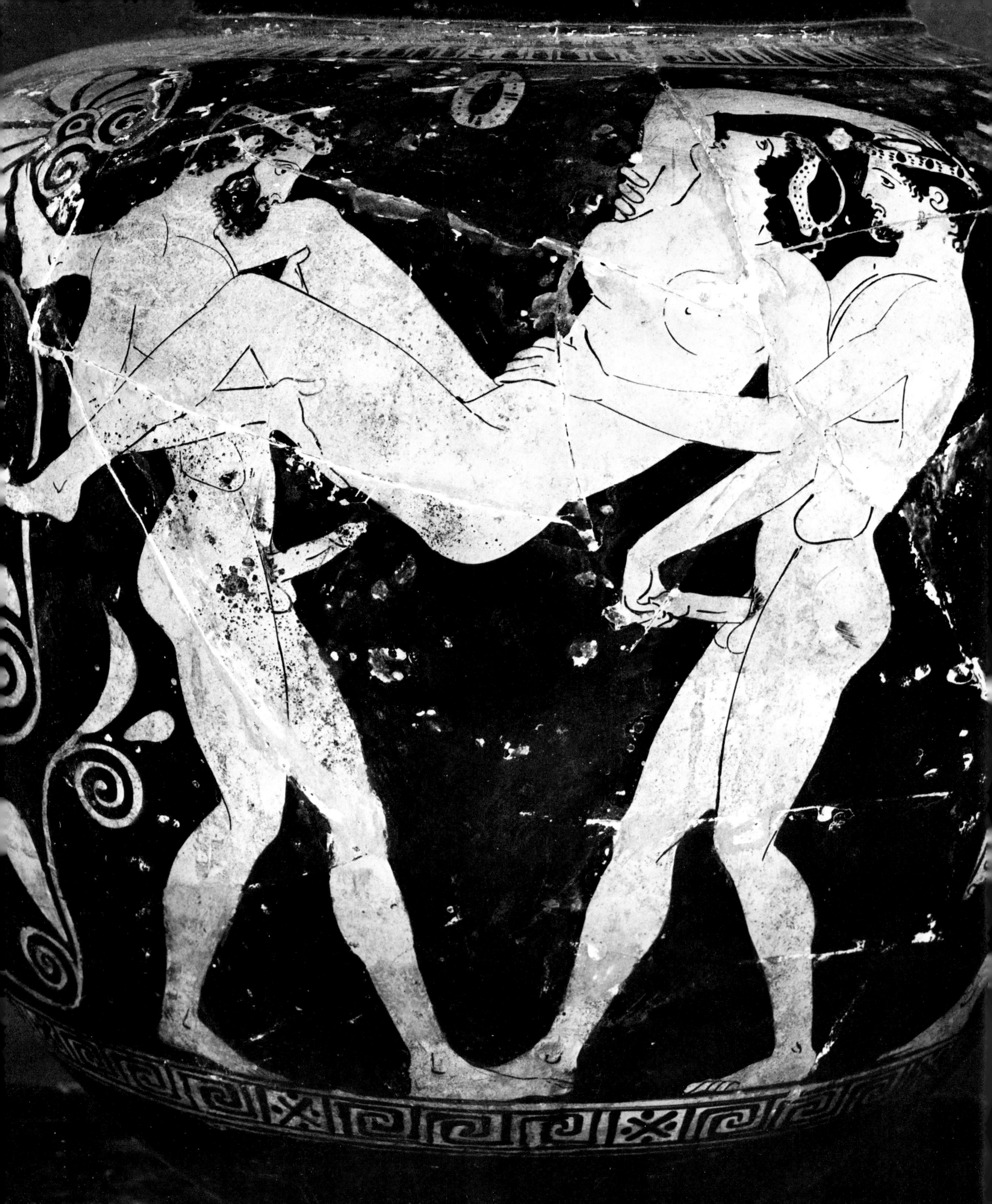

CHAPTER 1

The Classical World

The early history of Europe and the Mediterranean is still being explored by scholars. The works of Homer, Herodotus and other classical writers and the folklore and mythology that have been mostly transmitted by word of mouth give occasional, indistinct glimpses of the past, to which archaeologists have gradually added fragments of fact. Interpretation is difficult, but it has become clear that two main sources of civilization met and mingled about four thousand years ago.

From the Middle East and Asia Minor primitive Stone Age people, who had learned how to plant and grow their food and who therefore tended to make settlements and grow prosperous, gradually moved westwards by short sea passages to the islands of the Aegean Sea and to Crete. These relatively peaceful, farming communities, living in settled homesteads, were matriarchies: the procreation of children and the civilized comforts that women could provide made the mother figure of paramount importance. Her fertility and her womanly attributes could be seen to be vital for the community. Throughout a wide area there were mother goddesses with many different names. Statuettes of these were universally portrayed with large breasts, large buttocks, wide hips and quite frequently a pregnant abdomen. Some show the goddess exhibiting and drawing attention to her vulva as an indication of her fertility role. Remnants of this artistic expression of fertility continued through many centuries. Other figurines show simple, doll-like men and women, without any emphasis on their sexual characteristics. Those of the mother goddess may have had some erotic effect, but in the main they were probably the object of religious awe and respect for the fertility which they symbolized. Artistic remains from the focus of the matriarchal society in Crete, however, a great civilization that arose around the palace of Minos at Knossos, show little significant Minoan art of an erotic nature.

4 *Sheela-na-gig*. Stone carved corbel, 13th century. Kilpeck Church, Herefordshire, England

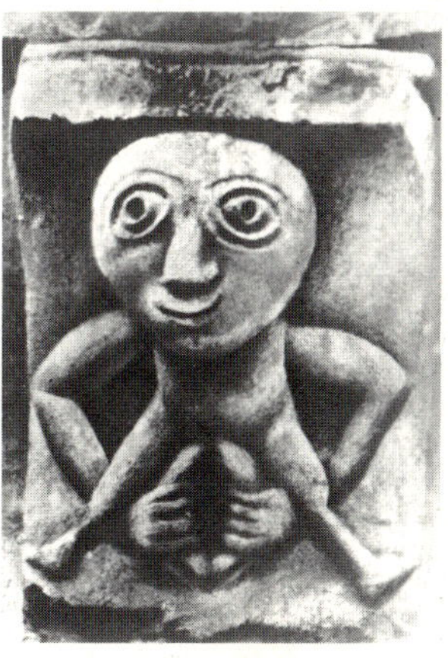

At the same time, from the great plains north of the Black Sea, nomadic hunting groups, who had domesticated the horse and used it as their means of transport, moved slowly west and south across the Danube towards the mountainous lands of Greece. The nature of their life and the need to hunt made them skilled in the arts of war, and they valued the courage, strength and virility of their men. They were a patriarchal society, with predominantly male gods who were

3 *Men with Prostitute*. Attic red-figure stamnos by Polygnotis, c.430BC. Louvre, Paris

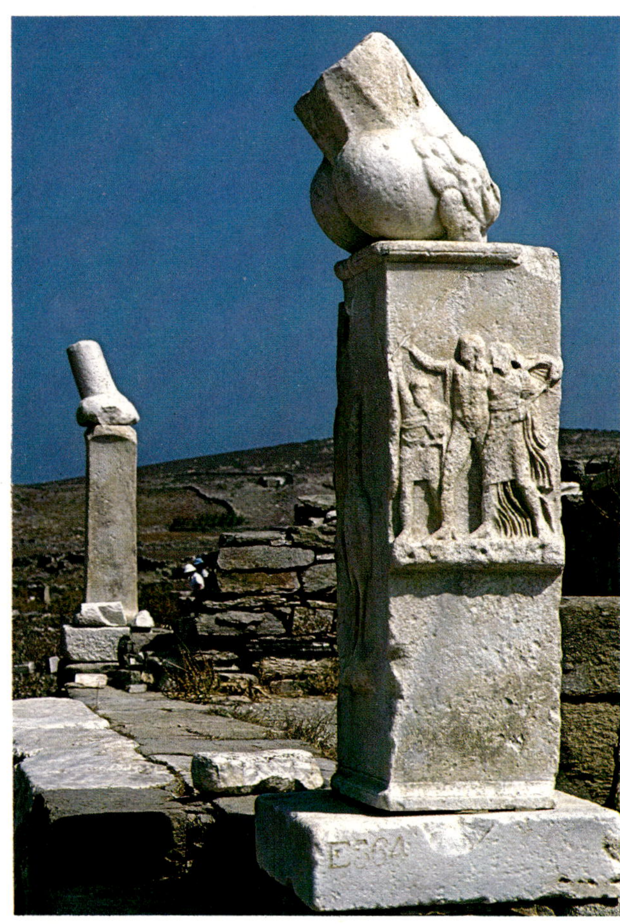

5 *Phallic monuments in the Avenue of Priapus*. Stone, 3rd century BC. Island of Delos, Greece

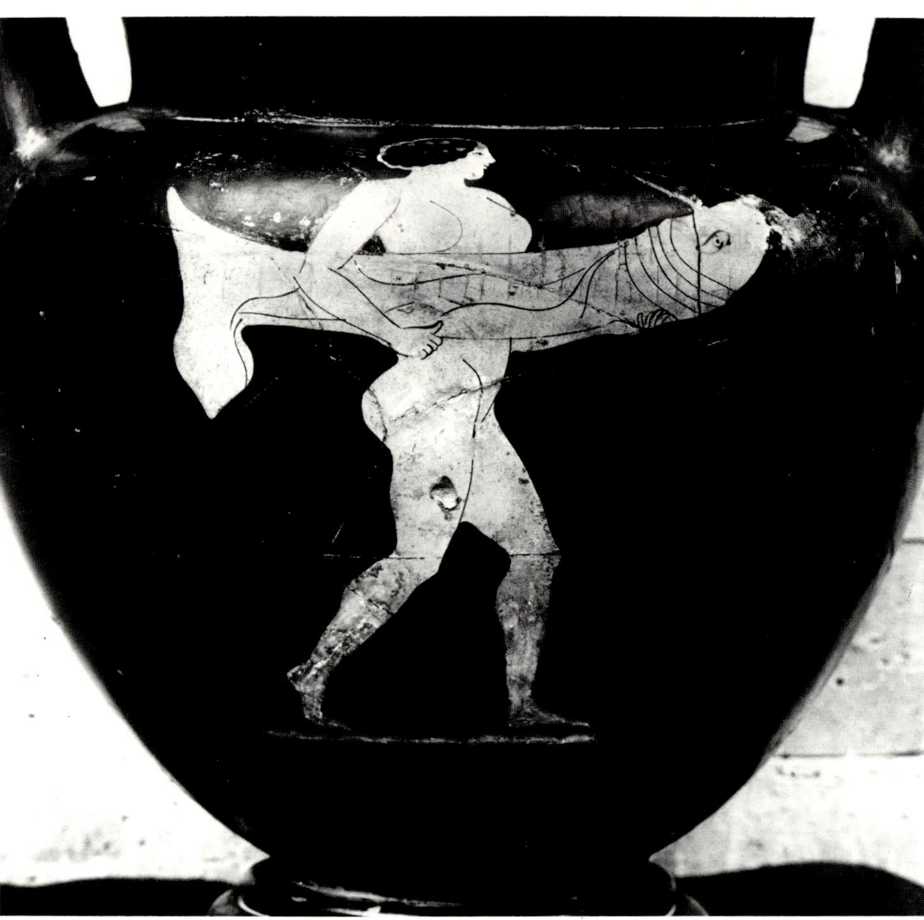

6 *Naked woman carrying model of giant phallus*. Column crater by the Pan Painter, Greece, c.530BC. Staatliche Museen, East Berlin

thought to live in the mysterious peaks of distant mountains. When these nomads reached Mount Olympus it naturally came to be regarded as the abode of Zeus.

In Southern Greece, where these warlike northern people met and mingled with a southern farming community, a powerful civilization formed at Mycenae. It overran and destroyed the Minoan civilization about 1450 BC, only to be conquered in its turn about 1100 BC by a further wave of Greek-speaking warriors from the north who were to found Greek city-states all over the eastern Mediterranean. This was a male-dominated society, but many of the goddesses of the Minoan and Mycenaean pantheon were taken over and added to those of the Greeks, as were also many of the ancient myths and superstitions concerning fertility and religious rites designed to ensure the success of each community. Ancient ceremonies, which in matriarchal times had been secret and confined entirely to women, were now widened to admit men and, in the name of the god Dionysus, became drunken, sexual orgies. There were religious processions in which enormous models of the phallus were carried, painted with an eye. The eye itself was regarded as a strong protection against a malignant 'evil eye' and phallus and eye together were thought to bring good luck, to promote fertility and to protect against calamity. A painting

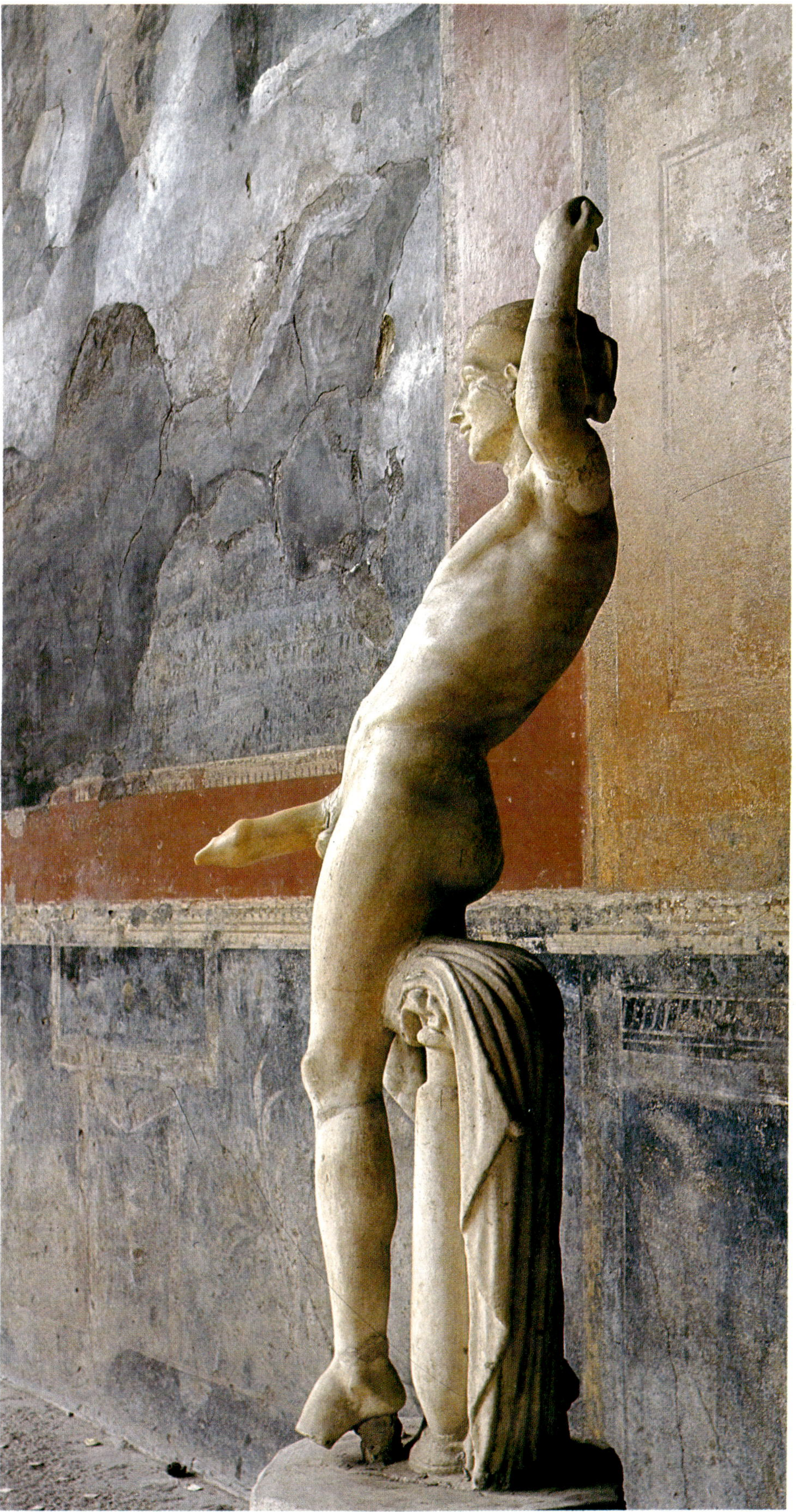

7 *Fountain in the form of an ithyphallic figure* (the phallus serving as a waterspout). House of the Vettii, Pompeii

on an Attic vase of 500 BC shows a nude woman carrying a phallus. It would have caused no surprise but merely approval, since in such ceremonies the priestess or the acolyte was often nude and it would not have been thought erotic. The magical, protective power of the erect phallus was taken for granted for hundreds of years before this picture; in many parts around the Mediterranean today there are people who believe in the evil eye and ward it off with phallic amulets and phallic gestures with the fingers. Plate 5 shows the Avenue of Priapus at Delos, which is decorated with huge phallic monuments of stone. Far from being shocked at seeing what they regarded as a normal part of the human body, the people who saw such monuments regarded them with religious awe.

Outside the religious context, the actors in Aristophanes' comedy *Lysistrata* were regarded with hearty amusement when they appeared on stage with exaggeratedly enlarged phalluses, as were those in the comic scene from the play *Iris* by Archaios in which a Silenus, with similar make-up, is trying to grab a priestess of Dionysus. A comic painting on one side of an amphora (illustrated)

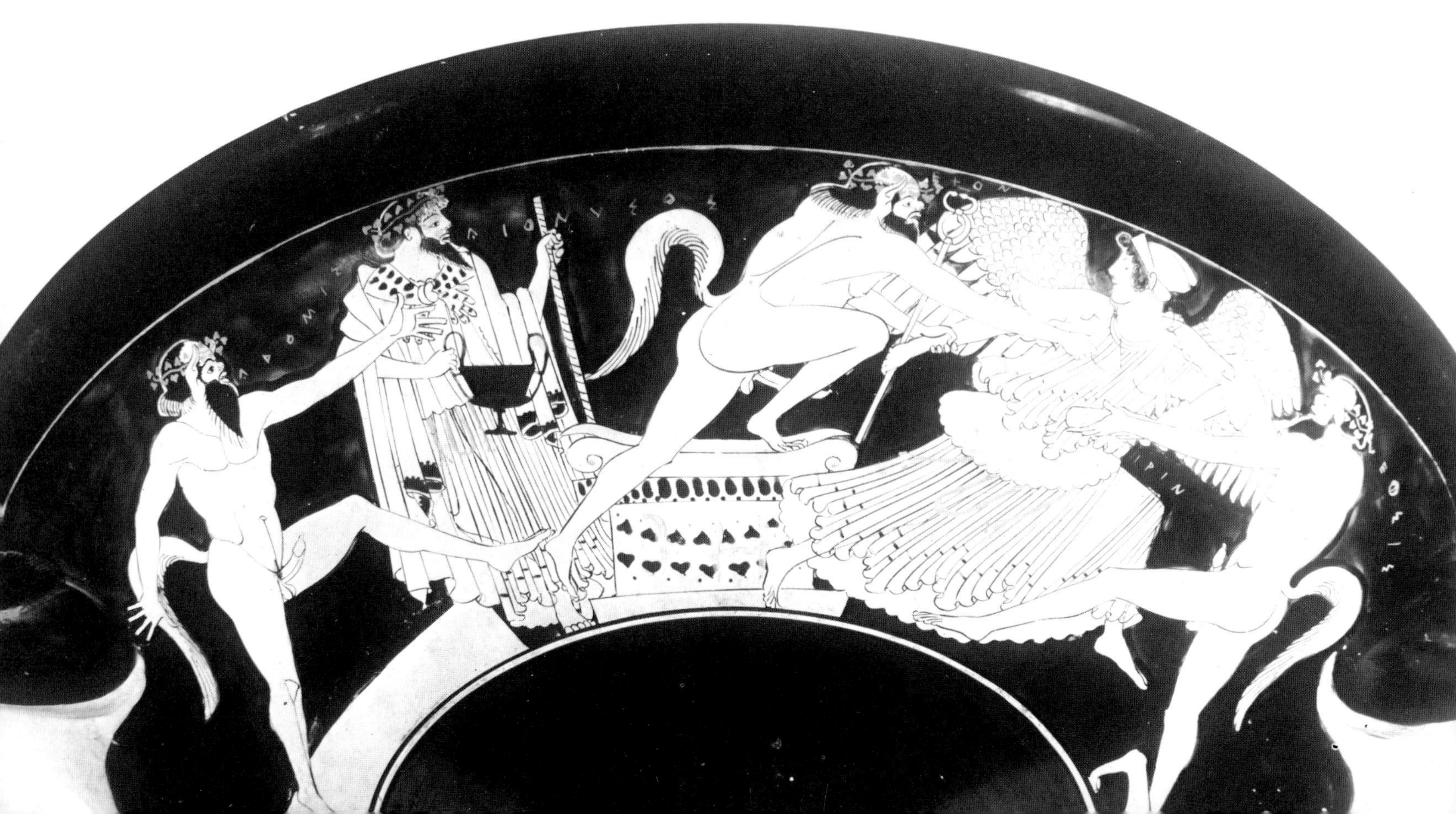

8 *Scene from the Iris of Archaios*. Attic bowl, Greece, 5th century BC. British Museum

shows a satyr masturbating an enormous phallus. A similar picture on its opposite side shows another satyr sadly eyeing an equally large but flaccid organ. The people of archaic Greece were an earthy, bawdy population who were not offended by natural functions and who thoroughly enjoyed phallic humour.

The influx into the already developed civilization of Mycenae of a highly intelligent people with great powers of organization led to the rapid development of one of the greatest cultures the world has ever seen. The technique of every craft increased with prosperity; the rivalry between different city-states maintained the athleticism of the men and their prowess in the martial arts. Each community knew that its life and freedom was dependent on the strength and courage of its warriors and the states themselves were sufficiently small for each man of talent to be known, to be recognized and to be heeded. By 500 BC the idea of democracy displaced the tyranny of previous chieftains.

The ancient Greeks considered sexual pleasures of every kind as highly desirable, life-enhancing experiences. Indeed, they thought that every man ought to take such pleasures wherever he could find them. It is true that most men preferred to use the professionally trained prostitutes or, if they could afford it, one of the celebrated courtesans, who were considered to be imbued with almost divine gifts. However, there were many other opportunities for heterosexual activity outside marriage, including those offered by religious prostitutes. Men were not expected to confine their attentions solely to their wives.

The position of the married woman had sunk to a very low ebb. The mother figure, in times gone by, had borne and reared the children and had also provided all the comforts in the homes of agrarian societies. She was now living in a society where men preferred to spend most of their time with other men, outside their home. A prosperity considerably dependent on slave labour enabled the men to engage in athletic pursuits, intellectual discussions or sometimes in battle. The home had become an expensive social obligation to provide men with a mechanism for rearing children. The Greek poet Palladas summed it all up by his cynical epigram, 'Marriage brings a man only two happy days: the day he takes his bride to bed and the day he lays her in her grave.' As Demosthenes

9 *Masturbating Satyr.* Black painted amphora, 6th century BC. Staatliche Museen, East Berlin

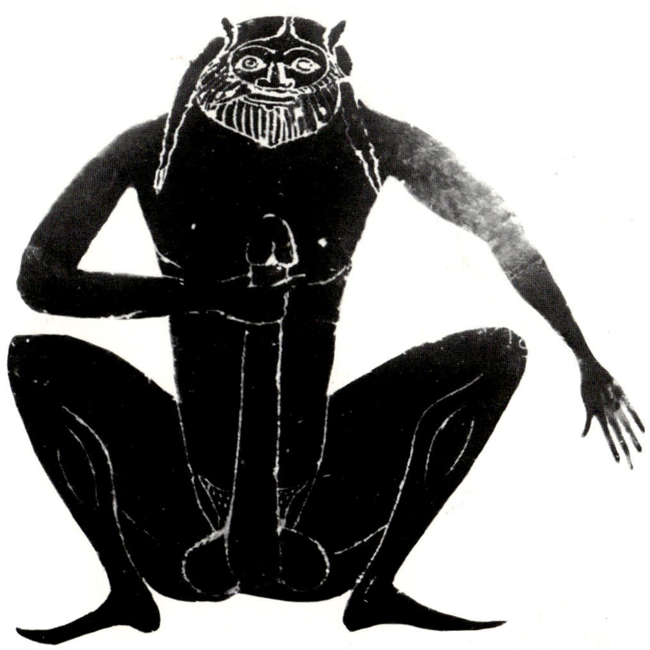

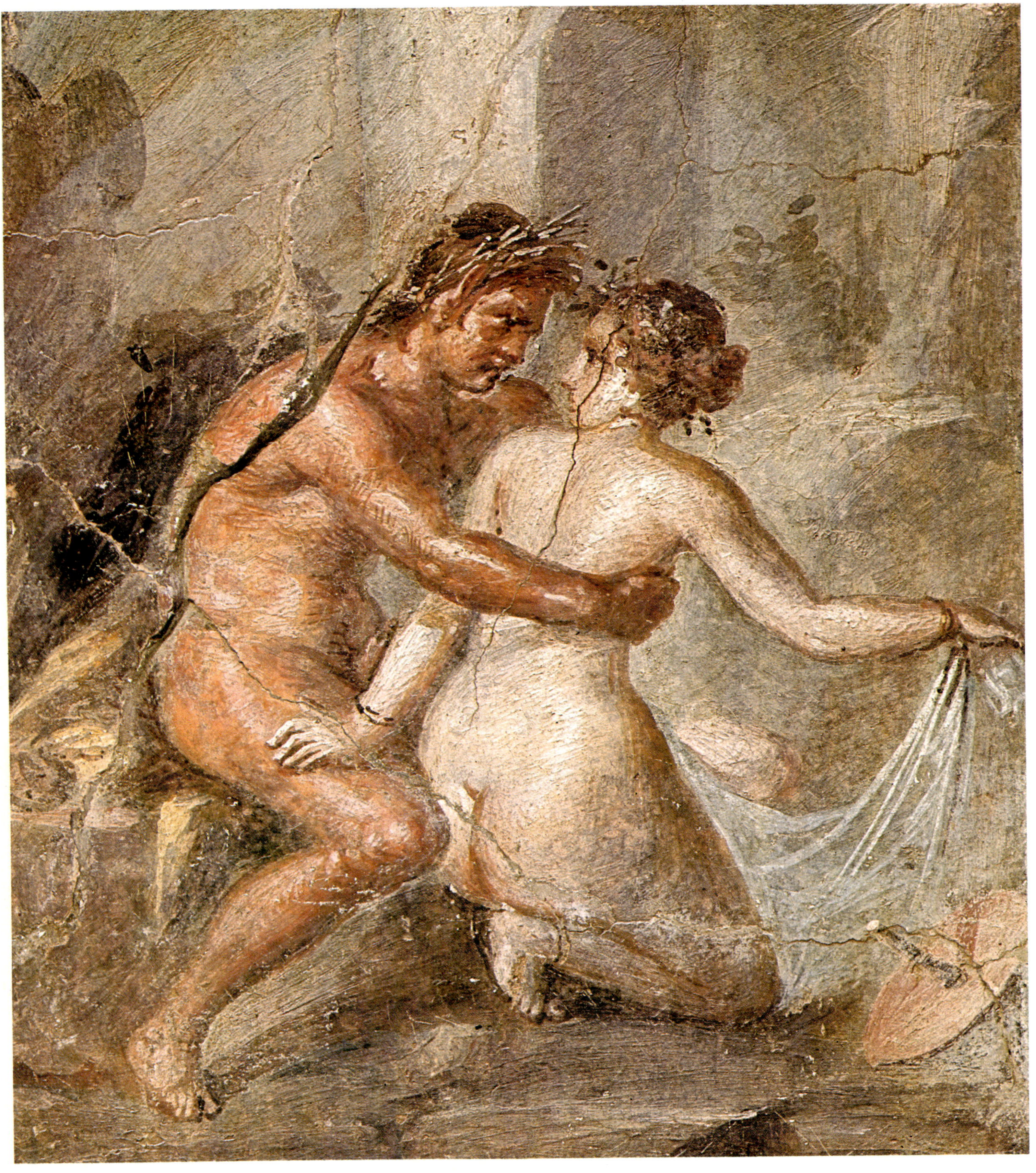

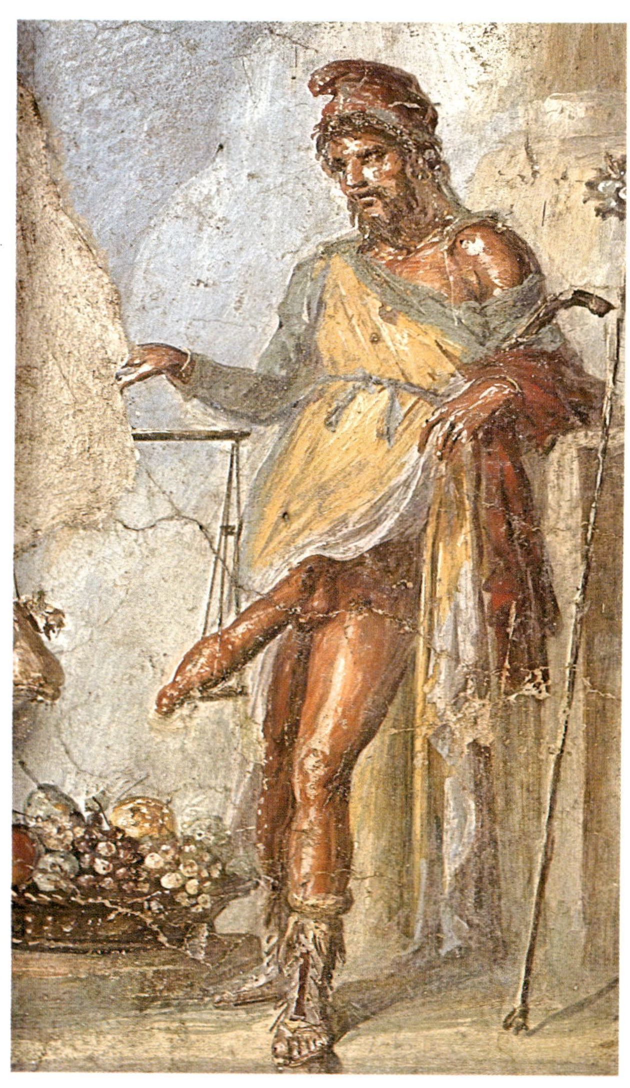

10 *Satyr and Maenad*. Wall painting from the House of the Epigrams, Pompeii, 1st century AD. National Museum, Naples

11 *Priapus weighing his phallus*. Fresco from the House of the Vettii, Pompeii, 1st century AD

put it, in a court oration, 'Mistresses we keep for pleasure, concubines for daily attendance upon our person and wives to bear us legitimate children and to be our housekeepers.' These were over-simplified statements, but nevertheless women were not in general educated to be companions for men but mainly to look after the households. On the other hand, as the play *Lysistrata* shows, the housewife had many ways of keeping her husband at home, and there are many individual stories of great affection and devotion between husband and wife.

The Greeks, who had won and kept their freedom and authority by the strength and courage of their fighting men, admired an athlete. Watching the competitors at the games or in the gymnasium, men acquired a passionate appreciation of the naked human body. In Greece there was also a special form of homosexuality. From archaic times there had been a traditional military grouping of pairs of warriors with an older, more experienced soldier training the younger man. The two would become comrades in arms who would support and encourage each other in any situation. To this end they were expected to establish sexual relations to create an additional bond. History records the exploits of famous groups composed of these two-man units, which showed superb fighting qualities and in which no man was prepared to shame his comrade. In later and more peaceful times, it became fashionable among the ordinary heterosexual male community for men to acquire a connoisseur's appreciation of beautiful adolescent boys as well as an appreciation of good wine, good poetry and the merits of different courtesans. Mature men were expected to become the patrons of young boys and teach them philosophy, ethics and other subjects which, in general, would lead them in the ways of civilized life. In many cases men would show all the symptoms of an infatuation for some handsome youth, of a kind usually associated with men in love with women. It was realized, however, that the feelings would only be transient and that they would only last until the boy's beard began to grow. Some who praised such relationships, including Plato in his later books, were against overt homosexual practices, but these undoubtedly occurred quite frequently. Homosexual relationships between mature men also took place, as in other communities, but these were quite a separate phenomenon.

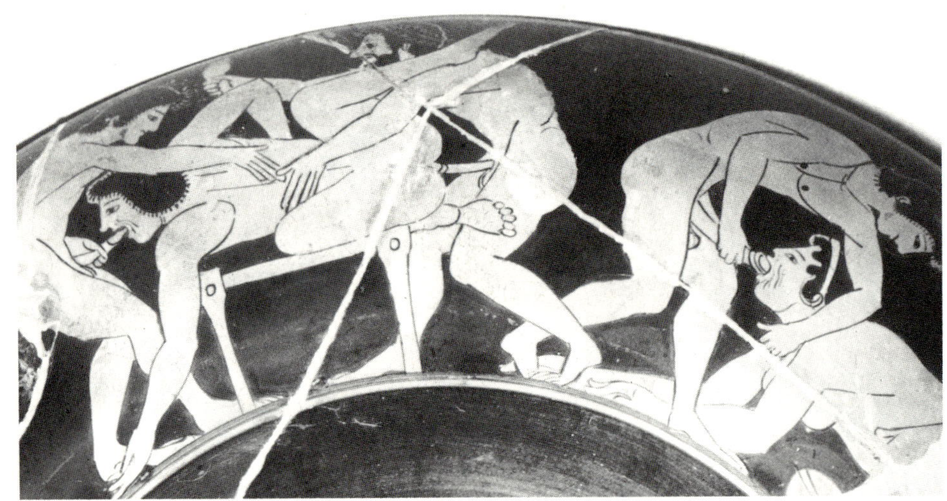

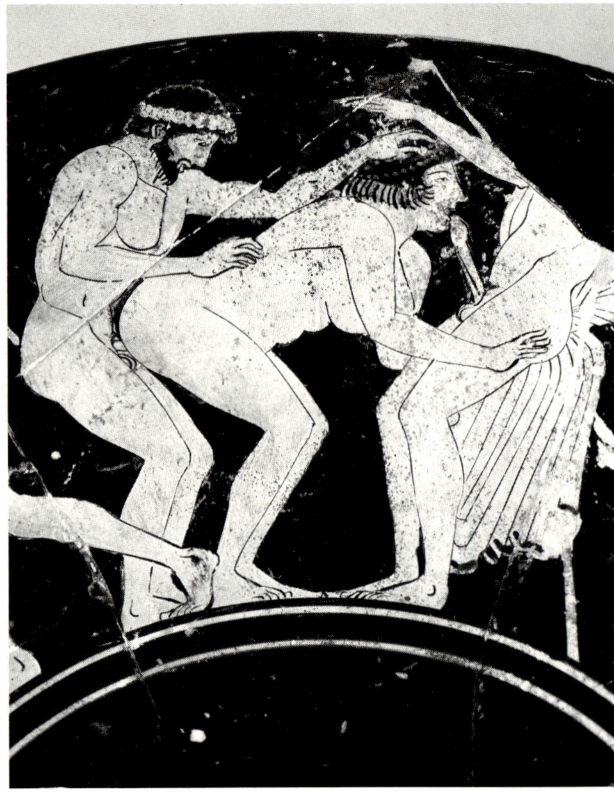

12 *Orgy Scene.* Greek cup painted by Pedeius, 5th century BC. Louvre, Paris

To artists a beautifully proportioned body became the image of divine perfection. Their early attempts to paint or sculpt their mental vision were stiff, stylized and lifeless figures. Gradually they learned how to imbue these with a relaxed, natural grace and with perfect proportions. By doing so they created a standard of bodily beauty which has never been surpassed. From time to time it was forgotten and other styles of beauty took its place, but it has always been rediscovered.

The Greek civilization reached its peak about 500 BC, when its cultural and political achievements attained near-perfection. At least for its aristocracy, life was intellectually and physically exciting, and men lived it to the full. In the evenings the Symposium with talk, wine and finally the services of highly trained prostitutes or courtesans provided the fashionable entertainment. Most of the paintings and sculpture of the period have perished, but one durable art form remains. For the well-to-do customer ceramic objects of high quality were produced, decorated with paintings by named and celebrated artists. Many of these have been found and have provided fascinating glimpses of the life of those days. Among them are some with erotic pictures.

Plate 3 is on the side of a large vessel. Others, particularly during the period of thirty years either side of 500 BC, were painted on the sides of wine bowls. More often they were placed on the inside or the outside of the round base of a wine cup, where they could be seen

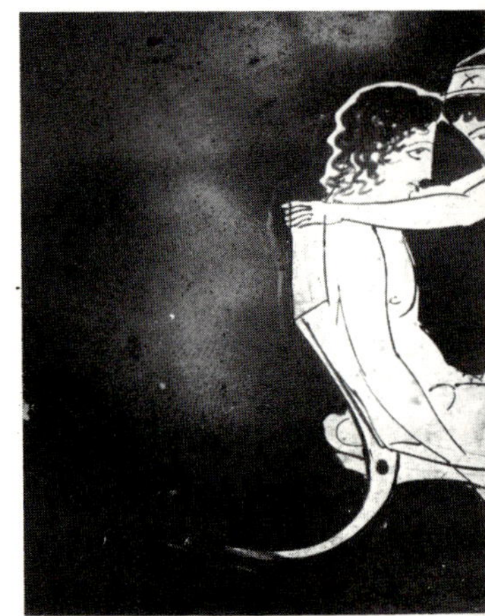

13 *(Top) Erotic Group.* Detail from red-figure cup by the Brygos Painter, c.480BC. Museo Archeologico, Florence

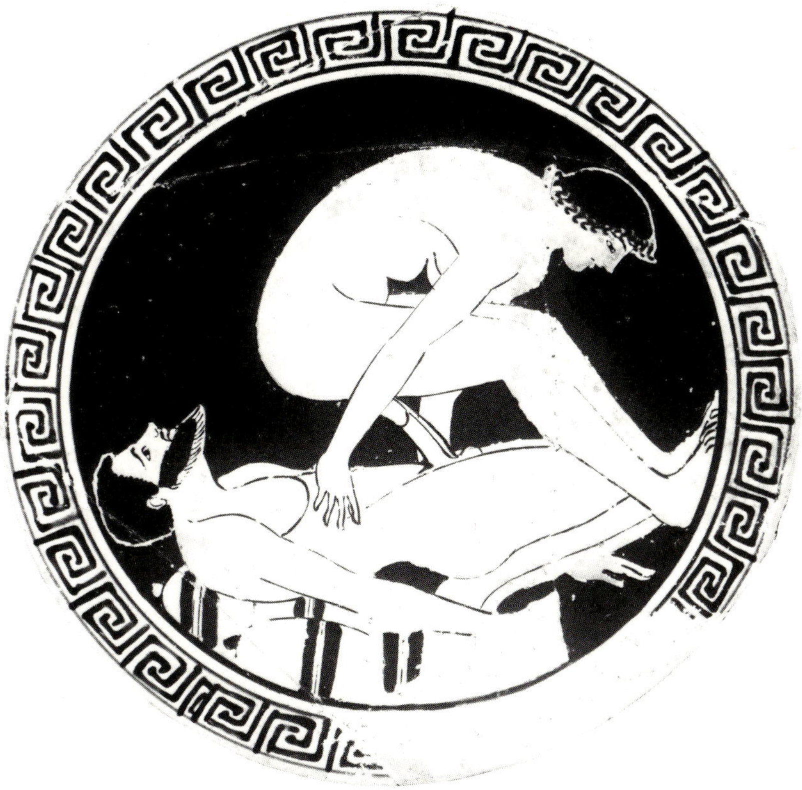

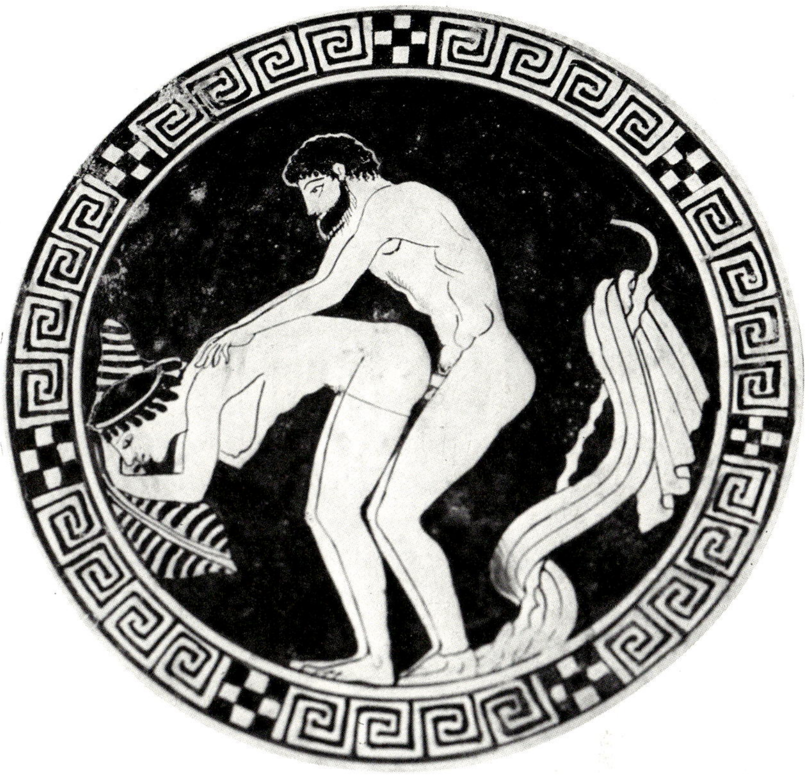

15 *(Above left) Courtesan and Client*. Attic cup, 5th century BC. British Museum

16 *(Above) Erotic Scene*. Attic red-figure cup by the Briseis Painter, c.470BC. Museo Nazionale, Tarquinia, Italy

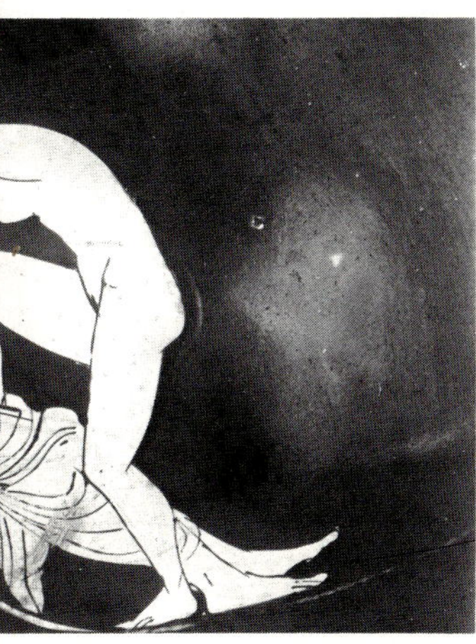

14 *(Above) The Lovers*. Red-figure scene on a jug by the Shuvalov Painter, c.420BC. Antiken Museum, West Berlin

when the cup was empty. Plates 15 and 16 are examples which show intercourse between a man and a prostitute in various positions. Erotic painting on circular shapes was a highly developed art form, and the pictures are skilfully composed with the figures expertly placed so that the act is explicit: to show this posed a difficult problem for the artists to solve. Usually, as in these examples, the man is mature, the girl much younger and there is no suggestion of any affection between them. A painting on the side of a jug has become famous because it shows a rather charming couple who are both young, who are looking into each other's eyes and give the impression that they are in love.

Satyrs were mythical wild creatures of the woods, half-man and half-beast, who chased after their female counterparts, the maenads, whenever they had the opportunity. Almost always the maenad would refuse their advances, and a crestfallen satyr was a subject for humour. Plate 17 shows a maenad repulsing one with a thyrsus, a pole capped with a pine-cone. There is also a very skilful engraving on the front of what would once have been the highly polished surface of a bronze mirror.

Erotic art of this kind was not confined to mainland Greece and it was either exported to or made in surrounding countries. One of these was Etruria in northern Italy. No one is certain where the Etruscans came from, but they appear by the eighth century BC. At that time they were more powerful than the Romans and were greatly

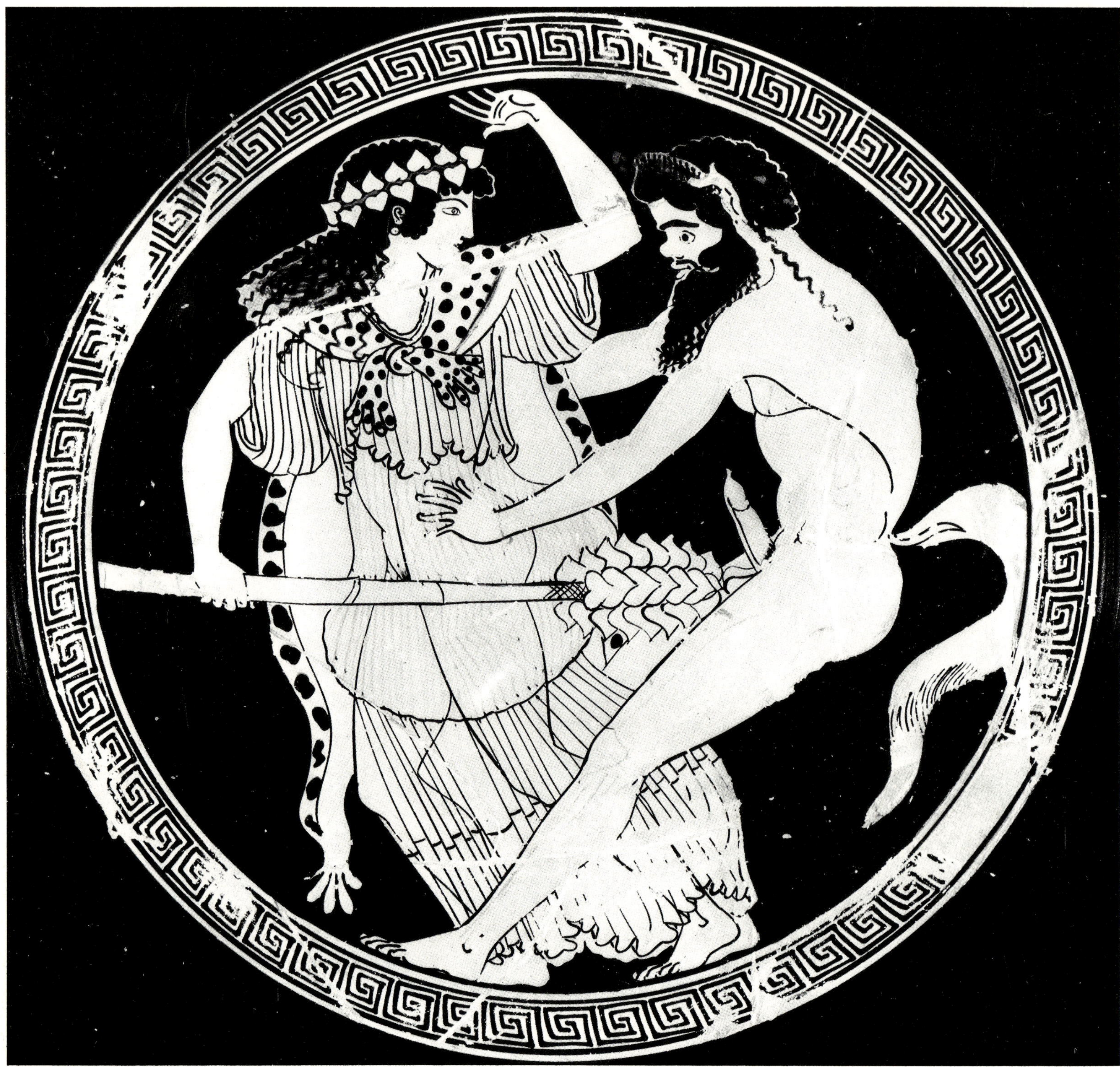

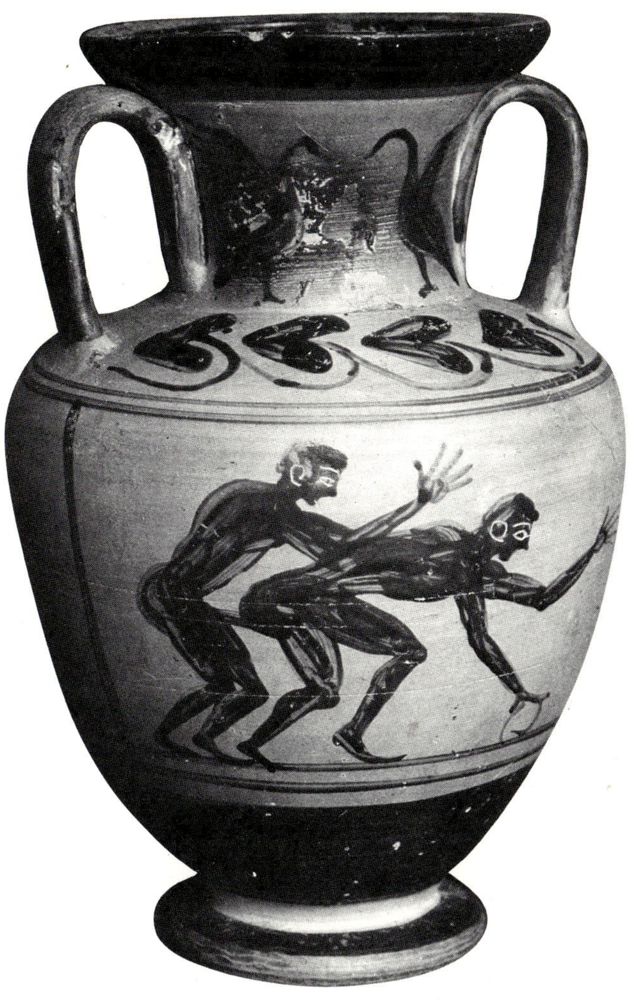

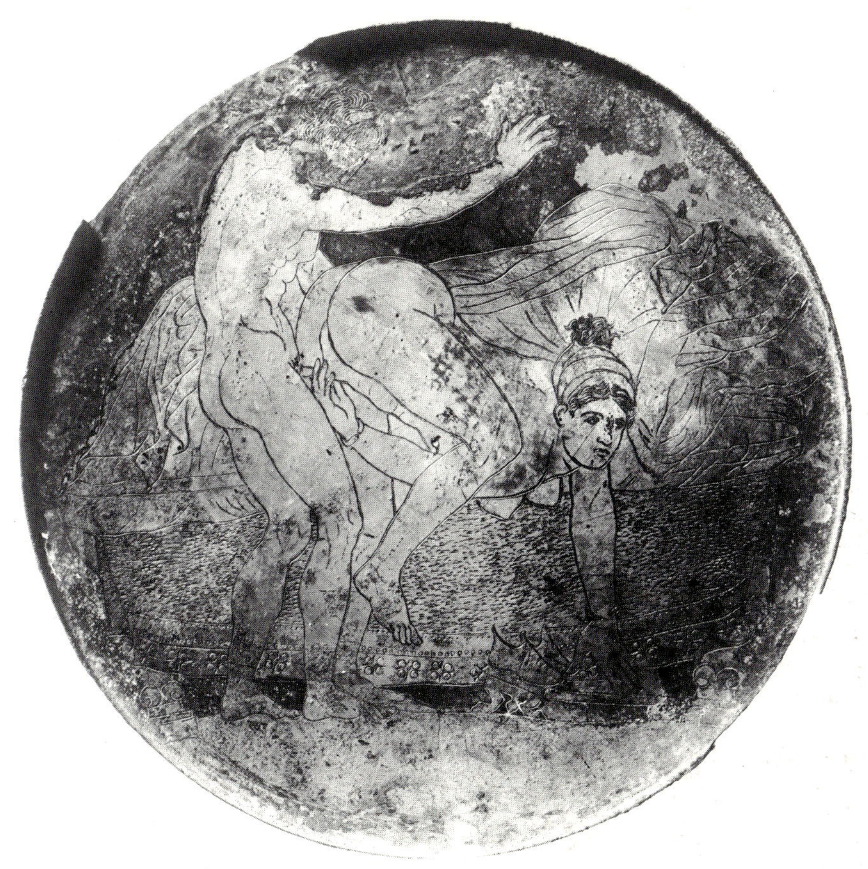

17 *(Left) Maenad Defending Herself with a Thyrsus.* Red-figure cup by Makron, c.480BC. Staatliche Antikensammlung und Glyptothek, Munich

18 *(Above) Erotic Scene.* Black-figure Etruscan amphora, 6th century BC. 24cm high. National Museum, Naples

19 *(Right) Erotic Scene.* Bronze mirror from Corinth, c.325BC. 17.5cm diameter. Museum of Fine Arts, Boston (Gift of E.P. Warren)

influenced by the Greeks. An Etruscan amphora is decorated with a painting in the early Greek, black-figure style. Little is known of Etruscan religion but the famous Tomb of Bulls at Tarquinia, thought to date from the second half of the fifth century BC, contains a frieze on which couples are shown having intercourse. This, and other erotic objects found in Etruscan tombs, may have been placed there in the hope of enhancing the sex life of the buried person in another world.

In 490 BC and again 480 BC the Greek warriors, in great exhibitions of martial courage and ability, defeated two invasions by the previously unbeaten, and much larger, Persian army. These victories brought an immense surge of confidence and justifiable pride to

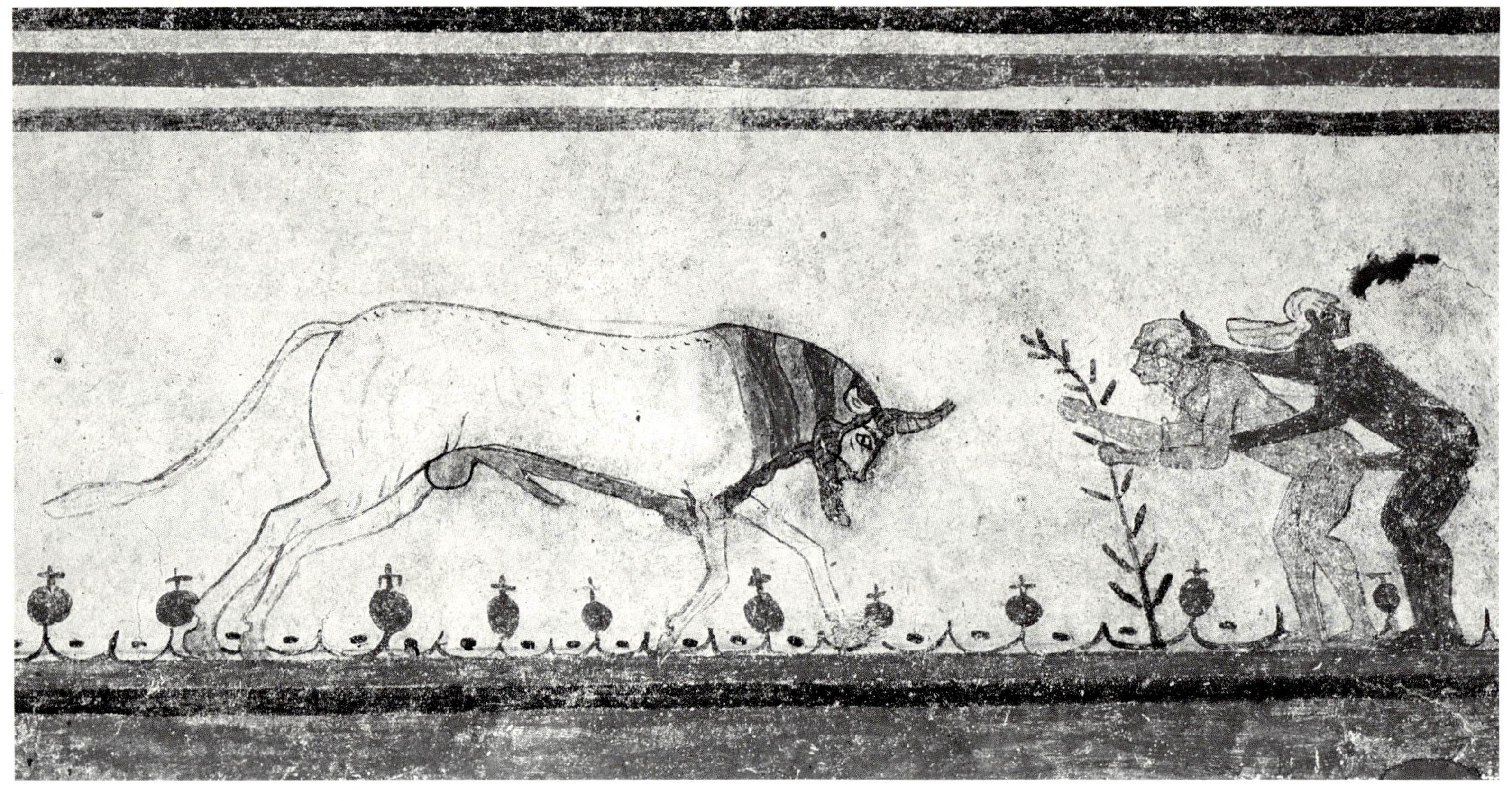

20 *Erotic Scene*. Detail from the Bull Tomb Frieze, Tarquinia, 5th century BC

every Greek. Prosperity grew and art flourished, with a corresponding increase in patronage.

While the athletic male body had long been regarded as the embodiment of beauty and nobility, women were much less frequently portrayed. A female statue was usually clothed, albeit with clinging garments. By the end of the fifth century BC, however, we have evidence, from copies of the rare, undraped *Esquiline Venus*, that a concept of the beautiful naked woman was evolving. By 350 BC, in the island of Cnidos, Praxiteles produced a female nude masterpiece. He also created a scandal, for not only had he broken the accepted rule that female statues should be clothed but he had also taken as his model his mistress, Phryne. She was a very beautiful girl who was to become one of the most famous of the Greek courtesans. Later, when she was accused of impiety and her cause seemed in doubt, Hypereides, her defender, in a dramatic gesture, stripped away her garment to reveal her beauty to the judges.

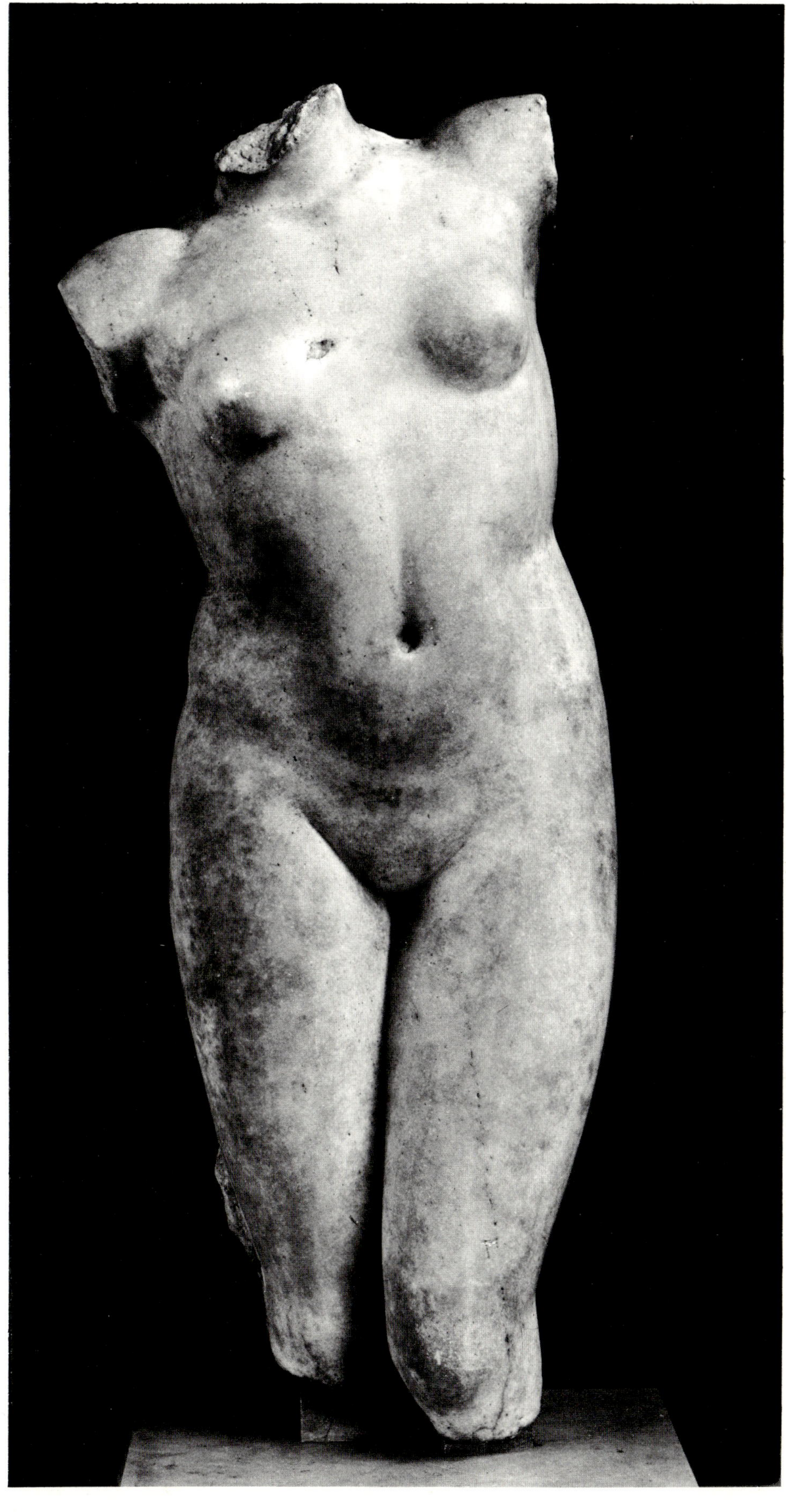

21 *Esquiline Venus*. Marble, 5th century BC. Louvre, Paris

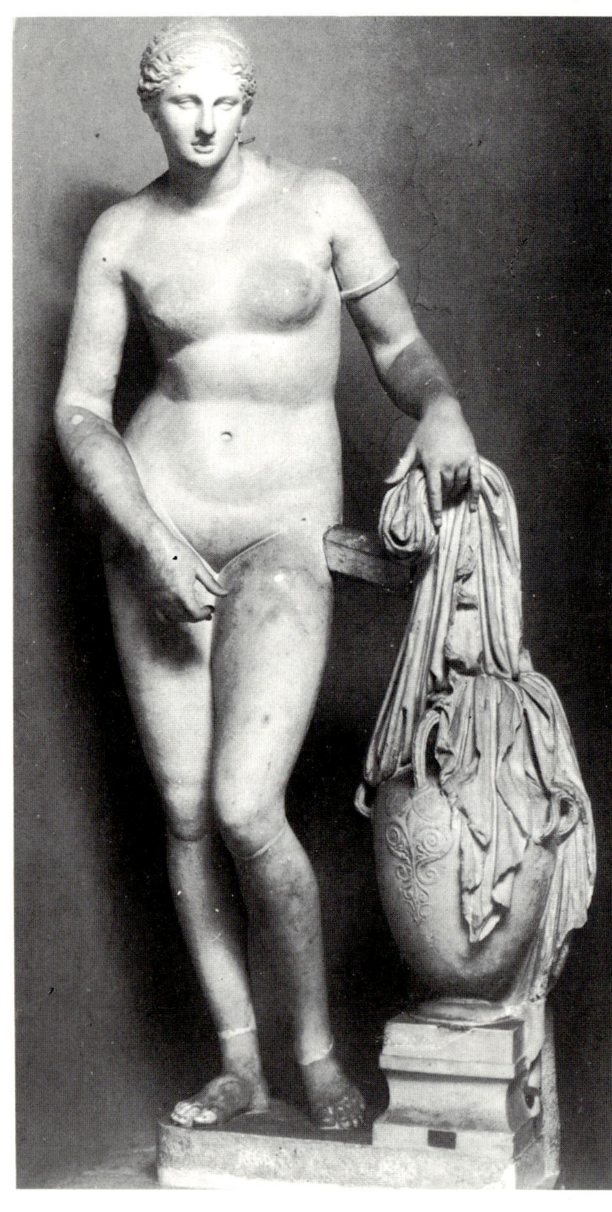

22 *Venus of Cnidos*, Roman copy. Marble, c.350BC. 203cm high. Vatican Museum, Rome

Overwhelmed by what they thought could only be divinely given beauty, with which no man must quarrel, they acquitted her.

Victorian artistic opinion reached the extraordinary conclusion that Classical Greek nudes were not erotic because they were in some way defused by the very fact of their being 'Classical'. This was certainly not the view of the young men who first saw the Venus of Cnidos. One ran forward and embraced her. Another tried to make love to her in the night. As Kenneth Clark so aptly commented about her, 'No one questioned the fact that she was the embodiment of physical desire and that this mysterious, compulsive force was an element in her sanctity.' Everyone who saw the statue thought it a thing of great beauty and it was widely copied around the Mediterranean.

About a hundred years later another artist produced the equally beautiful *Venus of Cyrene*, who is standing beside a dolphin to indicate her connection with the sea. About 100 BC came two further masterpieces. The first was the *Crouching Venus*, a copy of which is one of the treasures of the Vatican Museum. The second is the statue found on the island of Milos, which has become accepted as one of the most beautiful sculptures of a woman ever made. All these statues were intended to depict the Goddess of Love and to arouse erotic feeling, which was felt in itself to contain something of the divine. Indeed, the Greeks believed that sexual desire, which they felt could sometimes take the form of an irresistible madness, was something from which no man was immune and from which the gods themselves were not exempt.

Rome developed as a small city-state and at first was dominated by its larger neighbour, Etruria. However, by 400 BC it was strong enough to win a victory over the Etruscan army and during the next four hundred years it gradually conquered the Greek Empire, Gaul, Spain and most of Britain. By 200 BC plundered Greek art became fashionable in Rome. Copies of Greek paintings and sculpture were a status symbol for the rich Roman families. Pictures of Roman victories and portraits of Romans in the Greek style were to follow.

In the fifth and fourth centuries BC Roman domestic life was very similar to that in Greece and wives were expected to be no more than faithful housekeepers. However, the natural temperament of the Romans was hot-blooded and lusty and they were not inhibited by any sense of sexual sin. Gradually 'love' and sex developed into a

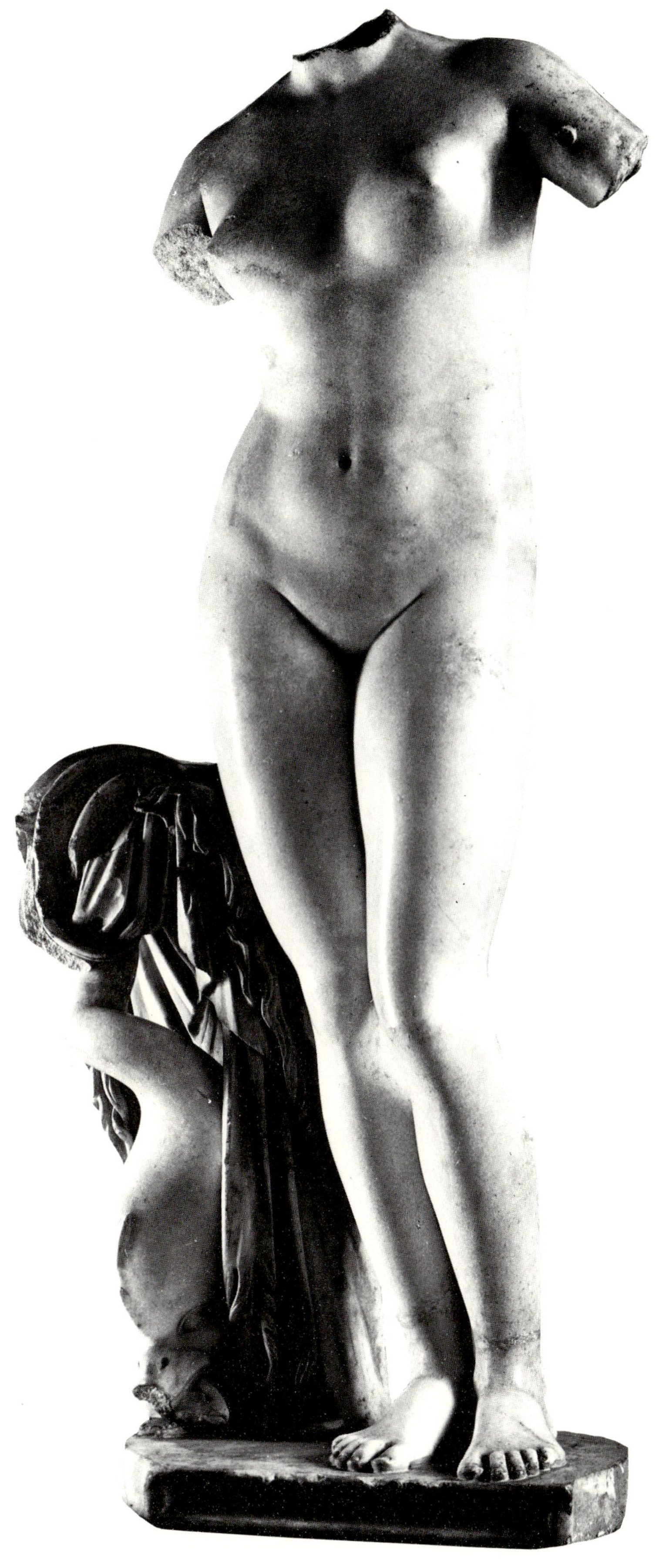

23 *Venus of Cyrene*, Roman copy. Marble, c.250BC. Museo Nazionale, Rome

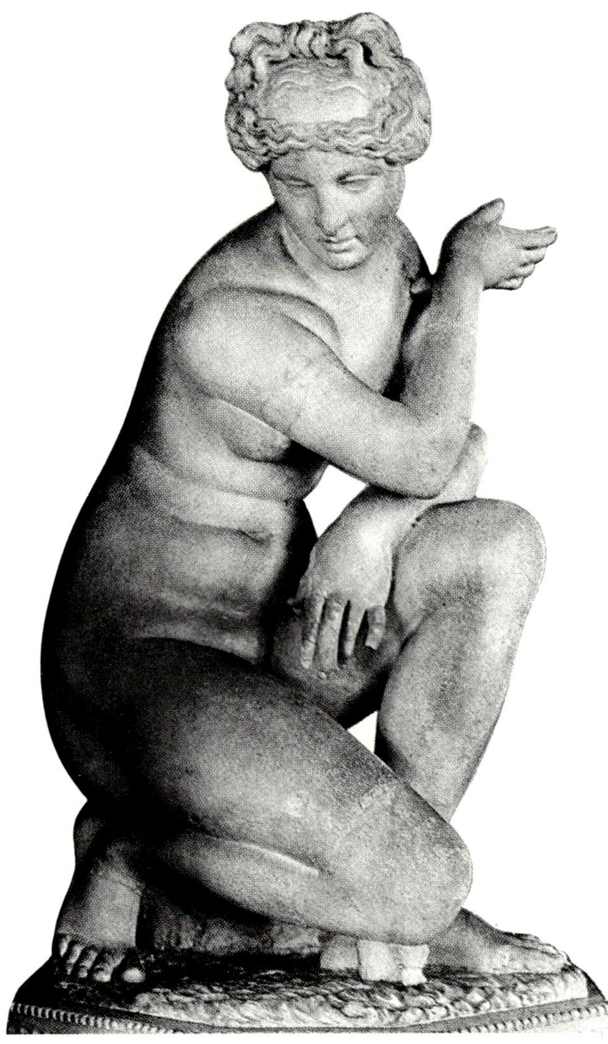

24 *Crouching Venus.* Marble, c.100BC. Vatican Museum, Rome

national sport, in which the object of each man was to seduce his neighbour's wife, while she was supposed, in turn, to find ways of deceiving her husband. Marriage and divorce were quick and easy, but danger from irate husbands remained and was thought to add a thrilling spice to the proceedings. The lovers themselves developed ingenious methods of revenge when their paramours turned their attentions elsewhere. As social disapproval of unfaithful wives dwindled, the women became more licentious than the men. Young women married rich old men and, having become rich on the death of their husbands, proceeded to take innumerable lovers and even to

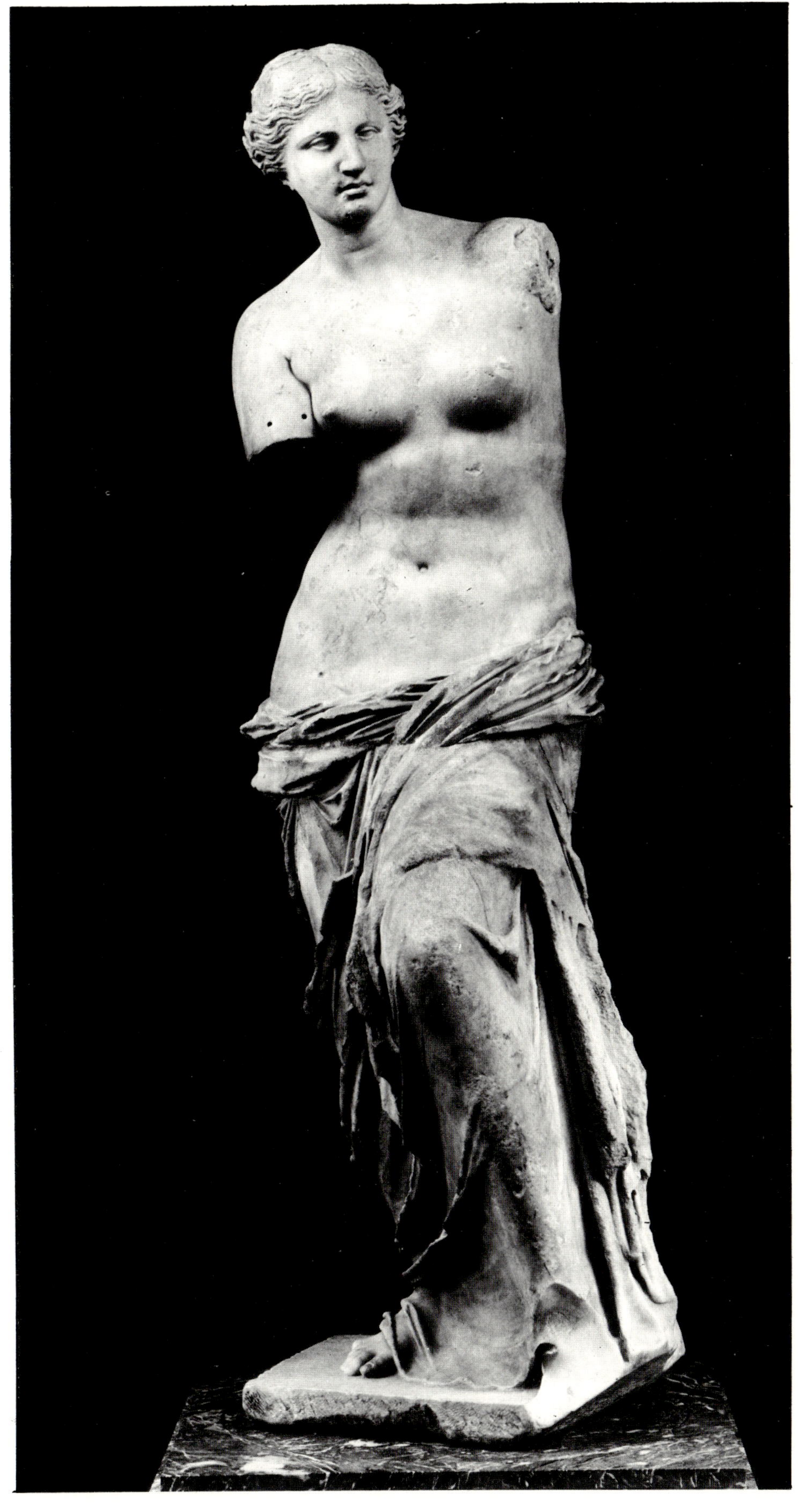

25 *Venus of Milos*. Marble, c.100BC. 208cm high. Louvre, Paris

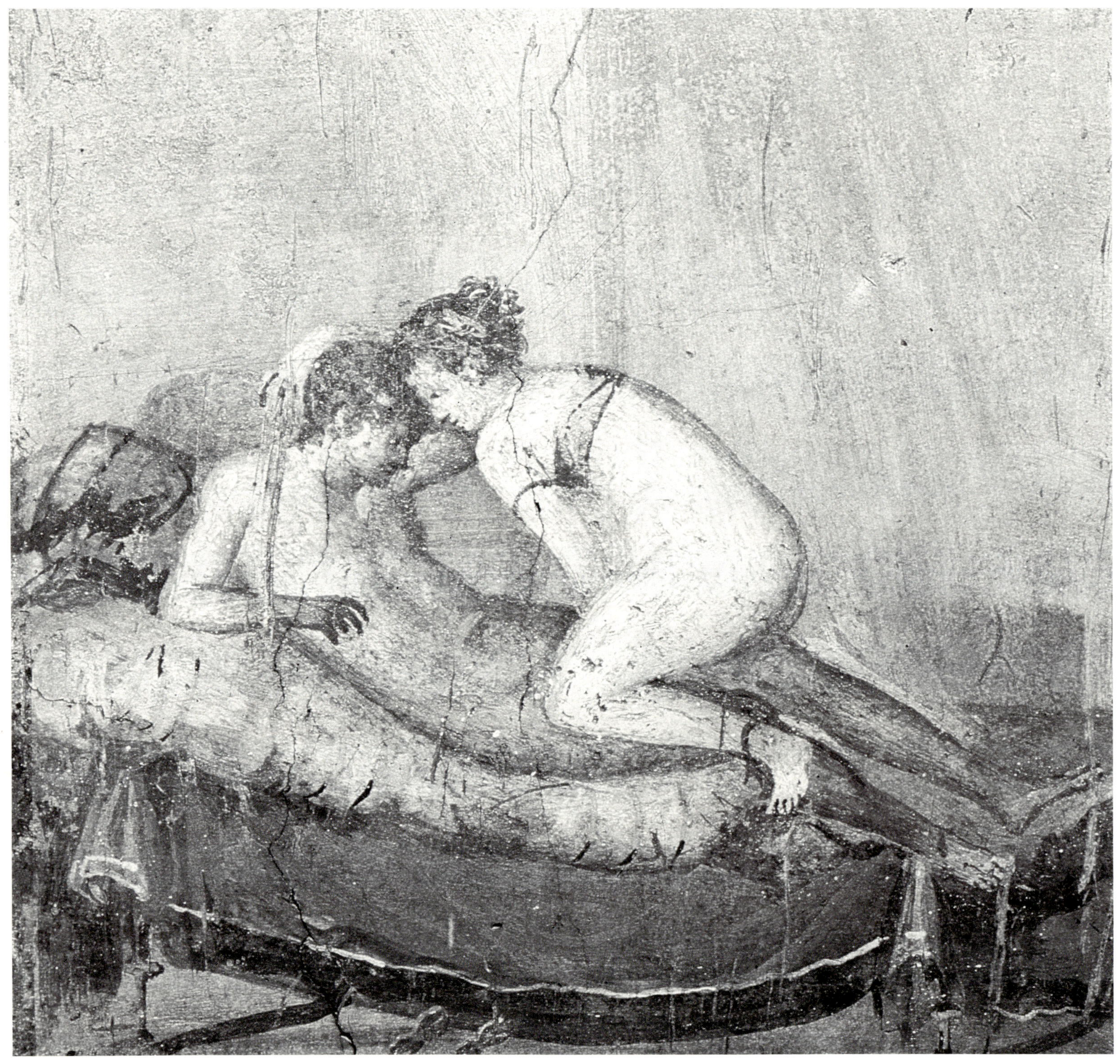

become part-time prostitutes to increase the number. When Ovid wrote *Ars amatoria* (The Art of Love), an adulterer's handbook, the Emperor Augustus, whose daughter and granddaughter, both called Julia, had been banished for notorious multiple infidelity, regarded the book with disapproval. Ovid was banished in his turn when he was found to have been one of the many lovers of the younger Julia. By AD 116 Juvenal could write, 'a woman with only two lovers is a paragon of virtue'. Girls were given the same education as boys, but it was noted that they seldom persisted in literary or artistic pursuits. Instead they revelled in the game of love, and increasingly wanted little to do with their traditional role of child-bearing and child-rearing. Olive oil was used in contraception, abortion was frequent and increasing numbers of unwanted babies were left on mountain-sides to die. Among upper-class Romans a steady fall in the birth-rate was noticeable all over Europe.

The factors which had made Rome successful and powerful were dissipated. The upper classes became corrupt, the lower classes became lazy, with endless leisure provided by slaves. Power began increasingly to pass to the successful generals. In the days of prosperity the quantity of art of all kinds increased, but technical standards tended to decline. Depictions of the erect phallus, frequently in a very stylized form, produced to ensure protection and good luck, abounded everywhere but were not considered erotic. On the other hand erotic objects were made in very large quantities, particularly in the form of ceramic lamps decorated with copulating couples, and amulets with similar scenes, but the quality was poor. In the first century BC, in the district of Arezzo, a higher standard of pottery was produced. These Aretine bowls, with moulded, appliquéd embossing, were decorated with gracefully sculpted couples having intercourse and were doubtless bought by a richer, more discriminating clientele.

Most Roman paintings have perished, but in AD 79 Vesuvius erupted and created a 'time capsule' in Pompeii. As archaeologists gradually disinter the town we have been able to see many examples of art which have been preserved. The best paintings were not of erotic subjects. Most of the erotic ones were not very well conceived or well painted and they are usually in a very damaged condition. The subjects were mainly individual couples having intercourse. Plates 10

26 *Erotic Scene*. Wall painting, 1st century AD. House of the Centenary, Pompeii

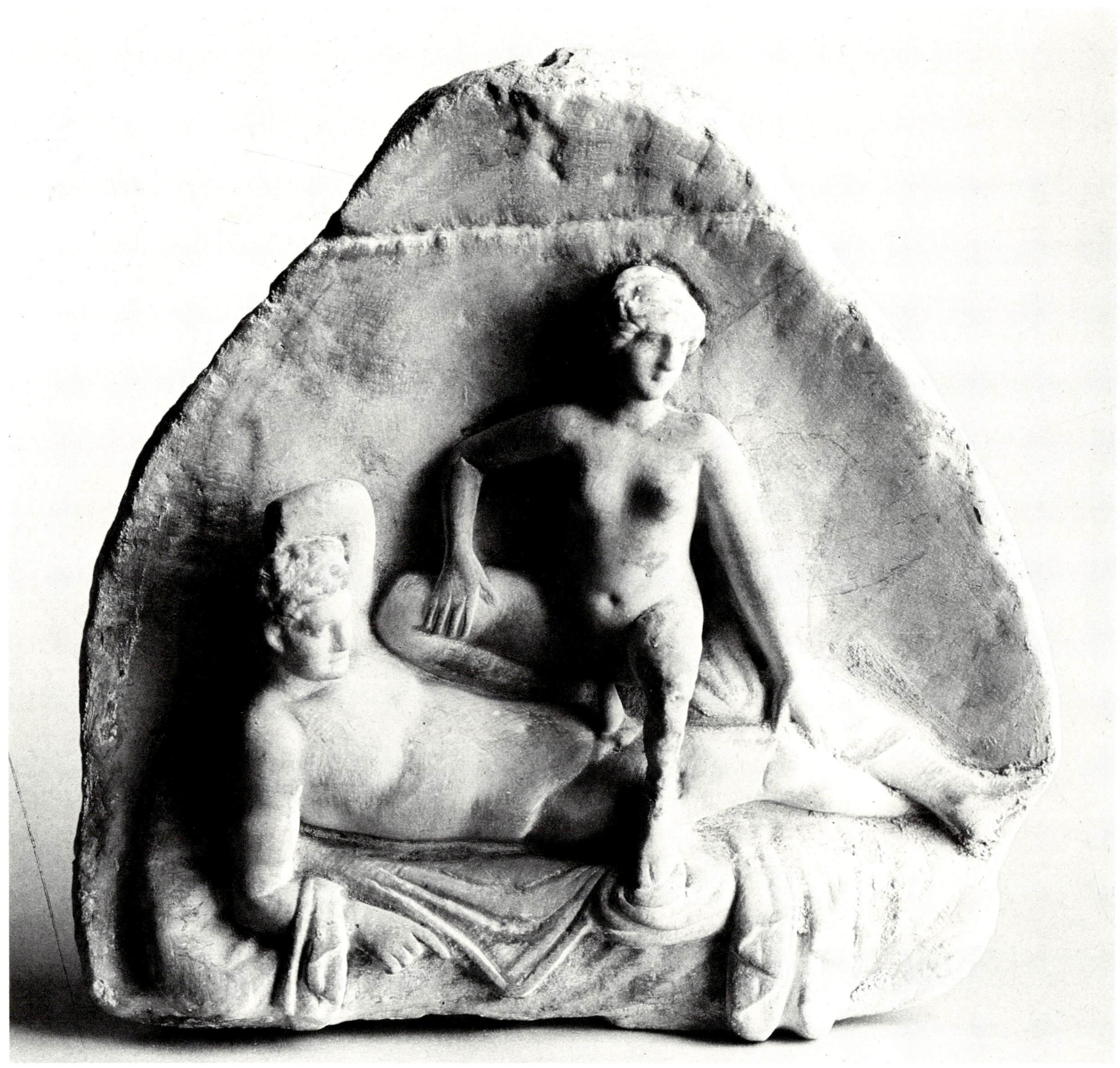

and 26 have been chosen for illustration because they were of better quality and have remained in much better condition. Plate 11, showing Priapus weighing his phallus, is of special interest because the subject is a rare one. The fountain (Plate 7) may well have been regarded as a humorous conversation-piece, but it is skilfully sculpted. Plate 27 was undoubtedly intended to be erotic.

Rome was now becoming weak. Tough, strong, warlike peoples had never ceased to migrate slowly westward from the Ural mountains and then southward towards the Mediterranean. In 375 AD northern Italy was invaded by the Huns. In 41 AD Rome was captured and sacked by the Goths, an event unthinkable to the Roman citizens of five hundred years before. The classical civilization was at an end.

27 *Erotic Scene.* Marble bas-relief from Pompeii, mid-1st century AD. National Museum, Naples

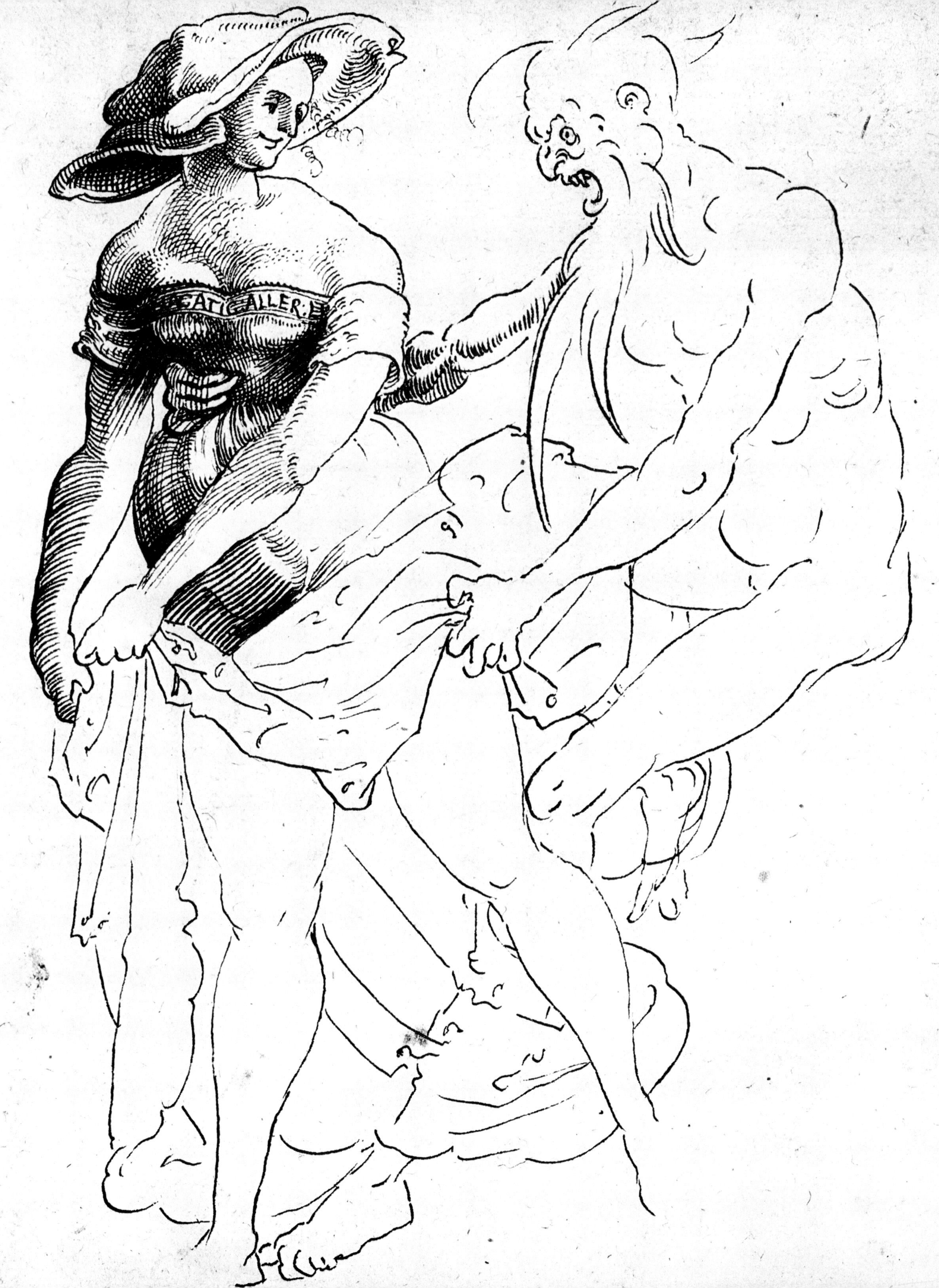
GATIC ALLER

CHAPTER 2

The Middle Ages

Even when a style of art has been brought to a high pitch of perfection over a prolonged period there is a tendency for it to change, or to be replaced by something new. When it has also been the expression of a great civilization, which is itself destroyed, the changes are likely to be very great. The period after the downfall of the Greek and Roman empires has been aptly described as 'The Dark Ages', and the cultural blackout which followed was so profound that it lasted for many hundreds of years. It is true that a decline in the standard of art had begun before the Roman empire was overrun by the barbarian hordes. Provincial artists and sculptors of little talent had attempted to copy the masterpieces which had been achieved at the peak of the Greek era. Where sculpture was concerned, for example, the beauty and subtle eroticism of the originals was lost and, as it dwindled, interest in the art also declined.

The invasion of the classical world by tribes of warlike, insensitive barbarians might well have seen the replacement of one attractive mental image of the human body by another. Instead an astonishing thing happened: artists all over Europe seemed to develop a mental block which prevented them from even thinking about the nude at all. As in the case of incest, the thought of which most people put from their minds, the nude male and female body, which had previously symbolized to the artist all that was noble, beautiful and divine, became a subject which people could only contemplate with difficulty. There seems little doubt that the main cause of this dramatic change was the form in which the Christian religion was preached by the early Christian Church.

After the crucifixion of Christ, St Paul, along with other Christians of the day, was under the impression that the end of the world would soon occur. He therefore counselled Christians against sex because he believed that this would interfere with their spiritual progress. Although Christ had been indifferent to them Paul also supported the ideas that were then very prevalent in many religions around the Mediterranean, which emphasized conflict between the spirit and all forms of bodily enjoyment. During the centuries which followed, these ideas were intensified by the ascetic, celibate churchmen of the times, who proclaimed that all sexual pleasure was sinful. They also denounced women as a sex, whom they blamed for the fall of man and the origination of sexual sinfulness. 'Woman,' said Tertullian,

28 Urs Graf: *Lust and the Young Woman*, c.1518. Pen, 19.6×14cm. Öffentliche Kunstsammlung, Basle

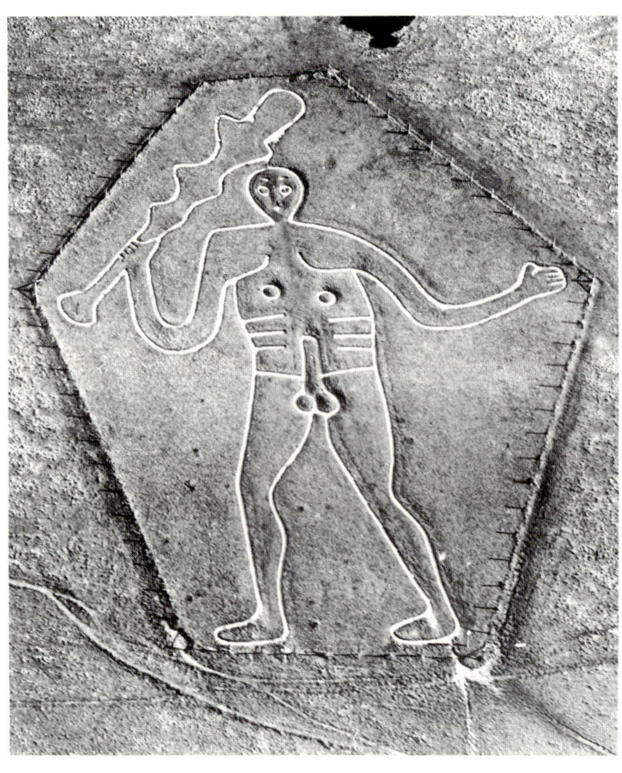

29 *The Cerne Abbas giant*, figure cut in chalk. c. 2nd century AD. Dorset, England

who was one of the great married clerics, 'you are the gateway of the Devil.' Women were encouraged not only to be chaste, but to take perpetual vows of chastity even if they were married. One celebrated instance was that of Queen Etheldred: even though her husband Aethelberht, King of Kent, offered lands and money to St Augustine if that famous archbishop could persuade her to change her mind, she remained a virgin till her death and was canonized by the Church for her chastity. As a direct result of these teachings of the Church, the human body, and particularly any sexual pleasures it might provide, became a shameful burden which stood between mankind and salvation.

These feelings were graphically portrayed by Grünewald (d.1528) in his depiction of the punishment of lust. A couple are shown with all the hideousness of their sexual sins revealed through the effect on their bodies. They are being devoured alive by the most loathsome creatures the artist's imagination could conjure up.

As the influence of the Church became more powerful, further pronouncements severely limited days and times when normal, conjugal intercourse was deemed to be permissible, and 'When pleasure, not procreation, bears rule in this matter,' said Pope Gregory the Great, 'husbands and wives have cause to lament their embraces.'

The attitude of the Church to sexual pleasure was only one of many tribulations for mediaeval people. For the most part they lived throughout the Dark Ages under tyrannous governments in tiny kingdoms, in which the Church and the rulers supported one another to their mutual benefit. Life for the ordinary people was lived in toil, insecurity and poverty.

During this time high degrees of skill in craftsmanship and decoration were being developed, particularly where metal-crafts were concerned. The graphic arts were almost entirely restricted to religious subjects and those commissioned by the Court and the State. Very few forms of art with any sexual connotation have survived. One example is the famous figure of a man with a club and an erect phallus cut through the turf into the chalky hillside at Cerne Abbas in Dorset, thought to date from the second century AD. No one knows its origin and the phallus is more likely to have been symbolic of power and virility, in the primitive Celtic tradition, than to have had

30 Grünewald (attr.): *Pair of Lovers*. Panel, 65×39.5cm. Musée de l'Oeuvre Notre-Dame de Strasbourg

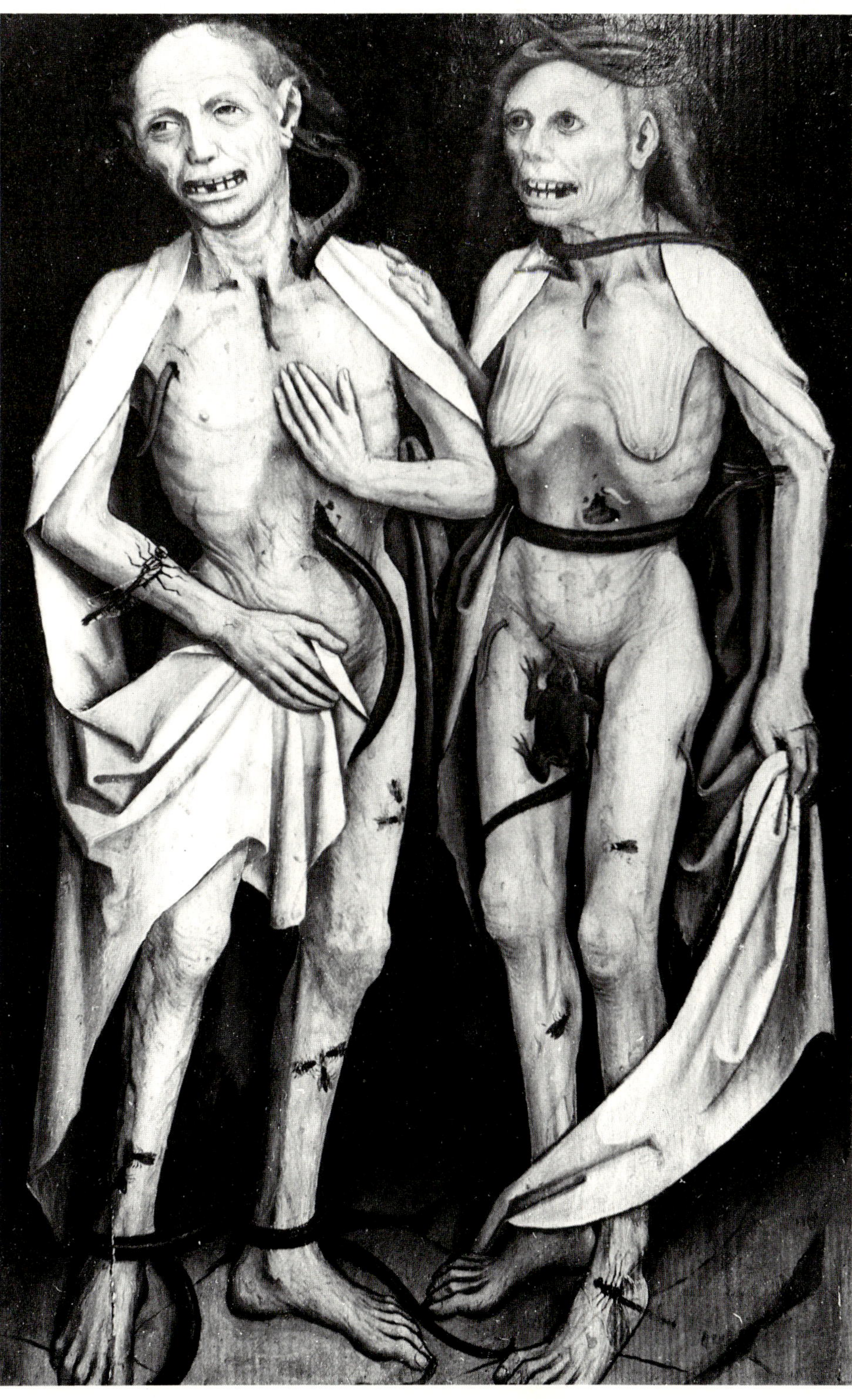

31 *(Overleaf)* Jacquerio: *The Fountain of Youth*, central portion. La Manta, Turin

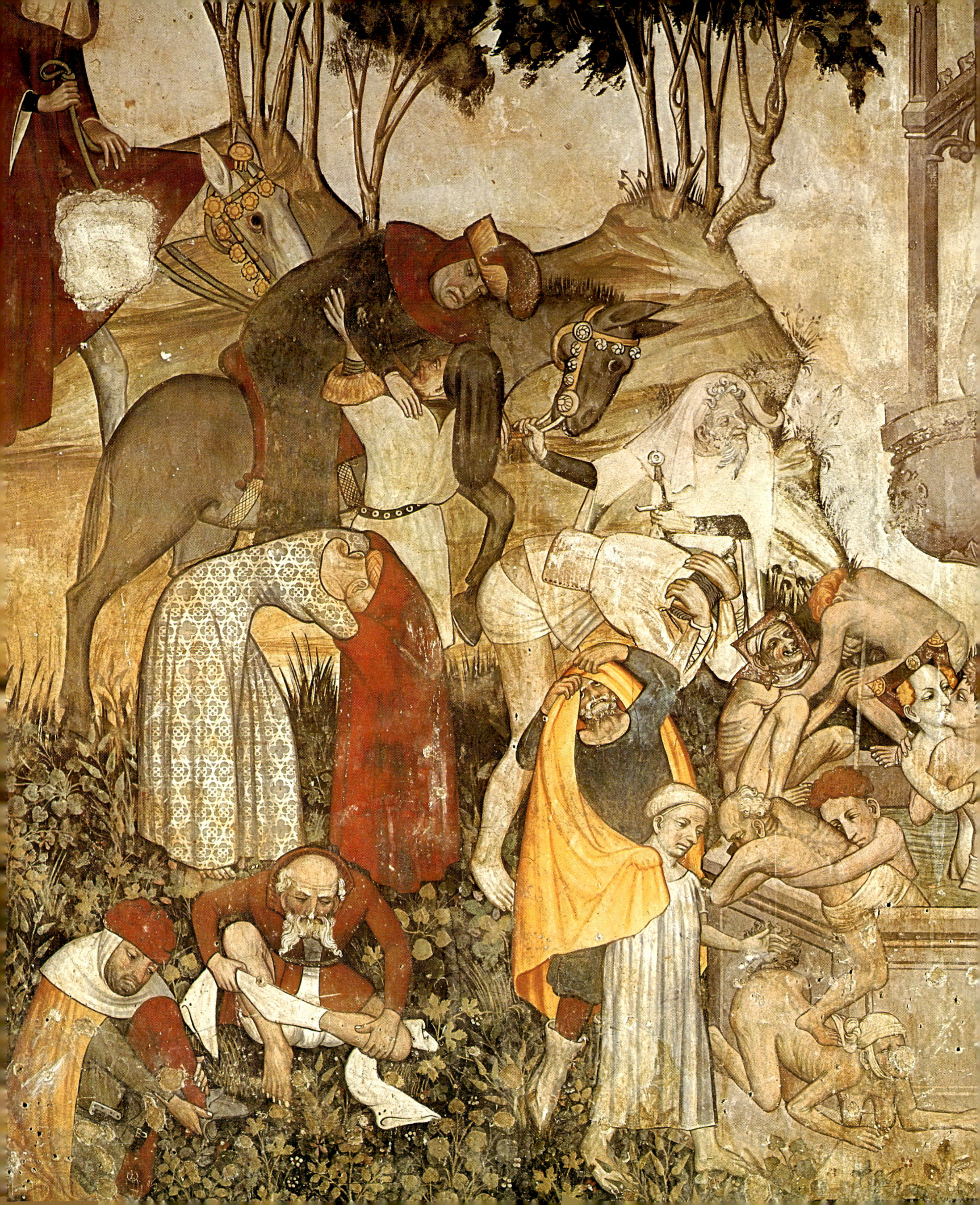

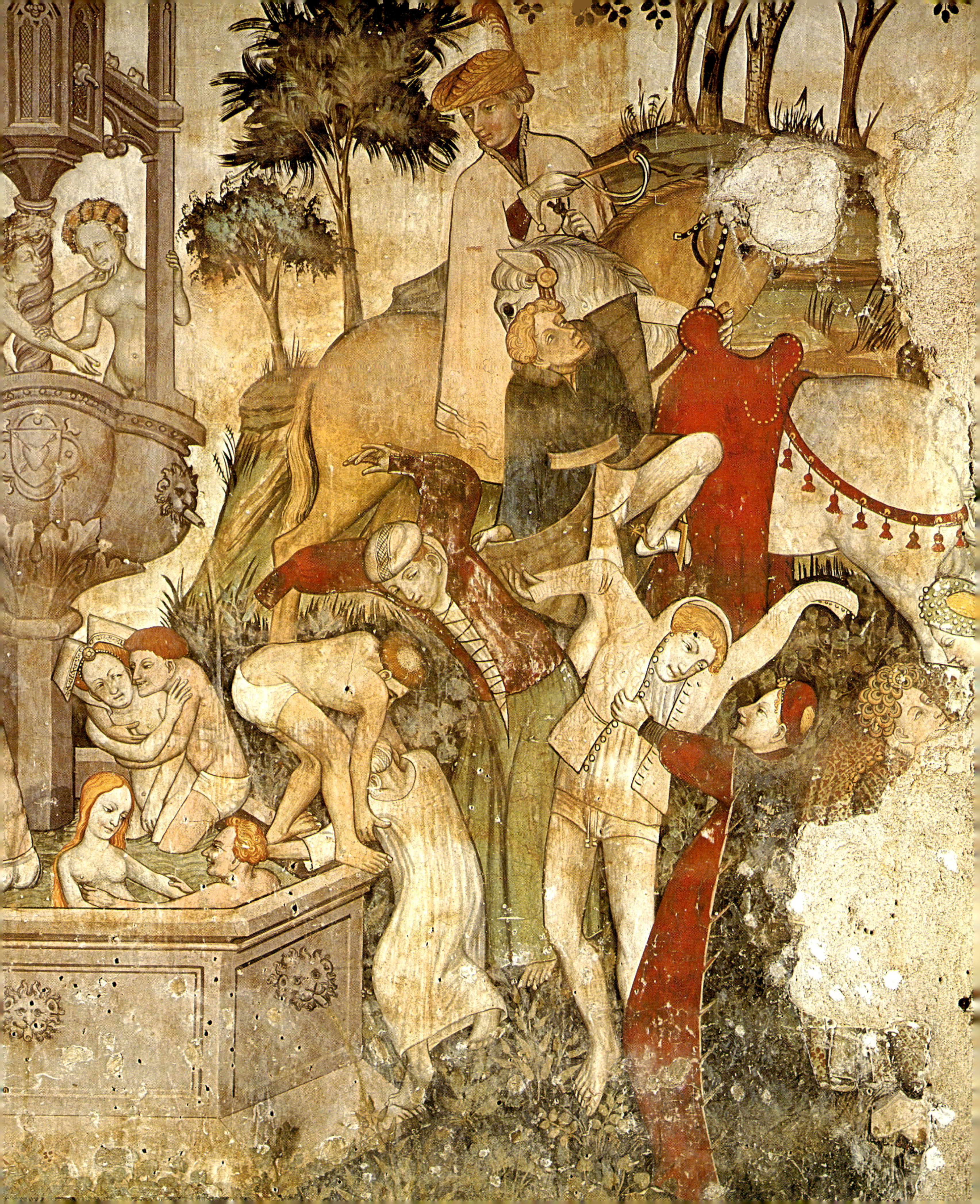

any erotic intention. Nevertheless, local traditions leave no doubt that it became a fertility symbol, and superstitious women suffering the sadness and, in those days, the shame of being barren are said to have spent nights upon its phallus in the hope of becoming pregnant.

32 Thomas Rowlandson: *The Timely Visit*. Aquatint, c.1810

Another example, a thousand years later, is found at Kilpeck Church in Herefordshire. This church is famous for the number and variety of its fanciful stone carvings, many of which form part of a series of corbels. One of these shows the Devil having intercourse with a witch; another (Plate 4) is a well-preserved example of a *Sheela-na-Gig*. Similar figures of a woman displaying her vulva have been found all over Europe and the Middle East dating back to at least 600 BC, and they were frequently used to represent fertility goddesses. A number have been found in Ireland and along the Welsh borders, but this representation at Kilpeck is later and was apparently included in the scheme of decoration because it pleased the artist and somehow slipped through the religious censorship of the time. Derived from fertility symbols, it may well have had erotic connotations at the time it was made.

The mediaeval age was a period in which few could read or write, and those who could had good reason to be very careful what they wrote. The stern views about the sinfulness of sexual enjoyment and the penalties to be incurred by any who transgressed are, however, well documented, and they must have affected the lives of many. Yet there is also extensive evidence, if only in the denunciations that were periodically made by the Church, that a large proportion of men and women continued to fall in love and live together, in and out of marriage, and that the natural instincts caused their sex lives to continue very much as they had always done. Moreover, poverty and insecurity, particularly in towns, meant that prostitution was frequently the only way in which many women could survive. Burford has described and documented, in the greatest detail, the brothels and the prostitution which existed along the south bank of the Thames by London Bridge, from Roman times right through until the seventeenth century. Incredible as it may seem, for much of that time many of the brothels and much of their revenues were owned by the Church and the Crown. There were even occasions when brothels were the property of convents of nuns! He also records

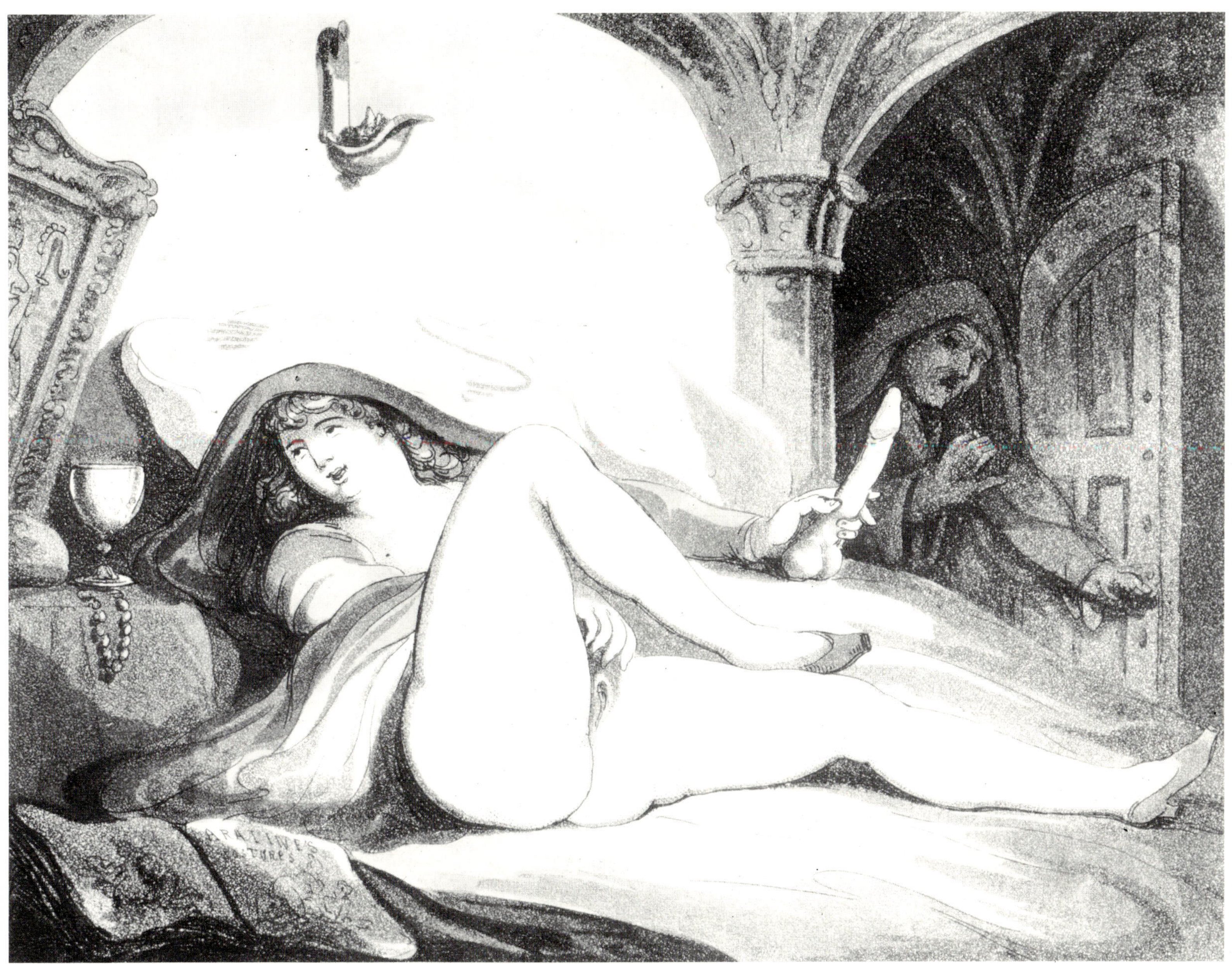

how, over hundreds of years, priests could buy indulgences which exempted them from their celibacy and allowed them to install 'hearth girls', although both the priests and the girls might also have to pay licence fees to the Crown. The south bank of the Thames represented only a tiny part of London, where prostitution was rife, and other records show that conditions were similar throughout the cities of Europe. Moreover, the evidence of literature, from the Canterbury Tales to the Decameron, leaves no doubt that where ordinary men and women were concerned the edicts of Church and State were never successful in curbing normal sexual activities, even if they did result in a great deal of guilt being attached to them.

As far as the clergy were concerned the penitential punishments for sexual transgressions were severe. For priests who had sexual

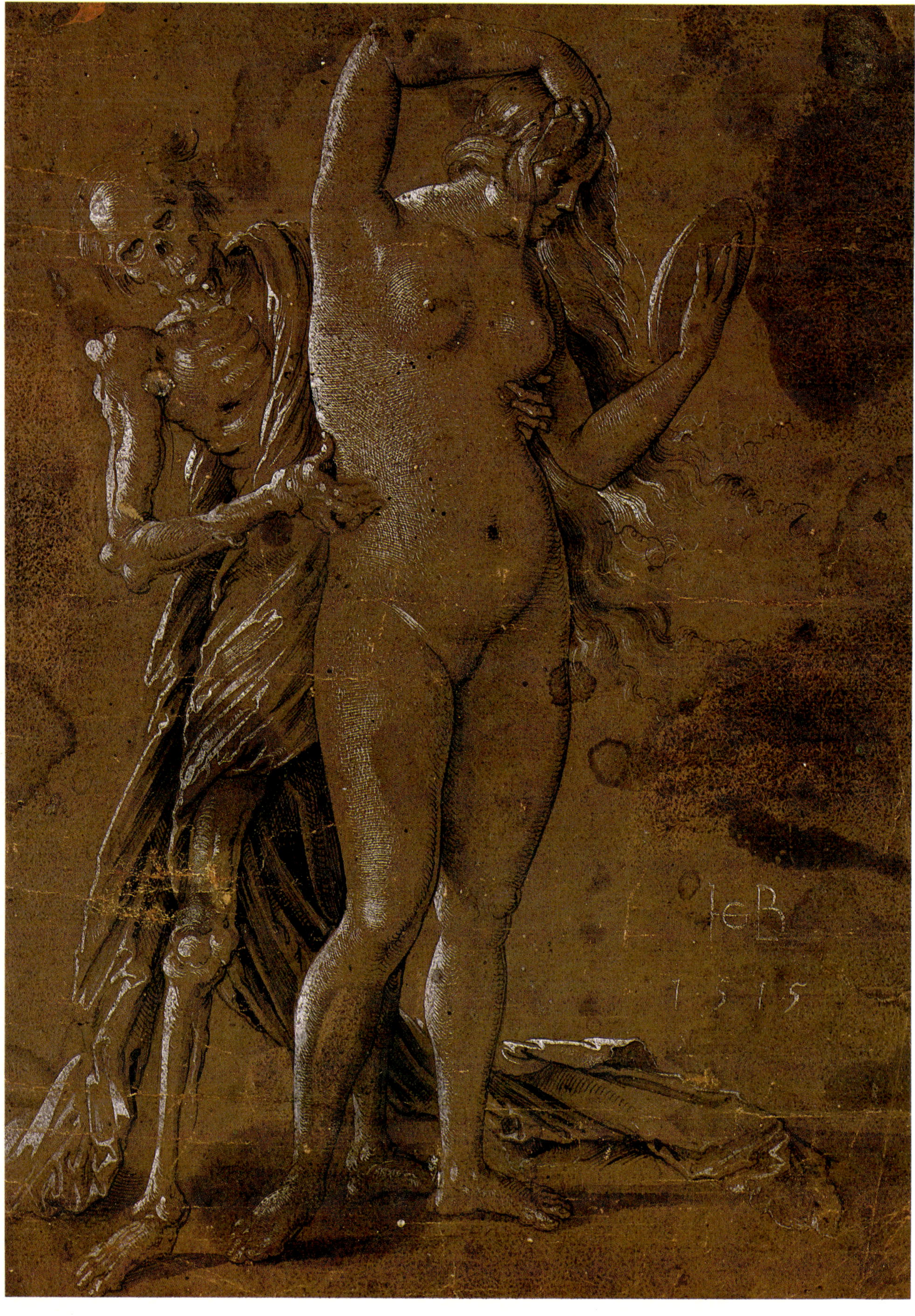

33 *(Left)* Hans Baldung Grien: *Death and the Woman*. Pen and black ink with highlights on brown paper, 1515. Staatliche Museen, West Berlin

34 *(Right)* School of Leonardo: *Leda and the Swan*, c.1500. Galleria Borghese, Rome

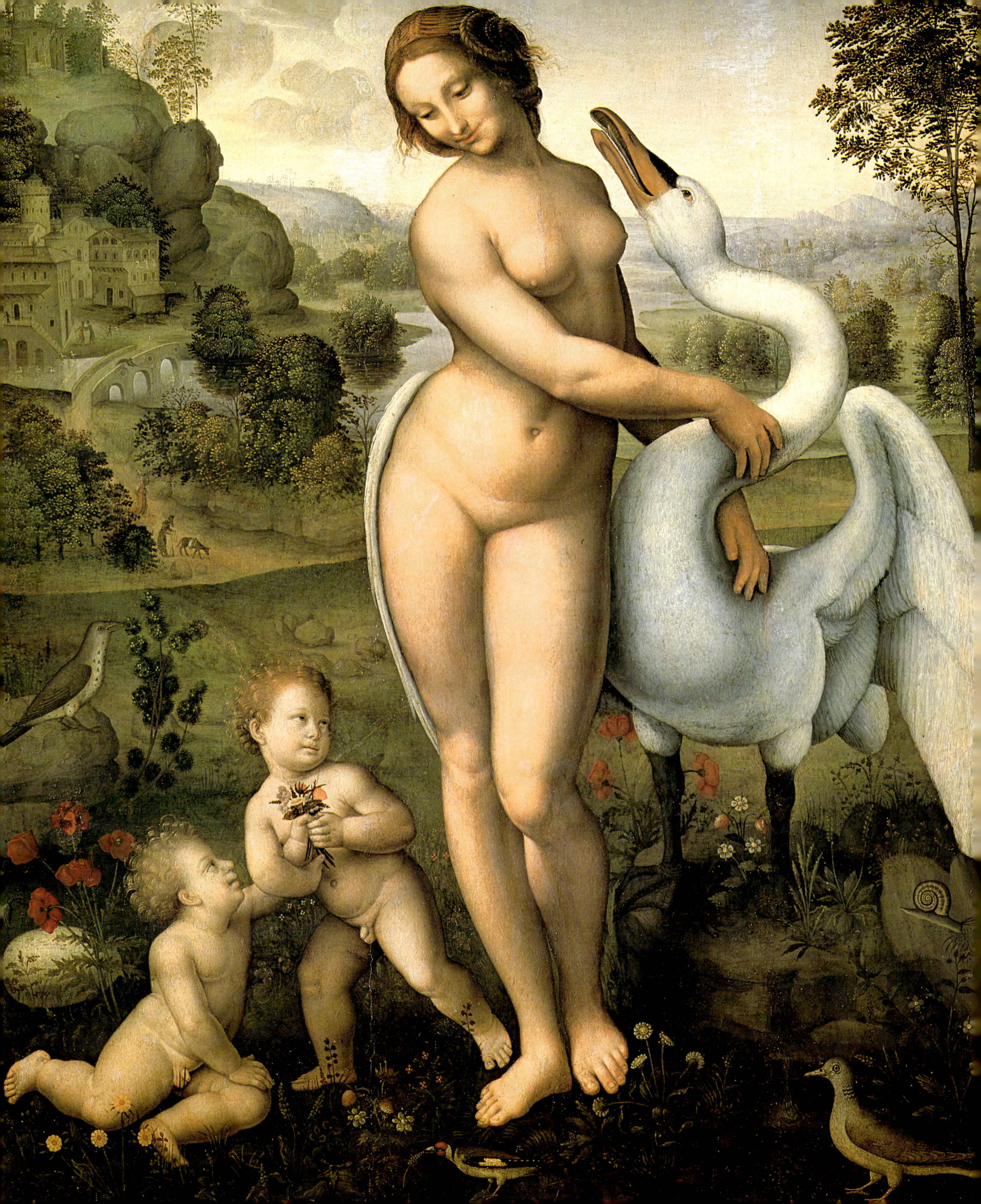

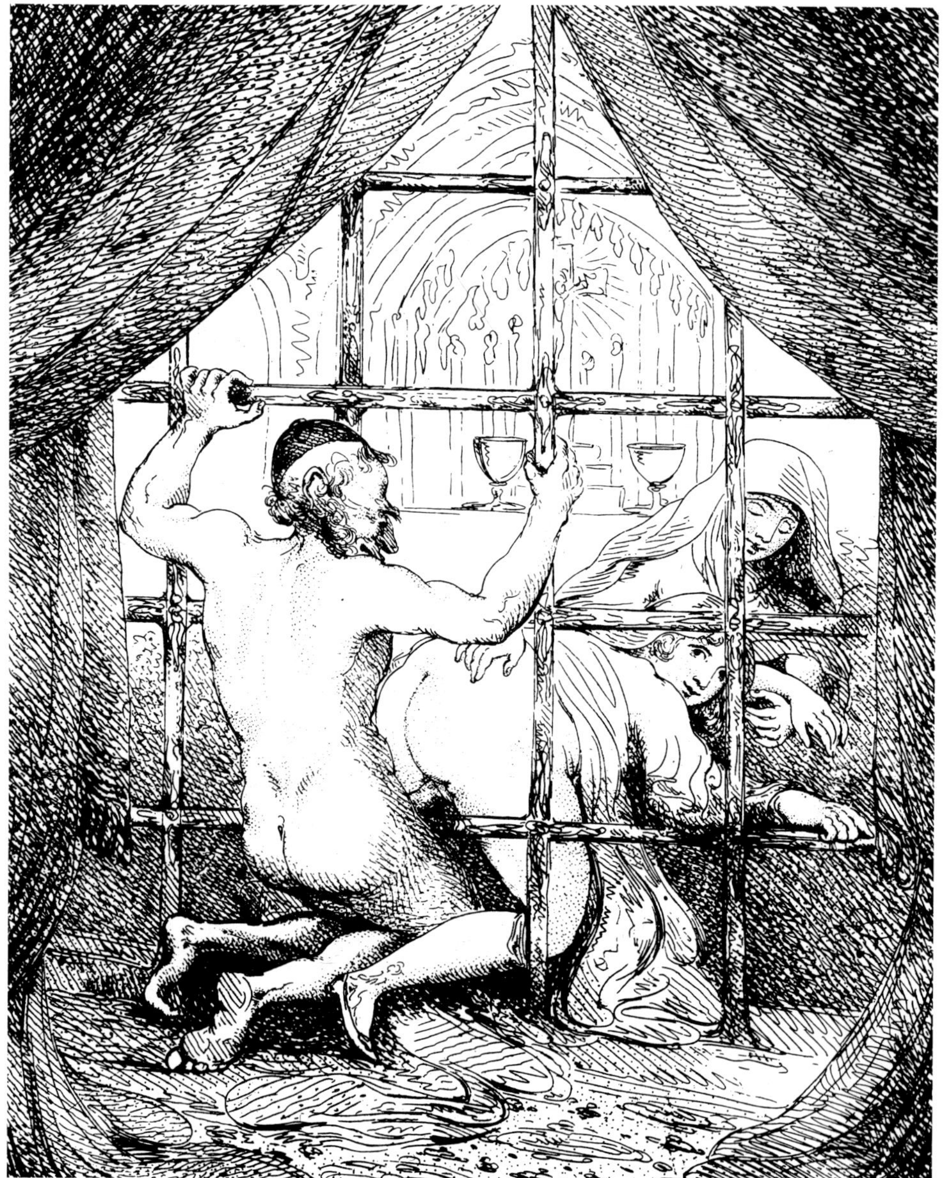

35 Thomas Rowlandson: *Intercourse with a nun.* Engraving, c.1810. British Museum

connection with a nun, for example, Dunstan pronounced a penalty of a ten-year fast with continual lamentation and no meat. Nevertheless, as the years passed and indulgences could be bought, the reputation of many of the clergy, particularly the friars, became notorious. It is hardly surprising, therefore, that under the constant pressure from anti-sexual Church teachings, ordinary people became particularly fascinated by any question of sexual transgres-

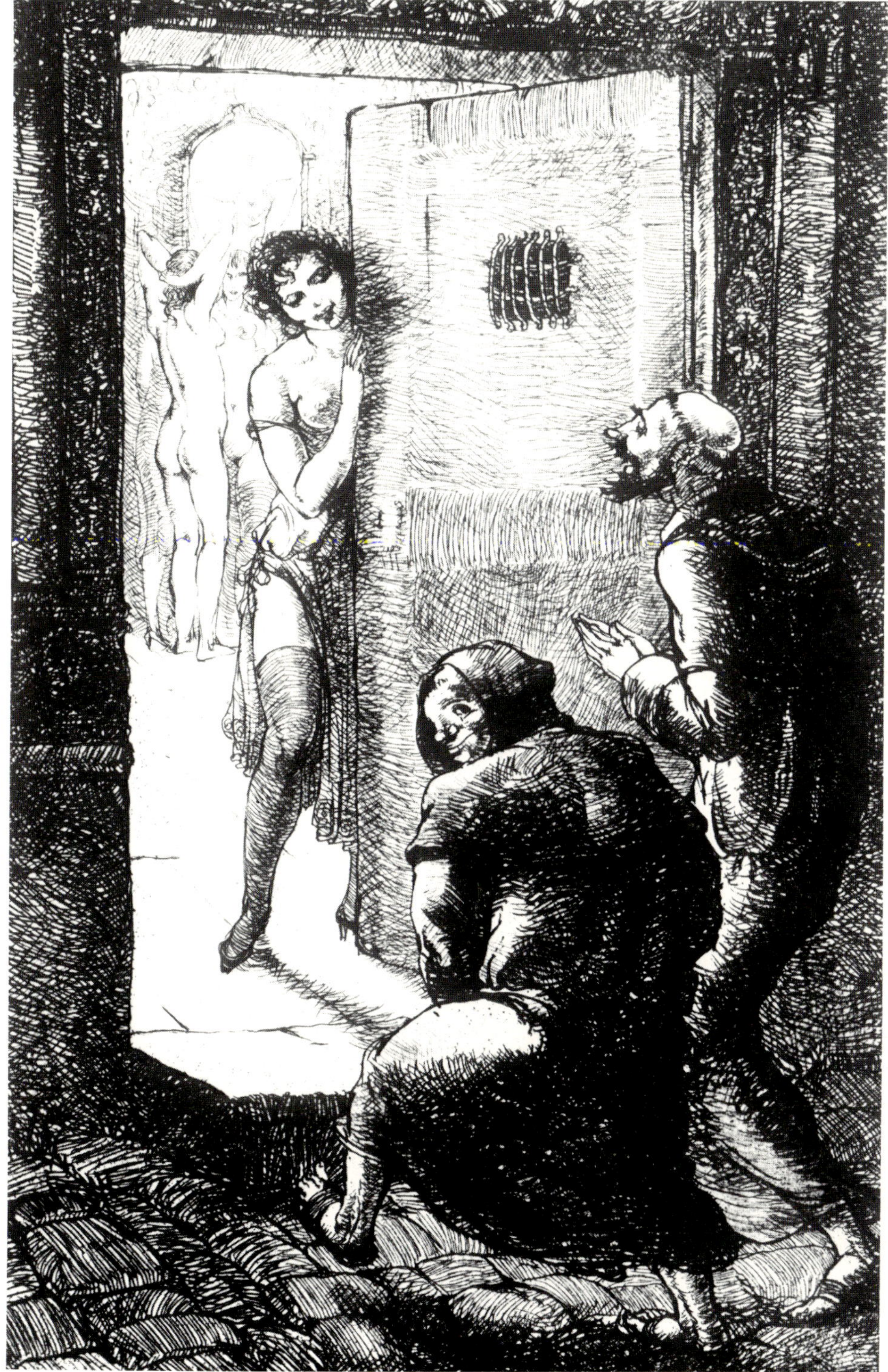

36 Viset: *Monks to the Brothel.* Illustration to the Marquis de Sade's *Léonore et Clémentine ou Les Tartuffes de l'Inquisition,* Paris 1930

sions by the clergy themselves. Indeed, this interest in the private lives of the clergy was to continue down the centuries. Mediaeval artists knew better than to depict such things, but later artists such as Rowlandson, in his pictures of the imagined sex-life of nuns, and the Belgian artist Viset, who showed two monks visiting a brothel, are typical of many. That Rowlandson's pictures (Plates 32 and 35) were not all that exaggerated, at least as far as some instances in mediaeval

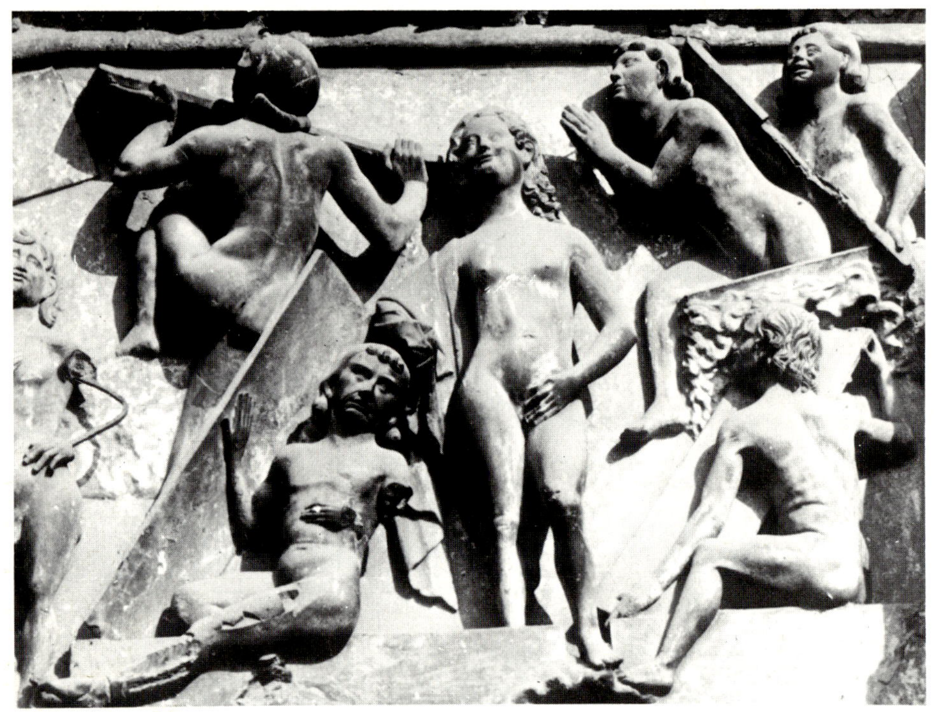

37 Detail from *The Last Judgement*, tympanum of Bourges Cathedral, France

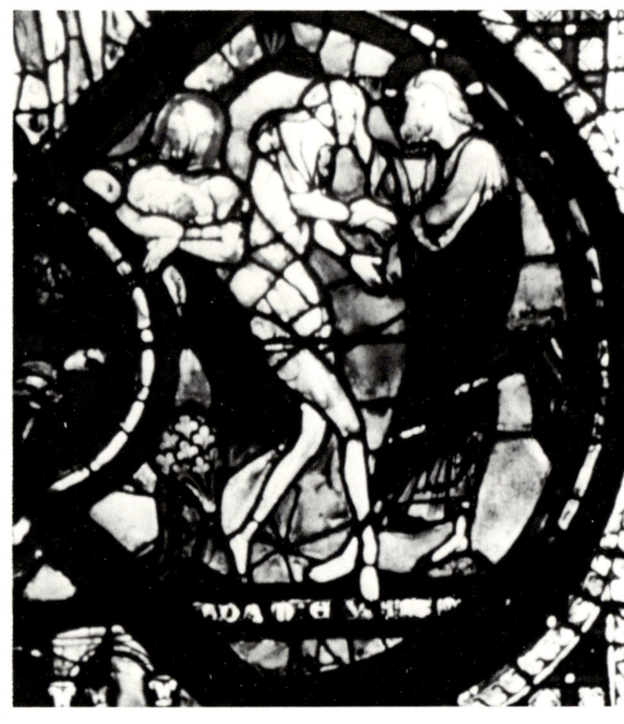

38 *The Creation of Eve*. Stained glass, detail from the Good Samaritan window, Chartres Cathedral

times were concerned, is borne out by the statement of Bishop Boniface on one occasion in the eighth century that 'the nunneries were no better than brothels'.

During the Middle Ages artists were commissioned to paint subjects, such as the martyrdom of saints or Adam and Eve in the garden of Eden, which inevitably involved painting the nude. How difficult they found this is demonstrated in the splendid stained-glass window at Chartres Cathedral, where God is shown creating Eve from one of Adam's ribs. Looking at the distorted figure of Eve one can only assume that the artist had never drawn a nude woman before and had never seen an illustration from which he could copy. On the other hand, at about the same time, in another part of France, a small artistic miracle occurred. Pictures of the Last Judgement had become a favoured theme, and although artists who were directed to depict the righteous as both nude and beautiful had complied by painting asexual, doll-like figures, in the thirteenth century at Bourges Cathedral an anonymous sculptor, in his tableau of the *Last Judgement*, introduced what was probably the most natural and most attractive nude figure of a young woman that Europe had seen for a

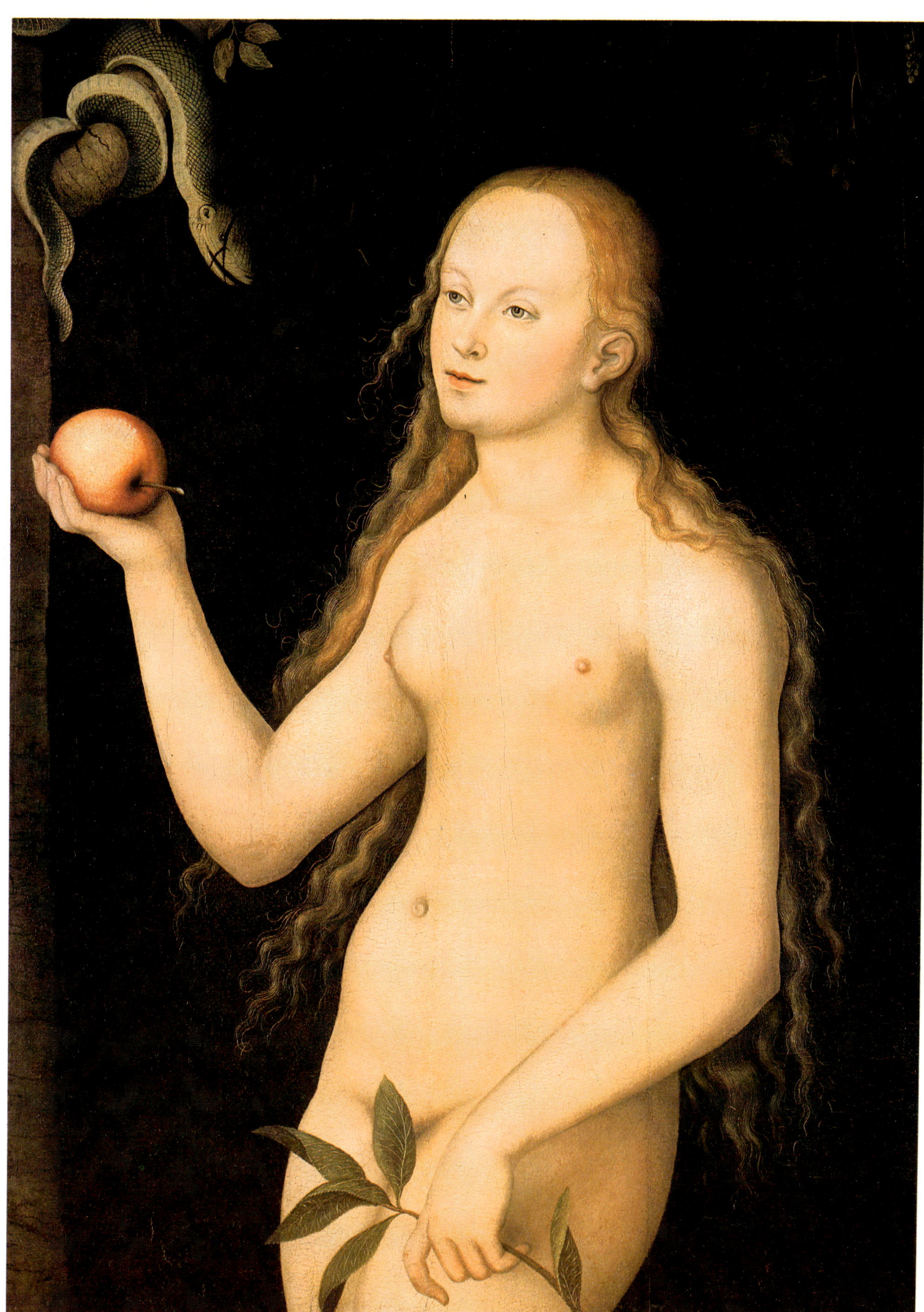

39 Lucas Cranach the Elder: *Eve*, 1553. 86.5×65.5cm. Koninklijk Museum voor Schone Kunsten, Antwerp

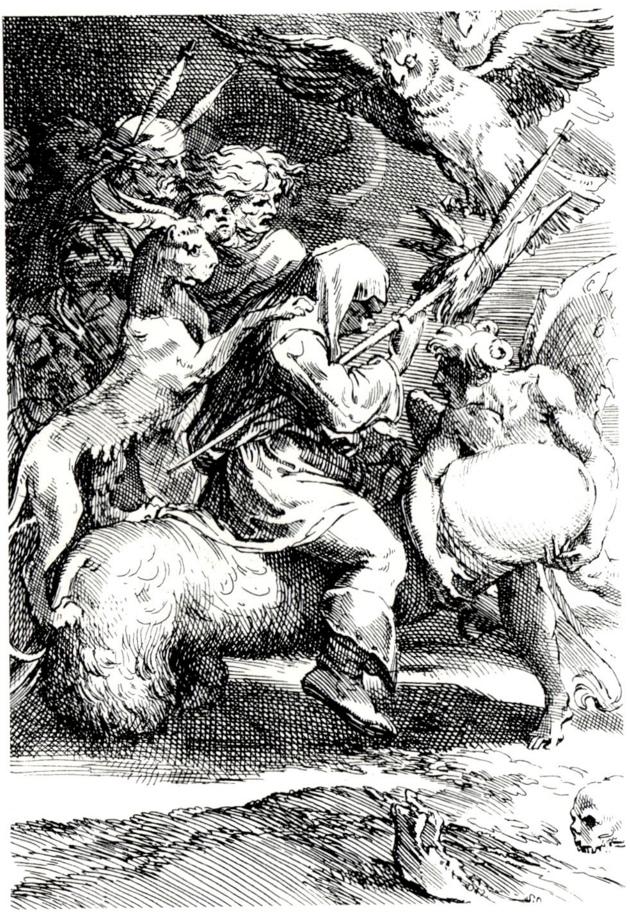

40 Parmigianino: *Witch's Sabbath*, engraving. British Museum

thousand years. He may have used a live model, although he placed her in a quasi-classical stance and gave her the fashionably small breasts expected of female nudes at that time. This was not a great masterpiece, but it was an expression of live womanhood and it must certainly have seemed very erotic and daring when it was created.

Jacquerio, a little-known artist of Turin, made the charming painting of the mediaeval conceit of *The Fountain of Youth* (Plate 31). This was said to be fed by the waters of a river which could endow those who bathed in it with youth and immortality. His picture shows old men bathing with amorous companions and climbing out with their youth and vitality restored.

As time passed the feudal hierarchy of Church and State began to lose its previously undisputed power. All over Europe men developed a degree of independence and with it came independence of thought. Increasingly the corruption and tyranny which abounded in the mediaeval world began to be criticized by groups and individuals, and the forces which eventually produced the Protestant Reformation began to grow. The Church warded off criticism by inveighing against heretics, and one variety of heretic to which attention could easily be deflected was the witch. From the fourteenth to the seventeenth century, all over Europe and latterly America, innocent men and women, but mainly women, were tortured and burned at the stake as a wave of popular hatred and fear led ordinary people to do terrible things to their neighbours and even members of their own families. Superstitious men were persuaded to believe that witches could fly, that they had intercourse with the Devil and that they were the cause of many of the misfortunes of the community. An enormous number of people were tortured into convicting themselves, and then cruelly put to death. Both then and during the centuries that followed artists frequently depicted the witch and included her erotic aspects. Parmigianino, in his *Witch's Sabbath*, showed her with her broomstick riding an enormous phallus. In 1775 an anonymous illustrator of de Sade's *Boudoir* showed *The Witch and the Devil* about to have intercourse, while *Intercourse with the Devil* is also shown in one of the brilliant series of illustrations by Joseph Smith in Erica Jong's excellent summary of the whole confused saga of witches throughout history. A witch was supposed to have her own particular demon, known as a familiar, which usually took the

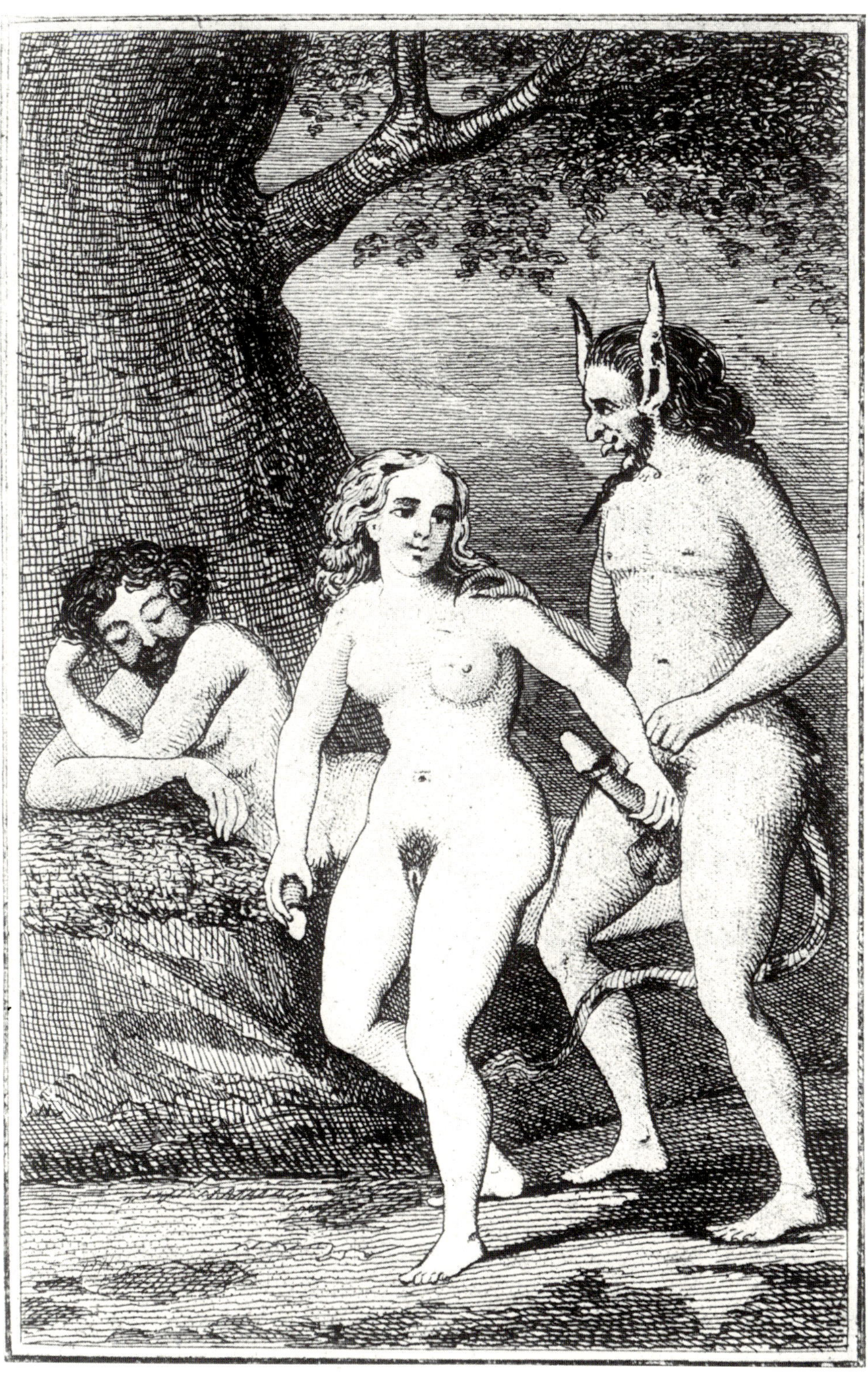

41 Anon: *The Witch and the Devil*, illustration from the Marquis de Sade's *Boudoir*, 1775

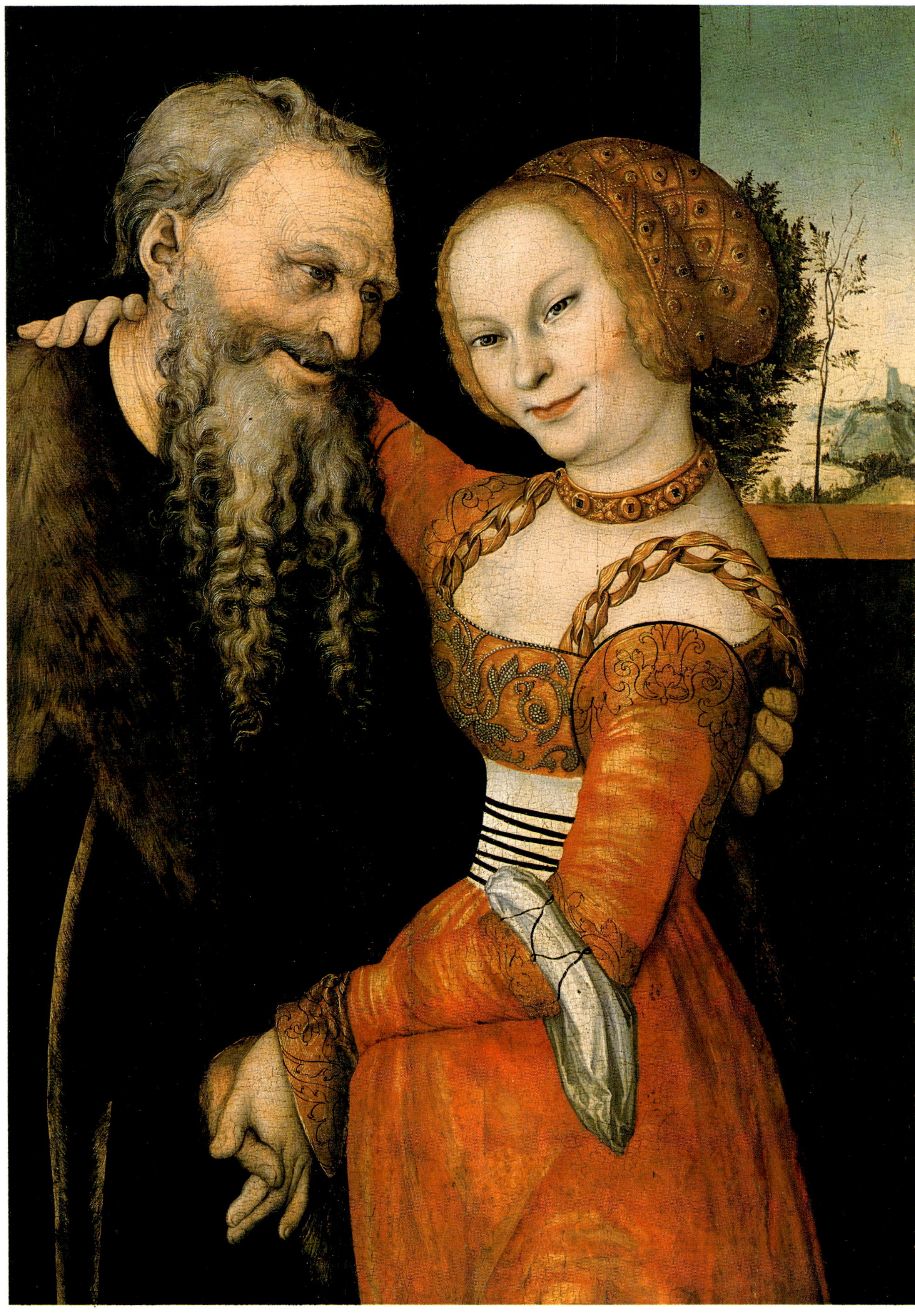

42 Lucas Cranach the Elder: *The Mismatched Couple*, c.1553. Germanisches Nationalmuseum, Nuremberg

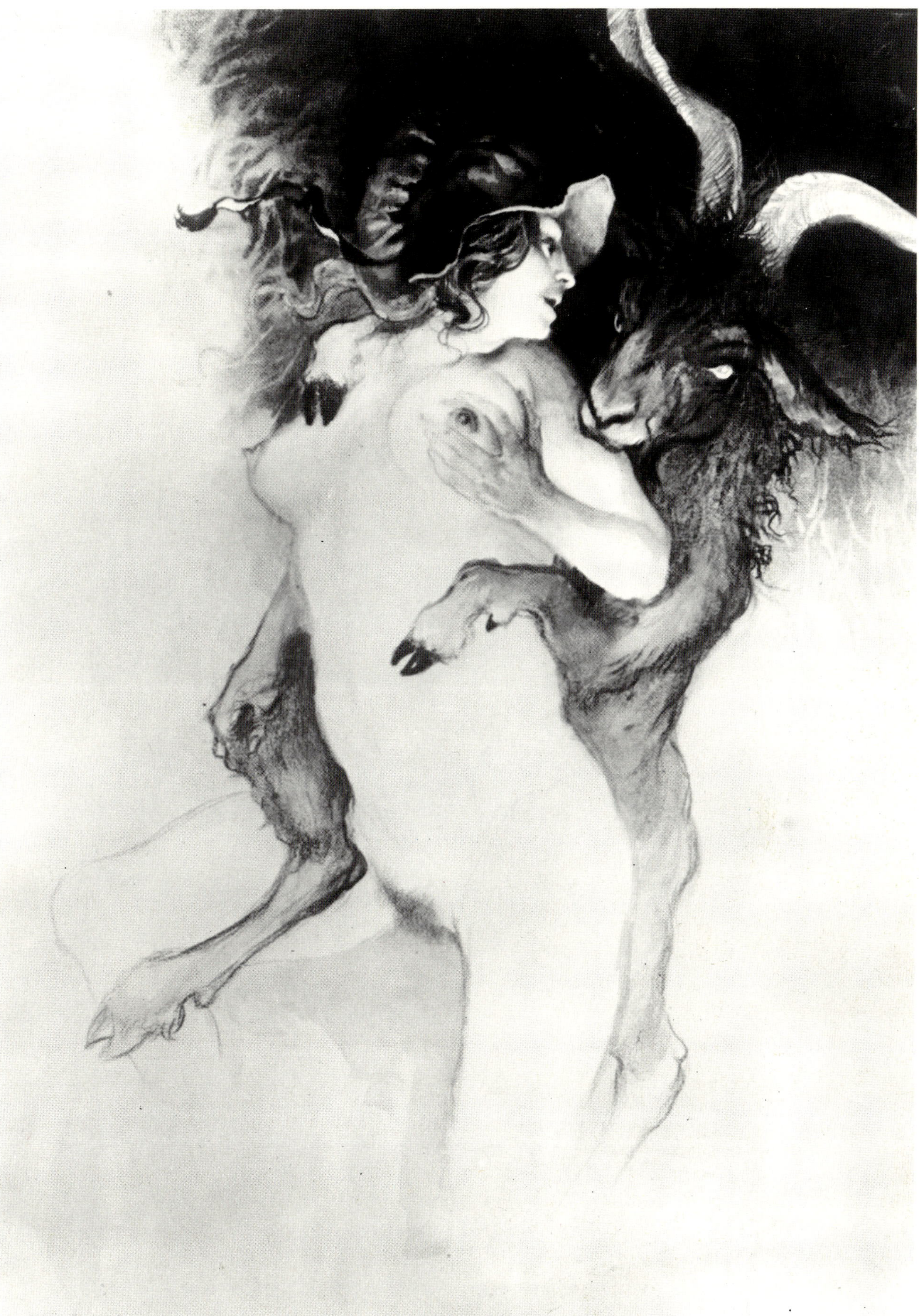

43 Joseph Smith: *Intercourse with the Devil*, illustration from Erica Jong's *Witches*, New York 1982

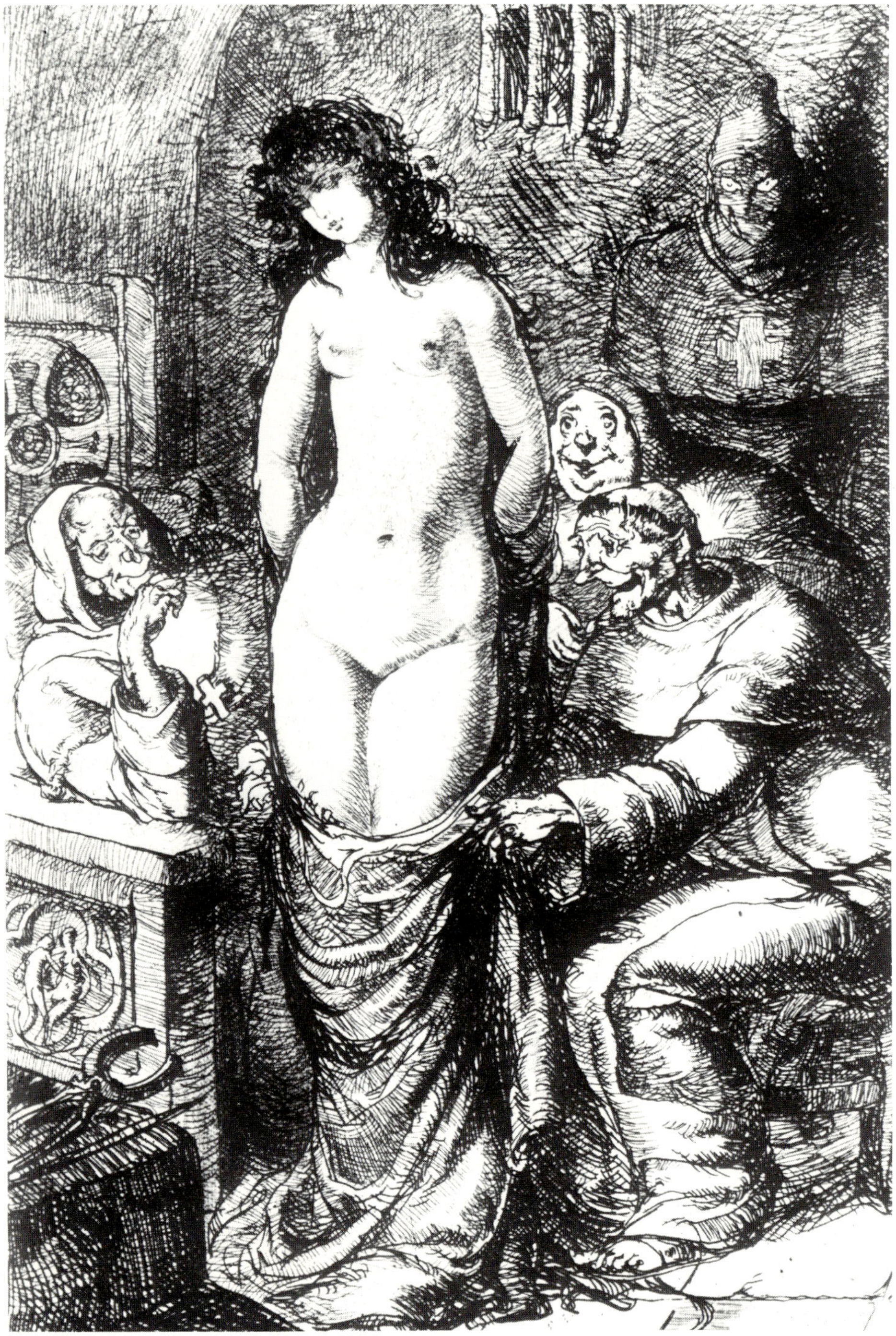

44 *(Left)* Viset: *Examination of the Witch*, illustration to the Marquis de Sade's *Léonore et Clémentine*, Paris 1930

form of an animal and was supposed to feed by sucking the witch's blood. When this occurred it left a mark upon her which was said to be insensitive to pain. It became part of the routine examination of suspected witches to search their bodies diligently for such marks. The Marquis de Sade in his story *Léonore et Clémentine* describes the very detailed physical examination of two of his heroines by members of the Inquisition, and Viset illustrates one of these examinations. Once again an artist has produced an erotic picture with the additional *frisson* of the juxtaposition of priests and a pretty, nude woman.

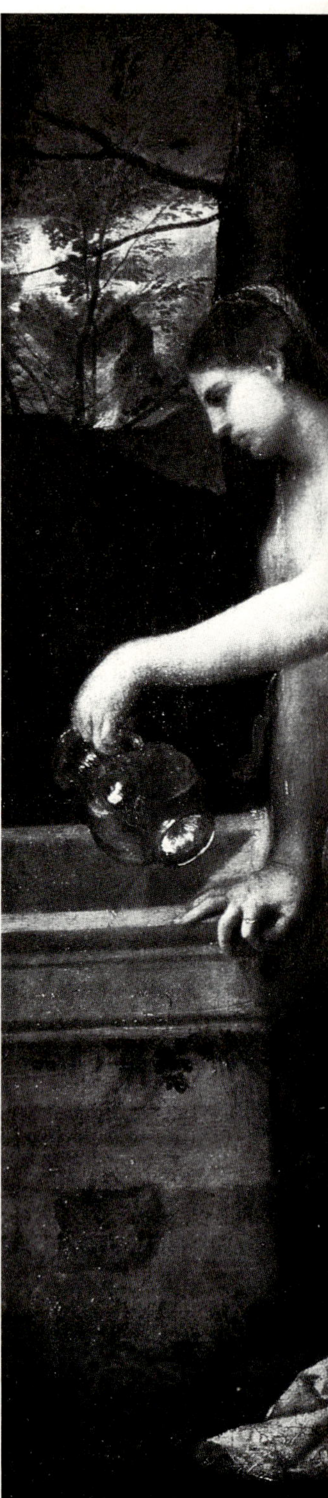

45 *(Right)* Giorgione (attr.): *Concert Champêtre*, c.1508. 109×137cm. Louvre, Paris

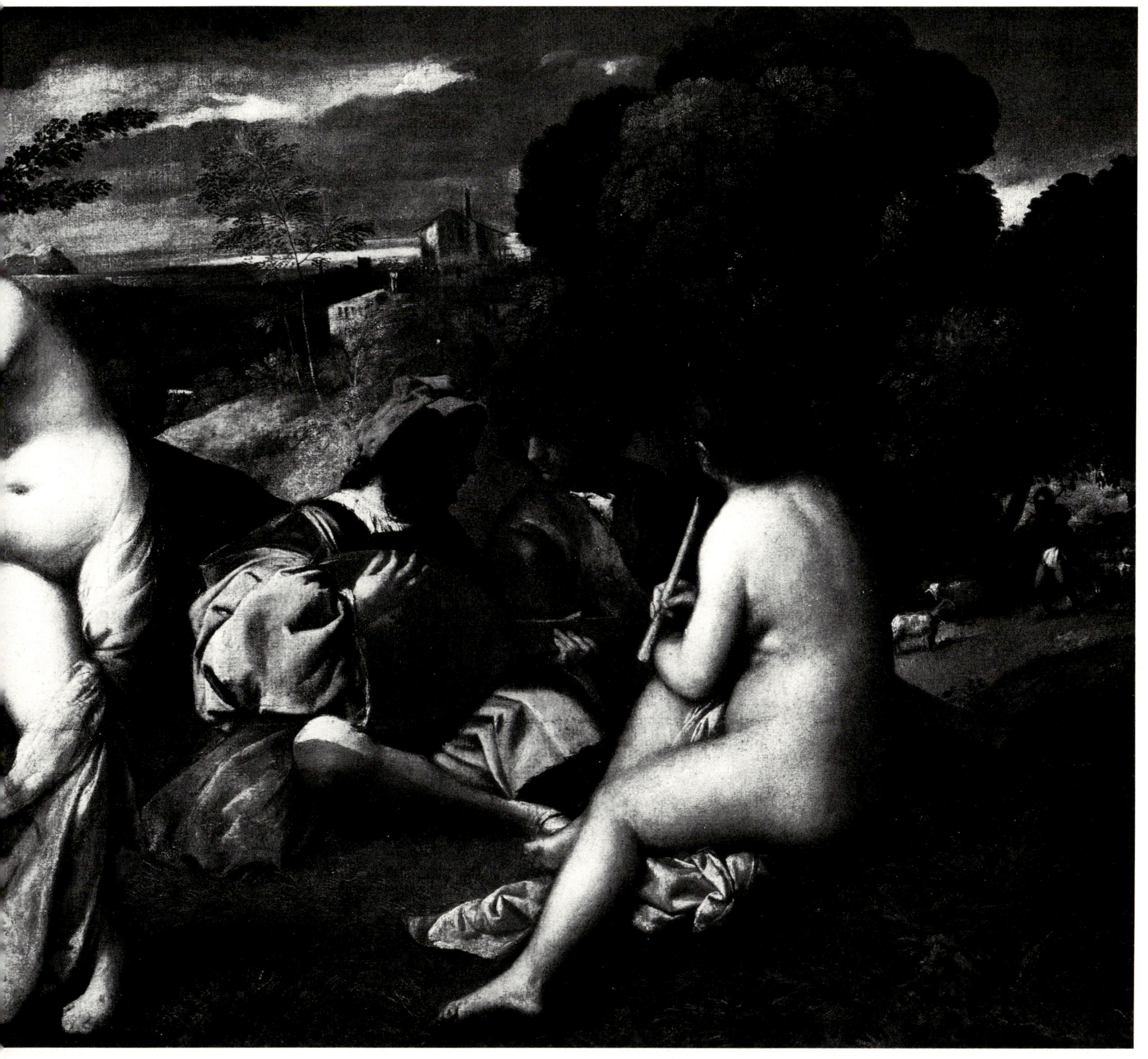

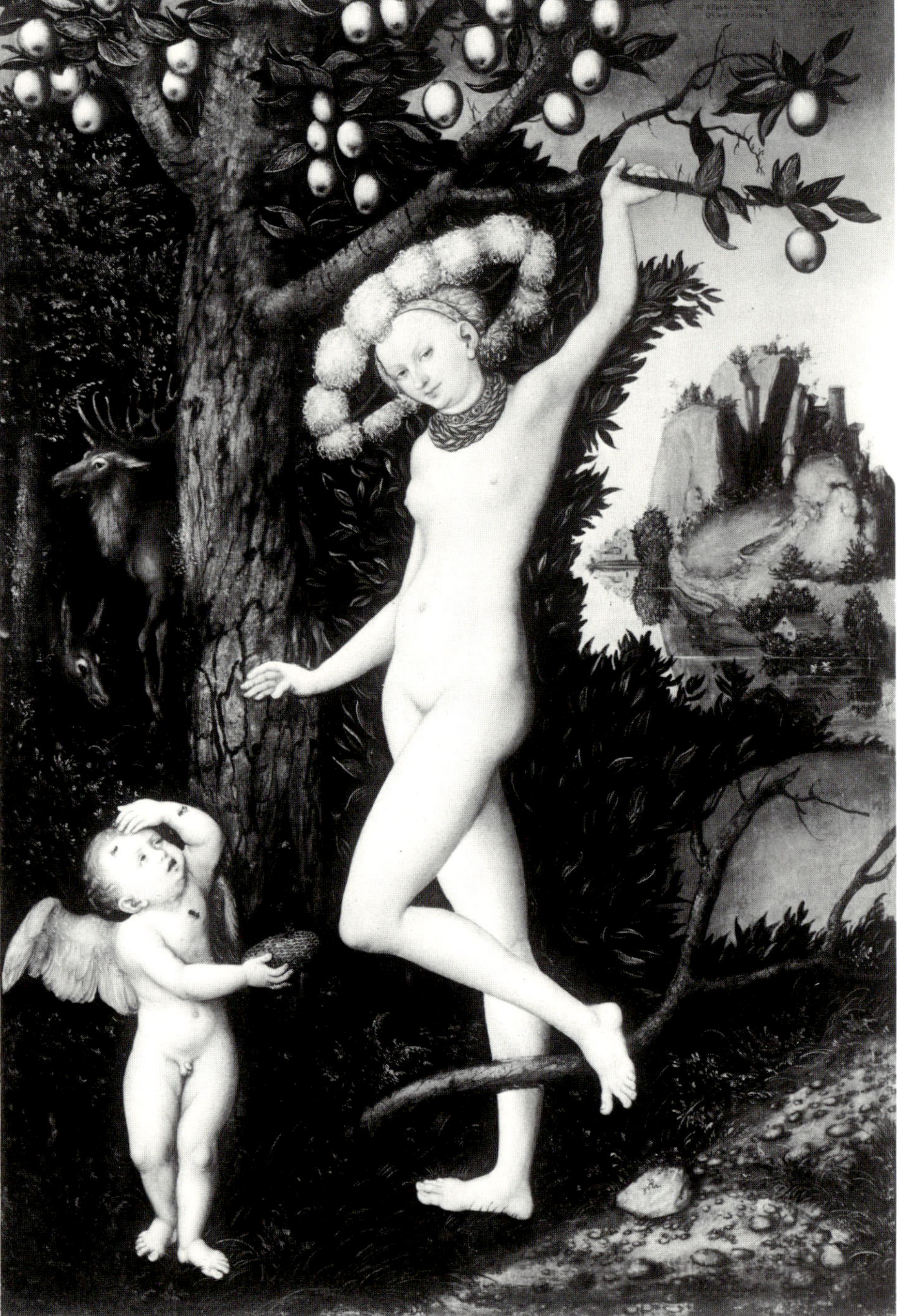

46 Lucas Cranach the Elder: *Cupid complaining to Venus*, 1553. Wood, 81.3×54.6cm. National Gallery, London

As the fourteenth and fifteenth centuries progressed a ferment of ideas sprang up all over Europe: men began to think for themselves and explore the world about them. In Italy, particularly in the field of artistic vision, men were inspired by the fragments of the Classical civilizations which were already displayed or were being unearthed. Cimabue and Giotto broke new artistic ground by bringing realism into their pictures in place of previous symbolism. A series of great artists brought back into painting the conception that men and women might be beautiful. The artists who followed, among whom

Masaccio and Botticelli were outstanding, re-introduced the nude figure, while still being careful to place it outside reality in the fairyland of mythology and allegory. It was Leonardo, with his painting of *Leda and the Swan* (Plate 34), who first added an element of eroticism, while Giorgione in his *Concert Champêtre* first painted beautiful nude women in an idyllic pastoral setting accompanied by men dressed in contemporary costume with no overt mythological excuse. Meanwhile the trend was spreading through the rest of Europe. In the first quarter of the sixteenth century several artists began to paint erotic pictures with religious and allegorical disguises. In Strasbourg, Baldung Grien (1484-1545) made a pen and ink drawing of *Death* together with a sensual woman consumed with vanity (Plate 33). In Vienna, Cranach, the close friend of Luther, had learned how to paint attractive nude women with a high degree of erotic skill. His picture of *Eve* (Plate 39) shows her as a warm, living creature of this world, fascinated by the phallic symbol of the snake and more than willing to tempt any man with her apple. His picture of *Cupid complaining to Venus* that he has been stung by bees from a honeycomb is typical of a long series of frankly erotic female nudes. In a couplet on the panel she tells him that 'Pain follows Pleasure', and standing seductively, dressed only in her eye-catching hat and her necklace, she leaves the spectator in no doubt about where that pleasure is to be found. Cranach was a superb artist and nowhere is this better shown than in his painting of *The Mismatched Couple* (Plate 42). The amused sensuality of the older man and the younger but experienced woman is, in its own way, more expressive and erotic than much of the more explicit erotic art of the present century. The Swiss artist Urs Graf was a draughtsman and engraver and his print of *Lust and the Young Woman* (Plate 28) has an unashamed expression of the subject, laced with humour and pathos. It provides a good example of how the climate of art had changed: artists concluded that they could now cautiously express the subject of sexual desire between men and women.

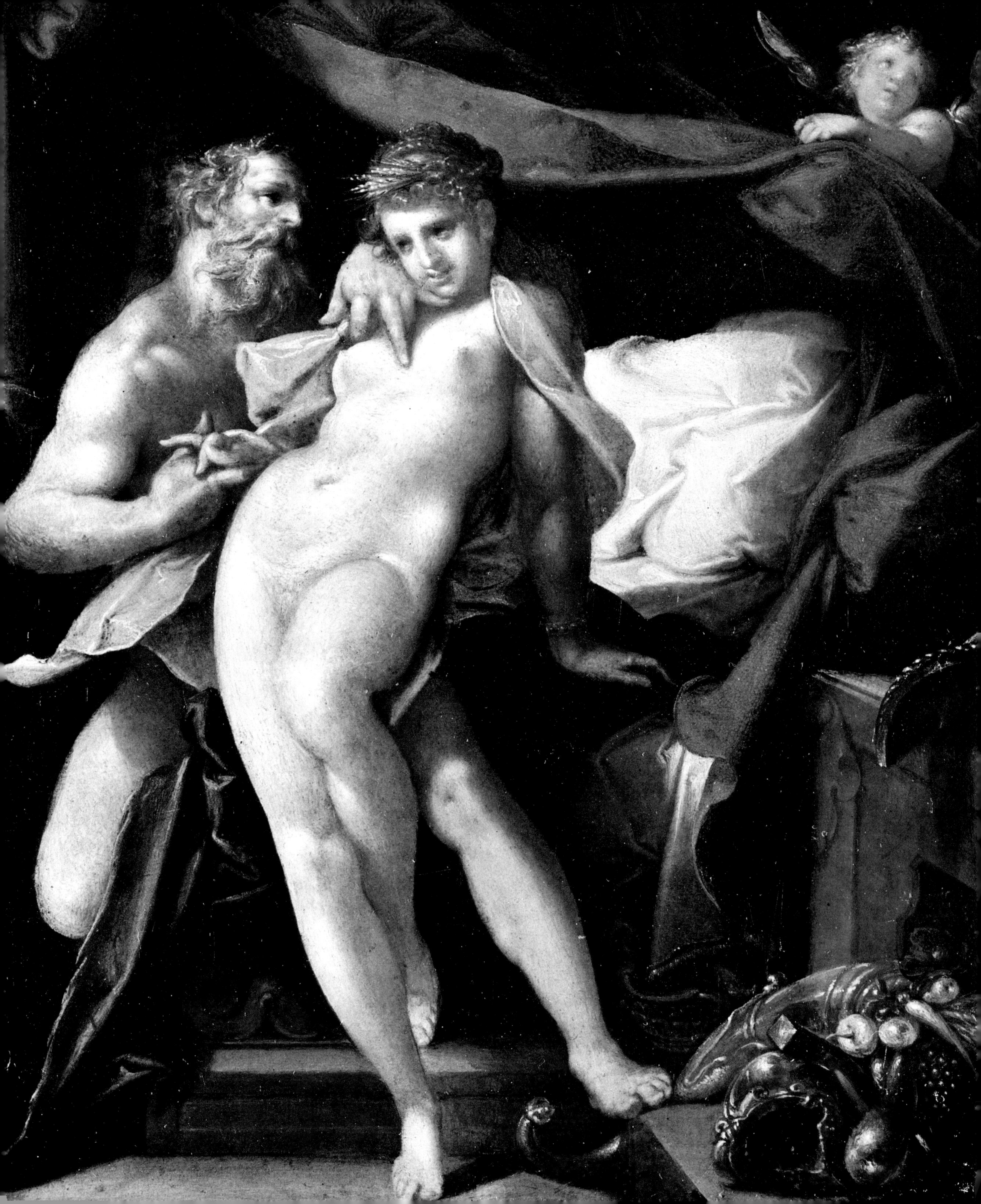

CHAPTER 3

The Renaissance

By the beginning of the sixteenth century, as a result of the civilizing and broadening effect of the Italian Renaissance on thought and vision, artists had rediscovered the beauty of the human body. They still tended to cling to the respectability of a connection with mythology, the Bible or the world of allegory. Nevertheless, nude pictures of women, painted with great skill, showed subtle but increasing eroticism. Sometimes they appeared on the same canvas as men. Increasingly it must have been found limiting to both the artist and his patron that no picture showed any couple making love. Suddenly, in Rome, there appeared a series of the most explicit erotic pictures that the West had seen since classical times.

It is a measure of the change represented by these pictures that the Church authorities and the Inquisition suppressed them so quickly and so thoroughly that none of the originals is known to exist today. What we know of them is due to four people. As a result of their actions it is almost certain that two good copies of the series are available today. The story of the four people and the parts which they played is a fascinating one.

The artist who produced the pictures was Giulio Pippi (1492-1546), who became known as 'Romano' because he was born and brought up in Rome. He had a natural talent for drawing and is generally acknowledged to have been Raphael's best pupil. In 1520, when Raphael died, Giulio Romano had been acting as his chief assistant in the decoration of the Vatican and he completed a number of Raphael's pictures. He is regarded as one of the originators of the style of Mannerism, which tends to exaggerate for effect, producing muscular figures in rather melodramatic situations. This style is well portrayed in his frescoes in the Hall of Psyche in the Palazzo del Tè at Mantua (Plates 61,67). A short time after Raphael's death, Giulio Romano made sixteen explicit, erotic pictures of men and women having intercourse. The scenes were indoors and show the naked participants obviously enjoying themselves without any suspicion that they might be observed. With considerable ingenuity the artist has placed them in postures which leave nothing to the imagination, although this has led later critics to pronounce the positions awkward. Those criticisms were probably made without consideration of the difficulty of composing an explicit sex picture.

47 Bartholomäus Spranger: *Vulcan and Maia*, c.1590. Copper, 23×18cm. Kunsthistorisches Museum, Vienna

It is not clear in what form these pictures were produced. There

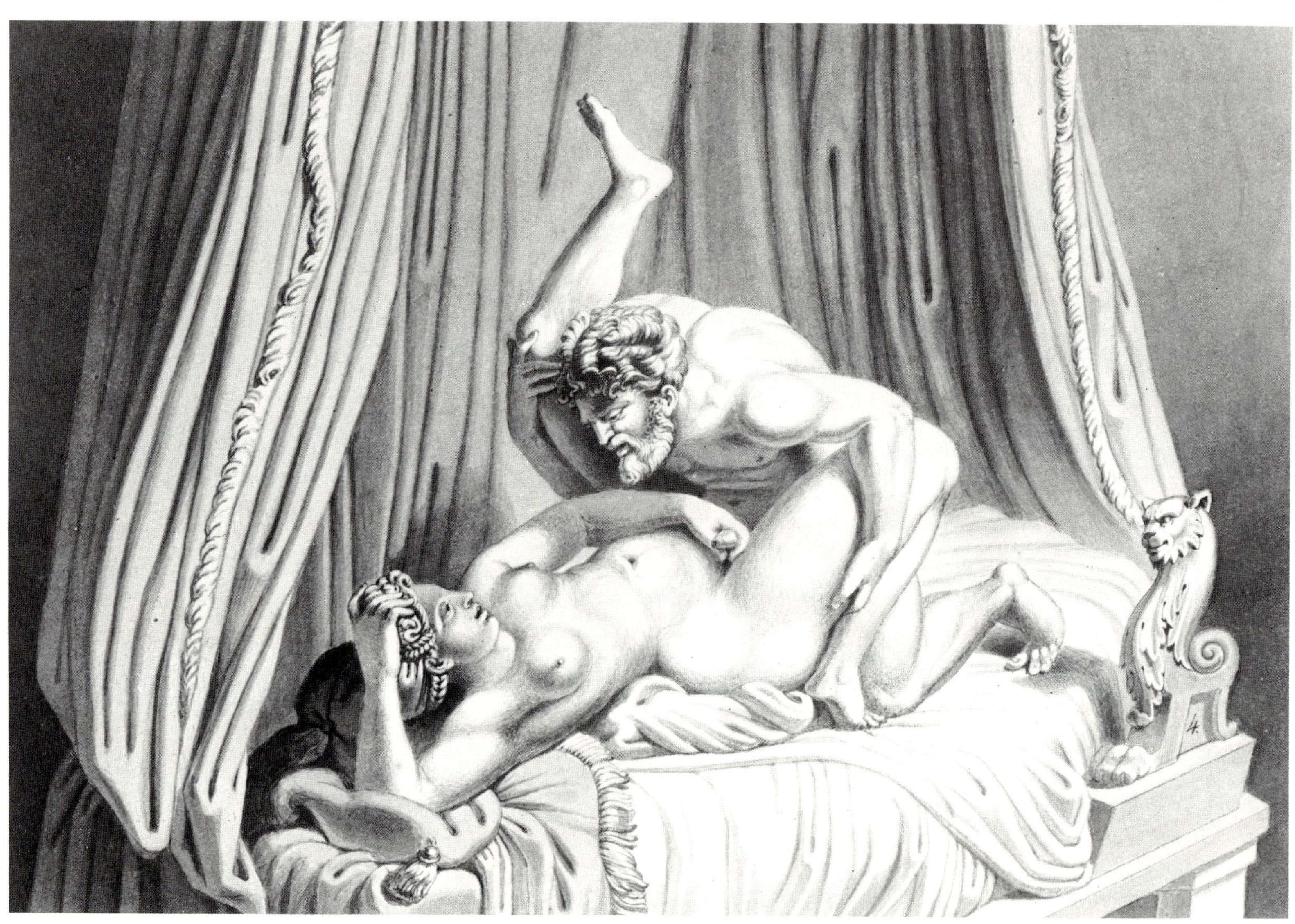

48 Waldeck (after Raimondi): illustration to Aretino's *Sonetti Lussoriosi*. Ink and wash, c.1831. British Museum

was a suggestion that they were painted on the walls of a room in the Vatican, when the artist wanted to protest that he had been kept waiting for payment. It is much more likely that they were drawings.[*] What we do know is that when the Church authorities became aware of them the original pictures were all destroyed, and Giulio Romano left Rome and went to Mantua, where he spent the rest of his life.

The second person in the story was Marcantonio Raimondi, who was an accomplished engraver, with commissions from many artists, and occasionally an artist in his own right. It is uncertain whether

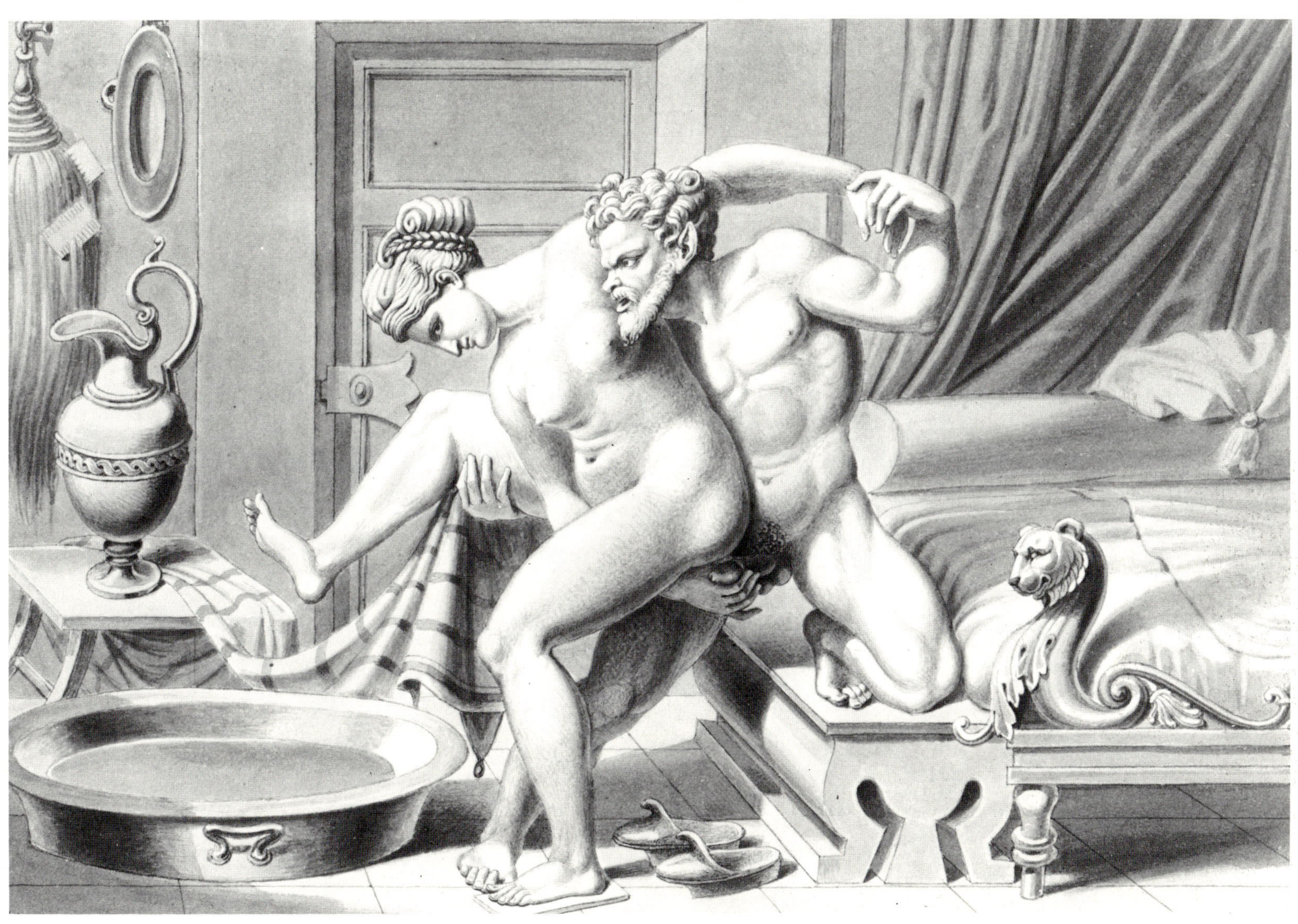

49 Waldeck (after Raimondi): illustration to Aretino (details as Plate 48)

Giulio Romano had commissioned him to make engravings from the original erotic pictures. Perhaps Raimondi made them on his own account, from his memory of the pictures he had seen. What is certain is that he did make sixteen erotic engravings based on Giulio Romano's pictures, which he published in 1523. As soon as the Church authorities became aware of these, Raimondi was imprisoned and every effort was made to destroy the engravings and the plates from which they had been printed. This time, however, many people had seen them. Various people later claimed that they had

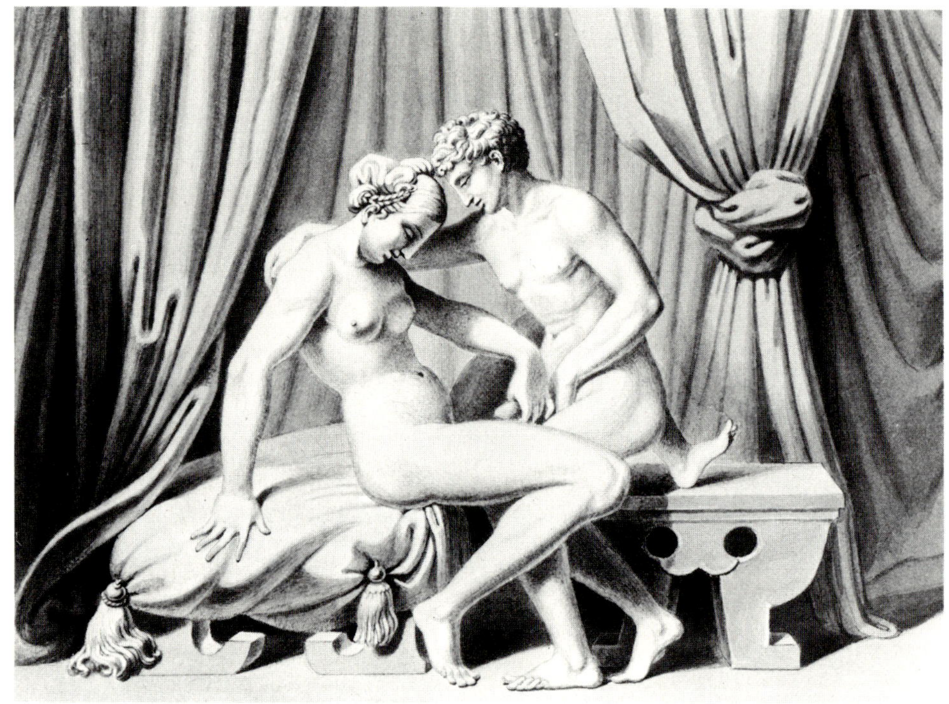

50 Waldeck (after Raimondi): illustration to Aretino (details as Plate 48)

played a part in obtaining Raimondi's release from prison.

The third person in the story was Pietro Aretino (1492-1556), a very independent-minded writer and commentator of the day who had become notorious throughout Europe. His outspoken criticism, laced with wit and satire, of those in power and authority had made him known as 'the scourge of Princes'. He was also a successful writer of erotic literature. It is evident that he was full of admiration for Raimondi's engravings, and he is one of those who claimed to have obtained Raimondi's release from prison. Following that release Raimondi and Aretino, apparently undeterred by what had previously happened, worked together to produce yet another version of the engravings together with a sonnet about each, written by Aretino and engraved by Raimondi. This new series contained four new subjects, making a total of twenty, but no one is sure about the origin of the four additional pictures. They may have been based on four previously unknown drawings by Giulio Romano or they may have been created by Raimondi himself. The new engravings and sonnets were published in 1527 with the title *Sonetti Lussoriosi* (Lustful Sonnets) by Pietro Aretino. Aretino, who had always lived

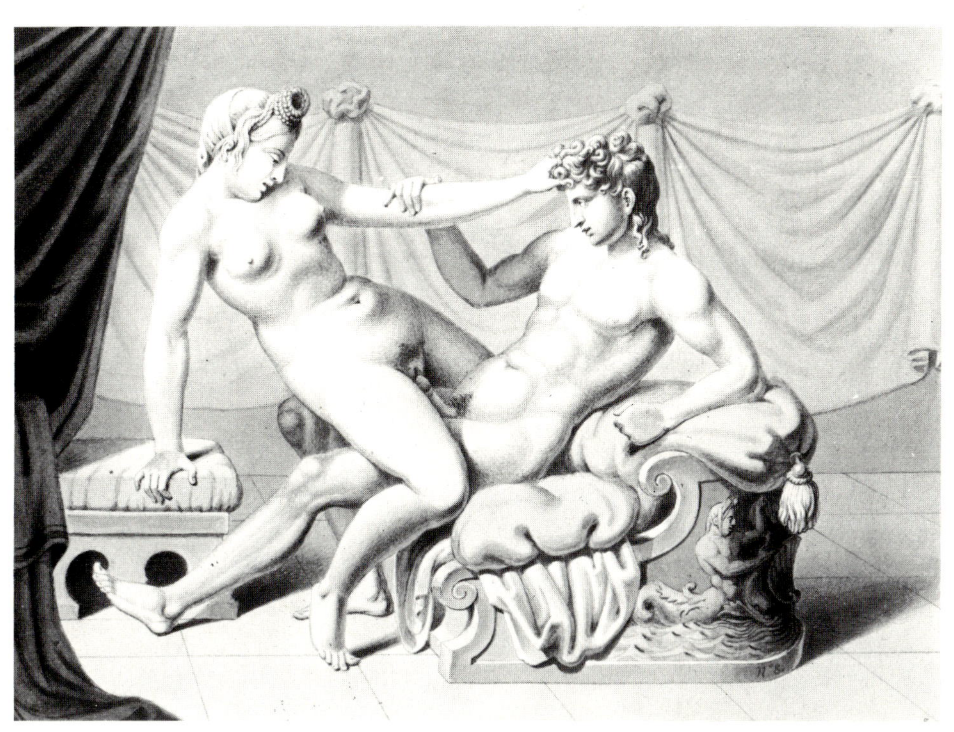

51 Waldeck (after Raimondi): illustration to Aretino (details as Plate 48)

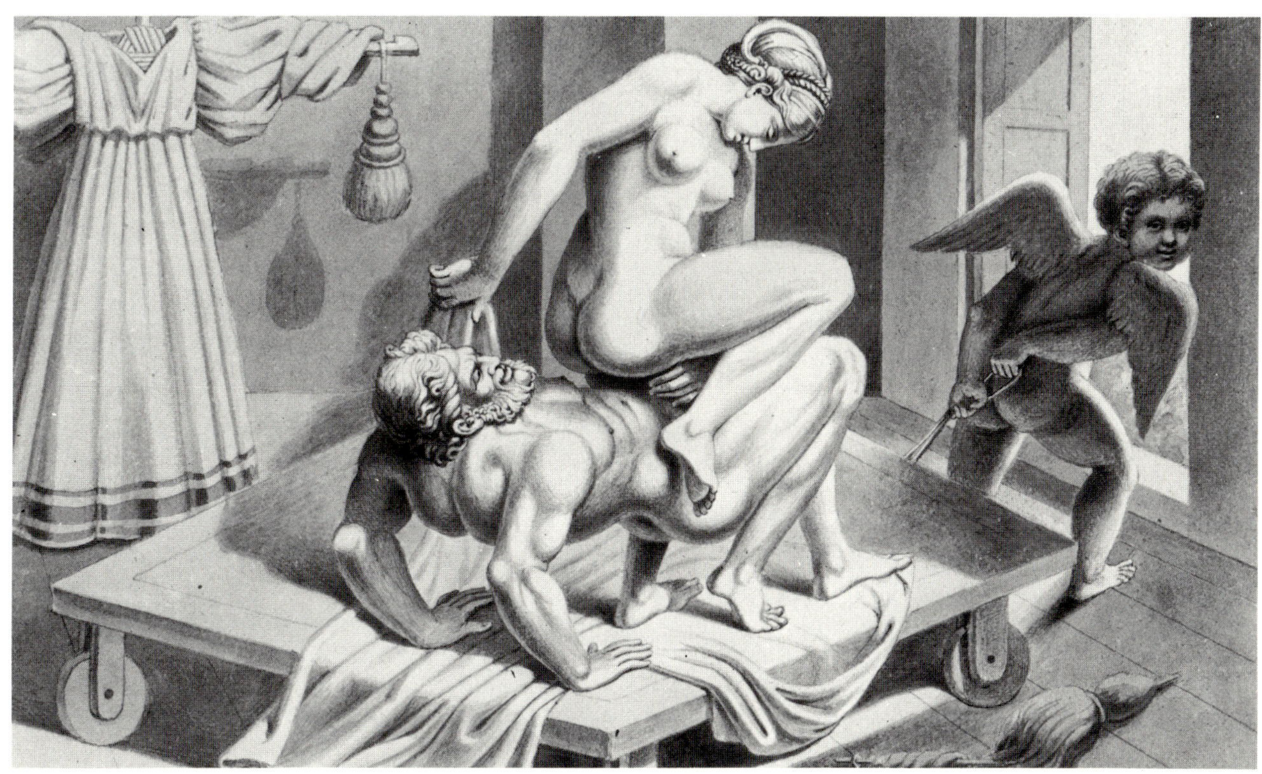

52 Waldeck (after Raimondi): illustration to Aretino (details as Plate 48)

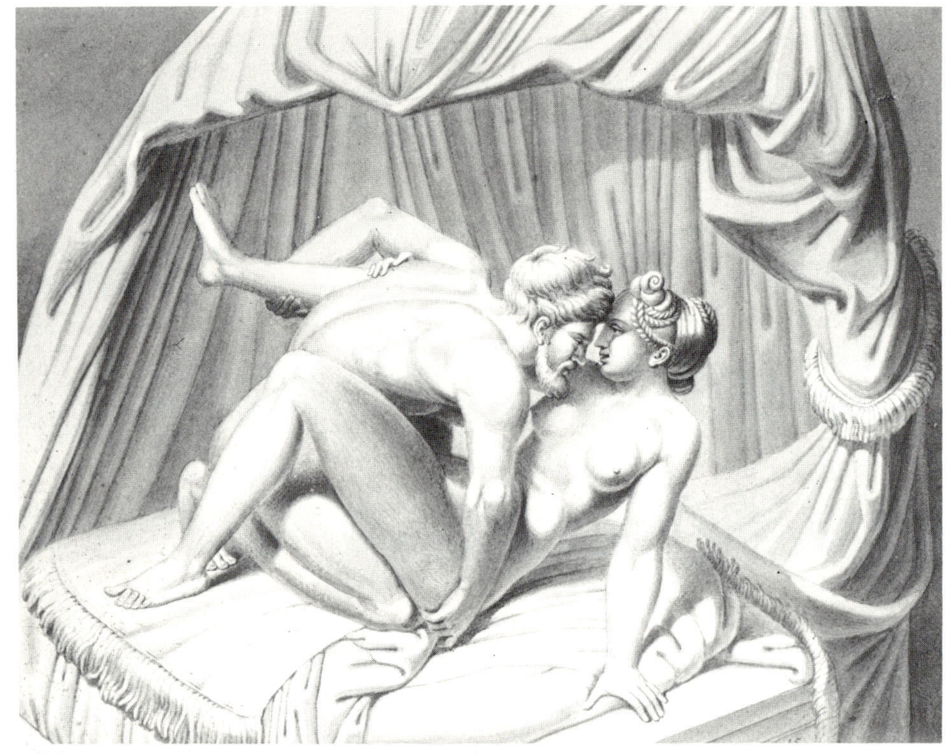

53 Waldeck (after Raimondi): illustration to Aretino (details as Plate 48)

by his wits, had departed for Milan and Venice before publication, which, since it took place in the year when Rome was sacked, occurred amid great confusion and destruction. The sonnets themselves have been applauded by some for their frank, honest, explicit and earthy themes and language and denounced by others for the same reasons. Their colloquial, bawdy language makes them difficult to translate into English. In spite of strenuous efforts to destroy them, sufficient copies of the book remained for it to have been seen and been influential throughout Europe, although no original copy is known to exist today. Two pages, each showing the same engraving, which are thought to have come from the book, are in existence. One is in the British Museum and the other in Vienna. The British Museum also has nine small pieces of engravings showing the heads and parts of the body of nine figures which are almost certainly small, expurgated pieces of the original pages. In addition, there is a series of fourteen woodcuts which are thought to have been copied from the original engravings about 1530. These are in the hands of a private collector in Switzerland.

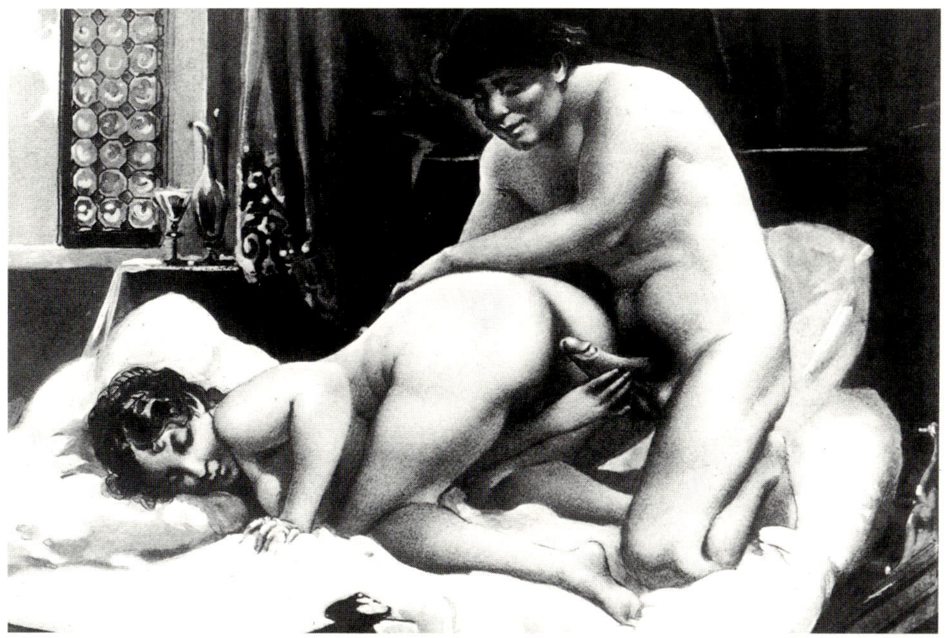

54 *(Left)* Anon: illustration to 19th-century edition of *Sonnets Luxurieux de l'Aretin*. British Museum

55 *(Below)* Anon: illustration to 19th-century edition of *Sonnets Luxurieux de l'Aretin*. British Museum

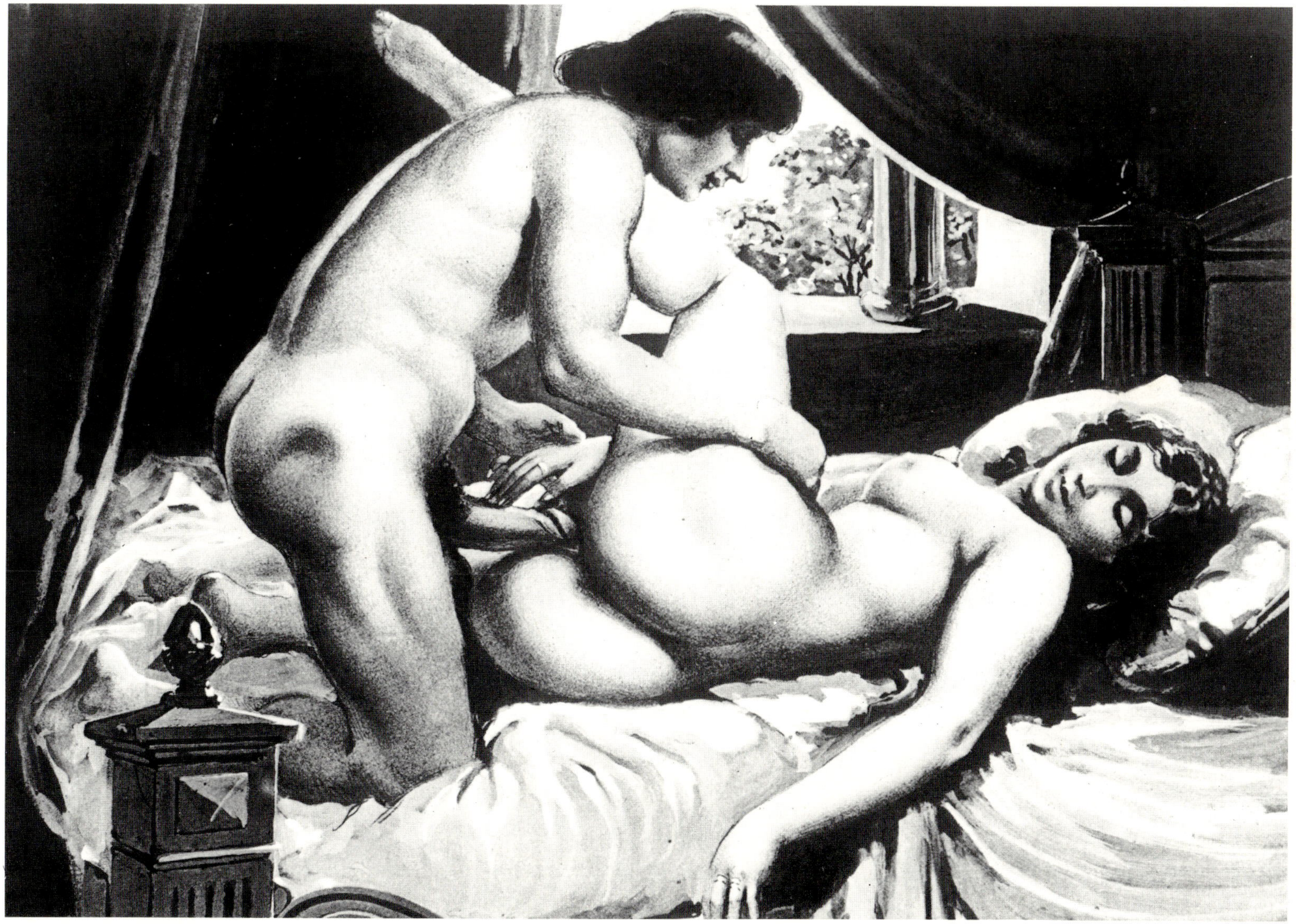

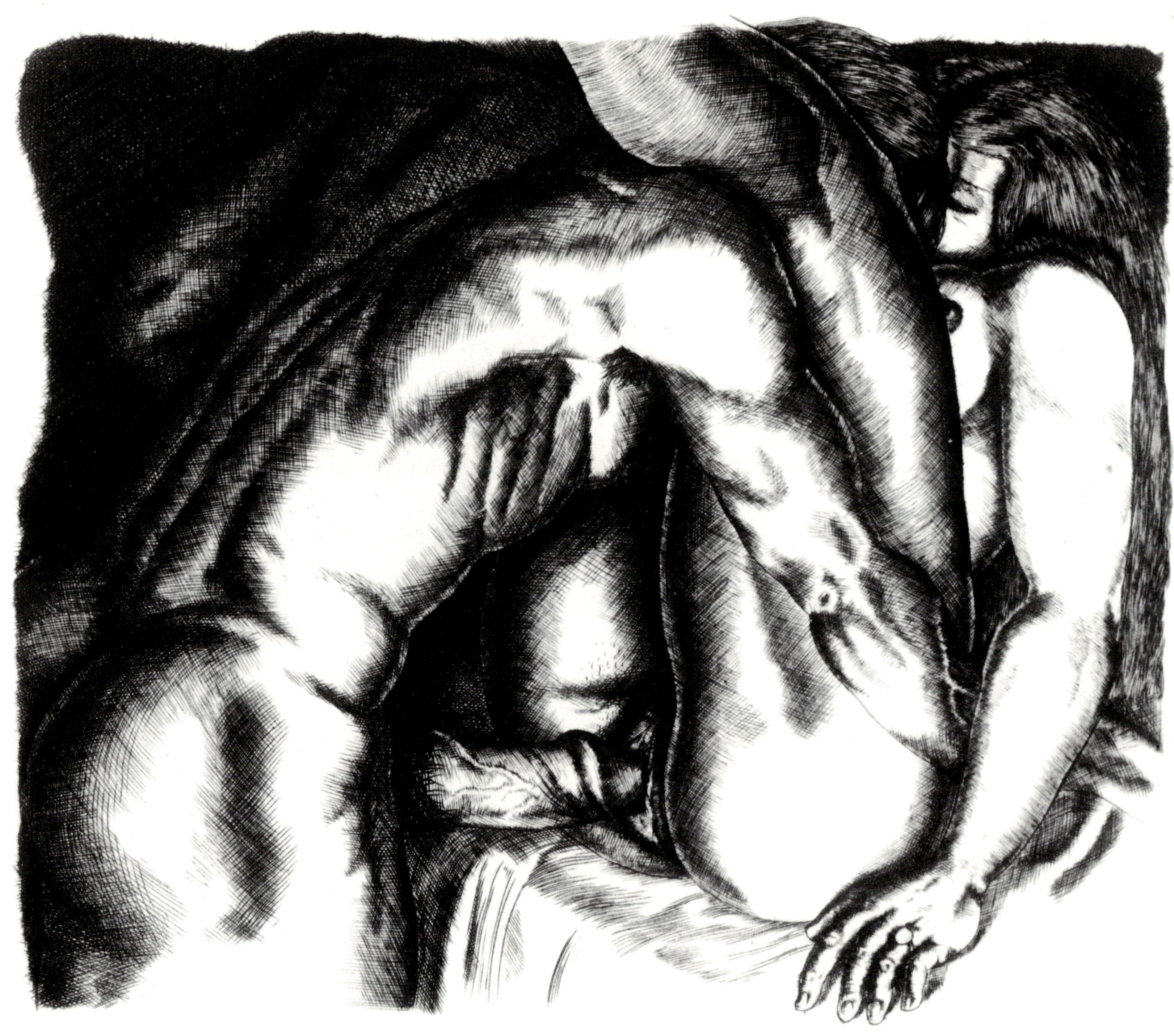

56 *(Left)* Anon: illustration to privately printed 20th-century edition of *Sonnets Luxurieux de Pietro Aretino dit l'Aretin,* copper engraving. France, 1948

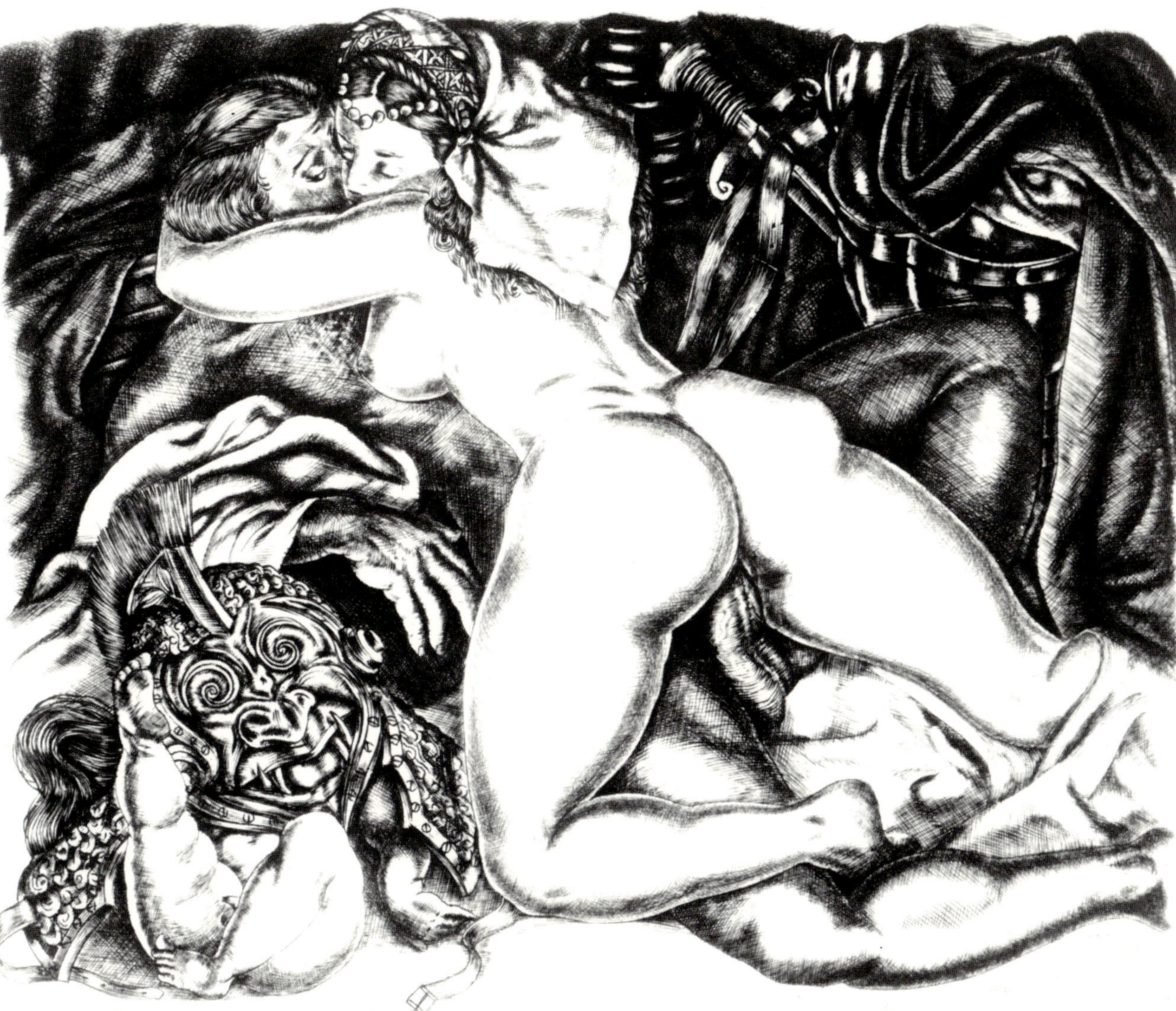

57 Anon: illustration to privately printed 20th-century edition of *Sonnets Luxurieux de Pietro Aretino dit l'Aretin,* copper engraving. France, 1948

The fourth person, who appeared much later in the story, was Baron Frederic Waldeck (1786-1875), who was born in Prague. Like many young men of his day he travelled widely through Europe and across the world to seek his fortune. He studied art under the French artist Vien in Paris, and became sufficiently skilful to be employed as an illustrator. He also led an adventurous life, following different occupations around the world. At the age of 65 he made the claim that in 1831 he had found a set of the Raimondi engravings in a convent in Mexico City and had copied them. At least two identical copies, which he had almost certainly made, are known. One is in the British Museum and the other in the Bibliothèque Nationale in Paris. Both are meticulously drawn in ink and wash in the classical manner which would be expected from a pupil of Vien. They correspond very well with the nine fragments of the original in the British Museum and are probably as accurate a copy as a professional illustrator could make them. Each set contains twenty pictures, and illustrated are six of these Waldeck copies. They show at once what a complete

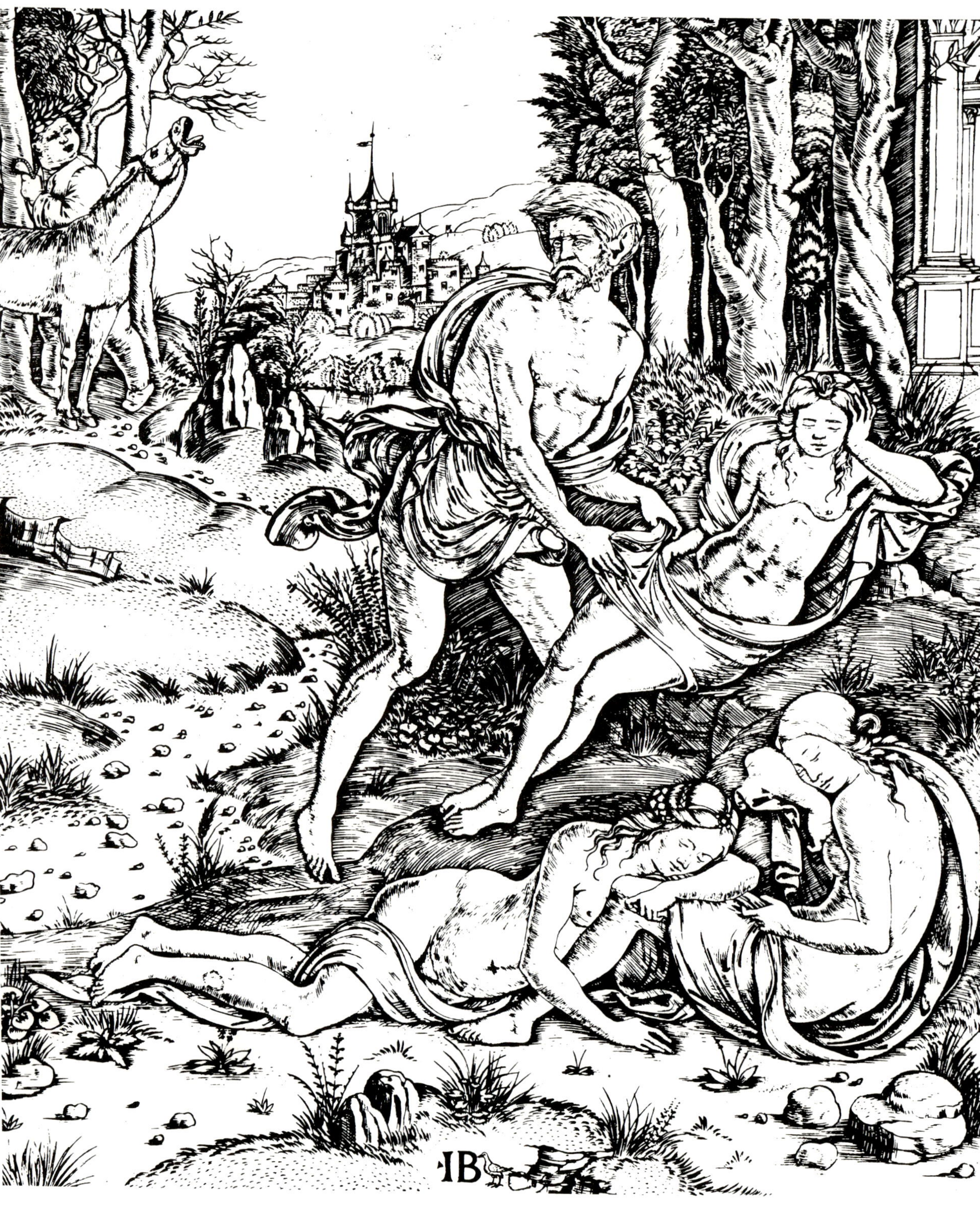

58 Giovanni Battista del Porto: *Priapus and Lotis*. Engraving, c.1525. British Museum

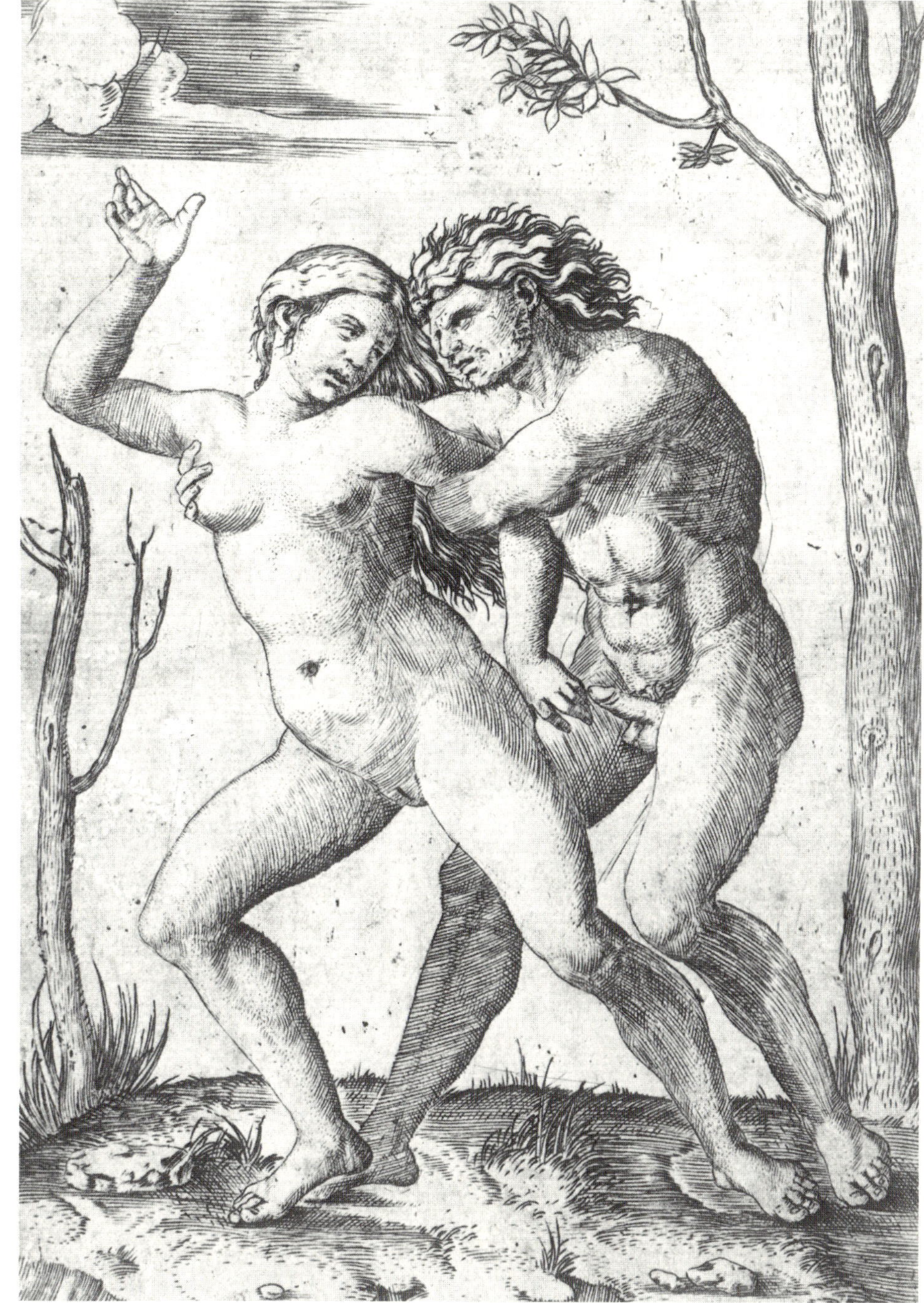

59 After Giulio Romano: *Erotic Scene*, engraving. British Museum

break Giulio Romano had made with the conventions of his day.

There have been a number of translations of the sonnets into different languages, some of which have been illustrated by new artists, but none of these were copied from the original book (Plates 54 and 55; 56 and 57).

Giulio Romano had made other erotic drawings besides this series, and Plate 59 is thought to be an engraving from one of them. This was probably contemporary with the artist and therefore gives a good impression of his style. Another explicit print of about 1525, which has been tentatively ascribed to G.B. del Porto, is *Priapus and Lotis*.

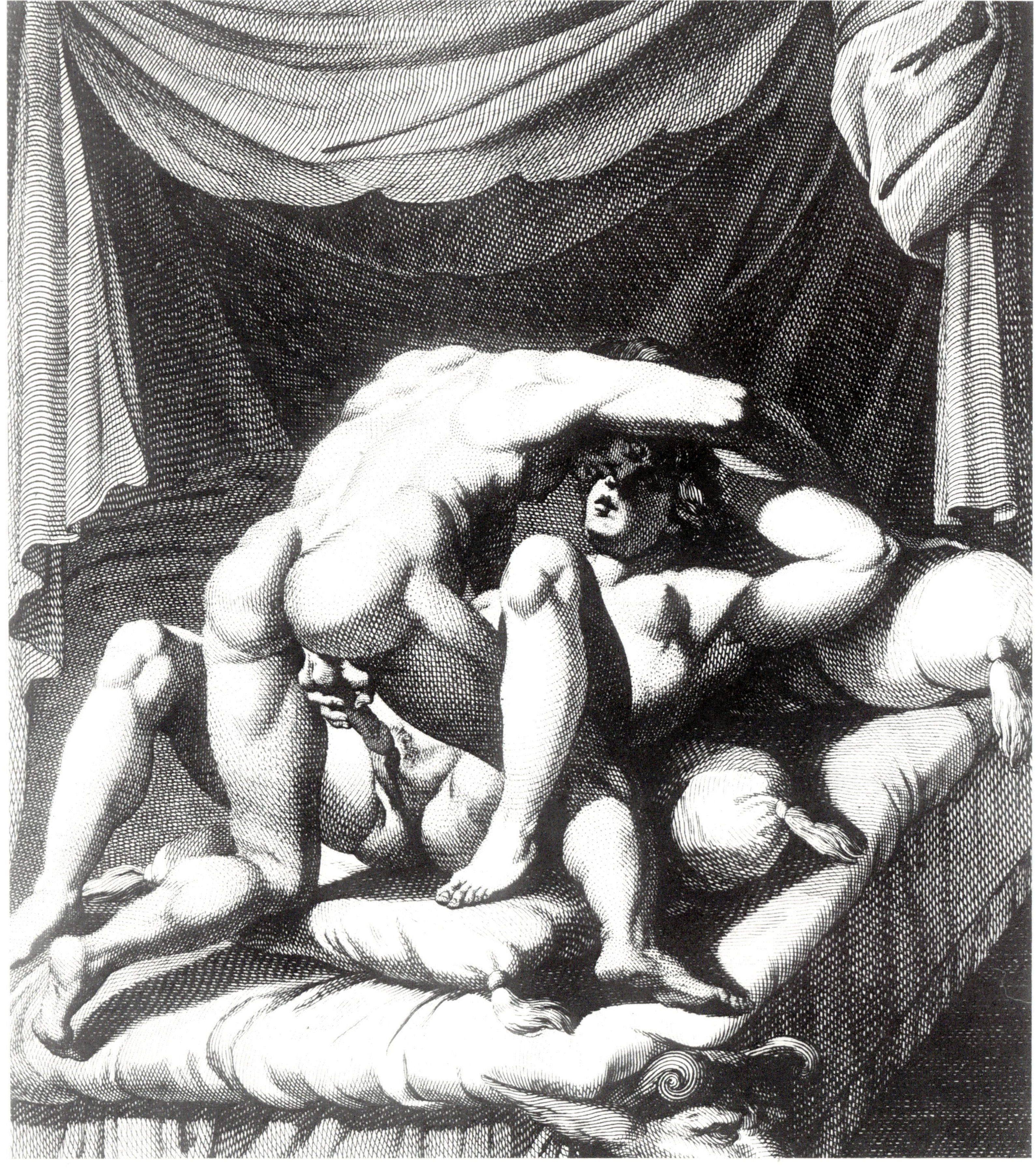

In Mantua Giulio Romano obtained the patronage of Duke Federico II almost as soon as he had arrived. He spent the remainder of his life supervising the architectural development of the town. Vasari, commenting on his many designs of chapels, houses, gardens and façades, was enthusiastic. The town, he said, had become charming and pleasant with the look of a 'new Rome'. The Palazzo del Tè was built for Federico II and is particularly connected with his love affair with Isabella Bouschetto. The centre of the building was the Hall of Psyche, and the upper walls and ceiling of this large room are entirely covered by Giulio Romano's pictures of an allegory of love with mythological figures. Plate 67 shows a detail from the *Marriage Feast of Cupid and Psyche* and Plate 61 shows Jupiter in one of his many disguises as a sea-god, about to make love to Olympia. In these paintings Giulio Romano had produced sexually explicit mythological painting for all the world to see. This did not mean, of course, that many similar pictures would be painted. The pleasures of sex are private pleasures and erotic art has almost always been produced in a form suitable for private viewing. What Giulio Romano had made clear to other artists was that explicit, erotic art was possible.

Titian (1487-1576) had little need to entice his patrons by providing erotic subjects. Not only was he a superb painter, he was also a very fortunate one. One by one the great artists of the Renaissance, who might have been his rivals, died. Giorgione, a fellow Venetian, whose style was particularly close to his, and who was only about ten years older, died of the plague in his early thirties in 1510. Titian was to spend the whole of his long and prolific life trying to keep up with the widespread demand for his paintings. He became rich and successful, and all the evidence shows that he enjoyed the pleasures of life and the society of pretty women. The erotic elements in his many paintings, however, were very few. Even his otherwise marvellous painting of *Danaë* shows a beautiful nude girl apparently oblivious of a seducing shower of gold. Apart from possible exceptions such as *Venus and the Organ Player* and the *Nymph and Shepherd*, which he painted in his old age, his most erotic painting was the *Venus of Urbino* (Plate 65). This he painted in 1538 as a direct commission from the future Duke of Urbino who described it as 'the naked woman'. In 1598 it was described by a later Duke of Urbino as 'lascivious' and the title of 'Venus' as only a courtesy one. Many years

60 Anon: *Ovid and Corinne*, detail of illustration to an edition of Aretino's *Sonetti lussoriosi*, engraving

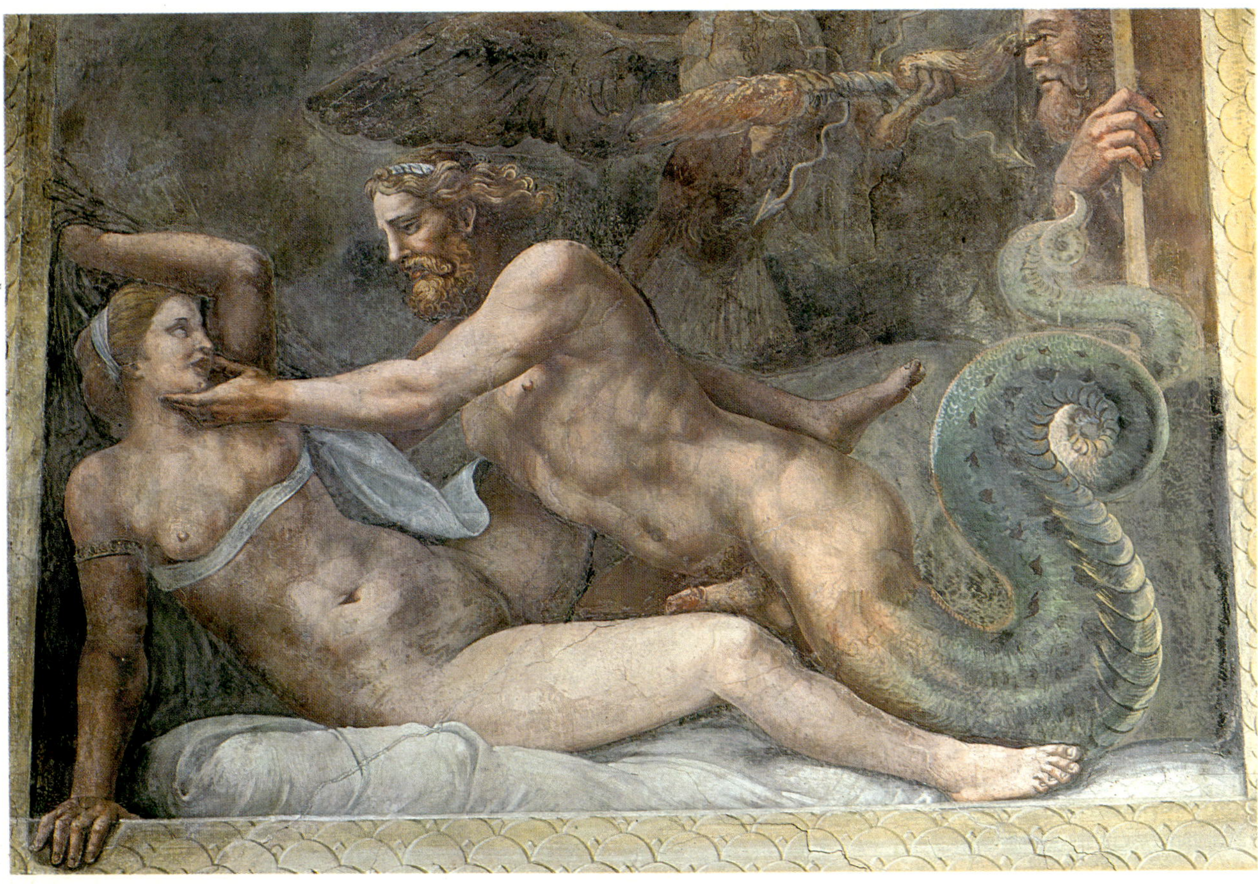

61 *(Left)* Giulio Romano: *Jupiter and Olympia*. Fresco, c.1528. Palazzo del Tè, Mantua

62 *(Below)* School of Fontainebleau: *Nymph and Satyr*, c.1550

63 *(Right)* Bronzino: *Allegory: Venus, Cupid, Folly and Time*. Panel, c.1542-5. 146×116cm. National Gallery, London

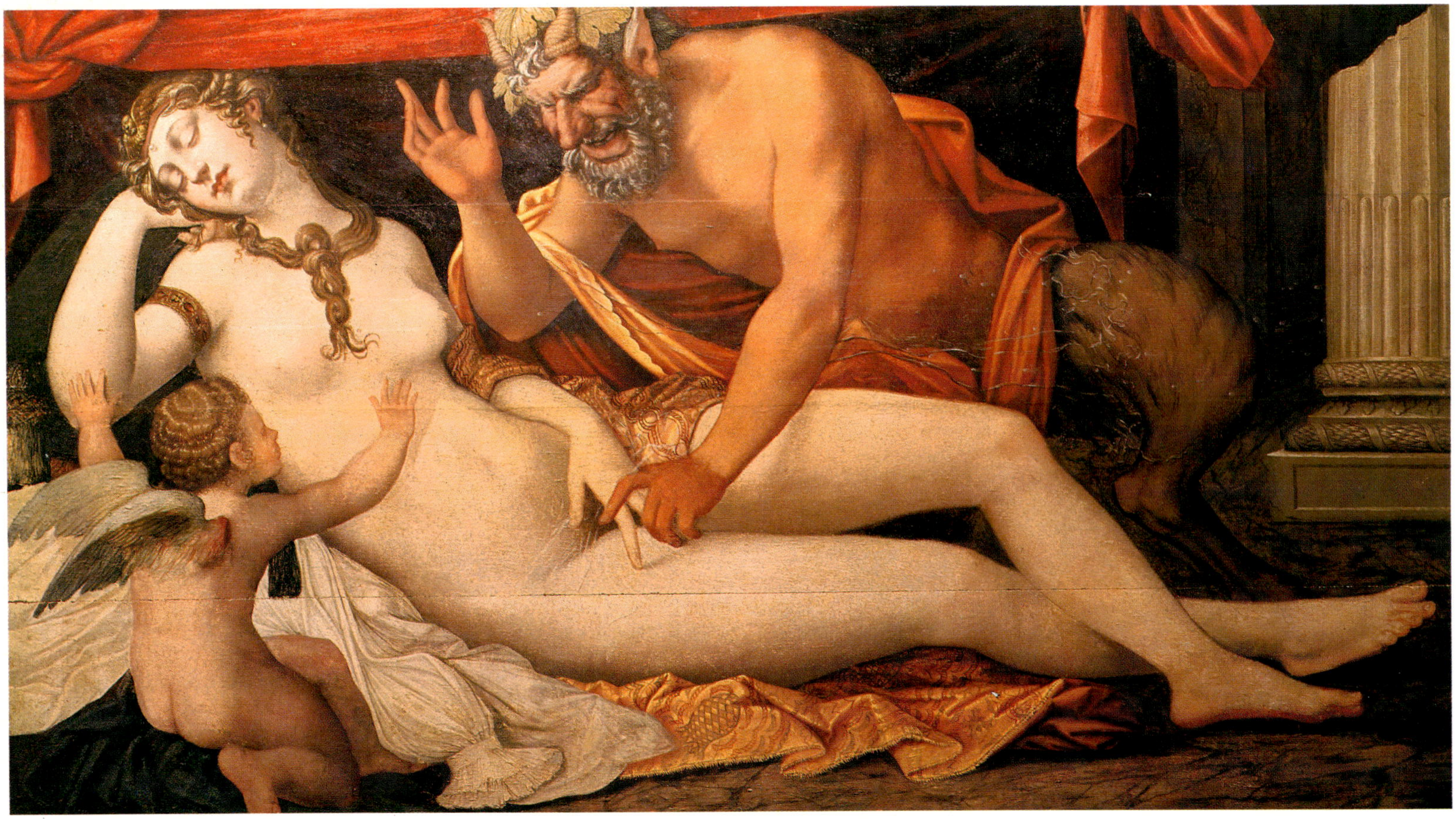

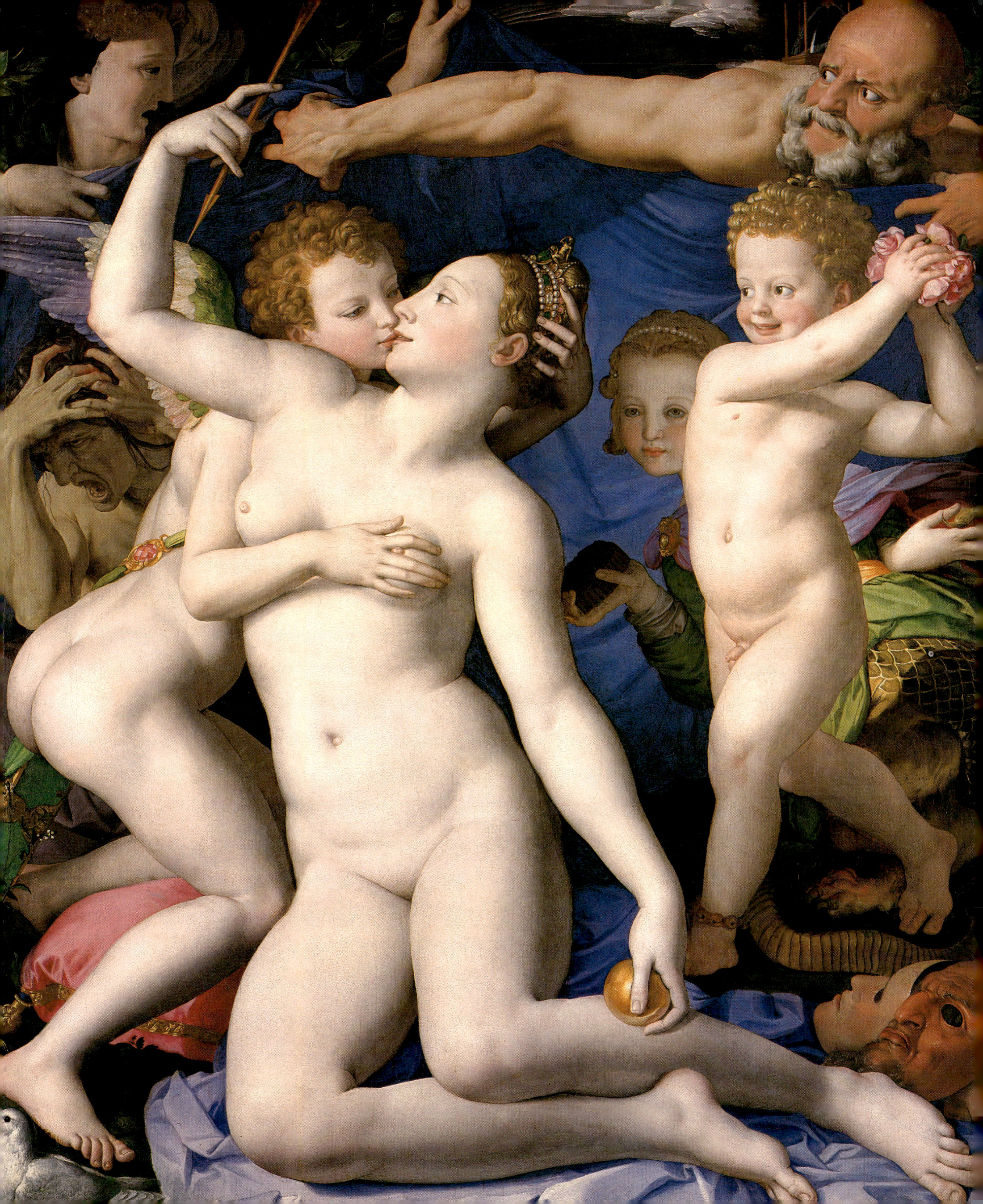

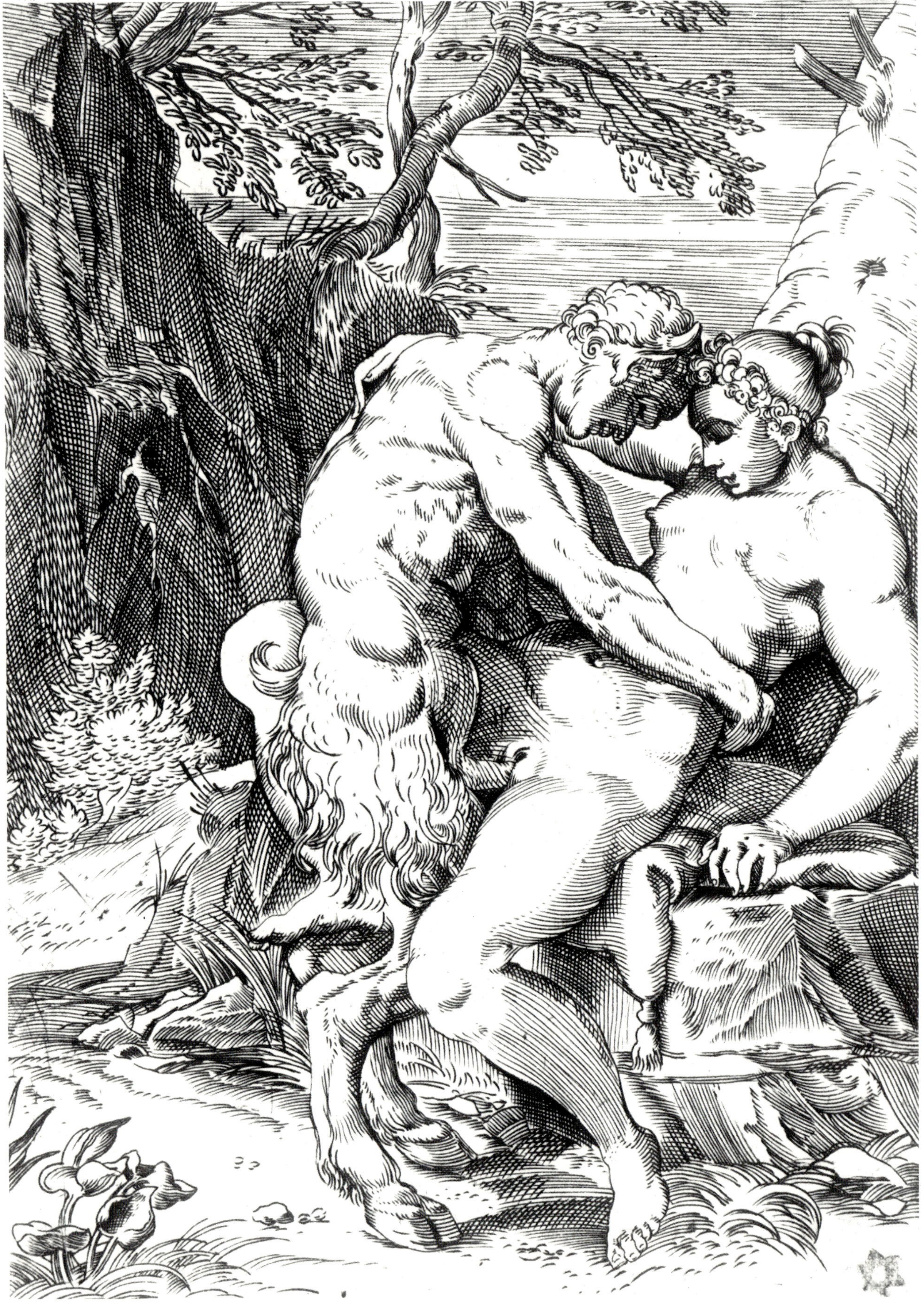

64 Agostino Carracci: *Satyr and Nymph*. Engraving, c.1585. British Museum

before, Titian is thought to have finished the background to the *Dresden Venus* of Giorgione. Comparisons between them are inevitable, since both show a beautiful nude girl lying in a rather similar position. Here the resemblance ends, for Giorgione's nude is completely unclothed, relaxed, asleep and safely separated from us by being placed in the golden, ideal world of rustic simplicity which Giorgione had invented for us. The girl in Titian's painting, on the other hand, lies naked on a bed, having decorated herself with earrings and a bracelet and with a bunch of flowers in her hand. She is wide awake and her gaze meets our own with an unabashed, quizzical look. The Duke of Urbino knew what he was talking about!

Garafalo (1481-1559) was known as 'the miniature Raphael', and was one of Raphael's assistants. His picture *Amor and Voluptas* (Love and Pleasure) openly asserts by its title that the two couples which it shows, in the presence of Cupid, intend to make love and recognize this as a source of pleasure. In terms of eroticism this was a considerable change from Giorgione's *Concert Champêtre*, where similar couples were intent only on playing music in the countryside.

Bronzino (1503-72), in his *Venus and Cupid*, produced the archetypal intellectual Florentine allegory. Venus, clad only in a tiara of pearls, is holding Cupid's bow while he embraces her. Pleasure, in the form of a little boy on the right, is about to shower them with roses. Behind them is the serpent Deceit, with a girl's head, offering a honeycomb in one hand while concealing the sting in her tail in the other. On the left, Jealousy, her face contorted with envy, tears her hair. The whole scene would have been concealed from us had not the forces of Truth and Father Time lifted the veiling blue drapery. Despite its complicated disguise, the picture has always been recognized as an erotic masterpiece. It was commissioned by the first Grand Duke of Florence and given to the amorous French king, François I.

In 1494 the French had invaded Italy and the French kings came to know it intimately. They could not fail to be impressed by the achievements of the Renaissance artists, and in 1530 François I, who was building himself the great palace at Fontainebleau, invited first Rosso, who was staying with Aretino in Venice at the time, and later Giulio Romano, who was decorating the Palazzo del Tè in Mantua, to come to France to work for him. Giulio Romano stayed in Mantua,

65 Titian: *Venus of Urbino*, 1538. 119×165cm. Uffizi, Florence

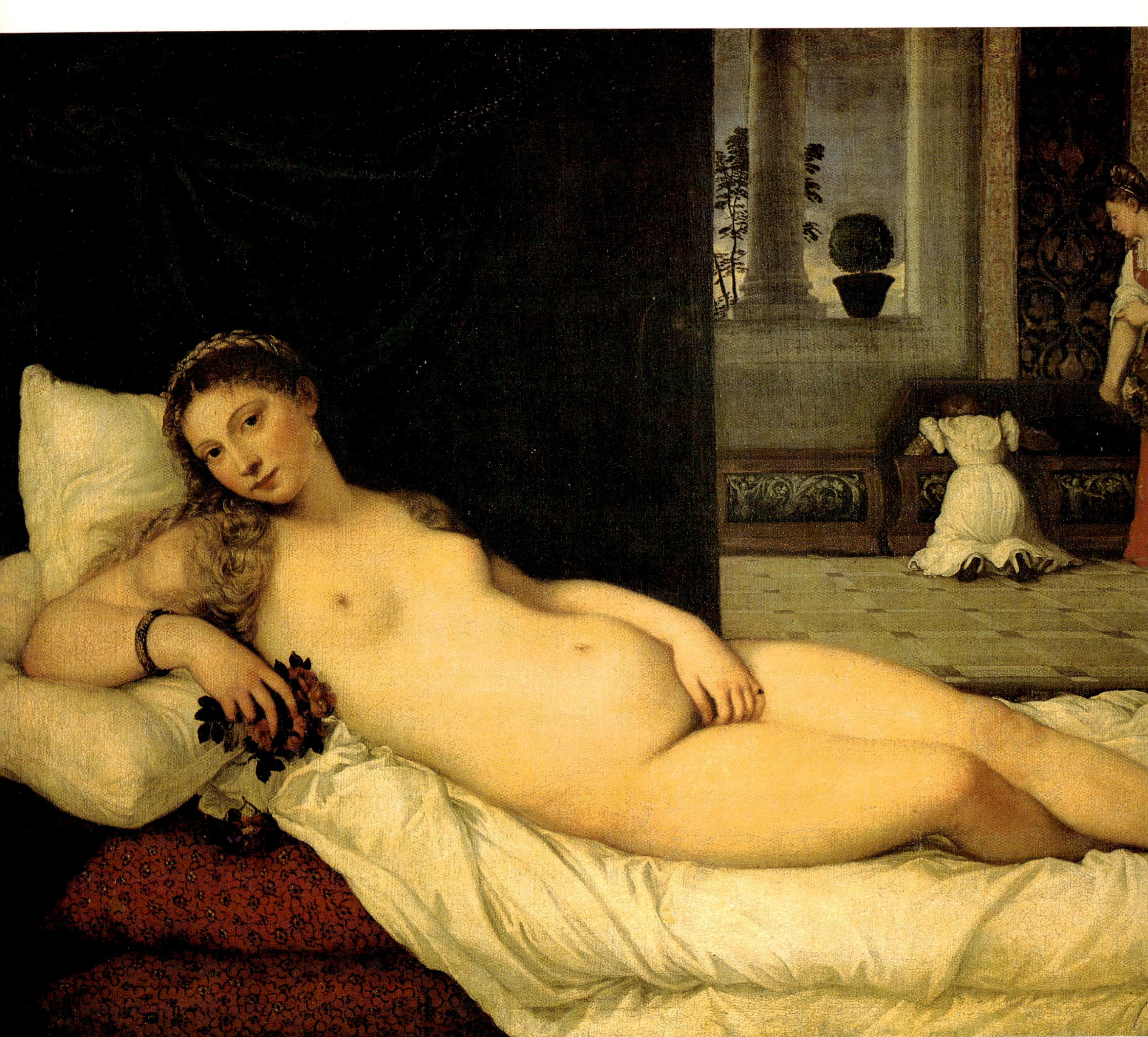

66 *(Right)* Garofalo: *Amor and Voluptas*, 127×178cm. National Gallery, London

67 *(Below right)* School of Giulio Romano: detail from *The Marriage Feast of Cupid and Psyche*. Fresco, c.1528. Palazzo del Tè, Mantua

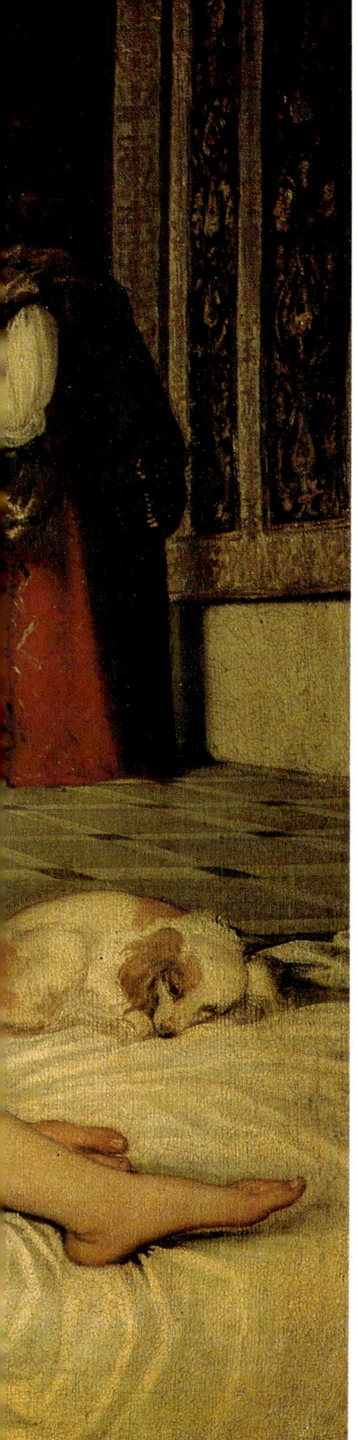

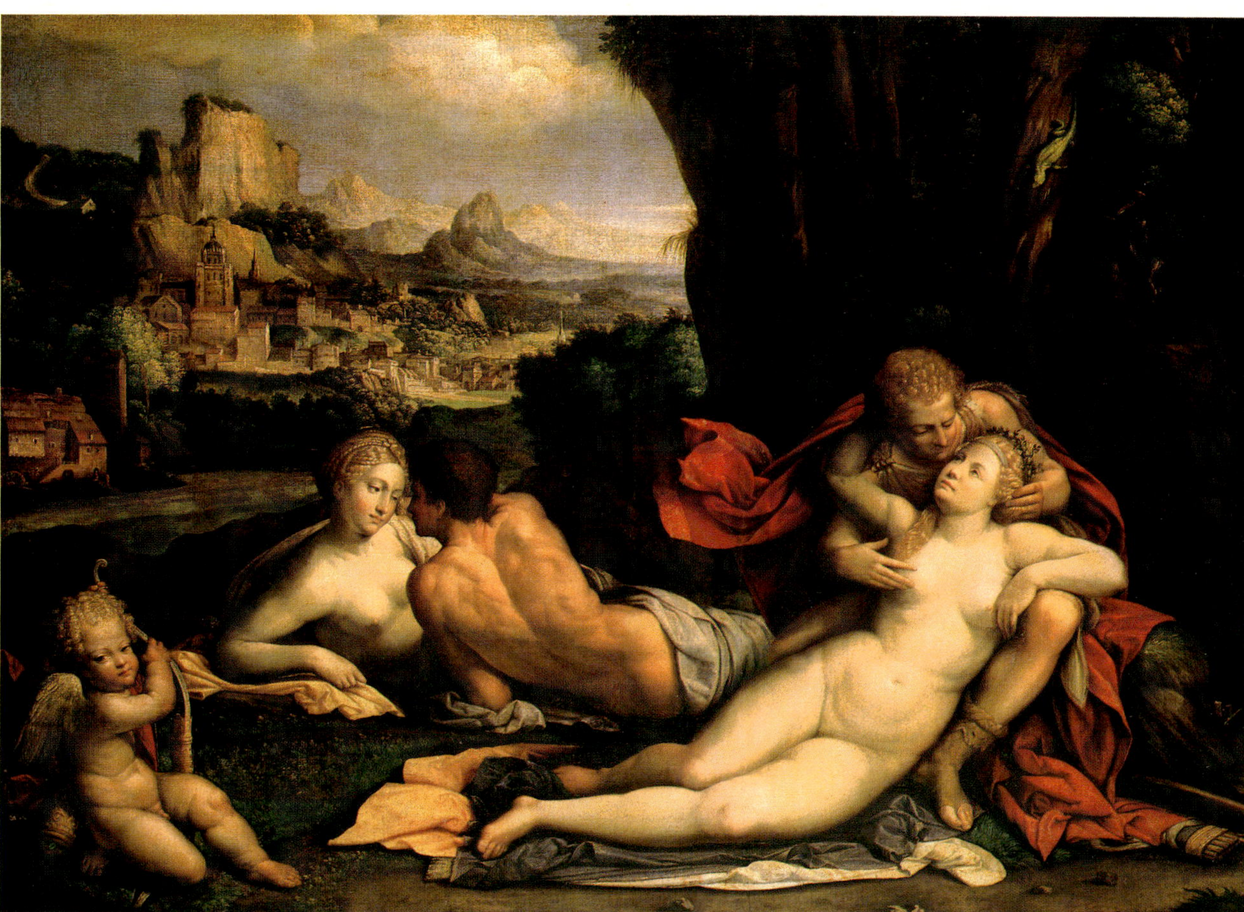

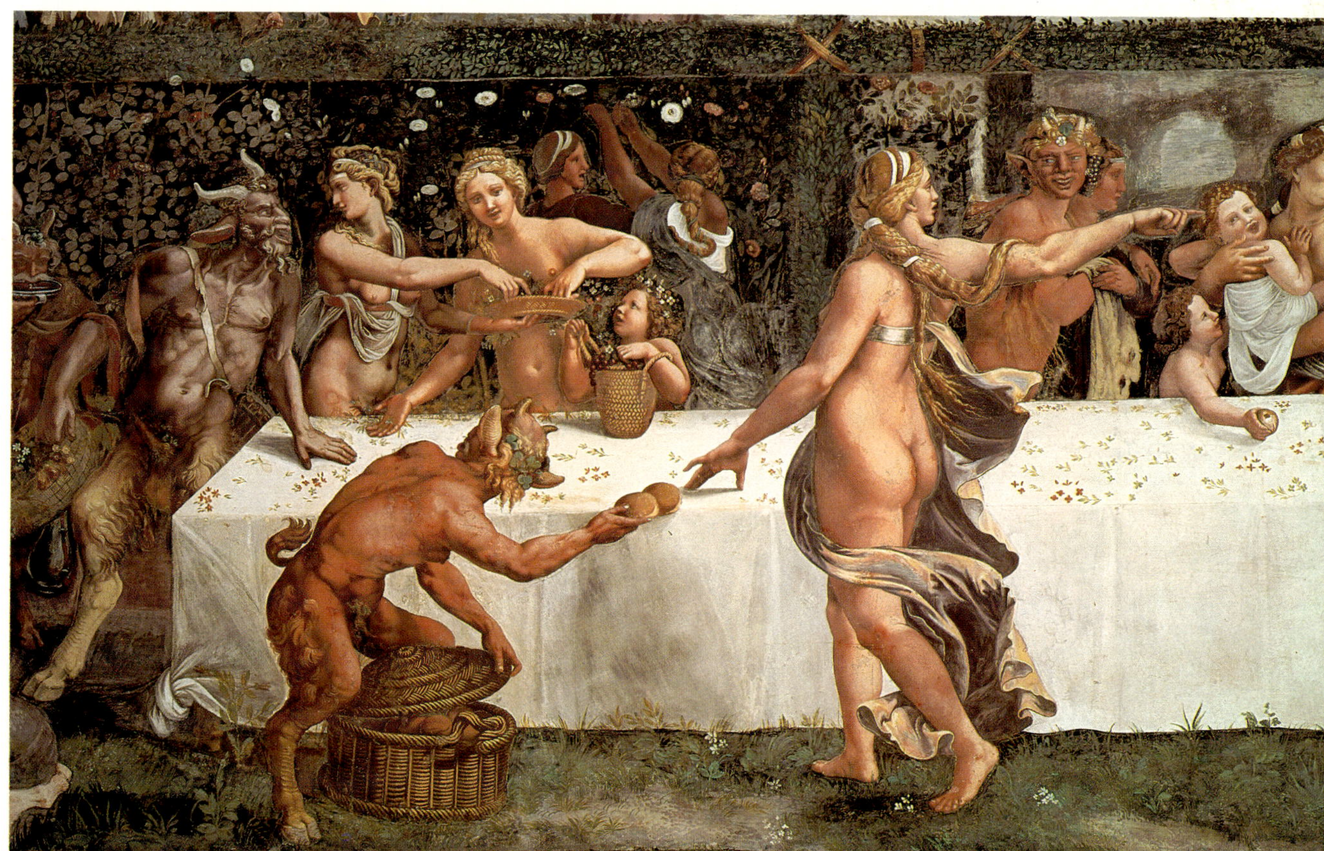

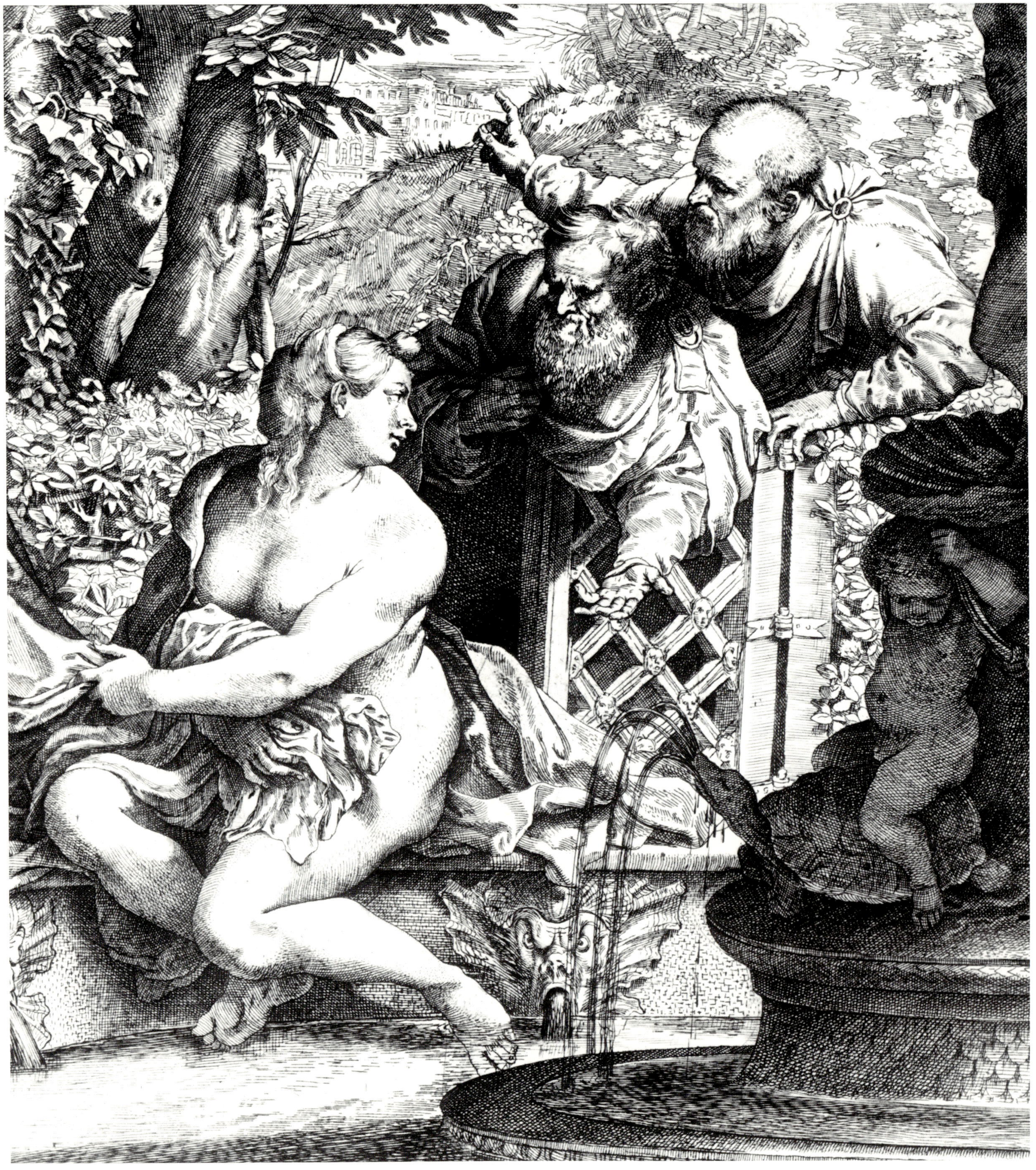

but his assistant Primaticcio went to France, where Rosso was already working. Together with Abbate, who joined them twenty years later, they were the main artists of what came to be known as the First School of Fontainebleau. They were not the greatest Renaissance painters, but they were well trained in the Mannerist tradition, well able to create the erudite, sensual paintings required by the French court and to introduce mythological in place of the biblical themes which had previously been the rule in France. *Mars and Venus* is a typical picture from the school, depicting the notorious liaison between the god of war and Venus, who was married to Vulcan. In the picture they are shown with Cupid, her son whom Vulcan had fathered. Another typical painting is *Nymph and Satyr* (Plate 62), in which a pointed-eared, horned satyr, who would have been equally at home on the walls of the Palazzo del Tè in Mantua, is being ordered away by Cupid from the sleeping, voluptuous girl. These and other pictures like them set the scene, in France, for the flowering of the *genre* which was to take place at the French court during the next two centuries.

In the painting of *Vulcan and Maia* (Plate 47) by Spranger (1546-94), it is Cupid who removes the screening cloth and discloses the pleading figure of the old Vulcan and the coy, teasing Maia. This was an exercise in provocative nudity, with a mythological title to give it a veneer of respectability. The theme of the young girl and the old man has always produced a certain erotic *frisson*. A favourite subject was the story from the Apocrypha of the virtuous Susanna: while bathing in her garden, she was spied upon by the elders, who tried to seduce her. When she refused them they were found out and eventually executed. Tintoretto (1518-94) used this theme in a painting. Agostino Carracci (1557-1602) was an accomplished engraver, usually working from the designs of others. However, he was also an artist in his own right and produced many explicit erotic works of which Plate 64 is an example.

By the end of the sixteenth century artists had mastered the techniques of their art and established that almost any subject was now available to them. Their need to cloak these subjects by placing them in mythical worlds had nevertheless held them back from achieving realism. This was to be the outstanding advance of the artists of the next century.

68 Agostino Carracci: *Old men surprising a girl*, engraving. Ashmolean Museum, Oxford

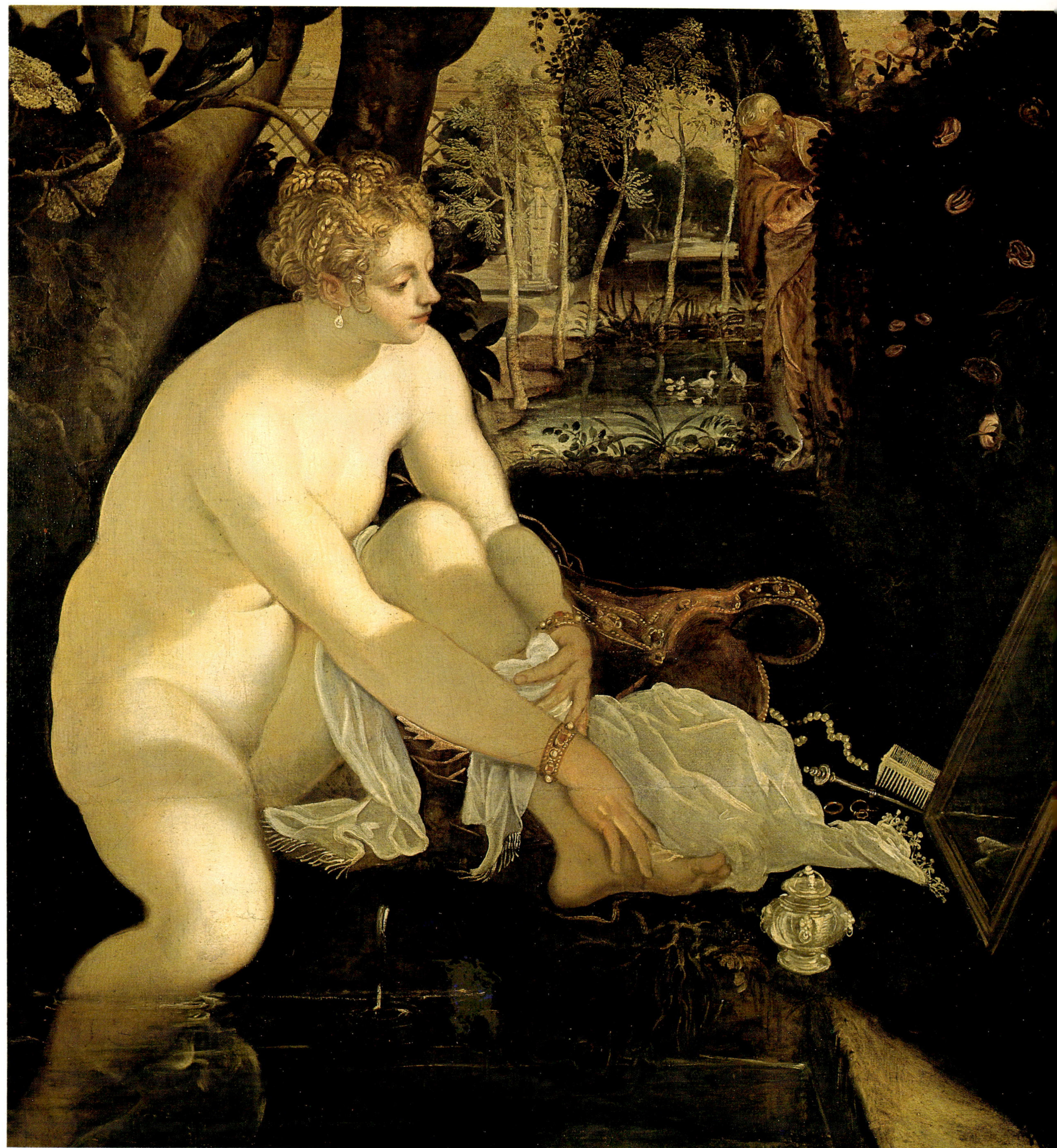

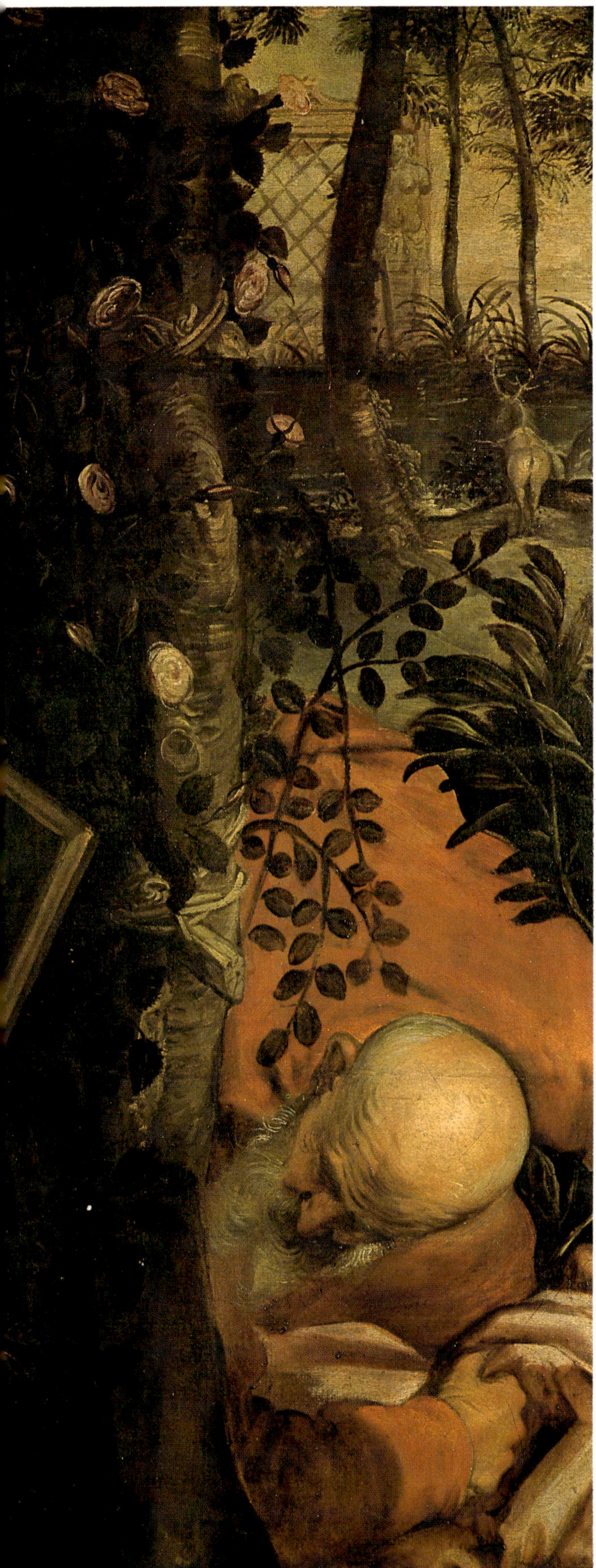

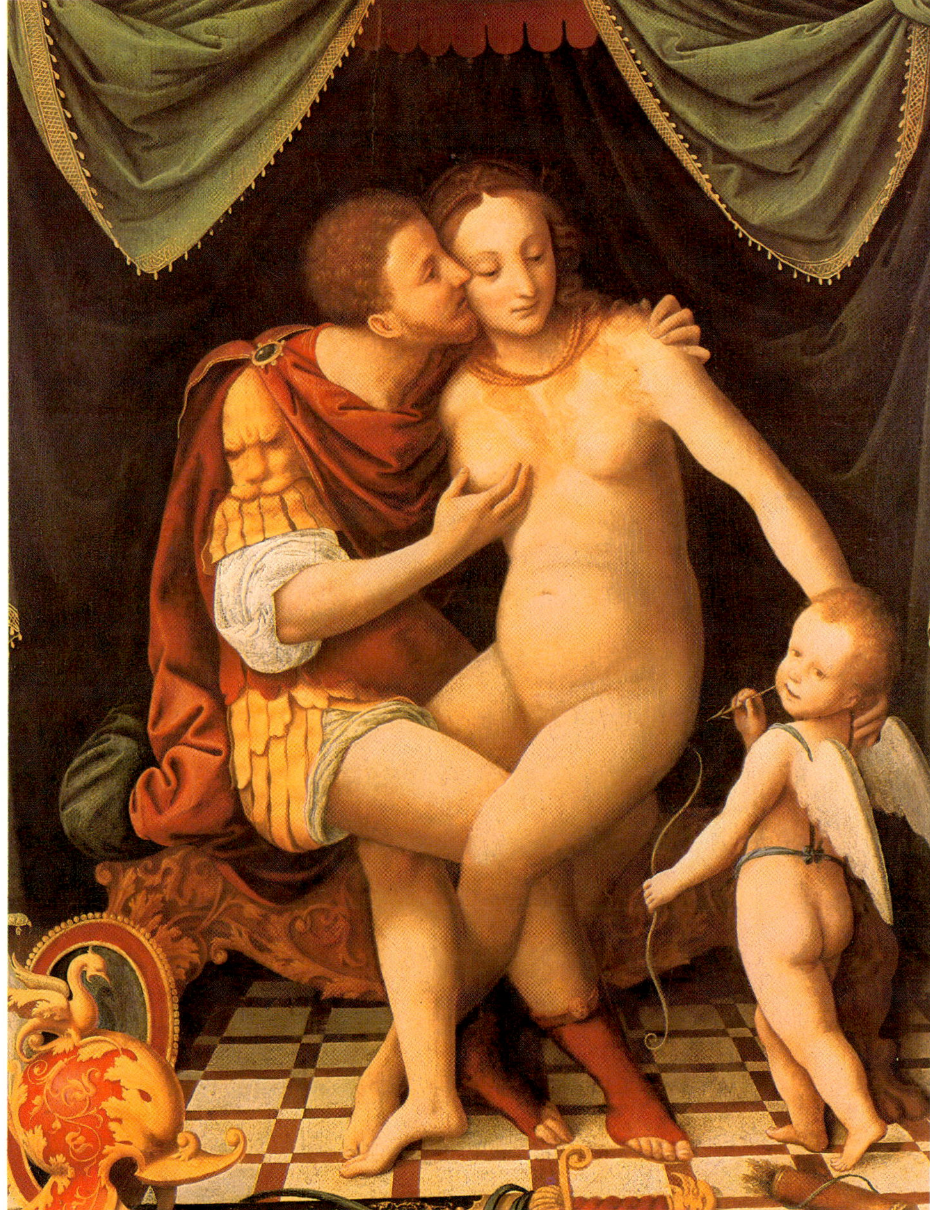

69 *(Left)* Tintoretto: *Susanna and the Elders*, c.1555. 146×193.5cm. Kunsthistorisches Museum, Vienna

70 *(Above)* School of Fontainebleau (attr.): *Mars and Venus*. Wood, 95.5×71cm. Musée du Petit Palais, Paris

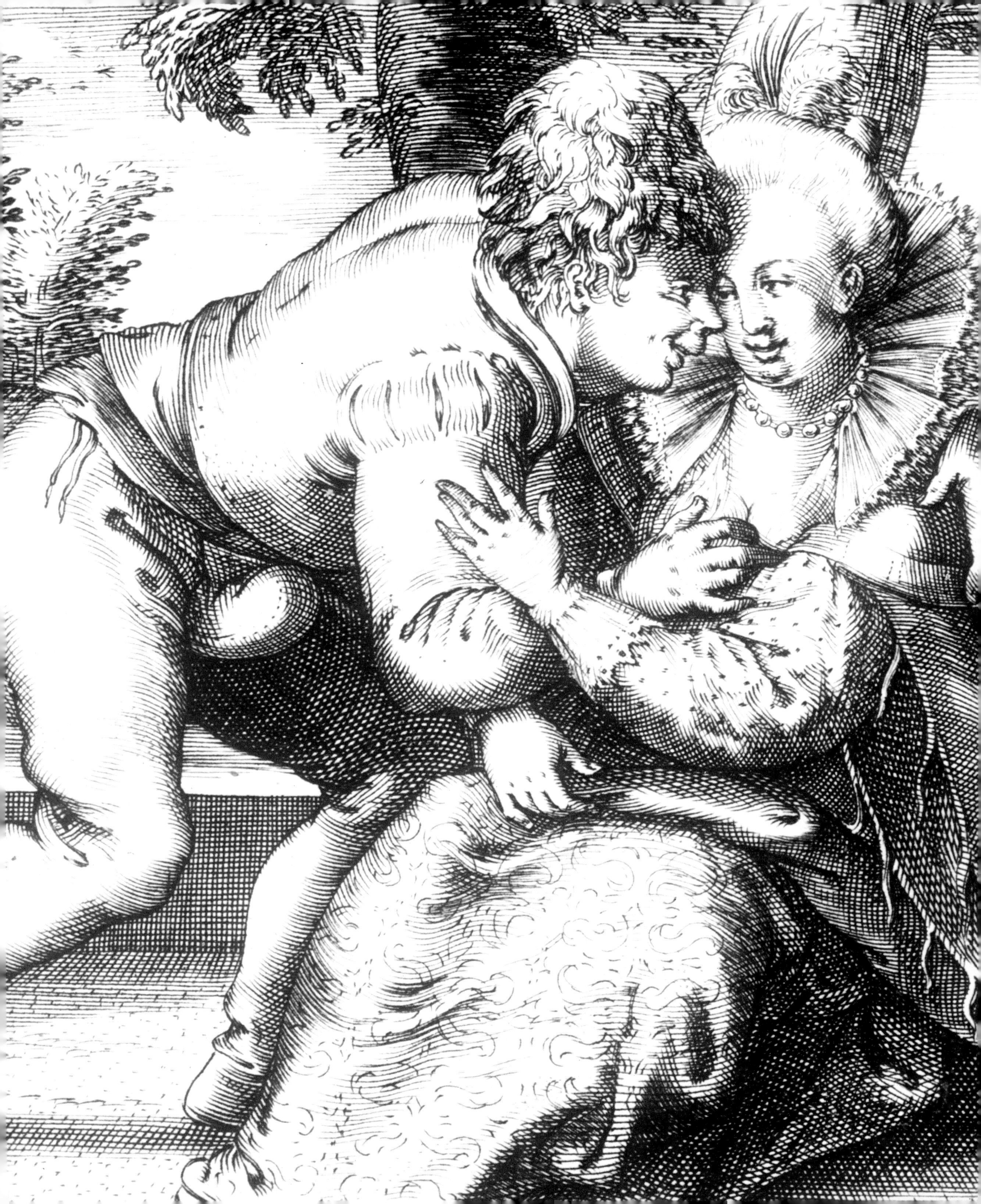

CHAPTER 4

The Seventeenth Century

The changes wrought by the Reformation in the sixteenth century, with sweeping gains for the Protestant movement spreading over wide areas of Europe, caused the Roman Catholic Church to make a major reappraisal of its activities. At the three Councils of Trent action was started to correct major abuses which had existed for centuries. By the beginning of the seventeenth century the Roman Catholics had already begun to regain much of their lost ground and were in a position to counter the Protestants. By the middle of the century most people in Europe had formed a firm allegiance to one church or the other. Thereafter the balance between the two contesting versions of Christianity was scarcely to change for a hundred years. Over the same period, political revolutions against the worst abuses of feudalism took place in many European countries. Nevertheless these revolutions invariably left behind them strong, autocratic governments and the lot of ordinary people changed very little.

Art remained one of the pleasures of those who were rich and powerful. They could now employ some of the most technically advanced painters Europe had yet seen. This new generation of artists had passed the stage where they were content to copy the best of their Renaissance predecessors. They sought for realism, and in particular wished to apply it to the people they depicted. In contrast with the beautiful idealized figures of Botticelli and Michelangelo, those that were to be seen in the works of Rubens, Rembrandt and Jan Steen seem of real flesh and blood. In pictures with an erotic flavour this new element of reality enhanced the effect, since a realistically pretty girl or handsome man could more easily evoke ideas of warm embraces and smooth skin.

Peter Paul Rubens (1577-1640) studied art, first in his native Antwerp, and then in Italy, before returning home at the age of thirty-one to become the appointed court painter to the Spanish Governor of the Netherlands. His innate talent, refined by his eight years in Italy, enabled him to paint a series of religious and mythological paintings which were notable for their beauty, vitality and skilful composition. He had, in addition, developed the North European skill of depicting textures and used it to great effect in the painting of human skin. His painting *The Rape of the Daughters of Leucippus* (Plate 72) shows two young men carrying off two girls. Leucippus, a king of Messene, had arranged a marriage between his

71 Pieter Bout: *The Amorous Pair*. Engraving (detail). Ashmolean Museum, Oxford

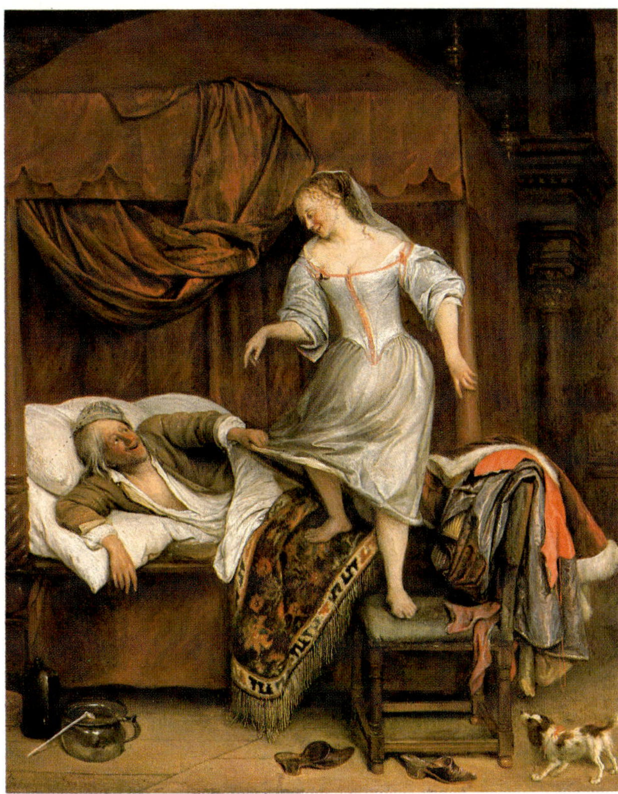

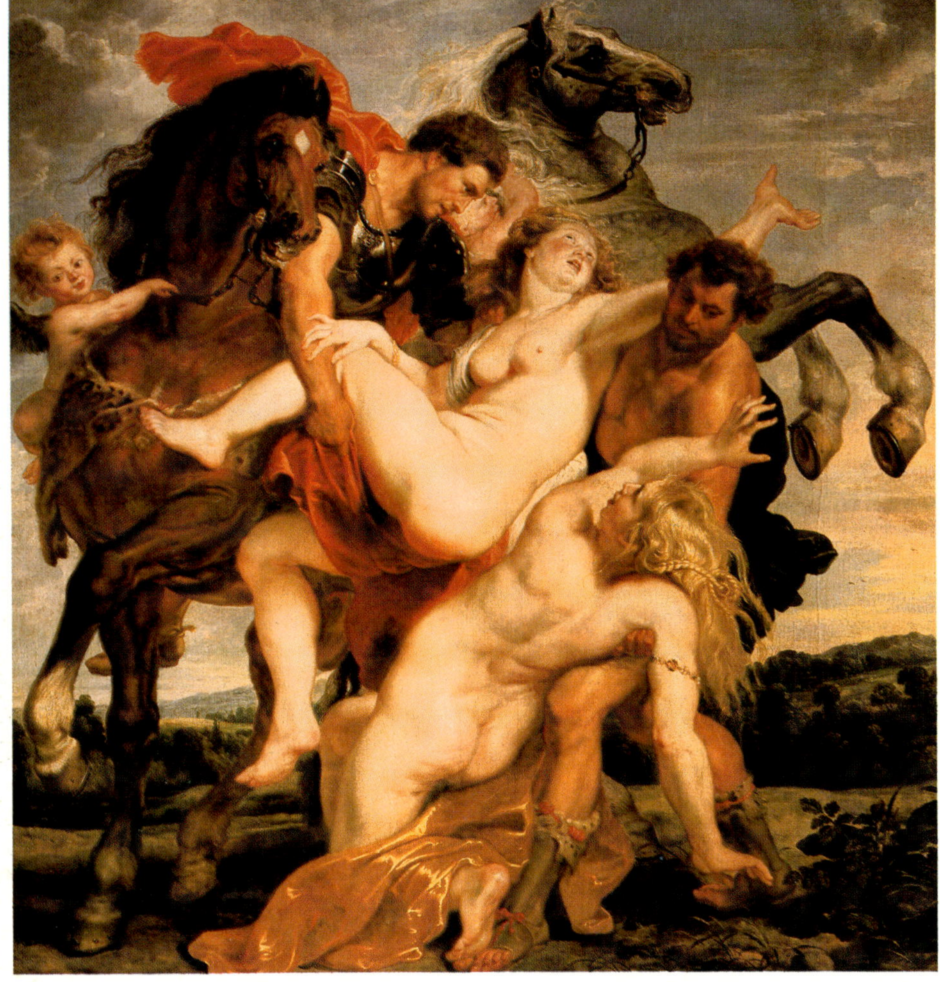

72 *(Left)* Rubens: *The Rape of the Daughters of Leucippus*, c.1616-17. 222×209cm. Alte Pinakothek, Munich

73 *(Above)* Jan Steen: *Bedroom Scene*. Panel, 59×39.5cm. Museum Bredius, The Hague

74 *(Right)* After Poussin: *Sleeping Nymph surprised by Satyrs*. 66×50.8cm. National Gallery, London

two daughters and their cousins. However, two other men, Castor and Pollux, had fallen in love with the girls. These new suitors abducted the girls, married them and a son was born to each marriage. The abduction was, in fact, a primaeval marriage rite and there is no reason to suppose that the girls were dissatisfied with the change in their marriage plans. It is significant that cupids are holding the reins of the horses.

Nicolas Poussin (1594-1665) was a French artist who began his painting in France, went to Rome at the age of thirty and, apart from one short interlude, spent the rest of his life in Italy. He was greatly influenced by the classical art of Greece and Rome, but learned also from the Italian art all around him. He developed his own restrained

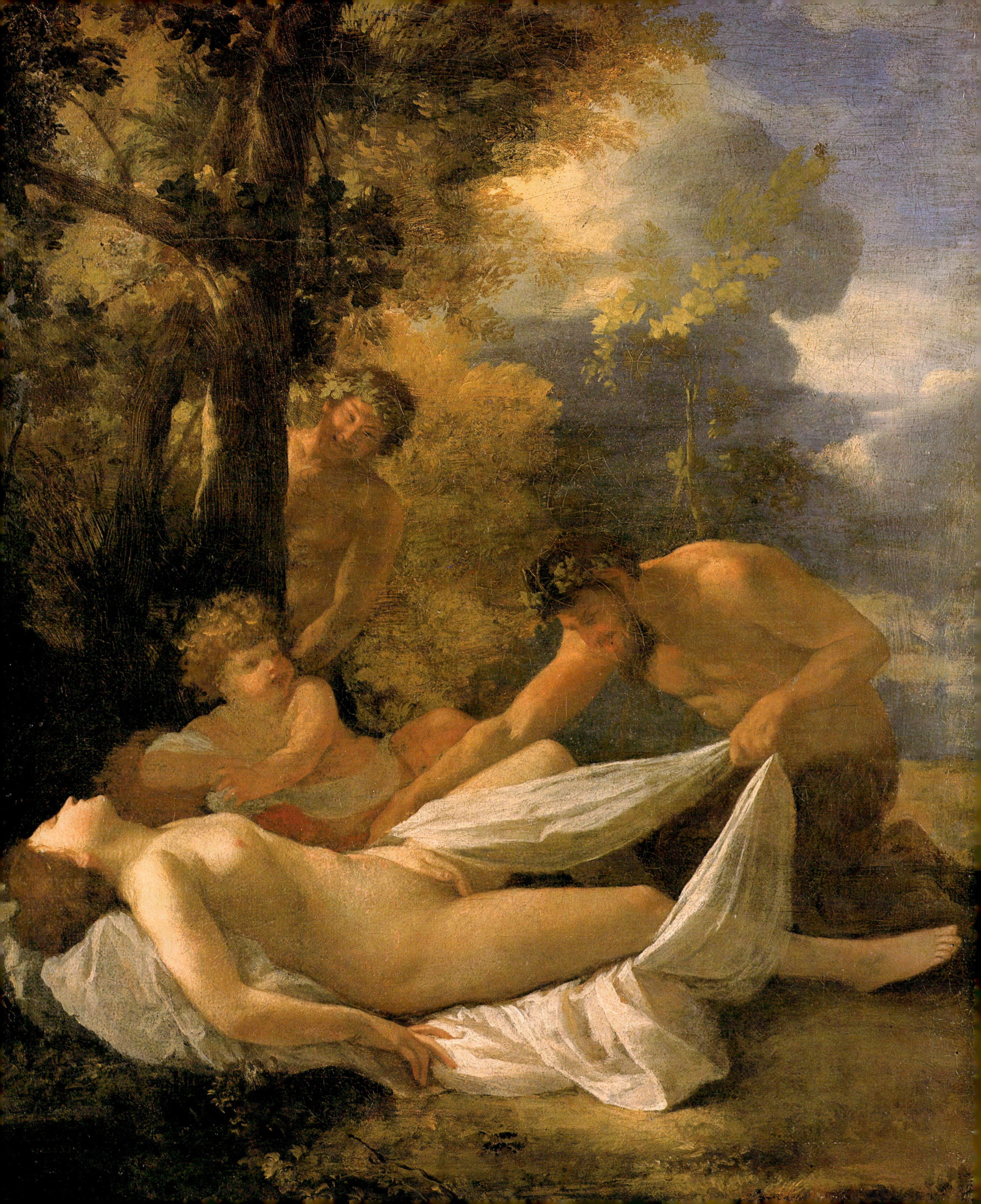

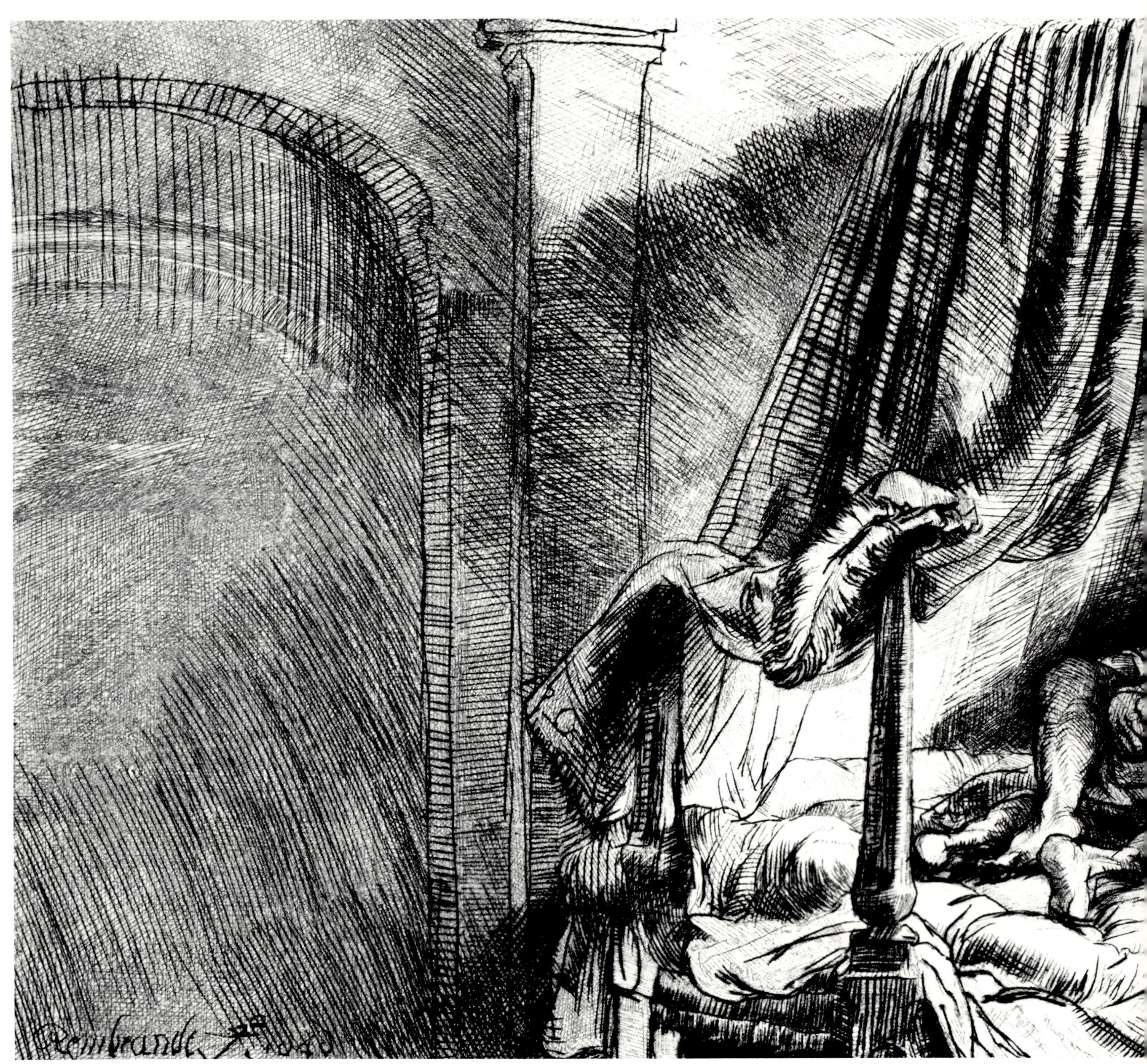

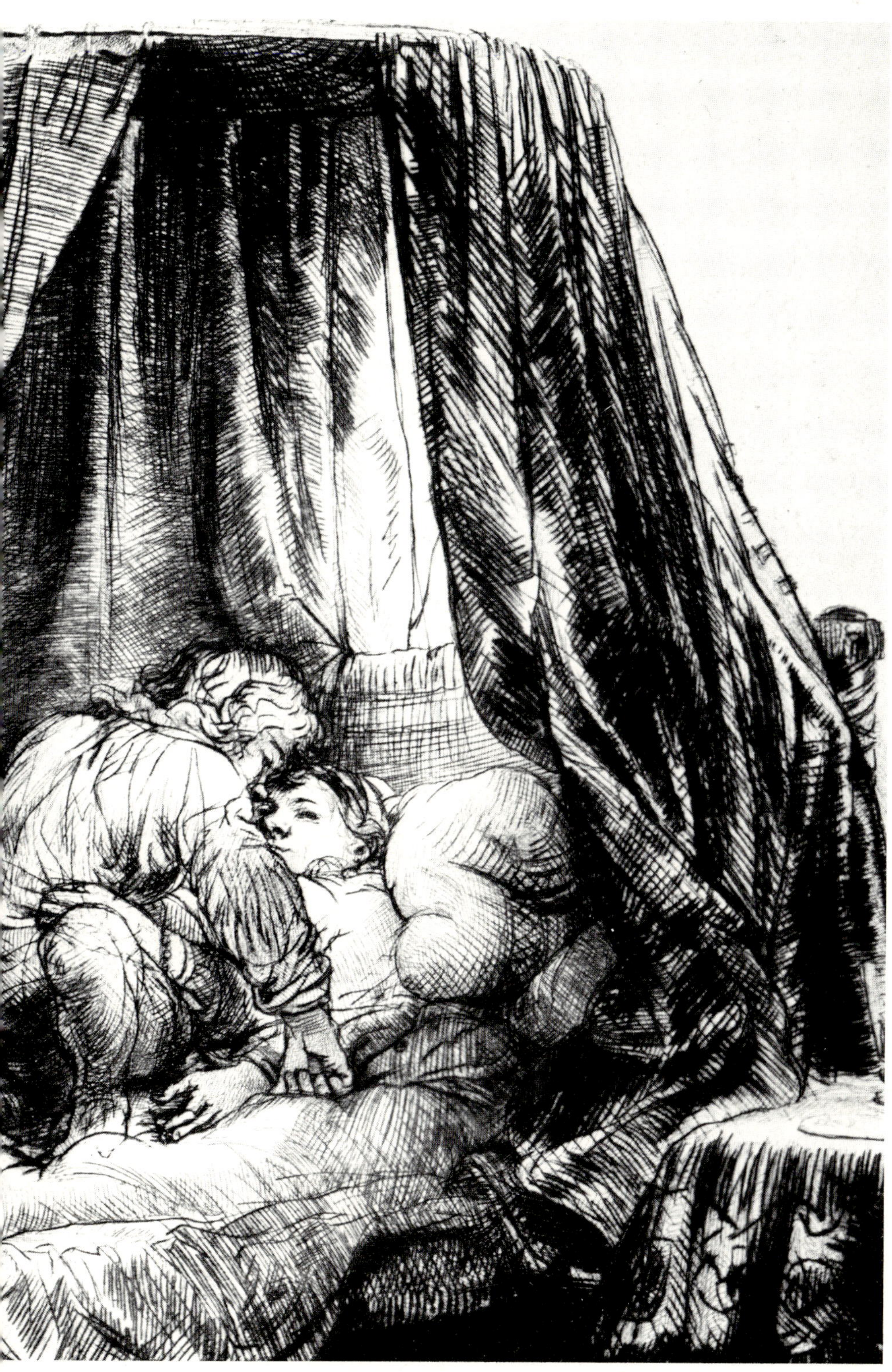

75 Rembrandt: *The Great Bed*. Etching, 1646. 12.5×22.4cm. Rijksmuseum, Amsterdam

and carefully contrived technique, one aim of which was to express reality. His painting *Nymph surprised by Satyrs* (Plate 74) is a straightforward erotic picture with the same theme as Plate 62. A comparison shows at once how skilfully Poussin has made an essentially classical subject something which is almost a scene from real life.

Rembrandt (1606-69) was another who pioneered the painting of reality, although he used an impressionist brushwork which has never been surpassed. Unlike Poussin, he did not apply the principles of classical art to his figures. By insisting on painting the truth he inevitably sacrificed the beauty which other artists could obtain by distorting it. There are few human beings who have the classical proportions of a Greek god, and, except in very occasional instances, Rembrandt did not seem to look for especially comely models. Indeed his 'anti-classical' stance, which led for example to his etching of Diana bathing, showing a nude woman with wrinkled paunch and flabby thighs, led to quite vitriolic abuse from some critics of the next generation. On the rare occasions when he depicts frankly erotic scenes he similarly aims at truth rather than erotic effect. In one etching he shows the back view of a monk having intercourse in a cornfield. In another which is famous, both because of its rarity and the greatness of the artist, he shows a couple having intercourse in *The Great Bed*. Rembrandt's wife, Saskia, had died when he was in his mid-thirties and this print seems to have been conceived a few years later, at or shortly before the time his young mistress, Hendrickje Stoffels, moved in to take her place. There is, unfortunately, no direct evidence of the identity of the young couple, who, relaxed and secure among the softness of the featherbed and pillows, are gently exploring their own sexuality.

It is interesting that when, ten years later, Rembrandt's possessions were being sold to satisfy his creditors, the inventory, still preserved in the State archives at Amsterdam, lists (No. 232) 'a book of erotica by Raphael, Rosso, Annibale Carracci and Giulio Bonosone'. Kenneth Clark has postulated that the erotica 'by Raphael' were more likely a set of 'the well-known engravings by Marcantonio after Giulio Romano'.

Jan Steen (1626-79), the prolific painter of over seven hundred pictures, was one of the most lively of the great Dutch painters. A tavern-keeper with his own brewery, he had a warm sympathy for people. Every person in his pictures is an individual, lovingly observed, from the life of his own time. He is noted for depicting intimate subjects and scenes in bedrooms and *Bedroom Scene* (Plate 73) intentionally creates an erotic effect by giving free rein to the imagination of the spectator.

Besides the expensive canvases by famous artists there were cheaper engravings for ordinary folk, some of which had erotic implications. The engraving by Pieter Bout (1658-1702) of *The Amorous Pair* produced a picture which is chiefly remarkable to a modern viewer because of its demonstration of the codpiece (Plate 71). This had originally been a piece of armour to protect the male organ, but by the sixteenth and seventeenth centuries it had become part of the conventional attire for a man. Indeed, it was an essential part of a tailor's job to ensure that his customer appeared well endowed. In the case of wealthy and powerful men a codpiece was frequently very impressive.

The seventeenth century had shown how nature could be represented in art but had also shown the limitations of verisimilitude. The next hundred years were to see the same talents used with the essential additions of imagination and charm by artists with a tale to tell.

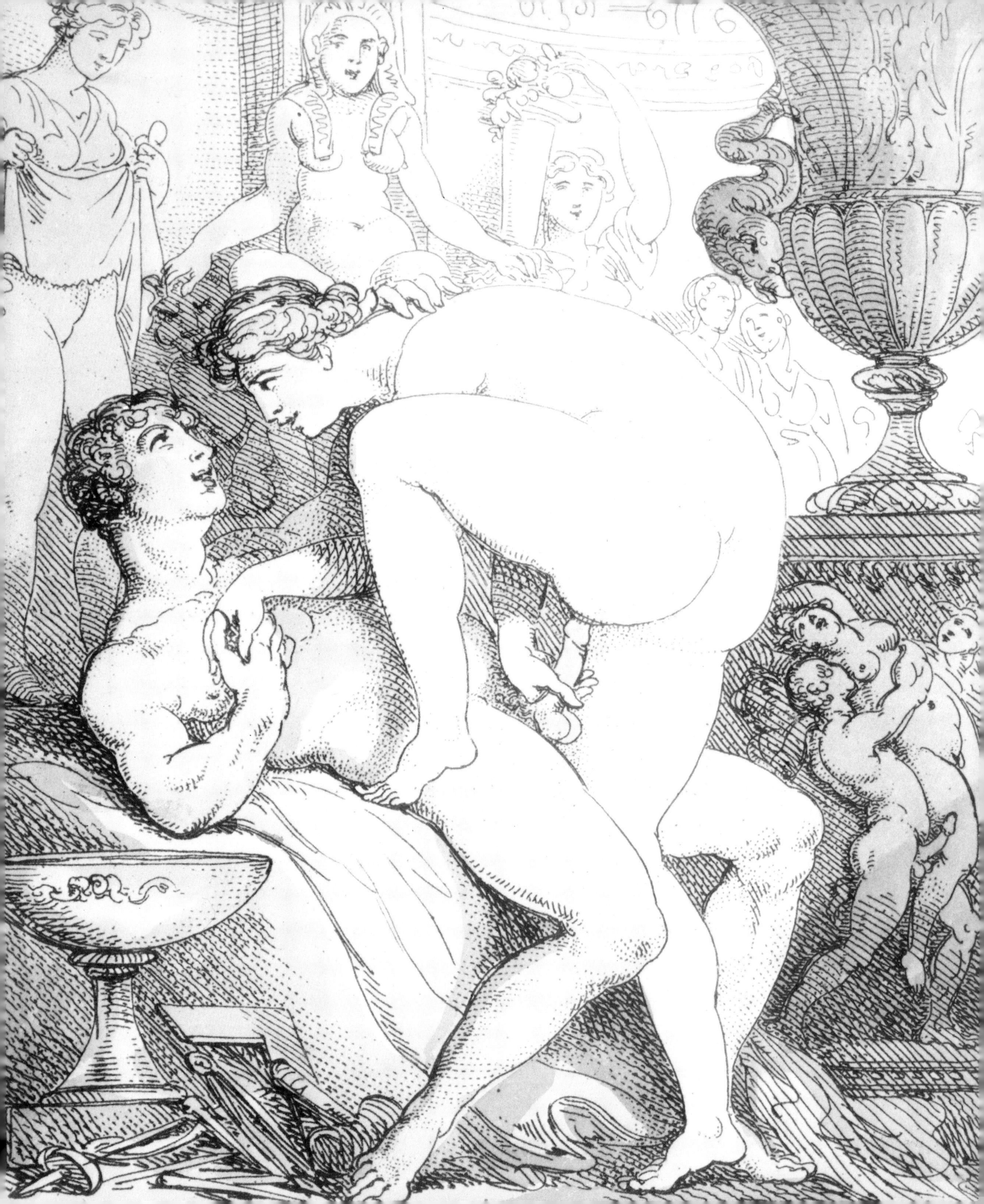

CHAPTER 5

The Eighteenth Century

The art of William Hogarth (1697-1764) showed the variety of eighteenth-century London life in all classes of society. Every picture seemed to illustrate a moral, whether it was the dangers of drinking gin, of idleness or of making a foolish marriage. These moralizing scenes were popular not only in his own day but also with the Victorians. Books of his collected engravings were careful, however, either to ignore two of the prints or to place them in a sealed envelope at the back. These pictures were titled *Before* and *After*. In the first all is excitement. A girl, in her bedchamber, is strenuously resisting an ardent suitor. We see that she has been reading *The Practice of Piety* but must view, with some alarm, that she has been 'getting ideas' from 'novels'. Worse still, we see a book entitled *Rochester* which doubtless contains some of that nobleman's notorious erotic poems. In the second picture all is changed. The pictures on the wall now stress a falling rocket and on the floor we see a quotation from Aristotle: '*Omne animal post coitus triste est*' (after coitus all creatures feel sad). This is a seduction without love or any happiness to follow, and it is scarcely an incitement to sex. With the double standards prevailing at the time, the girl would have been thought damaged and spoiled. Hogarth the moralist was still hard at work.

For the arts, in general, much of the eighteenth century was an era of French supremacy. The French economy was sinking gradually into bankruptcy but the all-powerful French court under Louis XV and the aristocracy continued to spend enormous sums of money on all forms of luxury.

François Boucher (1703-70) was well placed to express the tastes of the rich, artificial, pleasure-seeking world, which was focused on Versailles. At the age of thirty, married to a very pretty wife who was frequently his model, he was already a popular artist with an outstanding talent for painting pretty, nude girls. Passing through the fashionable salons and having transient affairs with young women, he met the future Marquise de Pompadour, who was later to lavish commissions upon him when she became the King's mistress. In the meanwhile he produced a seemingly endless succession of brilliant paintings on the subject of Venus or Diana, of which *Diana resting after her bath* (Plate 97) is a superb example. In 1752 he was to paint his famous and enchanting picture of the young girl Louison O'Morphi (Plate 96).

76 Thomas Rowlandson: *The ancients*. Tinted engraving, c.1810

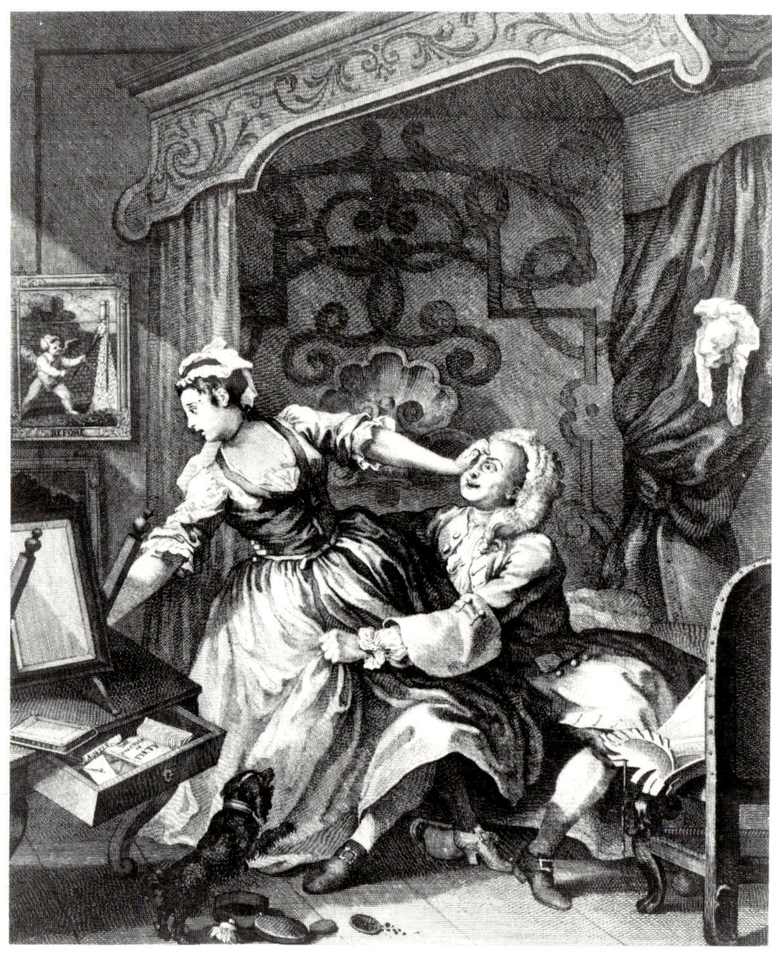

77 Hogarth: *Before*. Engraving, 1736. Print Collection, Lewis Walpole Library, Yale University

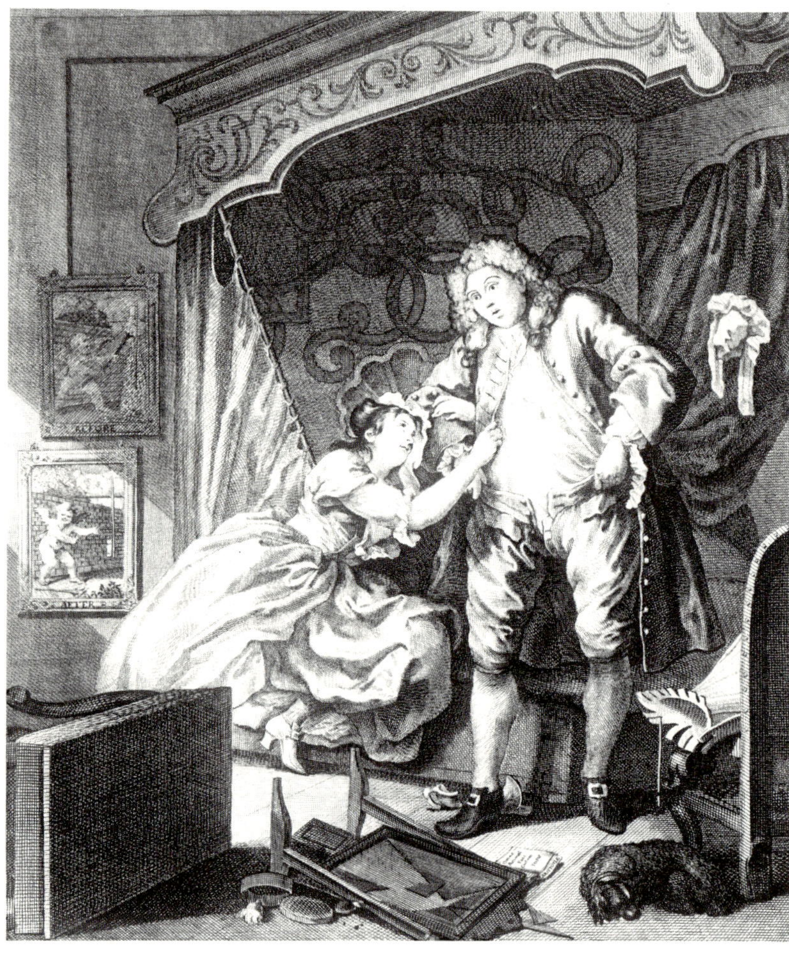

78 Hogarth: *After*. Engraving, 1736. Print Collection, Lewis Walpole Library, Yale University

Originally Louise O'Murphy, the pretty daughter of Irish parents, she had met Casanova when she was fifteen. He easily persuaded her to let him see her in the nude but, when he suggested intercourse, she asked for 25 golden louis. He regretfully decided the price was too high but claimed in his memoirs that, impressed by her beauty, he had introduced her to Boucher. She became the model for many of the pictures adorning the rooms of Madame de Pompadour, which were probably admired by the King. In 1753, at the age of seventeen, she became the King's mistress and later bore three royal children.

One of the most remarkable collections of erotic art ever made was gathered together and preserved in a beautifully bound album, now in the British Museum. This contains 68 watercolours of high quality, attributed to Charles Antoine Coypel (1694-1752), who became first

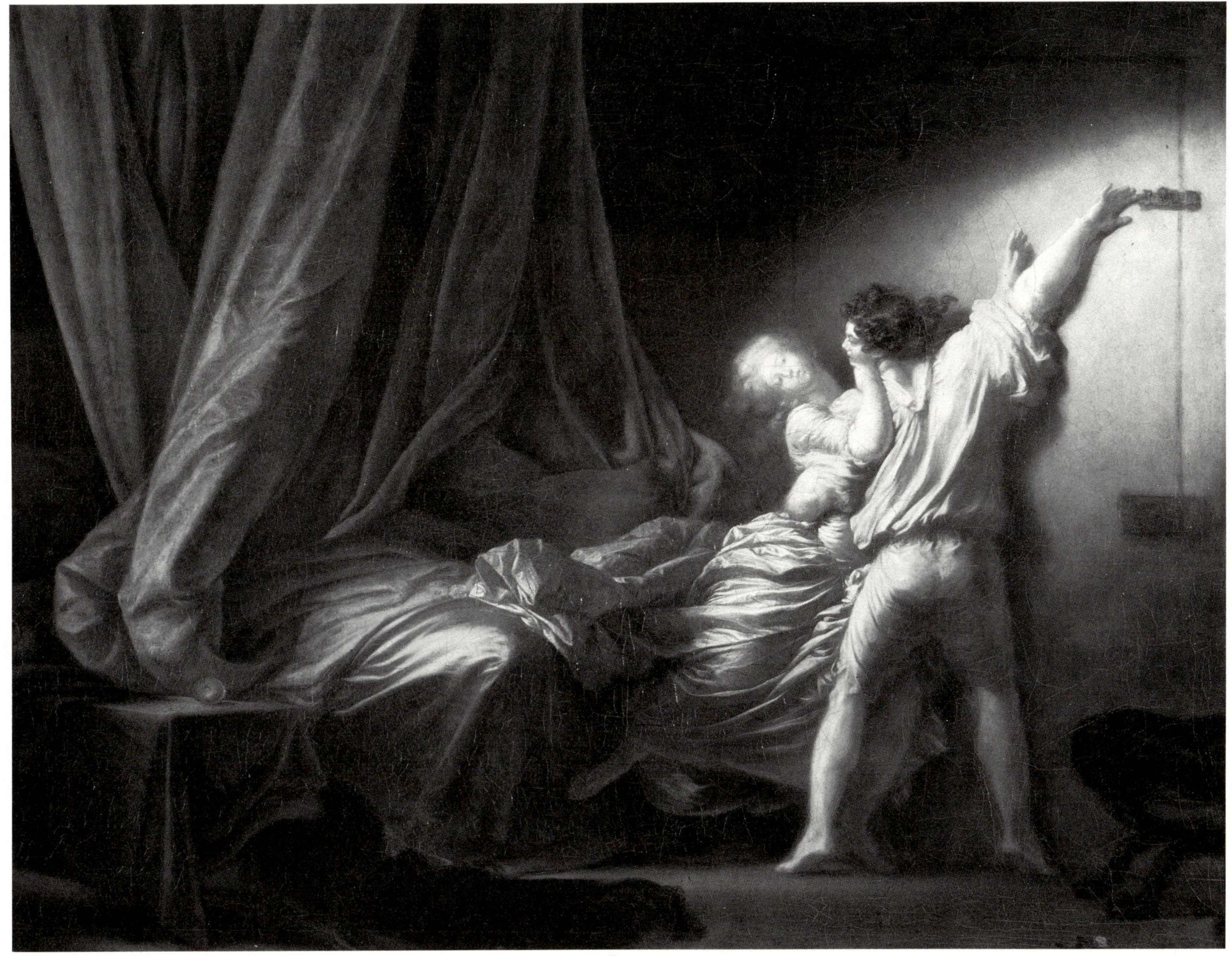

79 Jean-Honoré Fragonard: *The Bolt*, c.1784. Louvre, Paris

painter to the King in 1743. The album is ornamented with the arms of the dukes of Orleans and may have belonged to Louis, Duc d'Orléans (1702-52), the son of the Regent of France. The pictures show biblical or mythological scenes but what is so exceptional is that each is sexually explicit and leaves nothing to the imagination. Leda (Plate 92) is being seduced not by a swan but by a jovial Jupiter, and the same thing is happening to Antiope, whom he has surprised while she was asleep (Plate 102). These two pictures are typical and there is no comparable album in the Western world.

In 1764 Madame de Pompadour died and was followed as principal royal mistress by the Comtesse Du Barry. This was the opportunity for her *protégé*, Honoré Fragonard (1732-1806), to paint for her and for the aristocracy. In 1766 he was asked by the Baron de St Julien for a

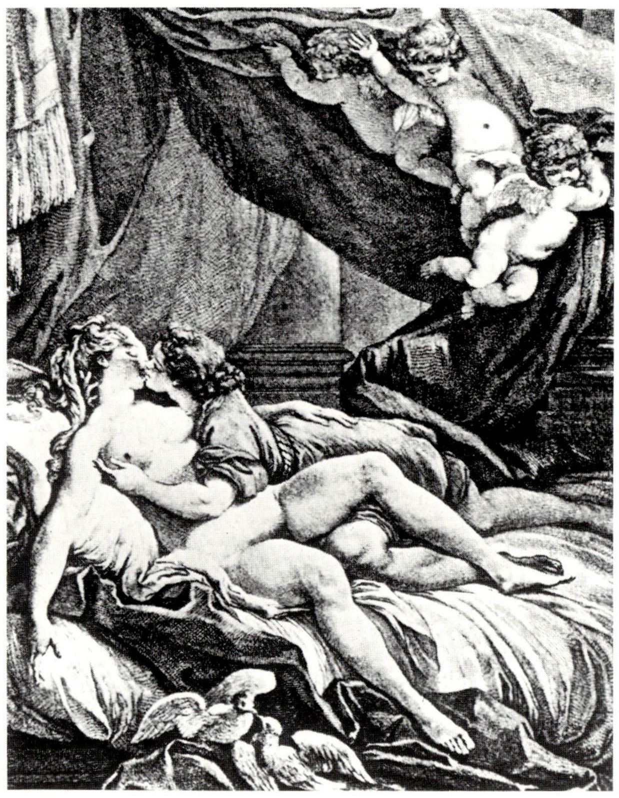

80 After Fragonard: *Man and woman in bed*. Engraving, late 18th century

picture to show 'my mistress . . . on a swing, which is being set in motion by a bishop. You must place me where I can have a good view of the legs of this pretty little thing . . .' It is a measure of the artist's skill and ingenuity that within these terms he was able to paint the delightful masterpiece of *The Swing* (Plate 98). He also made many paintings and engravings of erotic subjects, and his successful career lasted until it was ended by the French Revolution.

The middle of the eighteenth century saw the production of many sumptuous and expensive books for the small but well-to-do middle class in France. Some of these, with pictures by well-known artists, had erotic overtones: Prud'hon (1758-1828) made an erotic illustration for *Phrosine et Mélidor*. An illustration from *Contes et Nouvelles*, engraved by Charles Eisen (1720-78), shows a scene reminiscent of the painting by Jan Steen (Plate 73). A print by Pierre Antoine Baudoin (1723-69) shows a similar, titillating scene. Much more explicit erotic scenes were available in clandestine books such as *Satyra Sotadica*, published in 1749, and those from a later edition, published in 1782, with the title *Le Meursius François*, which has been attributed to Antoine Borel.

In 1789 the whole top-heavy edifice which had supported the French privileged nobility crumbled and was swept away by the French Revolution. For a time, in the resulting turmoil, there was little interest in erotic art. An anonymous artist produced a caricature of Cardinal Rohan, with erotic elements making up his features, which was doubtless intended as an insult, both to the man and to the type of cleric which he represented. Another artist (Plate 104) produced a humorous, if slightly rueful, expression of the talents of Napoleon's soldiery and the support they were receiving from the women of France.

About the beginning of the nineteenth century a painting was produced in Spain which is an undoubted erotic masterpiece, but which has been surrounded by an intriguing mystery ever since. The painter was Goya (1746-1828) and the painting was *The Naked Maja* (Plate 103). Spain was a bastion of the Roman Catholic Church, which did not favour female nude paintings. *The Rokeby Venus*, painted by Velázquez 150 years before, was the only notable predecessor. Moreover, Goya's painting was an obvious portrait of an actual woman and it had a companion painting of the same woman, lying in

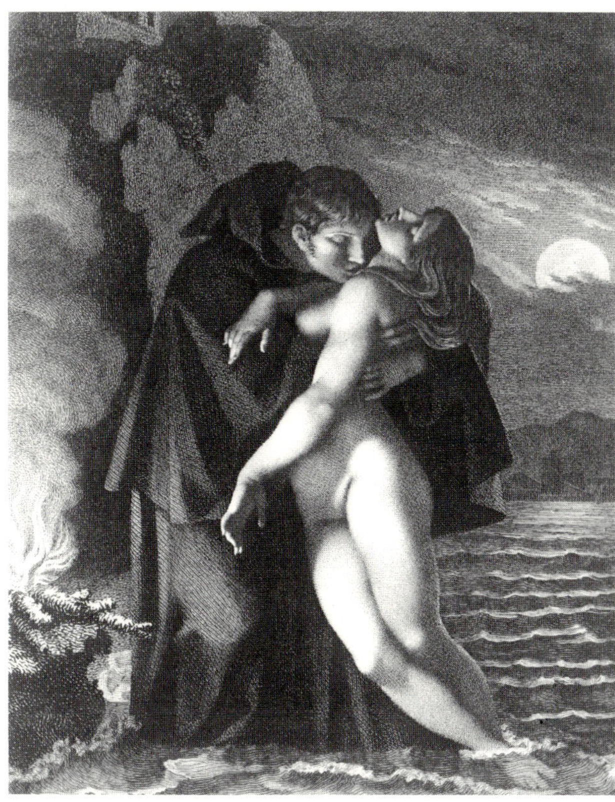

81 *(Above)* Prud'hon: *Phrosine et Mélidore,* engraving from *Gentil Bernard,* 1797. Metropolitan Museum of Art (Harris Brisbane Dick Fund, 1938)

82 *(Right)* Charles Eisen: *La courtesane amoureuse,* engraved by de Longueil, 1761. Philadelphia Museum of Art (Purchase: Seeler Fund from Rosenbach)

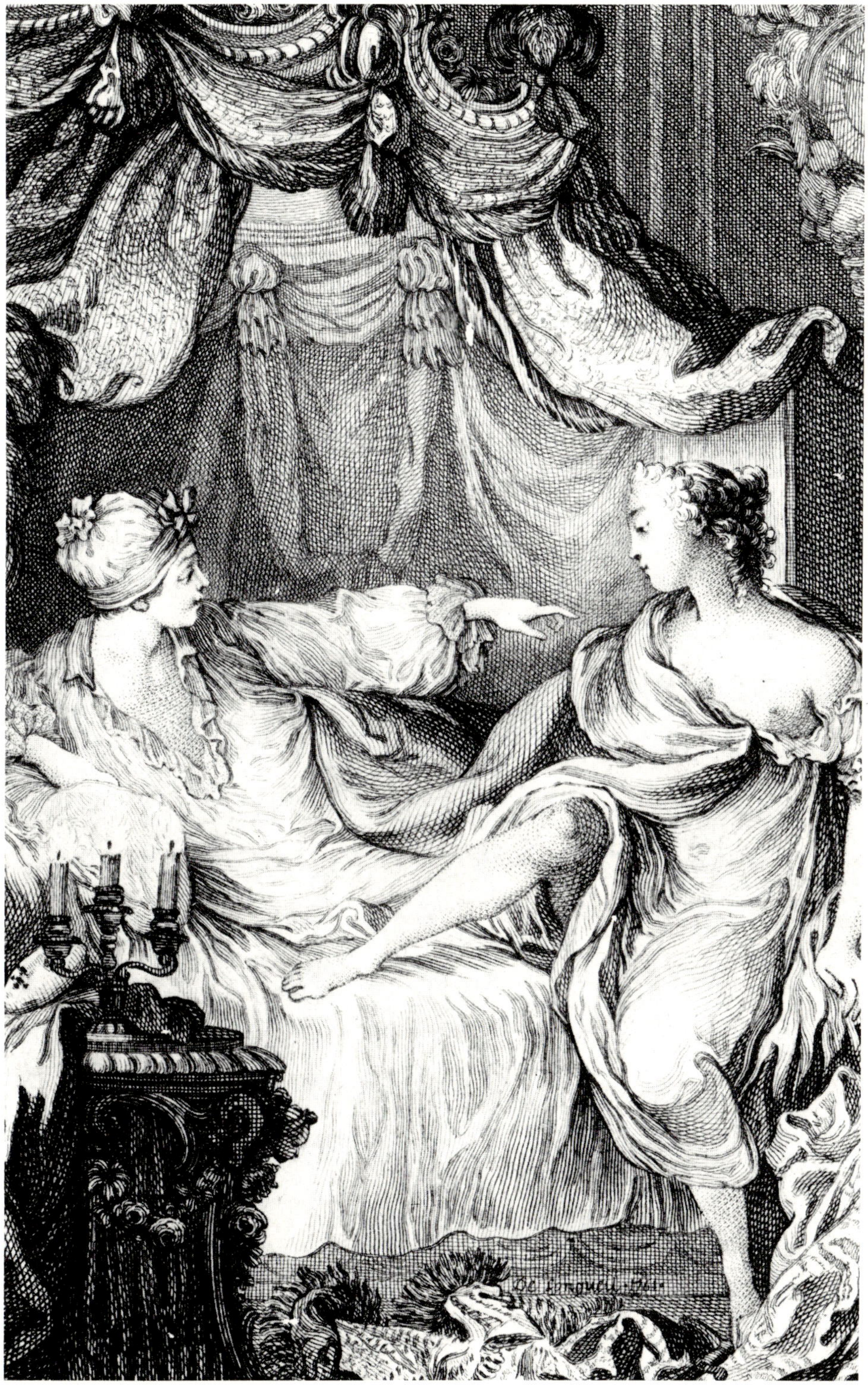

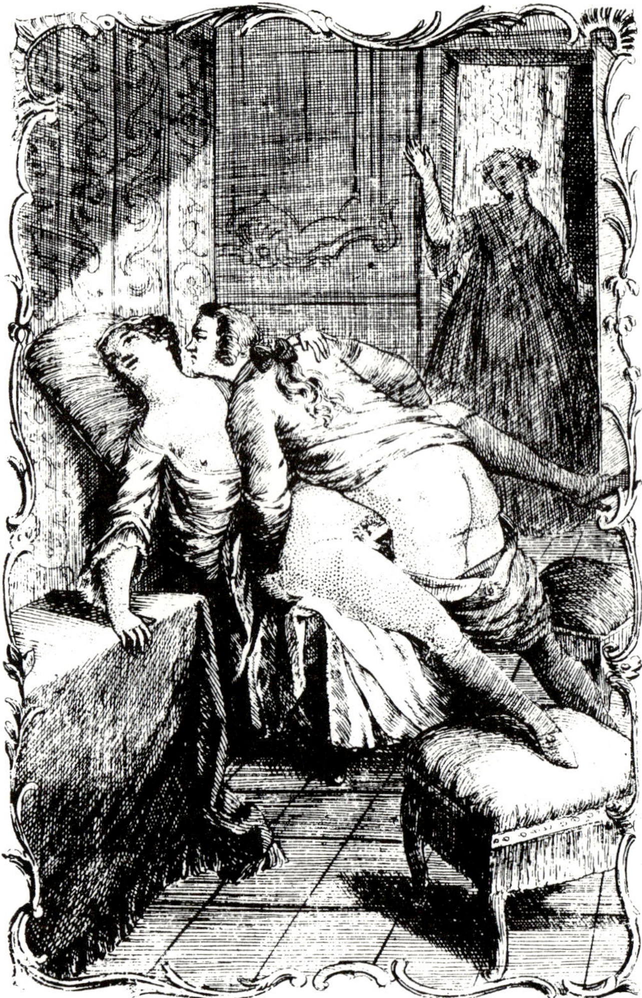

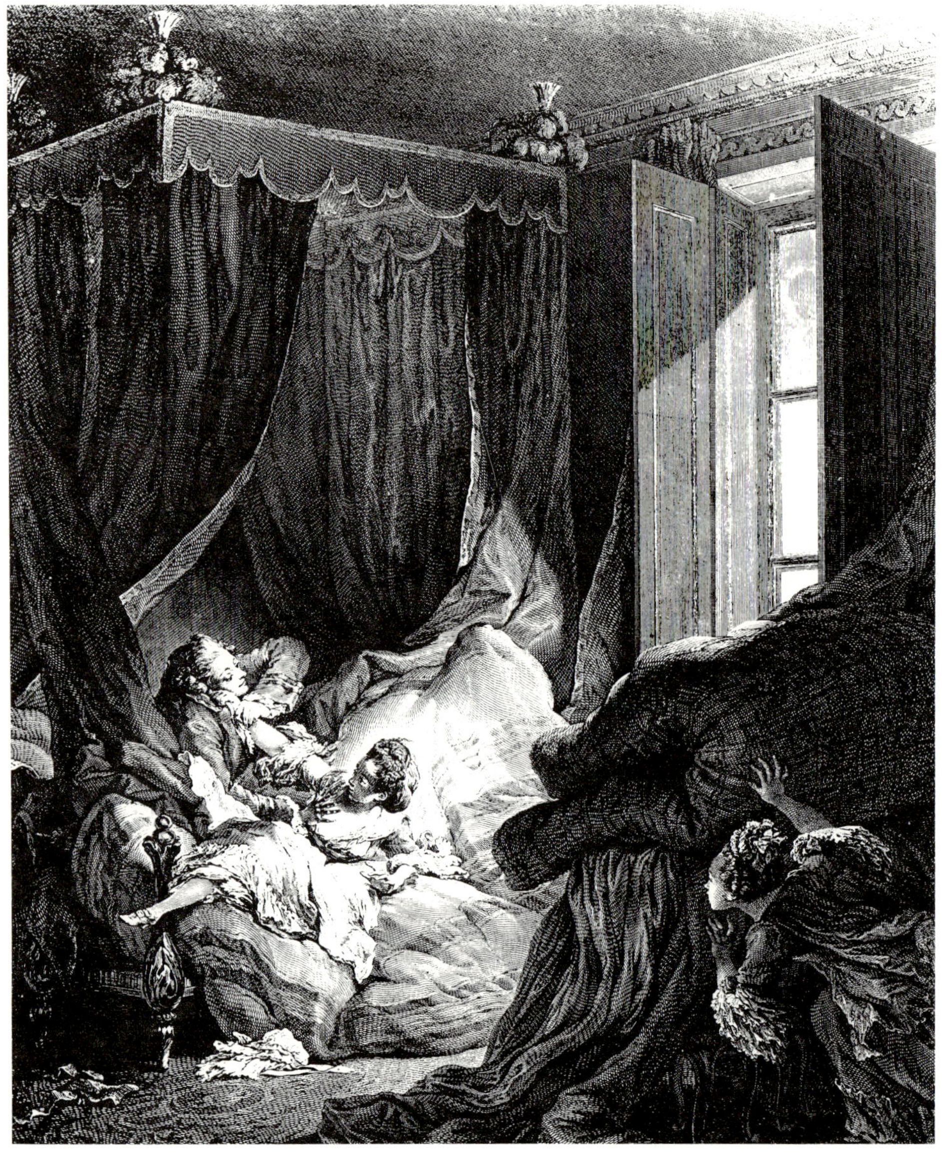

83 *(Left)* Baudoin: *The indiscreet wife*. Engraving, 1771. Bibliothèque Nationale, Paris

84 *(Above)* Antoine Borel (attr.): *Lovers with onlooker.* Plate from Meursius the Younger, *Nouvelle Traduction de Meursius, Aloisia ou l'Academie des Dames*, 1749. British Library

the same position, but clothed instead of naked. The existence of the two paintings was not known until they were found in the collection of Manuel Godoy, who had been Queen Maria Luisa's favourite, her reputed lover, and for a time the virtual governor of Spain. When found the paintings were indicted by the Inquisition for 'indecency' and it is lucky that they have survived. Goya had had a passionate and tempestuous affair with the Duchess of Alba, who was a wealthy and independent woman, notorious for the number of her lovers. It

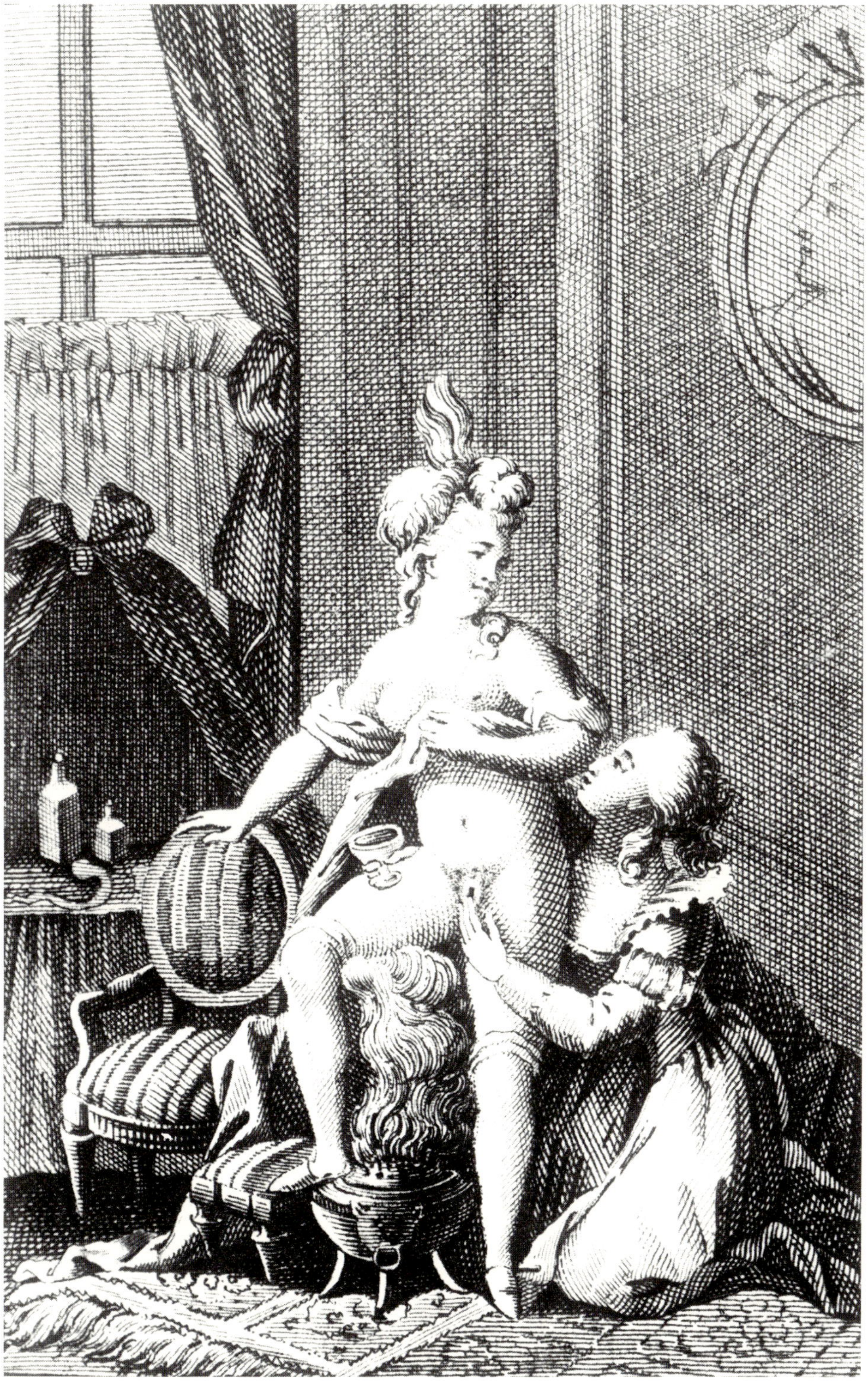

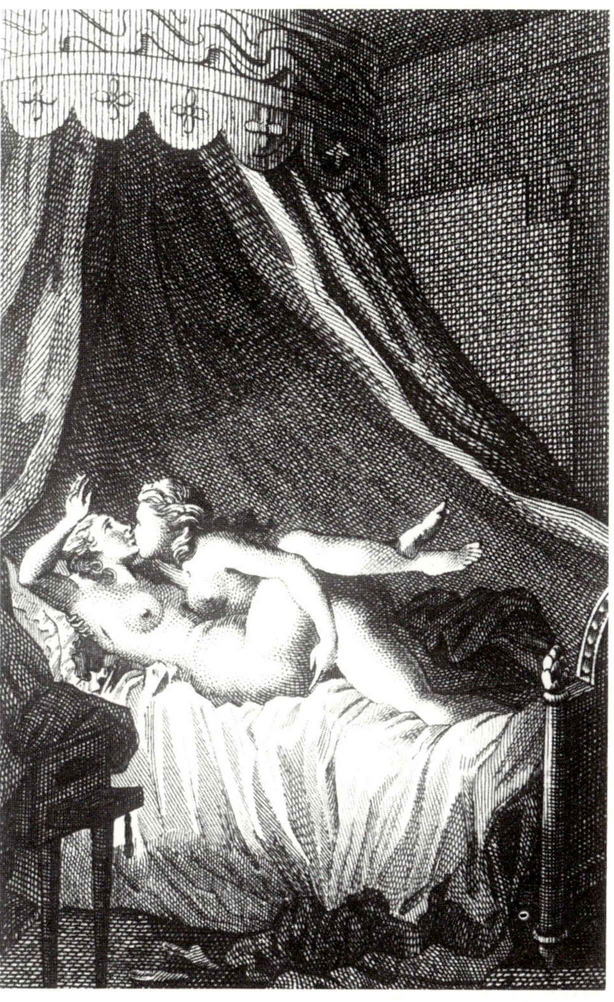

85 *(Left)* Antoine Borel (attr.): *Lady and Servant*. Plate from Meursius the Younger, *Le Meursius François*, 1782. British Library

86 *(Above)* Antoine Borel (attr.): *Lesbian Scene*. Plate from Meursius the Younger, *Le Meursius François*, 1782. British Library

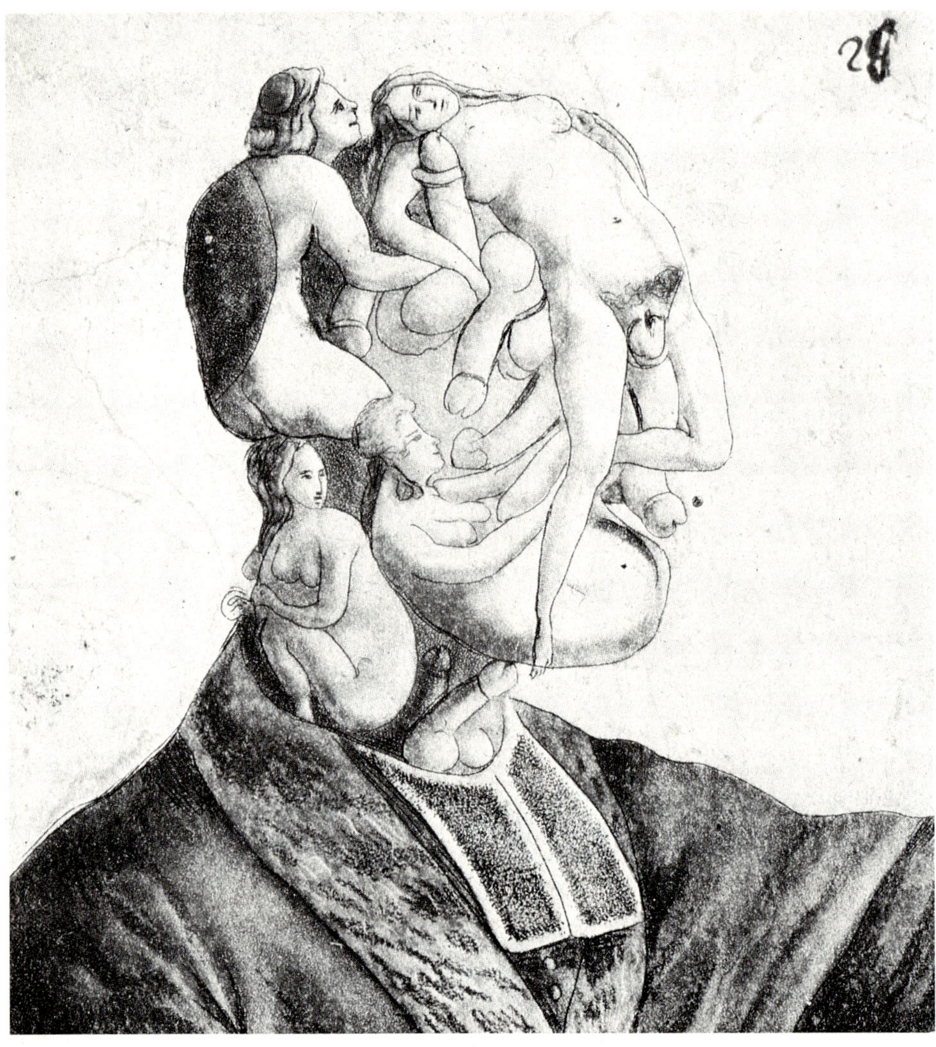

87 *(Left)* Anon: *Satirical portrait of Cardinal Rohan Soubise*, engraving. Coll. Gerard Nordmann, Geneva

88 *(Right)* Henry Fuseli: *Erotic Scene*. Pencil and wash, c. 1820

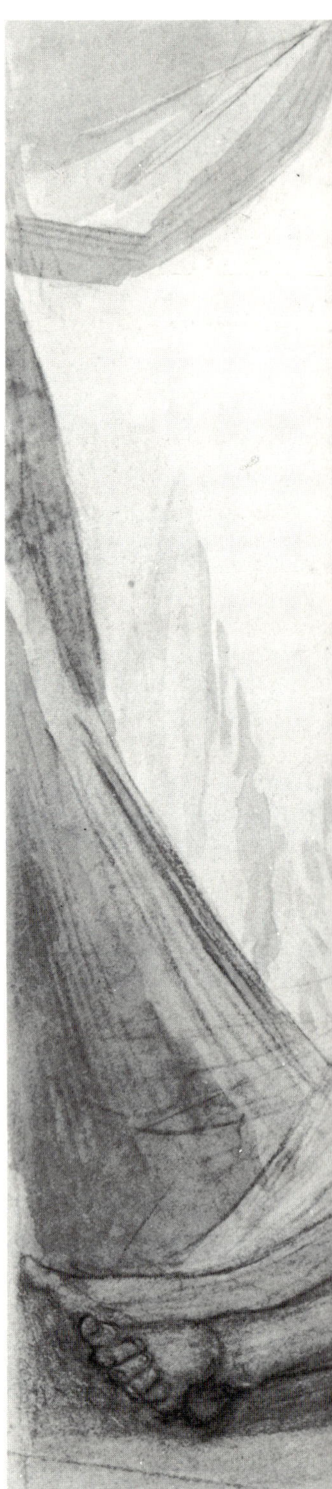

was suggested that she might have been the model. However, Goya was a superb portrait painter and a comparison with other portraits which he had made of her showed that she was not. The identity of the nude lady remains a mystery, but perhaps she was a mistress of Godoy and the clothed version was an alibi in case an inquisitive relation asked to see the portrait he had heard had been made of her lying on a sofa!

Some artists create erotic art for sale and some for themselves. One of the latter was the Swiss-born Henry Fuseli (1741-1825), a fine artist who was Professor of Art at the Royal Academy during the last twenty-six years of his life. In his youth he had evidently been subjected to strange influences, which left him with an obsessive interest in women's hair and a masochistic yearning for dominant women with whips in their hands. Analysis of his rather enigmatic public art has shown a suppressed eroticism. After his death a few explicit erotic drawings by him were found and one of these could, at first sight, be thought similar to Rowlandson's *Pasha* (Plate 93), in which one man is enjoying the attentions of a number of women. In

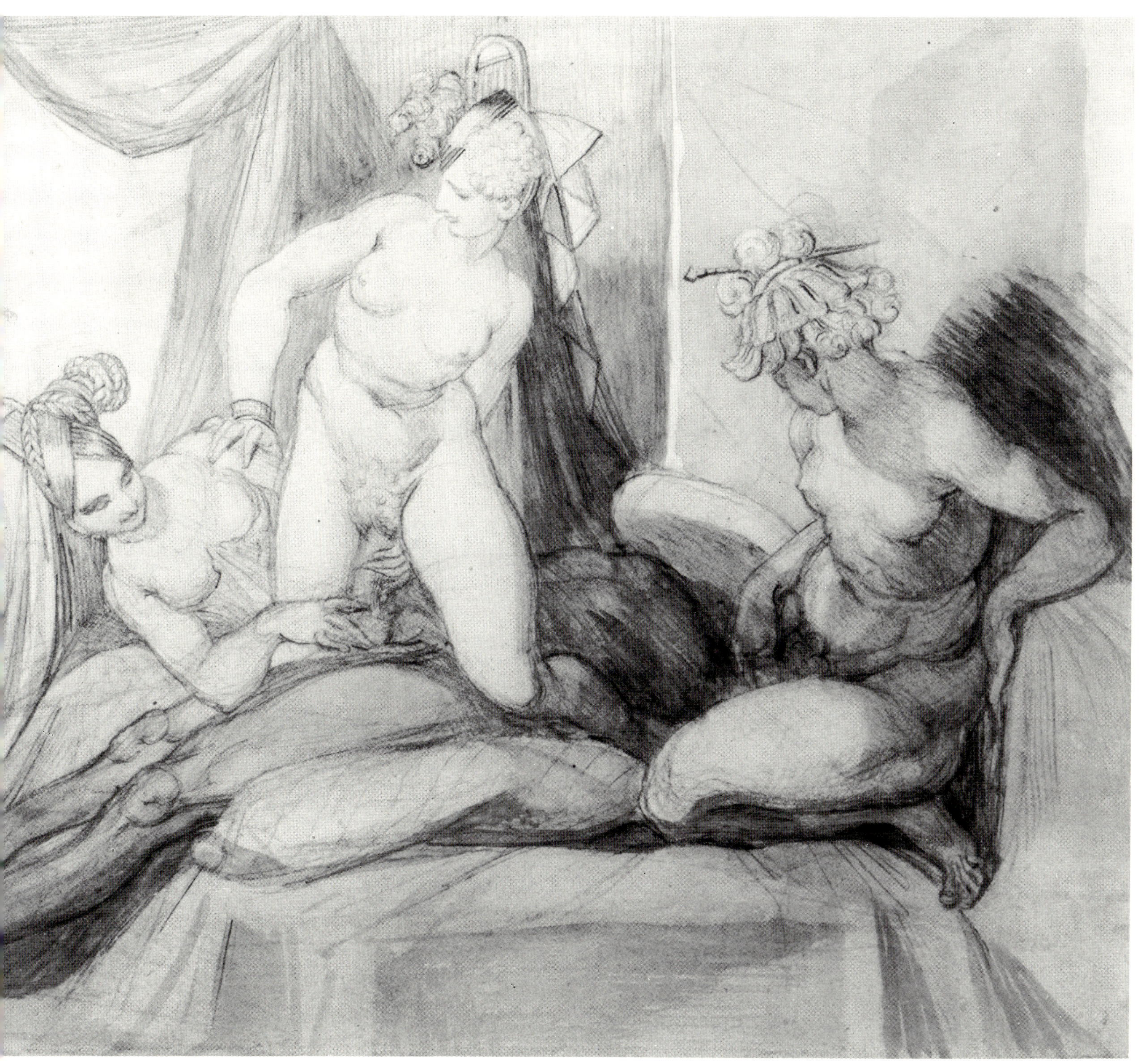

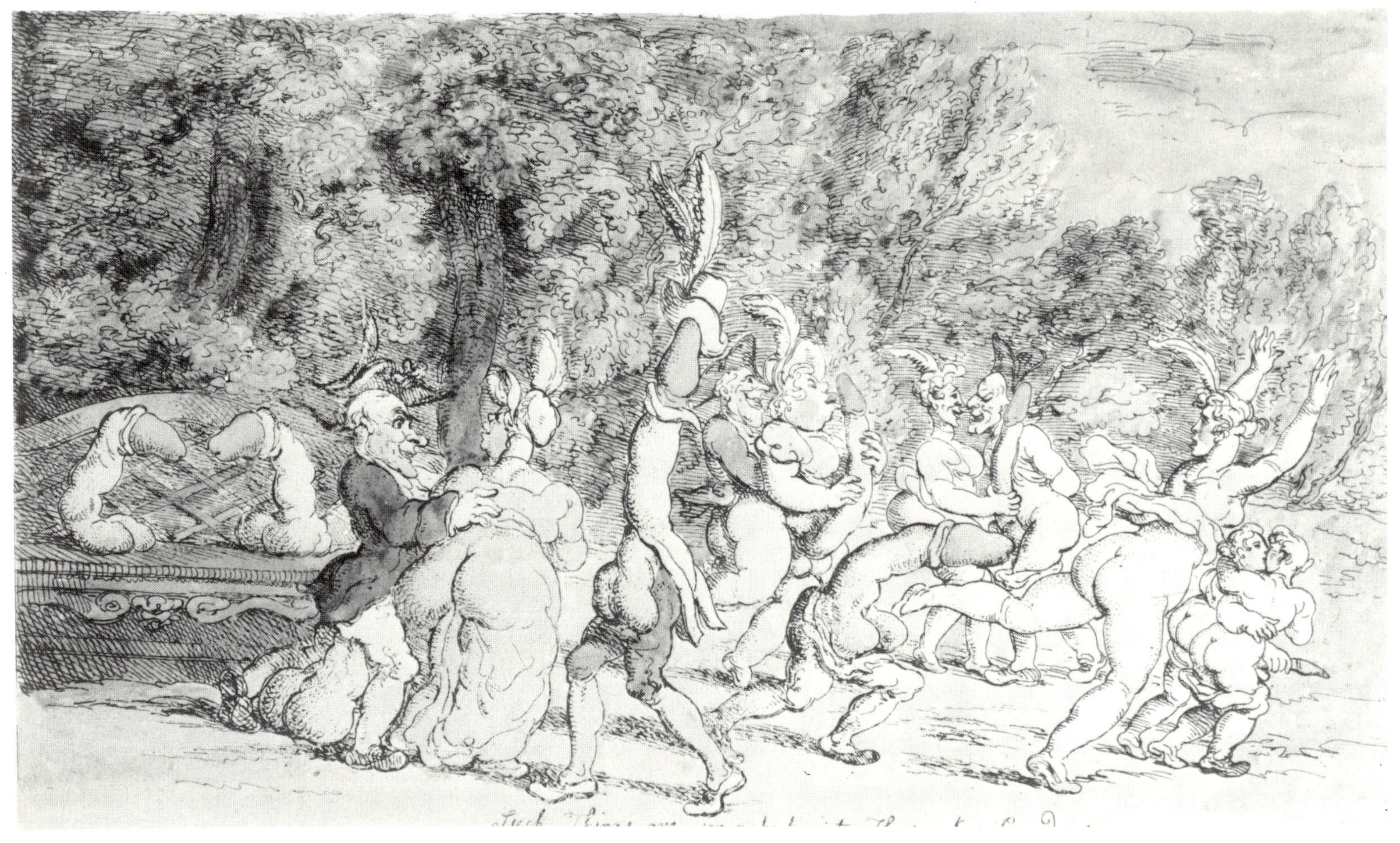

89. Rowlandson: *Such things are or a peep into Kensington Gardens*. Tinted engraving, c.1810

fact, it is inscribed with a quotation from *Prometheus* by Aeschylus: 'In such a way may love come upon my enemies.' This refers to an episode in which men were murdered by their brides on their wedding night!

Unlike Fuseli, Thomas Rowlandson (1756-1827) was an artist who was not ashamed to create explicit erotic art for sale and he is undoubtedly one of the most important erotic artists England has ever produced. He grew up in London, in a country which, in contrast to France, expected rich and poor to rub shoulders. The coaches and sedan chairs of the wealthy clattered over the cobbles of the narrow, twisted streets to meet a teeming multitude of freedom-loving individuals at the cock-fight, the gambling den, the inn or the coffee-house. This was a prosperous community which ate

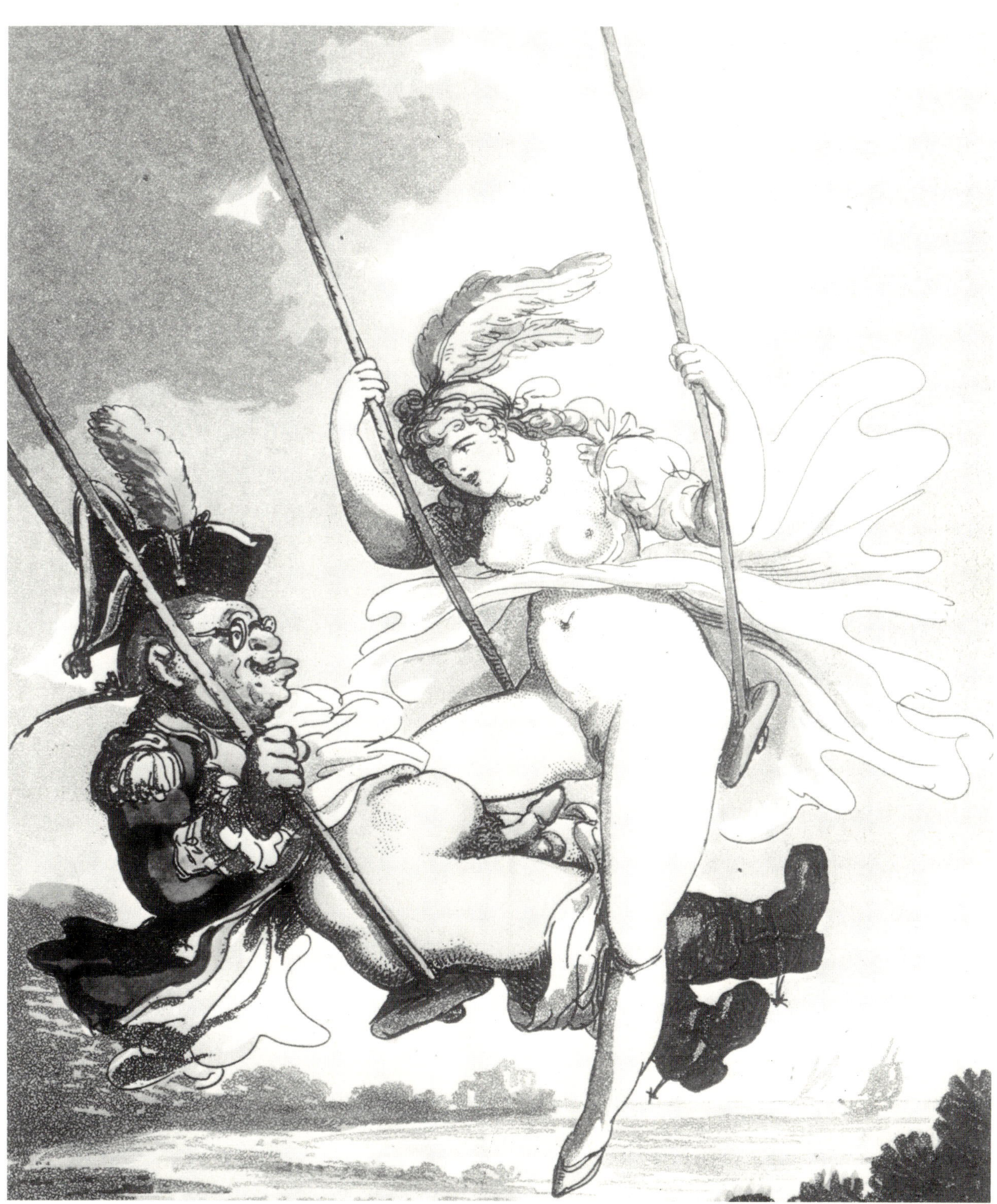

90 Rowlandson: *Love Play.*
Aquatint, c.1810

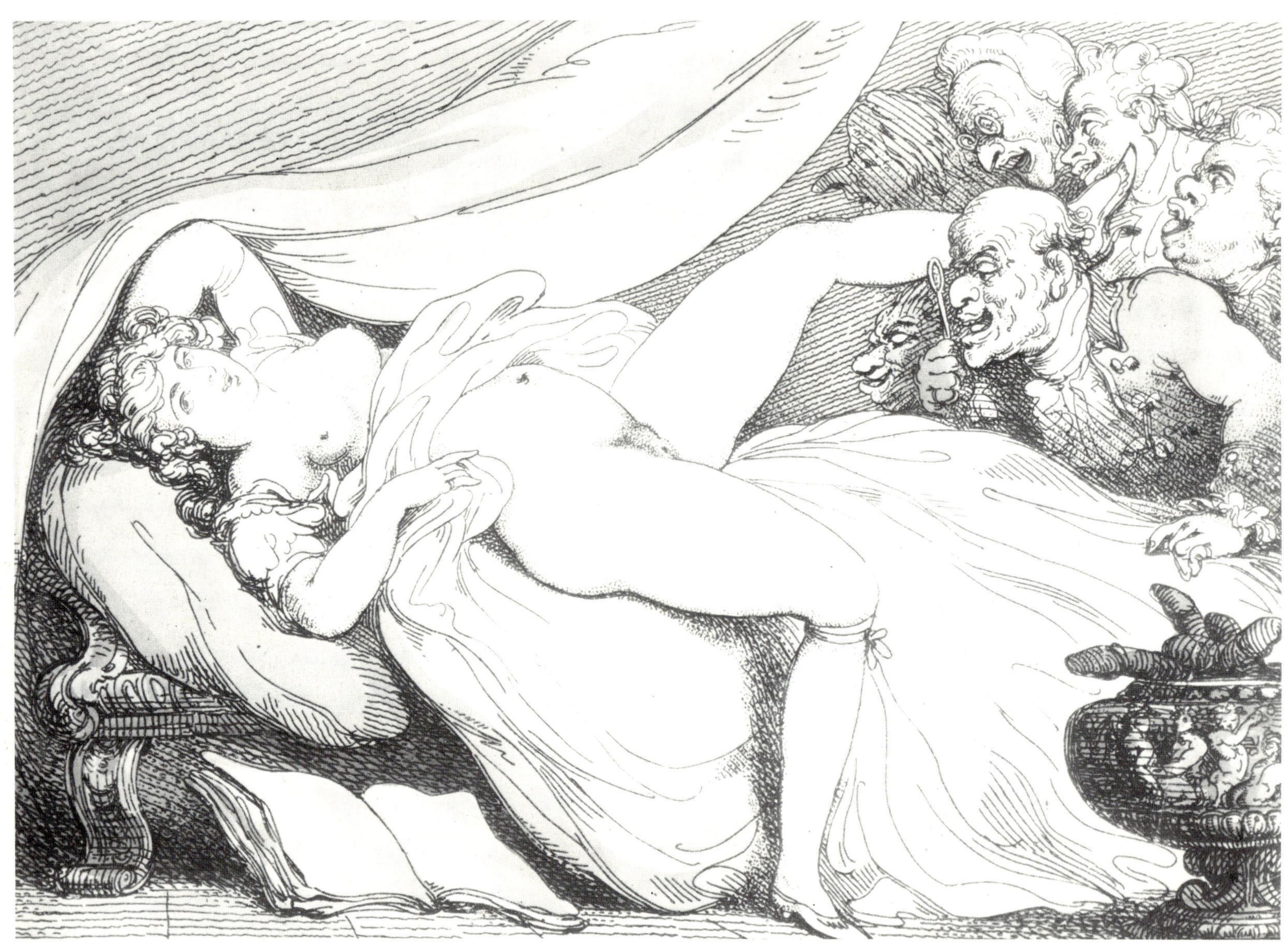

91 Rowlandson: *The Curiosity Seekers.* Tinted engraving, c.1810

and drank well, where a gallon of beer a day was not thought excessive for a working man. As a part of that prosperity art in England was reaching a peak.

Because of a well-to-do aunt who doted on him, Rowlandson was never short of money. He was able to travel abroad and, as a tall, good-looking young man, he enjoyed all the boisterous pleasures of the day. He was always fascinated by people and the variety of their lives. These he recorded in a stream of drawings and prints, each one

92 *(Right)* Charles Antoine Coypel (attr.): *Leda,* from *Histoire Universelle,* 1740s. British Museum

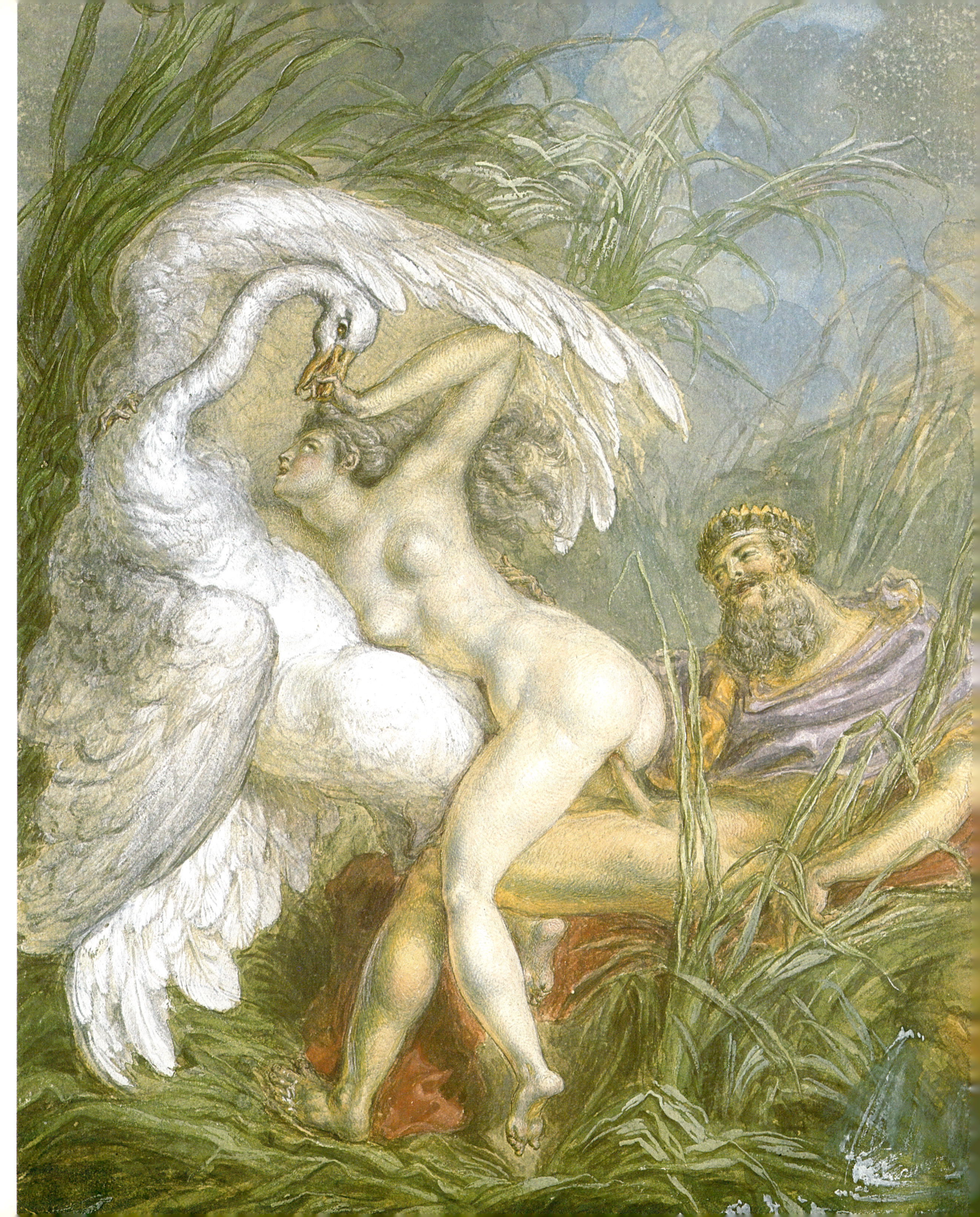

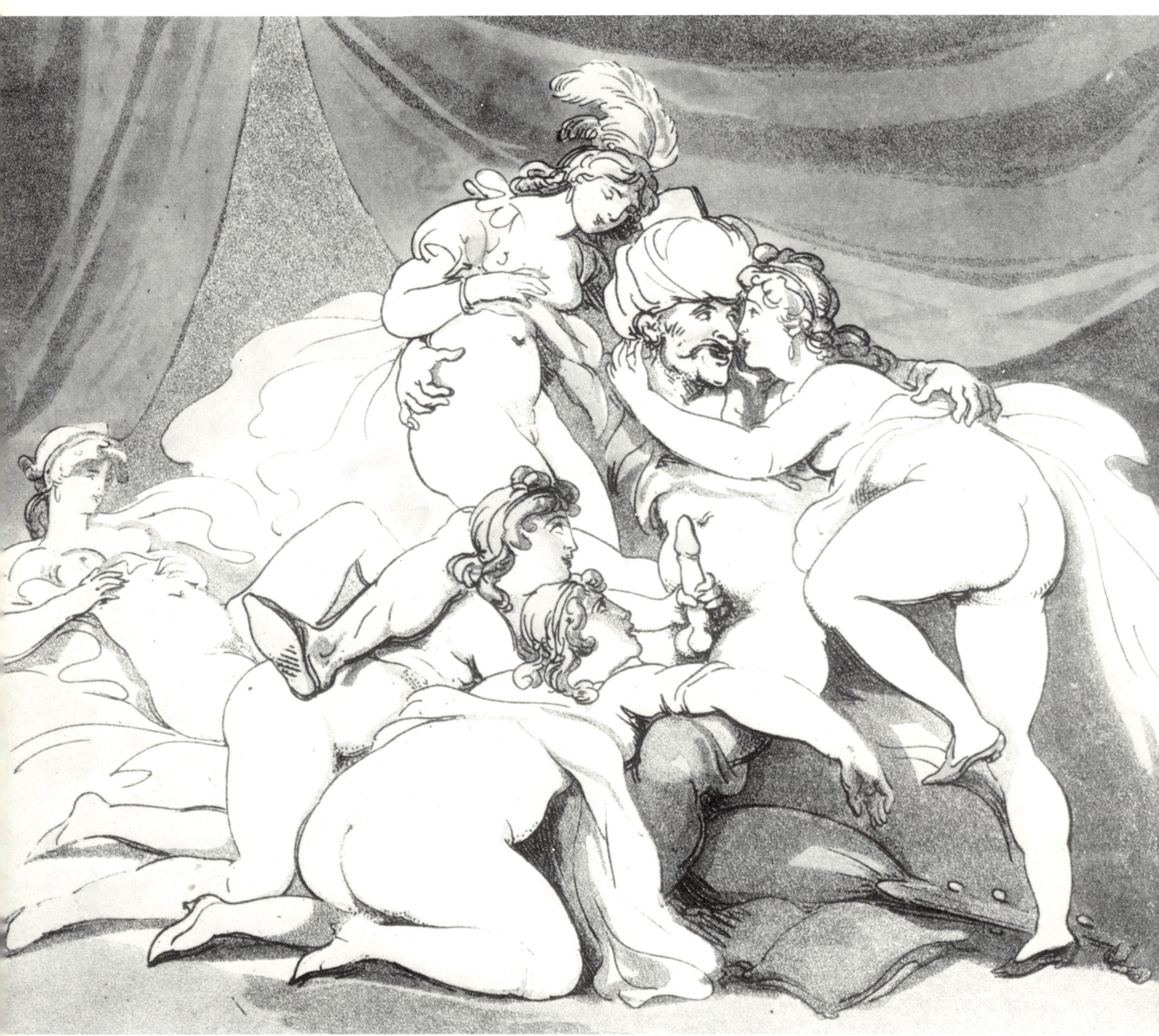

93 *(Left)* Rowlandson: *The Pasha*. Aquatint, c. 1810

94 Rowlandson: *The intruder.* Tinted engraving, c. 1810

95 *(Right)* Rowlandson: *The concert*. Tinted engraving, c. 1810

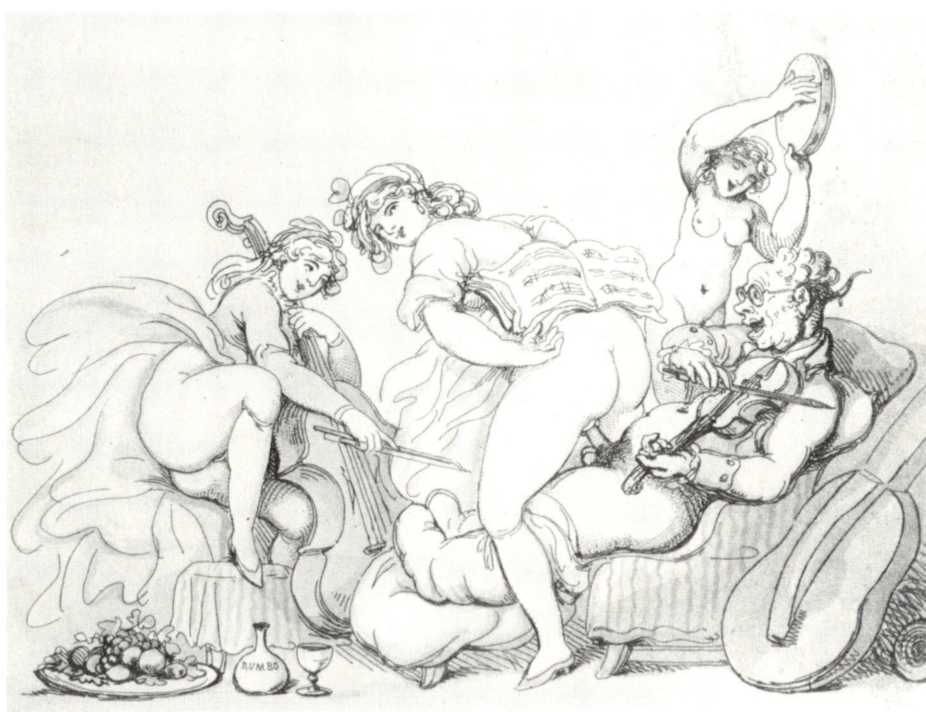

delighting the eye with brilliant draughtsmanship. He stressed the contrasts of youth and age, dignity and impudence, beauty and ugliness, leavening these with an inventiveness and a sense of humour which appealed to the bawdy fashions of the day.

Many of his drawings and prints had subjects which involved sexual innuendoes, but from about 1810 onwards he turned his attention increasingly to explicitly erotic themes, and in the years that

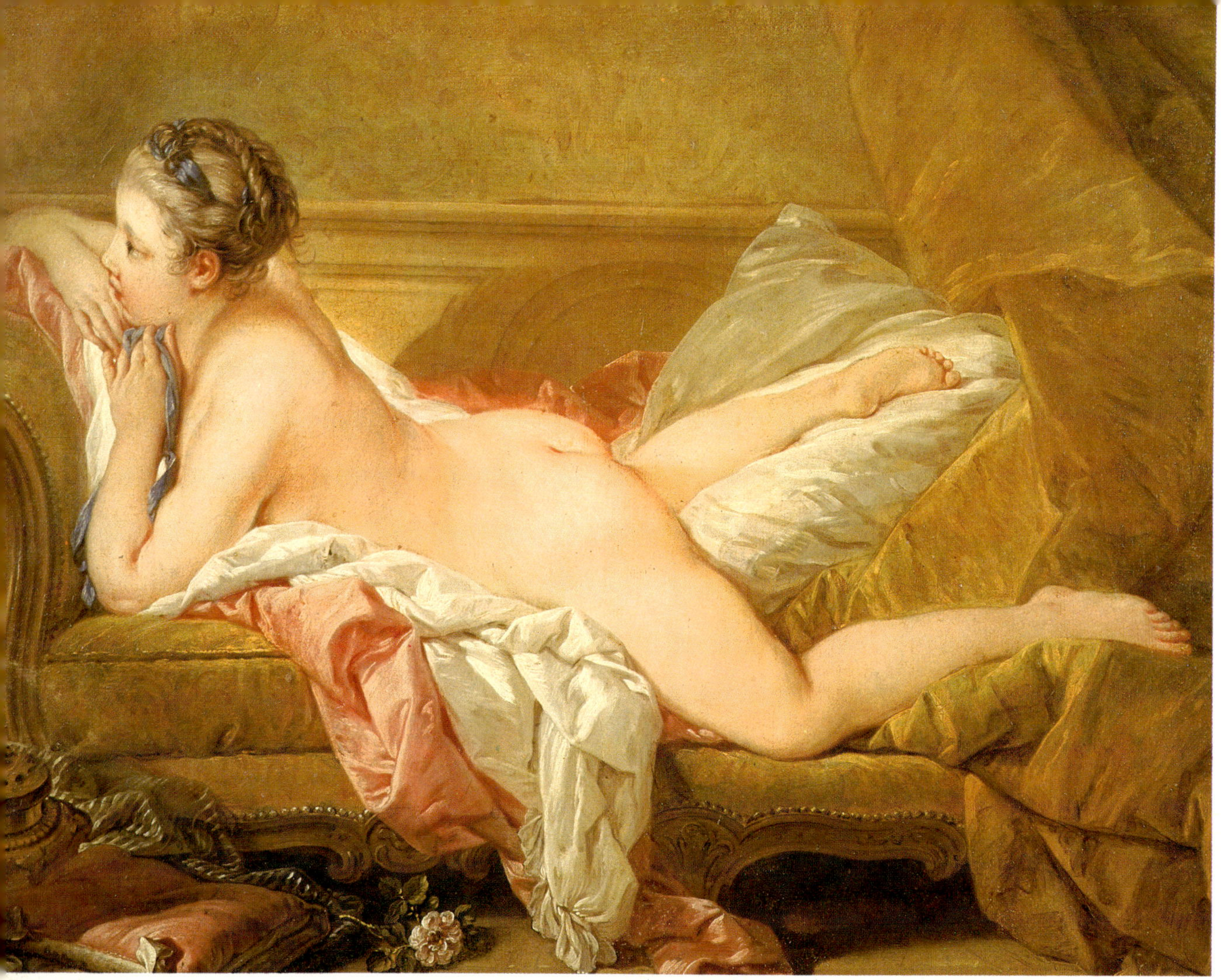

96 *(Left)* François Boucher: *Louison O'Morphi*, 1751. Alte Pinakothek, Munich

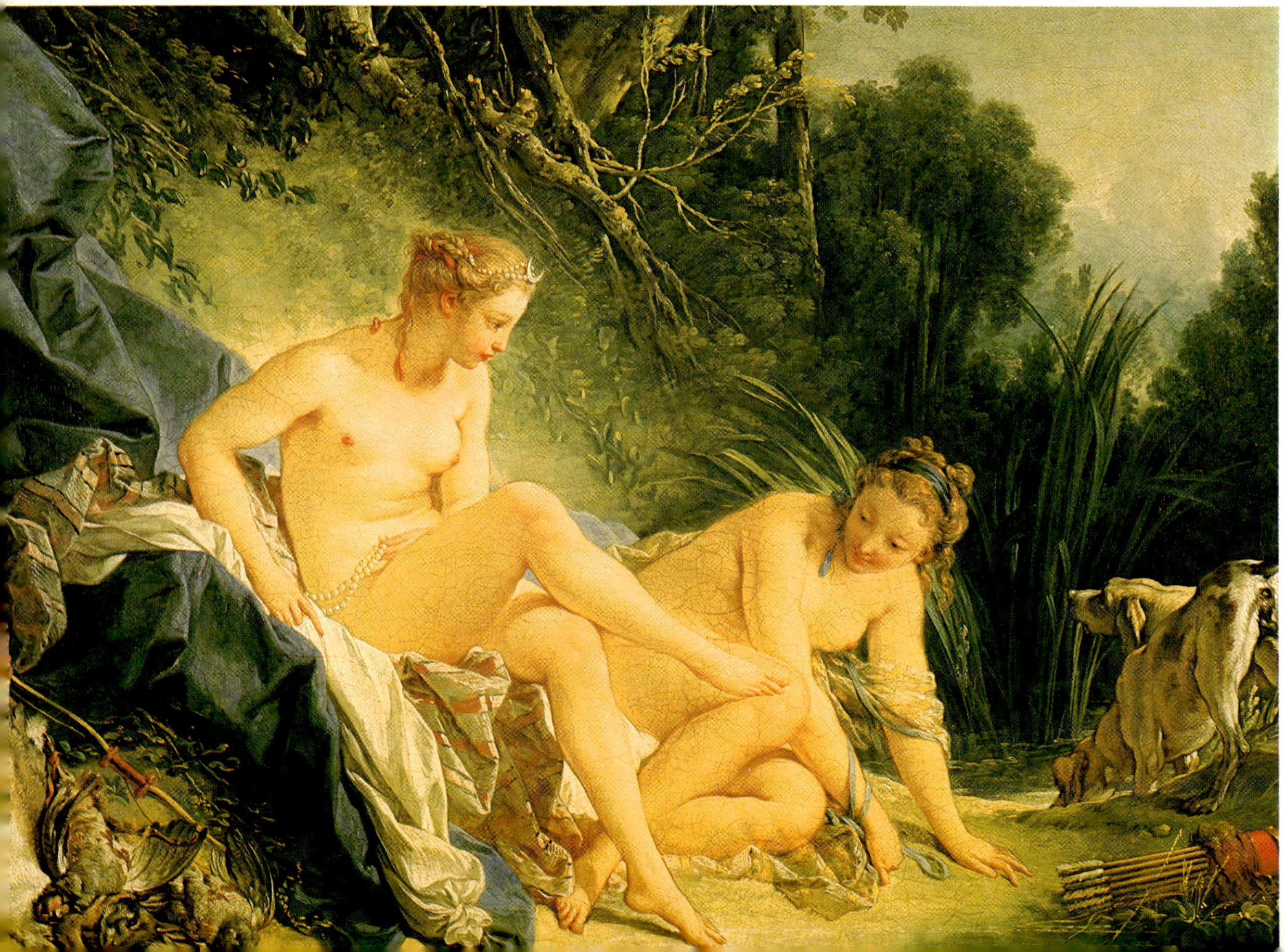

97 *(Left)* François Boucher: *Diana resting after her bath*, 1742. 56×73cm. Louvre, Paris

98 *(Right)* Jean-Honoré Fragonard: *The Swing*, 1768-9. 82.9×66cm. Wallace Collection, London

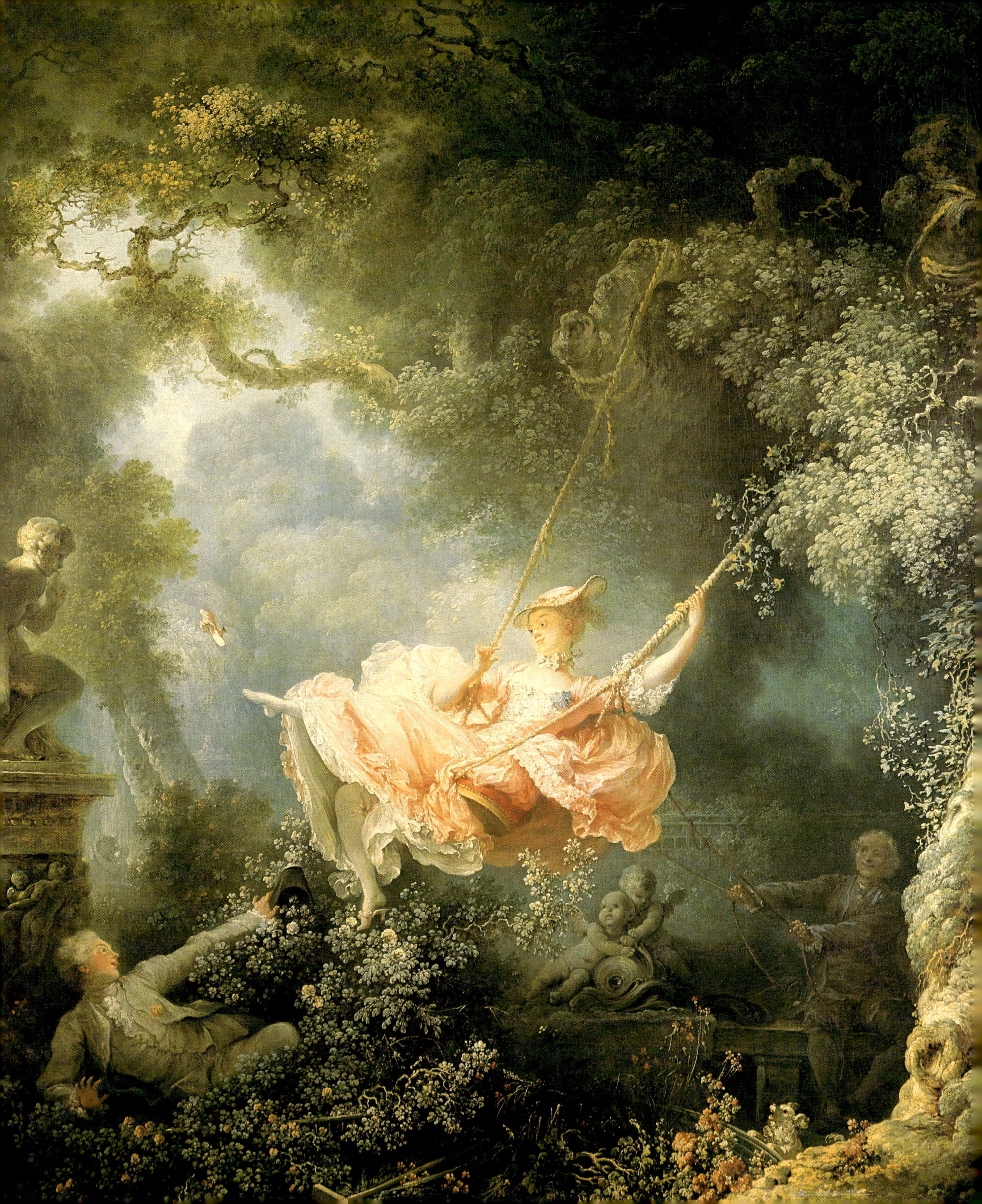

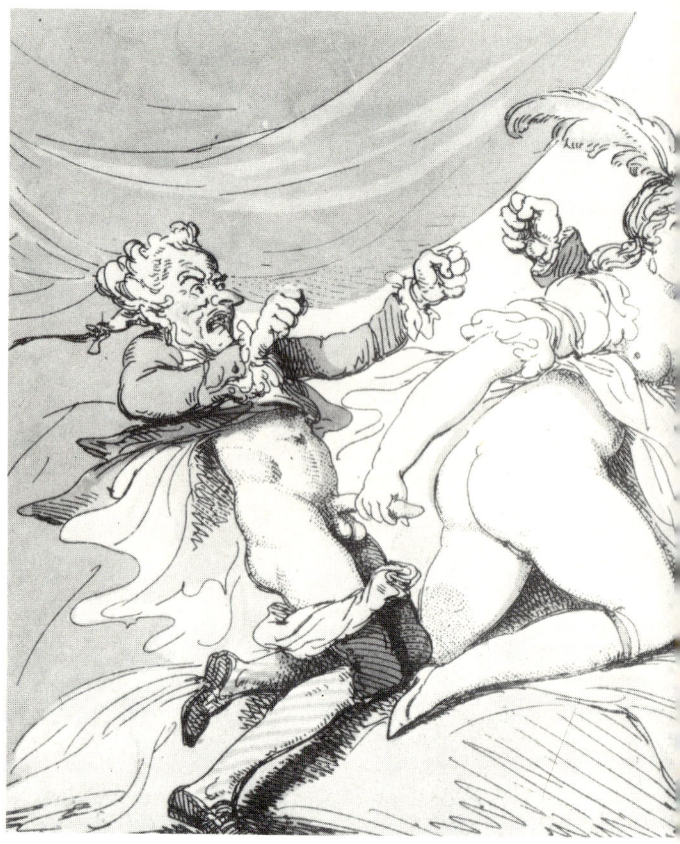

followed he produced more than a hundred prints which showed a wide variety of sexual activities in the frankest possible way.

In many of these he voiced the popular criticism of a supposed laxity in the morals of priests and nuns. Plate 32, for example, shows a young novice with a dildo who has just been reading Aretino's sonnets, and Plate 35 is still more dramatic. In another print he invented a landscape peopled with an incredible group of little phallic creatures, lying in wait for courting couples. He made several prints involving a pretty young girl on a swing and in one he added a typical contrast between her and an ugly old man. In another the contrast is between the elderly voyeurs and the unabashed nakedness of the young girl, who for no obvious reason has a bowl of dildos in her room. In *The Pasha* he created the male day-dream of a harem, which had become fashionable in the days when Brighton Pavilion was a novelty, and in *The Concert* there is another unbelievable scene which is nevertheless full of irrepressible gaiety and fun.

Rowlandson had visited France on several occasions and he probably drew on these experiences for his print of two English tourists quarrelling over a French prostitute. It was also in France that he may have developed his amused interest in cuckolds. It was commonplace in his day for a young girl to marry an old man. Rowlandson's attitude to this is well expressed in the text below one of his prints, where he poses the question: 'When an old man marries a young woman what is he to expect?' and answers, 'Why, to be made a cuckold of course.' In his print of *The Stargazer* the similar text reads: 'I have known many a man made a cuckold of in the twinkling of a star.' His reputation as a man-about-town leaves us in little doubt that he spoke from personal experience. He was living in a time of sexual laxity and his themes (Plates 76, 94, 101) were based on normal, heterosexual intercourse with a complete absence of the perversions which accompany sexual repression. It was ironic that within a few years of his death in 1827, Victorian decorum, gentility and hypocrisy were to sweep his erotic art out of sight, and it virtually disappeared from public gaze for over a hundred years.

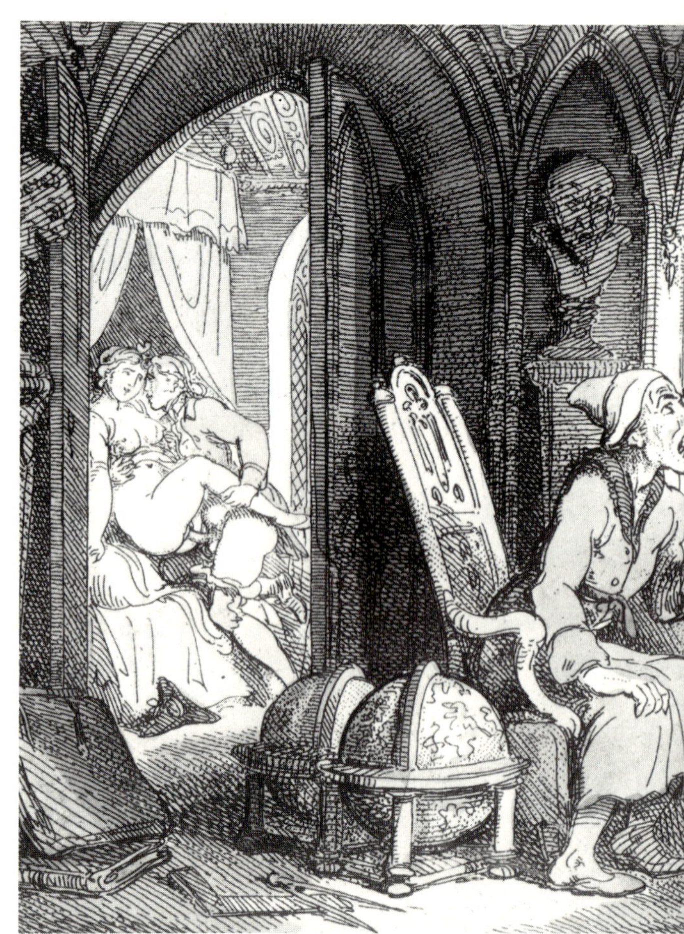

99 *(Centre, top)* Rowlandson: *The rural Knights or the Englishmen in Paris*. Aquatint, c.1810

100 *(Right)* Rowlandson: *The Stargazer.* Tinted engraving, c.1810

101 *(Far right)* Rowlandson: *Lovers*. Tinted engraving, c.1810

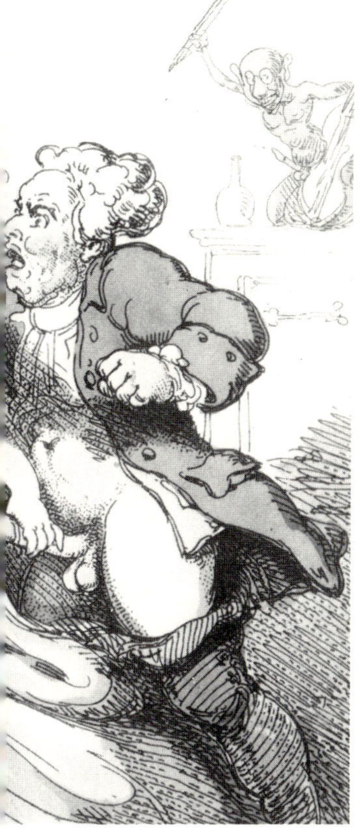

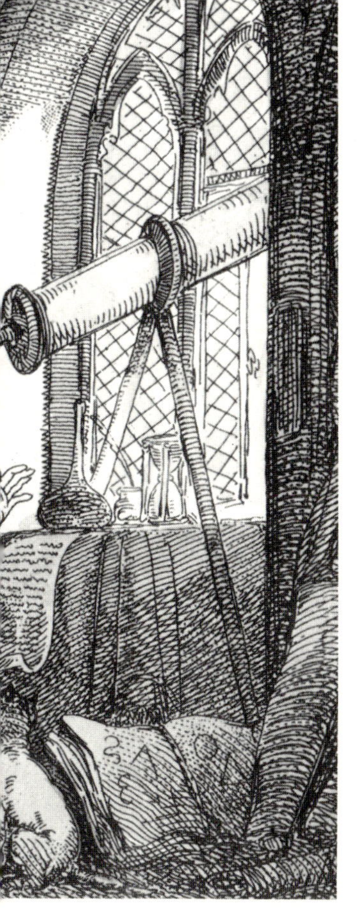

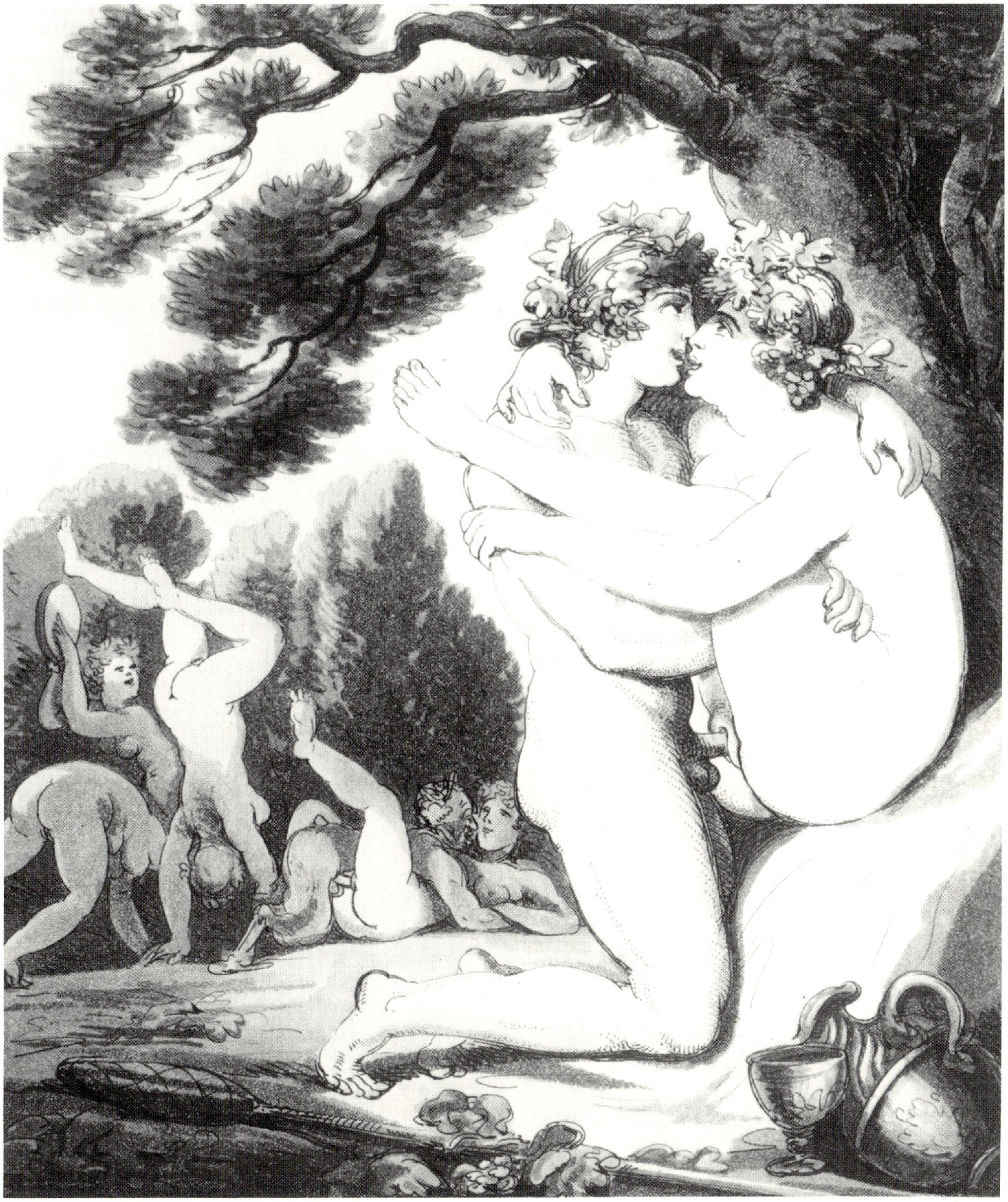

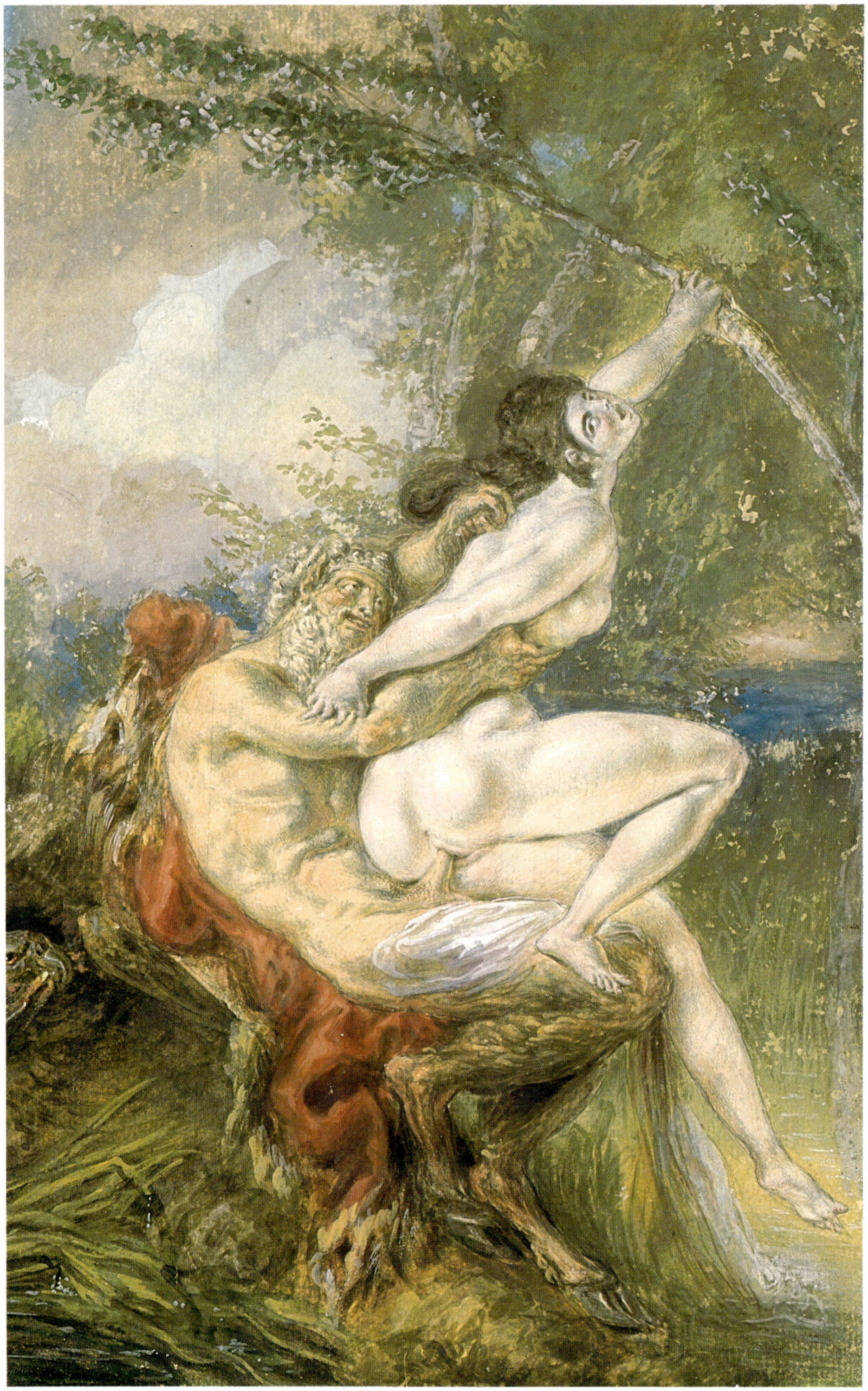

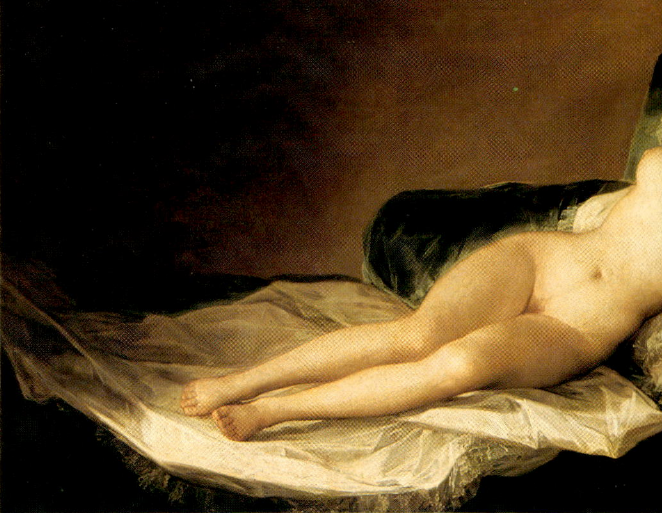

102 *(Left)* Coypel (attr.): *Jupiter and Antiope*, from *Histoire Universelle*, 1740s. British Museum

103 *(Above)* Goya: *The Naked Maja*, 1800-5. 97×190cm. Prado, Madrid

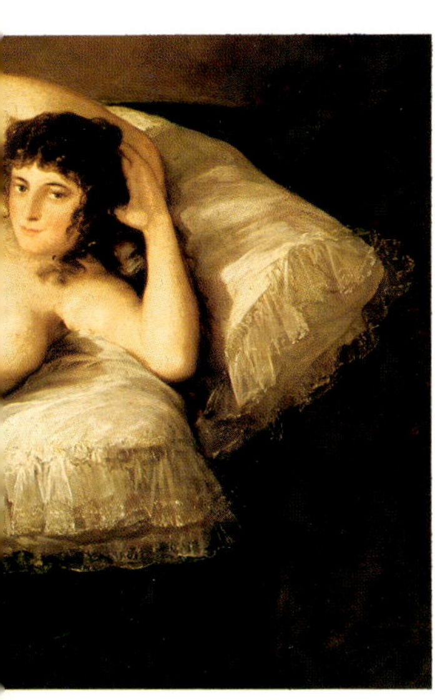

104 *(Right)* Anon: *The award of love,* watercolour. Coll. Gerard Nordmann, Geneva

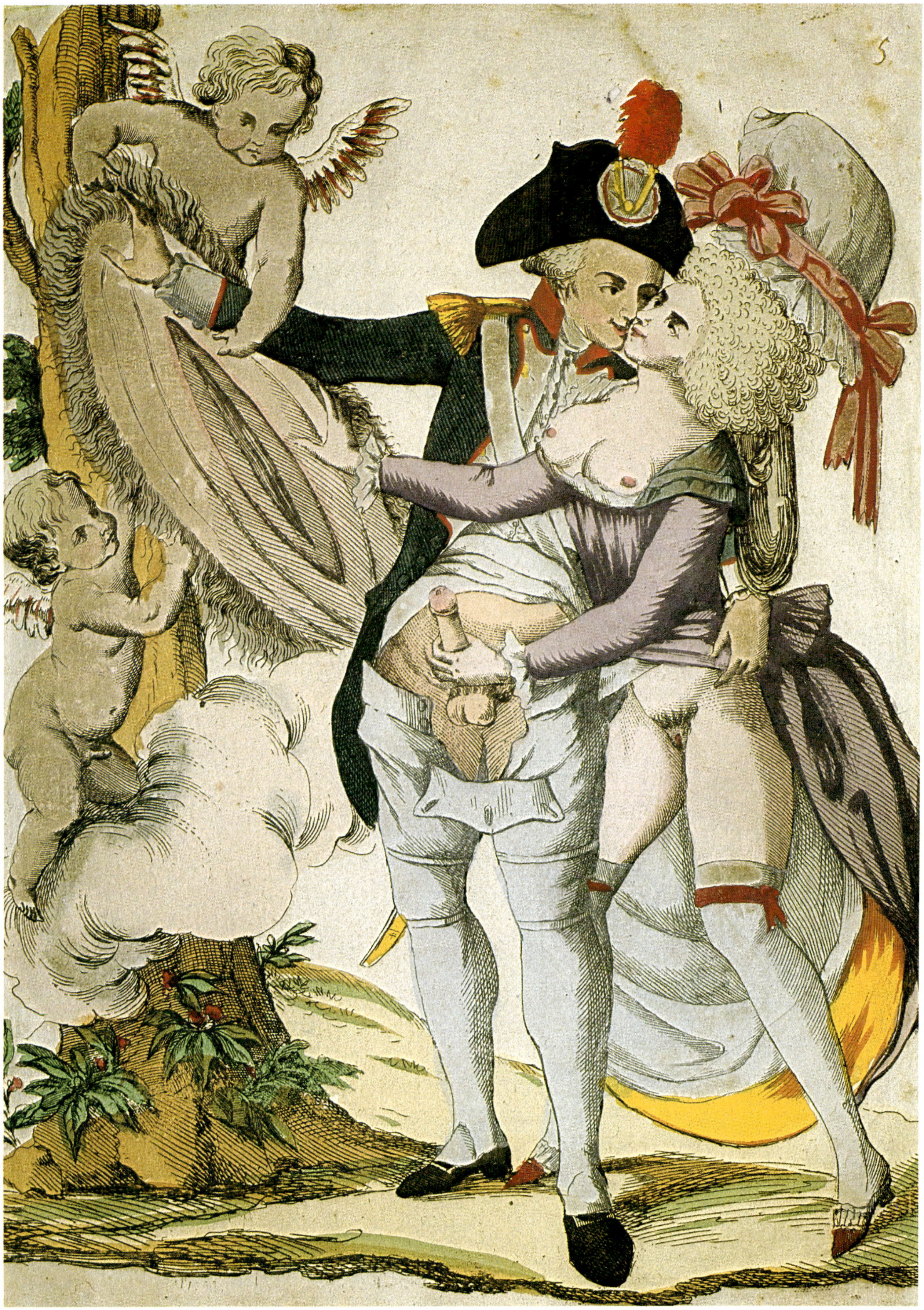

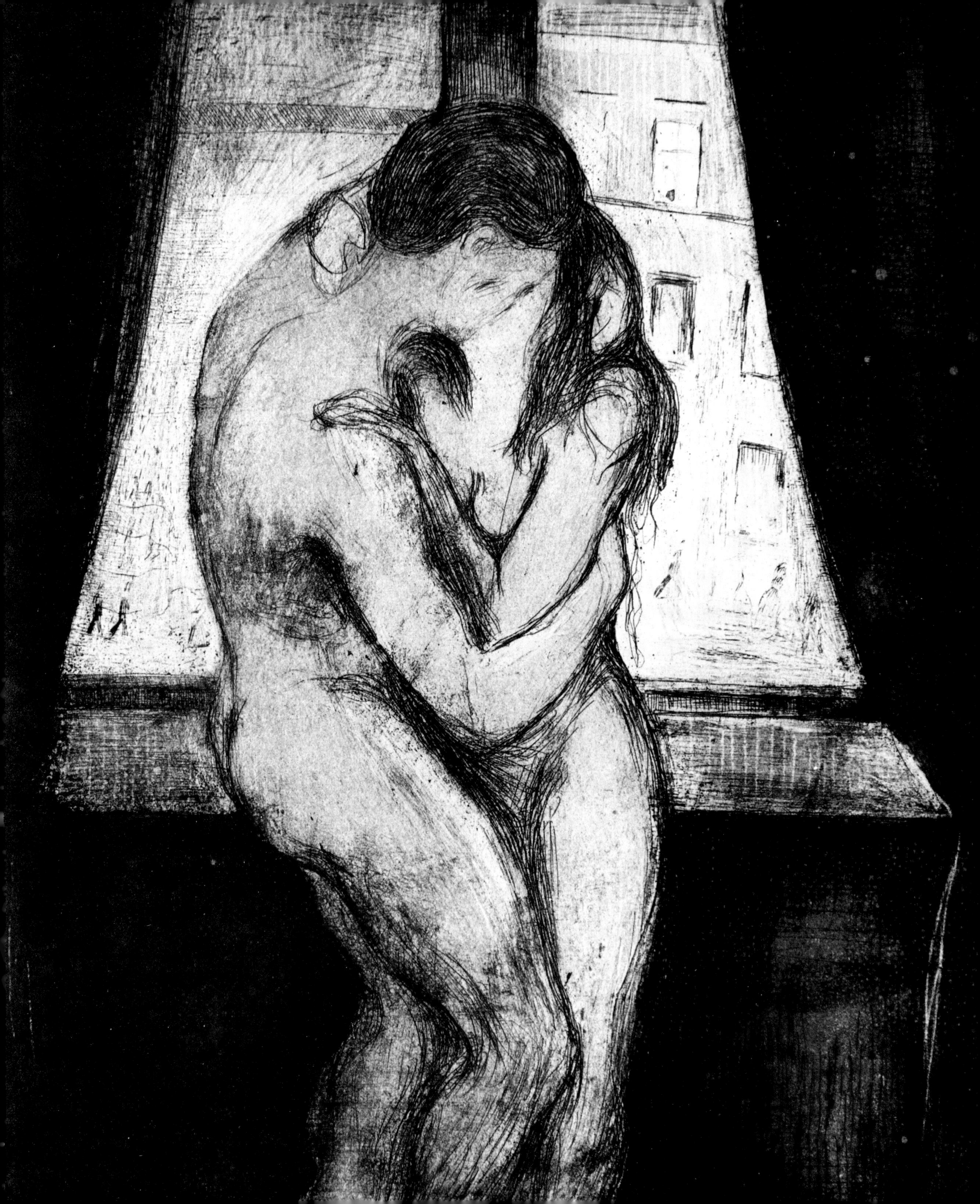

CHAPTER 6

The Victorians

When the nineteenth century began England was a prosperous country, sheltered by its navy from the revolutionary disruptions taking place in many parts of Europe. English artists were flourishing and Rowlandson and others were producing a high standard of erotic art. In Europe, on the other hand, Napoleon had seized power in France, when he became First Consul in 1799 and Emperor in 1804. From 1803 until the French were defeated at Waterloo in 1815, French armies and influence spread across the continent, meeting with strong opposition only in Spain and in Russia. This led to further rapid changes in countries already disrupted, in many cases, by previous revolutionary forces, and created much disorder and relative poverty.

These were not circumstances favourable to the production of erotic art, but in France Eugène Le Poitevin (1806-70), who was a skilled lithographer, produced a series of hand-coloured lithographs entitled *Les Diableries Erotiques* (Plate 106). These showed highly imaginative and humorous scenes in which devils played sexual pranks on innocent women, and sexual organs developed a life of their own. Achille Deveria (1805-57), another notable erotic artist, illustrated many books, including a small, privately printed edition of *Don Juan*. Among other pictures was a scene in which the hero watches two women engaged in cunnilingus.

After about 1830 the return to prosperity, particularly in England, was reflected in the growing numbers and increasing affluence of the middle classes. These people strove by every means at their disposal to distinguish themselves from those further down the social ladder. They began to adopt standards of morality and virtue higher than those of their predecessors and also of the upper classes, whom they hoped to emulate. They were pious people with good motives. Hard work, thrift and 'self-help' became the watchwords of a rising class that, by the middle of the century, had made England the richest country in the world. By the 1850s the middle classes had adopted both a highly artificial system of manners and an ambivalent attitude to simple facts of life. While, for example, it was considered most impolite to suggest that women had legs, it had become fashionable and 'respectable' to put skirts round the legs of pianos! At the same time, when visiting the Great Exhibition at the Crystal Palace, men and women alike were expected to admire marble statues of nude

105 Edvard Munch: *The Kiss*, 1895. Drypoint and aquatint, 29.8×34.7cm. Munch Museet, Oslo

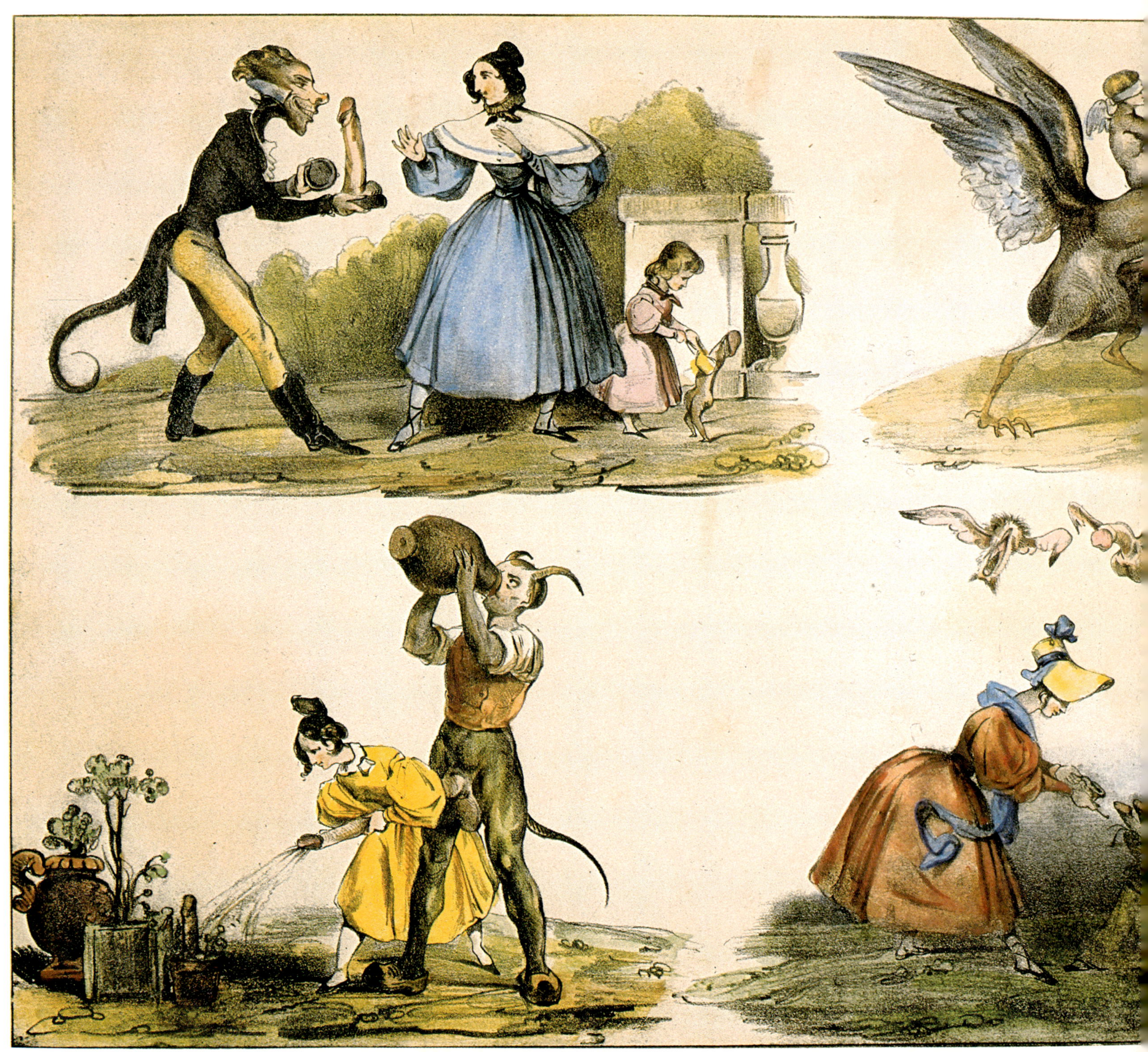

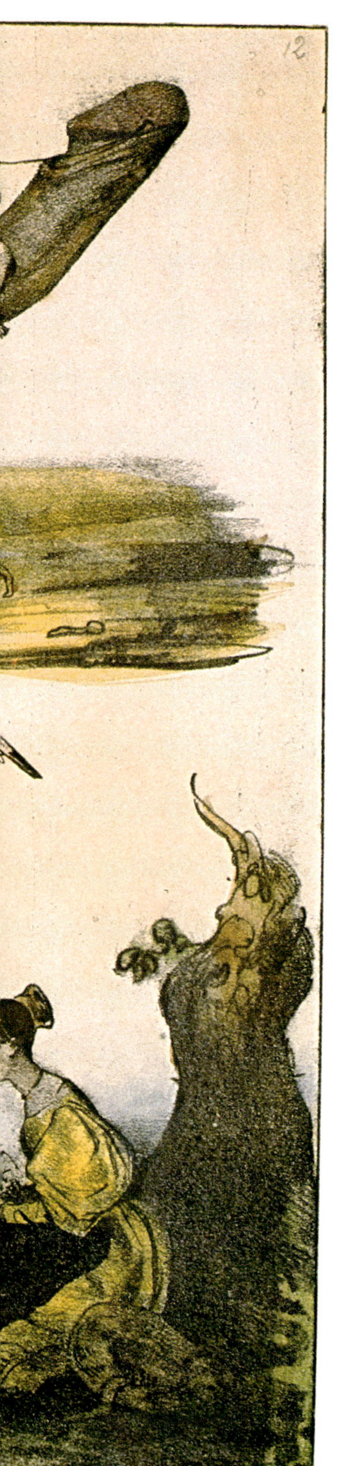

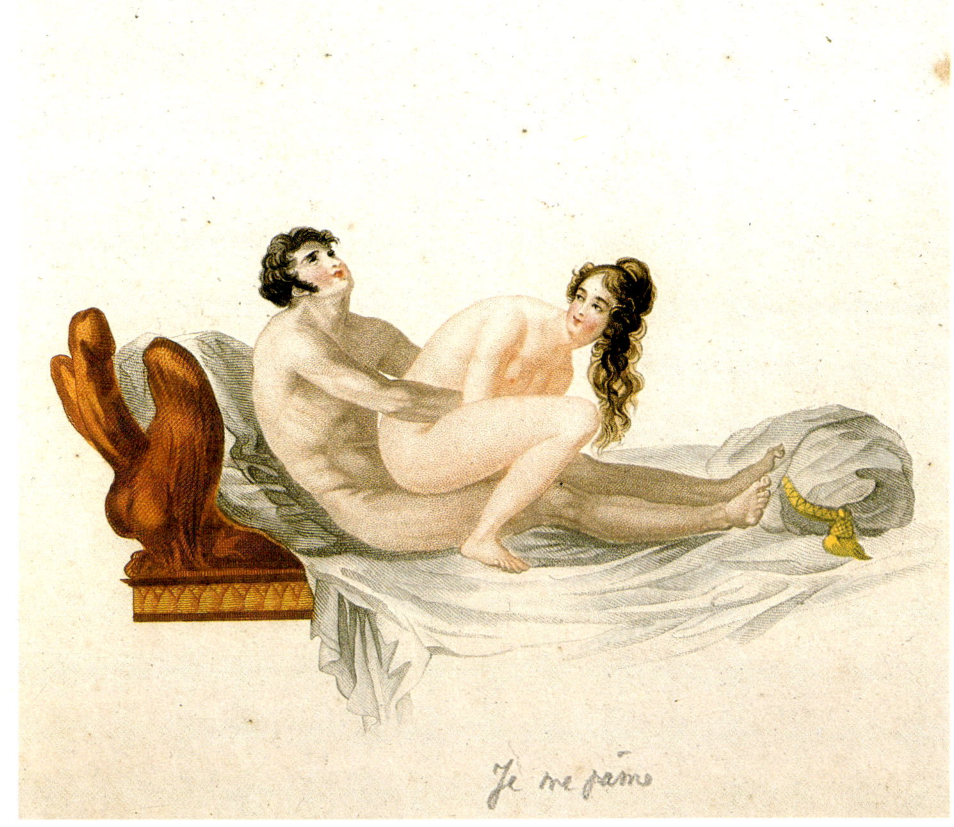

106 *(Far left)* Le Poitevin: *Les Diableries Erotiques.* Hand-coloured lithograph, c.1835. Coll. Gerard Nordmann, Geneva

107 *(Left)* Anon: illustration from *Les extases de l'amour,* hand-coloured aquatint

108 *(Below)* J.A.D. Ingres, *Odalisque with a slave,* 1867. 76×105.4cm. Walters Art Gallery, Baltimore

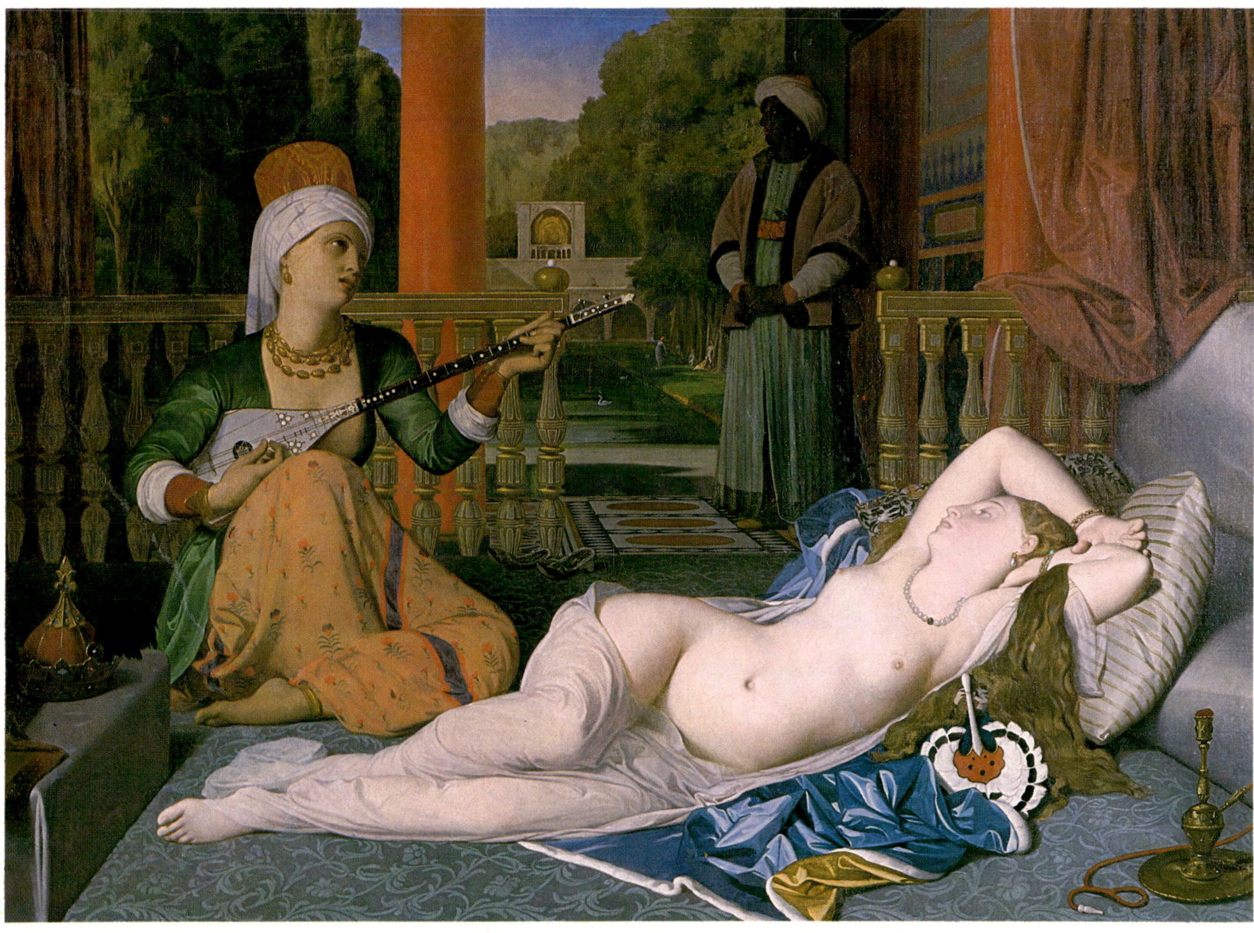

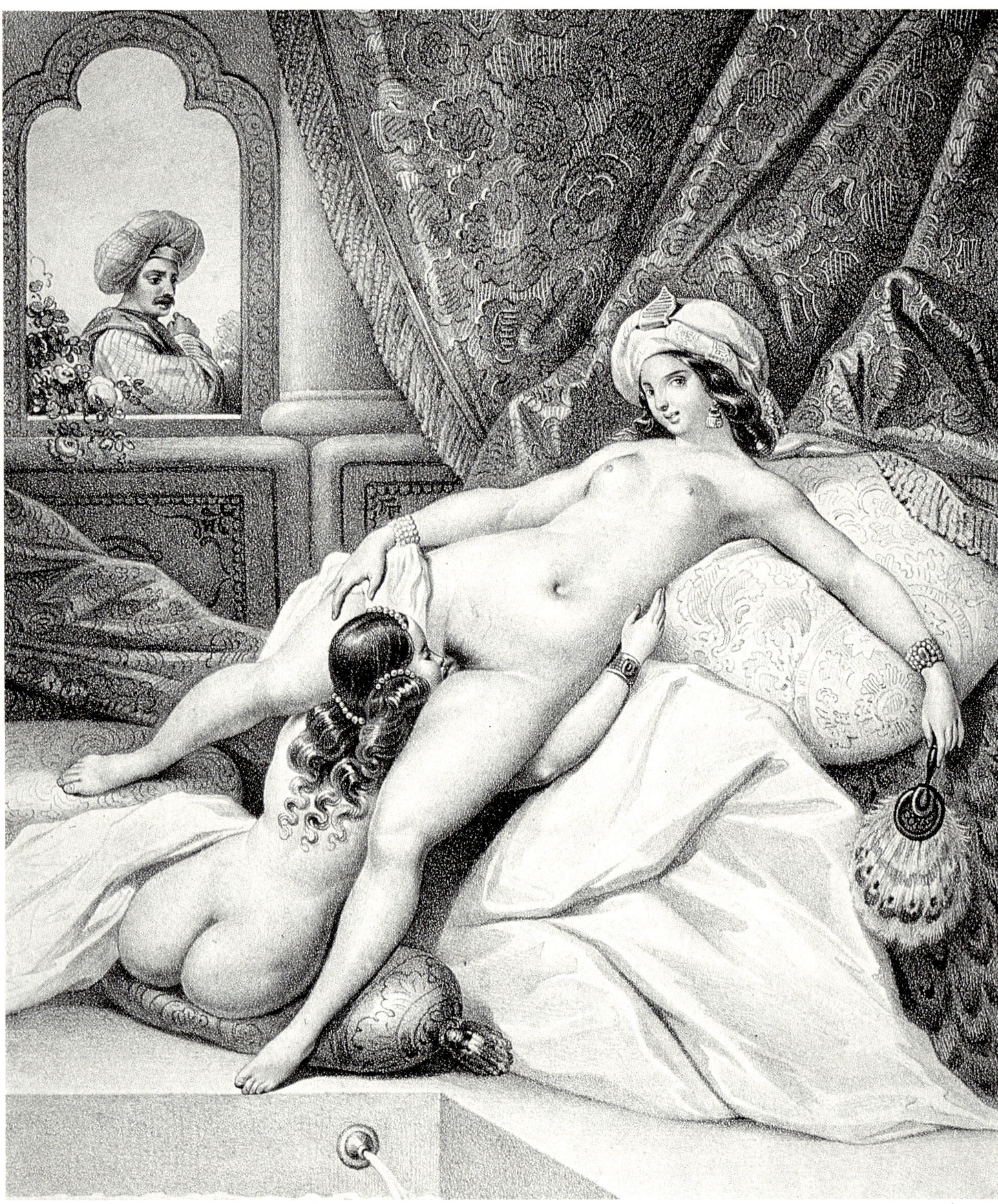

109 *(Left)* Achille Deveria: *The Harem,* lithograph. Coll. Gerard Nordmann, Geneva

110 *(Right)* Hiram Powers: *The Greek Slave*. China, 35cm high

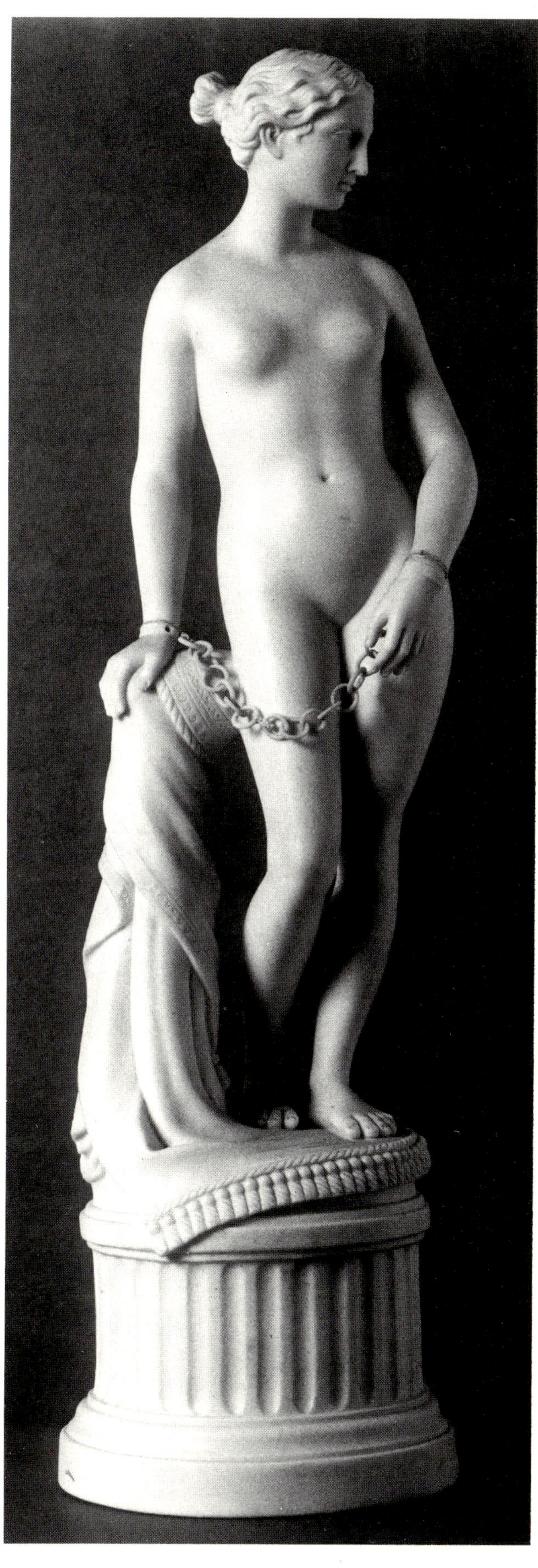

women, always provided that these conformed to what were considered to be classical canons of art. It was thought that the figures belonged to another time and another world, and were thus respectable and devoid of any erotic content. It is difficult, even with hindsight, to understand how so many people could have been prepared to sustain such an unnatural attitude for so long. The effort of forcing themselves to believe what they knew to be untrue carried inevitable penalties in its train.

A typical example of such a nude statue was *The Greek Slave* by Hiram Powers (1805-73). When exhibited at the Great Exhibition of 1851 it gave rise to controversy, not because it was nude but because the woman was chained. This made it an object of male fantasy, since it was held to depict her as a captive and therefore available female. The statue was, in fact, a beautiful one and the controversy may well have added to the popularity of the work, of which a great many white Parian china reproductions were manufactured. One of these, 14 inches high, is just the right size to stand on a Victorian mantelpiece, perhaps in the same room as a piano with skirted legs.

In painting, Ingres (1780-1867) learned to depict what popular taste in the nineteenth century would admire. A brilliant draughtsman who became a fashionable artist, he was in great demand as a portrait painter. He also delighted in painting female nudes and produced a steady succession of them for half a century. The precision of his correctly drawn outlines, his strong colours and his obvious interest in the subject have made many of these justifiably famous. *Odalisque*, which he painted at the age of 62, is typical both of his highly developed skill at producing a beautiful female shape and also of his preoccupation, at that time, with the captive women in Near Eastern harems.

Odalisque was greeted with approbation when it was first shown, but *Le Déjeuner sur l'Herbe* by Edouard Manet (1823-83), now much better known and acclaimed as a masterpiece, gave immediate offence when it was exhibited in the Paris Salon in 1863. Manet, who had taken his theme from Giorgione's accepted masterpiece *Concert Champêtre* (Plate 45) and had carefully depicted his nude girl in a pose copied from a picture by Raphael, knew quite well that by removing it from the classical world and placing it in contemporary France he would tear aside the artificial veil of prevailing prudery. He certainly

111 Gustave Courbet: *The Origin of the World*, 1866. Present whereabouts unknown

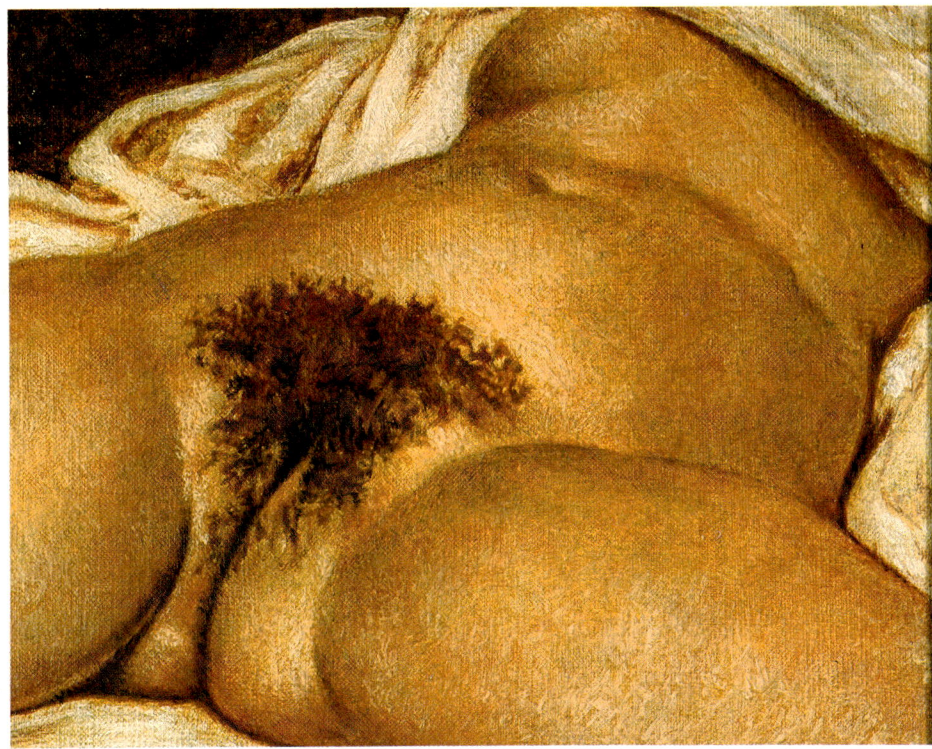

112 Edouard Manet: *Le Déjeuner sur l'Herbe*, 1863. 208×264.5cm. Louvre (Jeu de Paume), Paris

succeeded, and the public were shocked to see a naked girl sitting on the grass with two clothed men. The girl concerned was Victorine Meurend, Manet's favourite model. She is shown sitting beside his brother, and his future brother-in-law is lying opposite them. While the outcry may be surprising to us, it has to be accepted that the subject is an extraordinary one. Even today people would be surprised to come upon such a group on a walk in the country. The reaction did demonstrate, however, how sensitive was public opinion when nudity was denied the protection of Giorgione's Arcadian world.

Honoré Daumier (1808-79) was a humorous artist who kept Paris entertained from 1830 onwards with more than four thousand lithographic caricatures in *La Caricature* and *Charivari*, popular newspapers of the day. His work excelled with subjects involving political and social satire. He is not known to have produced much erotic work, but in April 1863 he made a quick pen and wash picture (Plate 2), which he signed and dedicated to 'my good friend Louise'. It was painted at a time when he was in financial difficulties, with his

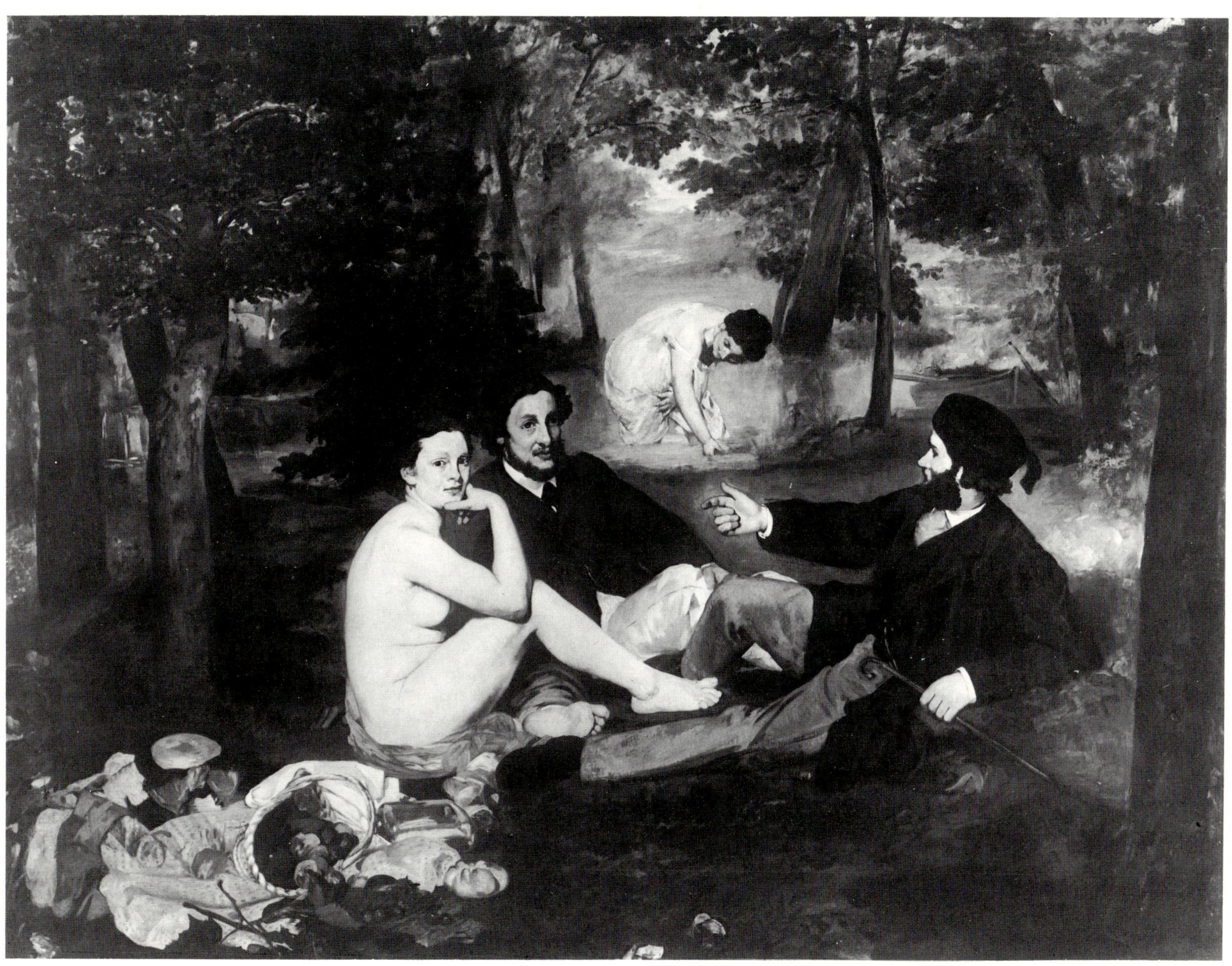

regular employment with *Charivari* temporarily interrupted, and he and his wife were constantly moving their lodgings. Nothing is known about the reason for the picture or the nature of the friendship between Louise and the artist.

Gustave Courbet (1819-77) earned the reputation of being an erotic artist because he insisted on painting the truth. He was one of a

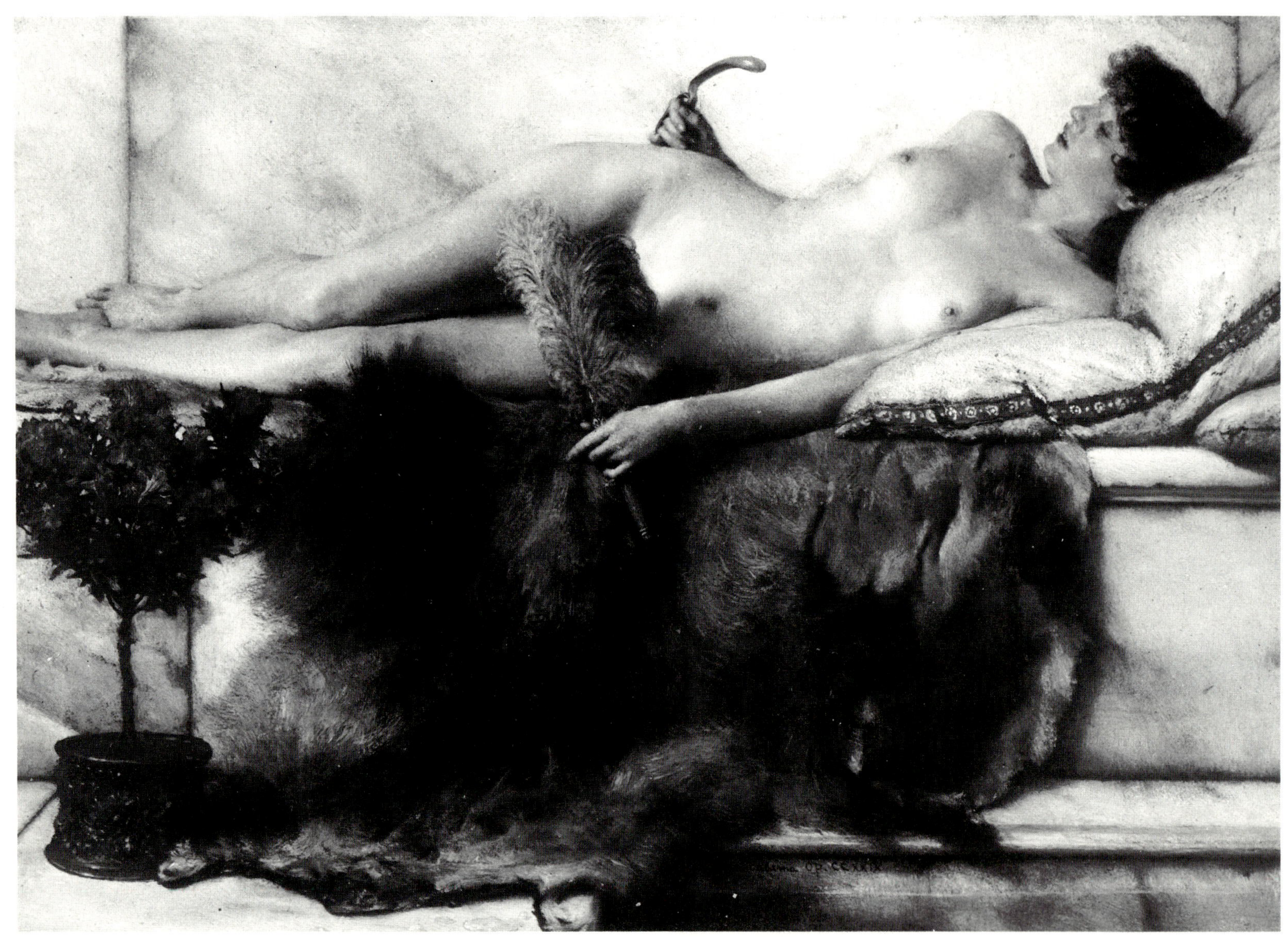

group of French artists and authors who thought they should, above all things, express the world 'as it is'. He believed, he wrote in 1861: 'Painting . . . can only consist in the representation of real and existing things.' While he painted many *genre* subjects he undoubtedly enjoyed painting female nudes and, when he did so, his naturalistic style almost always caused an outcry. He was like Rembrandt in refusing to produce beauty by artistic licence; his natural nudes were inclined to be ungainly or even ugly and were

113 Lawrence Alma-Tadema: *In the Tepidarium*, 1881. 24×33cm. Lady Lever Art Gallery, Port Sunlight

often not very erotic. He did, however, paint one most unusual picture. It was a commission from the Turkish ex-Ambassador to Russia and Courbet used his undoubted skill as a realist to paint, in the greatest detail, the sexual parts of an otherwise unidentifiable woman, *The Origin of the World* (Plate 111). The present whereabouts of the actual painting, which dates from 1866, is unknown and it has had to be reproduced from a photograph.

In mid-nineteenth-century England a small group of painters who were enthusiastic about the fresh, light colouring of the early Renaissance artists called themselves the Pre-Raphaelite Brotherhood. They were in revolt against the prevailing artistic tendency to give a brown tone to paintings in order to mimic the appearance of accepted old masters. They and their disciples painted many pictures using a meticulously detailed technique and bright, clear colours. *The Hireling Shepherd* (Plate 133) is a fine example. If William Holman Hunt (1827-1910), who painted it, had been asked he would probably have said that it showed a temporary farm-hand who, instead of diligently watching his flock, had chased and caught a death's-head moth. He is showing it, with undue familiarity, to a village maiden and causing her also to neglect her duties. In fact, of course, the artist has with great skill shown us the potential seduction of a not-too-reluctant young girl and has produced an undoubtedly erotic picture. Another example of a similarly ambiguous picture was painted by Sir Lawrence Alma-Tadema (1836-1912) and exhibited as *In the Tepidarium* in 1881. Alma-Tadema, a highly respected member of the Royal Academy, specialized in painting classical pictures. This shows a Roman patrician lady in the warm room, between the cold and hot rooms, of a Roman bath. By chance she happens to be gazing at a back-scratcher, which has a surprising resemblance to a phallus, in her right hand. The ostrich-feather in her other hand may well have given the impression, to the more libidinous gentlemen who viewed the picture, that they were looking at a fan-dancer on her day off, awaiting a visit from her lover. *The Tree of Forgiveness* (Plate 126) by Edward Burne-Jones (1833-99) is another ambiguous pre-Raphaelite picture. The subject is an obscure story from the classics. The girl in the picture is being turned into a tree because she had killed herself when she mistakenly thought that her lover, Demophoön, had deserted her. All the same her immodest behaviour in this picture, even purportedly in classical times, must have raised some strange thoughts in the minds of Victorian viewers and to many it must have been a frankly erotic picture.

In 1878 a little-known artist, Henri Gervex (1852-1929), painted a picture so striking that it has become famous. He entitled it *Rolla* (Plate 130), but the title tells us nothing and the spectator is left to make up his own mind about the drama which it depicts. What is certain is that with great technical skill he has produced a brilliant portrayal of passion on a hot afternoon.

It is, of course, impossible now to see the world from the viewpoint of those people who lived in England and America in the middle of the last century. The majority held unquestioning Protestant beliefs and were faced with the prospect of a judgement after death which might condemn them to eternal damnation and hell-fire. They were brought up in the Anglo-Saxon belief in justice and 'making the punishment fit the crime'. They were not in the least surprised if the wages of sin were in fact death or some very unpleasant retribution during their lifetime. While any form of sexual intercourse outside marriage was obviously thought sinful, many will have been less certain about the exact meaning of 'fornication'. The stronger the conscience, the stronger must have been the feelings of guilt. It was easy for the medical profession, which tended to uphold strict moral views, to teach that serious medical effects could follow from sexual practices which it felt were morally wrong. Dr William Acton publicized such views, with considerable effect. In several books, which were reprinted many times from 1843 onwards, he maintained that sexual intercourse was normal and essential within marriage but should be of limited frequency and limited duration. Outside marriage it was harmful. Why marriage should make a difference he did not seek to explain. He was particularly worried about what he considered the dangers of masturbation, which became known as 'self-abuse' and which many came to believe might cause blindness and madness. Belief in these mistaken views dwindled slowly until they were finally swept away by the Kinsey reports and the objective scientific evidence accumulated during the last thirty years.

While official Victorian opinion insisted that women should be 'pure' and chaste before marriage and 'modest' after it, it became increasingly accepted that they should have no interest in sexual

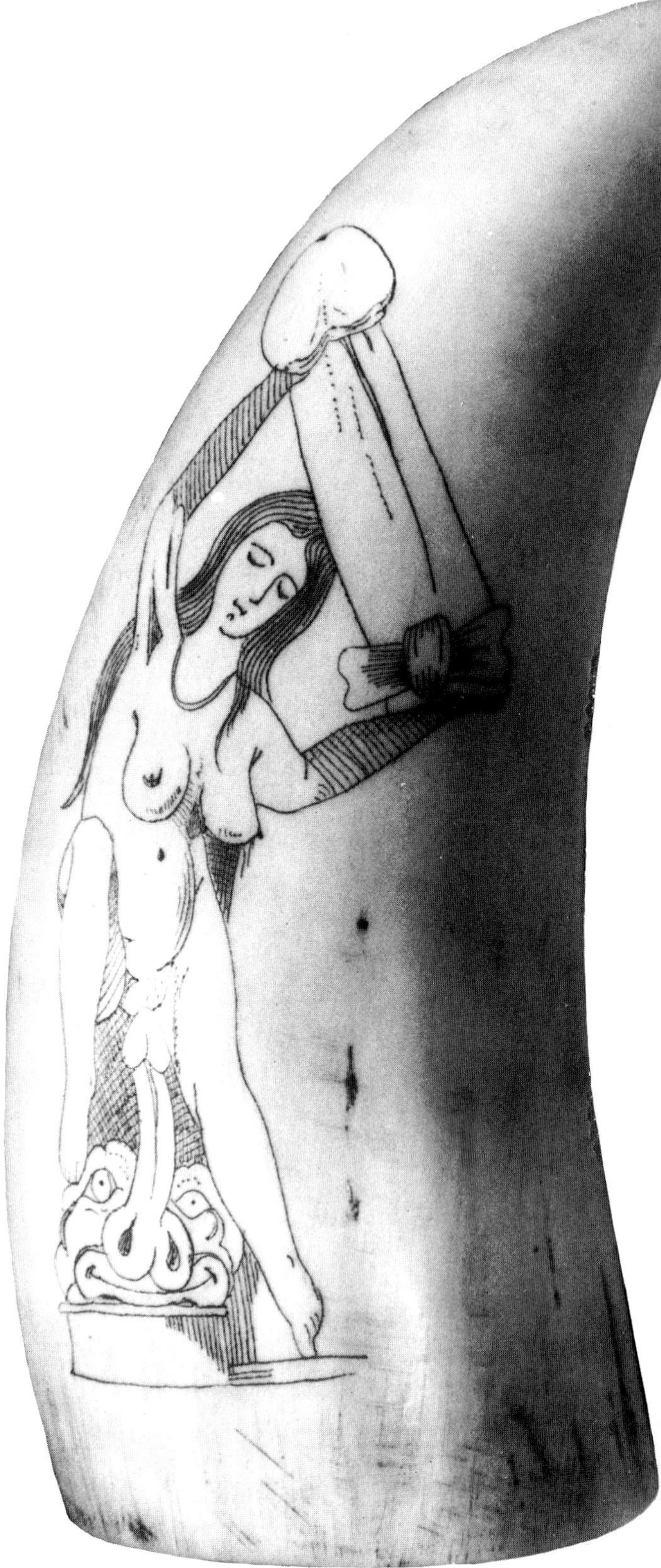

matters. Dr Acton stated unequivocally: 'The majority of women (happily for society) are not very much troubled with sexual feeling of any kind.' The Greeks and Romans, the men and women in Chaucer's *Canterbury Tales*, the ordinary men and women up and down the centuries of history would have thought he must be either joking or mad. It is still surprising that so many Victorians should have taken these opinions seriously. Partly as a result, a large number of young women were married without ever having had any instruction about intercourse or indeed, any knowledge of the male or female anatomy. Many husbands, who did not wish to force their apparently unwelcome attentions on the wives whom they admired and loved, felt it their duty to look for sexual outlets elsewhere. As usual, there were plenty of these available. A young girl in a back alley could easily earn as much in an hour as a labourer working hard for a week. Prostitution was rife and venereal diseases, for which there were then no effective treatments, were rampant. As the danger of venereal disease became common knowledge among Victorian women, a gradual change in their thinking occurred. Increasingly they sought the means and the knowledge to become the sexual partners that their husbands wanted, in order to keep them at home and away from the perils waiting for them outside.

At a time when perversions of all kinds flourished in the furtive, guilt-ridden atmosphere of the sexual underworld there was a flood of clandestine literature. This was usually poorly printed, badly written, pornographic hack-work but there was a smaller amount of clandestine erotic books of higher quality. Plate 134 was an illustration in an anonymous book, *The Exhibition of Female Flagellants*, and Plate 115 is an illustration of a work purported to be a biography of the Earl of Rochester. Both were published in London in 1860 and are typical of many. There were also many editions of John Cleland's *Fanny Hill* (Plates 128 and 129). An unusual erotic artefact of a similar date is the scrimshaw piece, a picture cut into a walrus tooth by a sailor, to while away the time on board ship. It would doubtless have found a ready market in London.

One artist who lived through the latter half of the nineteenth century and who has become well known as a fine erotic artist seems to have been quite exceptional in that he remained almost untouched by the prevailing guilty feelings about sex. Mihály Zichy (1827-1906)

114 Scrimshaw, walrus tooth decorated with erotic carving, 19th century. 10cm long

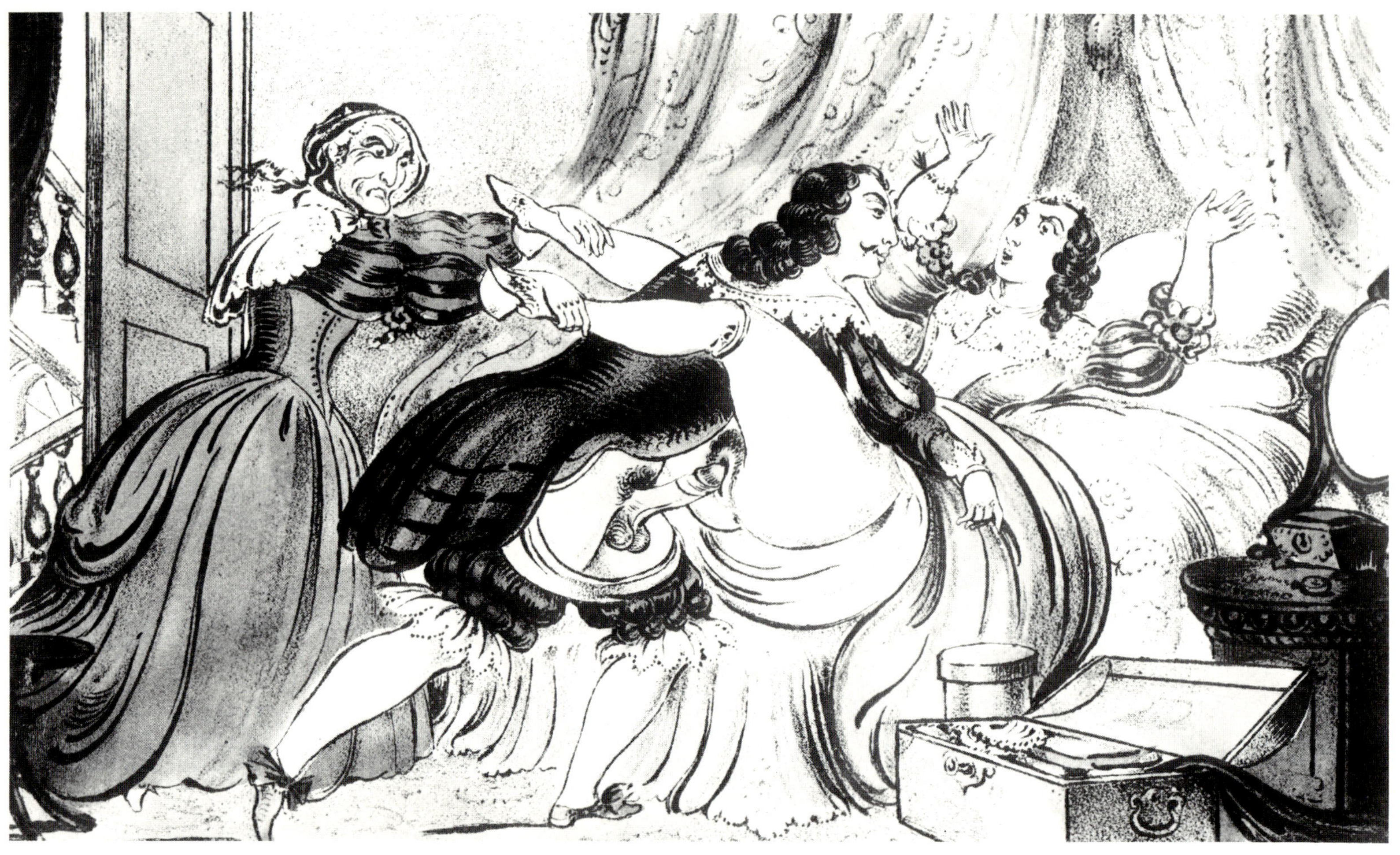

115 Anon: Plate from *The Singular Life*, a biography of John Wilmot, Earl of Rochester, c.1860. British Library

was born in Hungary, trained in the Vienna Academy of Arts and by the age of 20 had become drawing-master to a Grand Duchess in St Petersburg. In 1856, at the age of 29, he became court painter to Czar Alexander II and spent most of his life painting scenes and portraits for the Russian court and aristocracy. In 1874, however, he travelled to Paris and worked there for eight years, also visiting England and Hungary. It was probably during this period that he began to produce the 40 etchings for his book *Love*. He is said to have prepared these with the greatest care from numerous sketches. The subjects commence with a woman and her child, and show a wide variety of sexual practices, in childhood, between young people and between adults. The viewer becomes an onlooker in a quiet, relaxed, domestic scene. Plates 116 and 117 are typical of the series. *Hands* is probably one of the finest sets of drawings of the male organ ever made. All the drawings have a tenderness which points to the title 'Love' as being intended to describe the sex displayed as well as the feelings of the artist towards the participants. In 1882 he returned to Russia, was reinstated in his former appointment at the court and remained there until his death at the age of 79.

The last quarter of the nineteenth century and the beginning of the

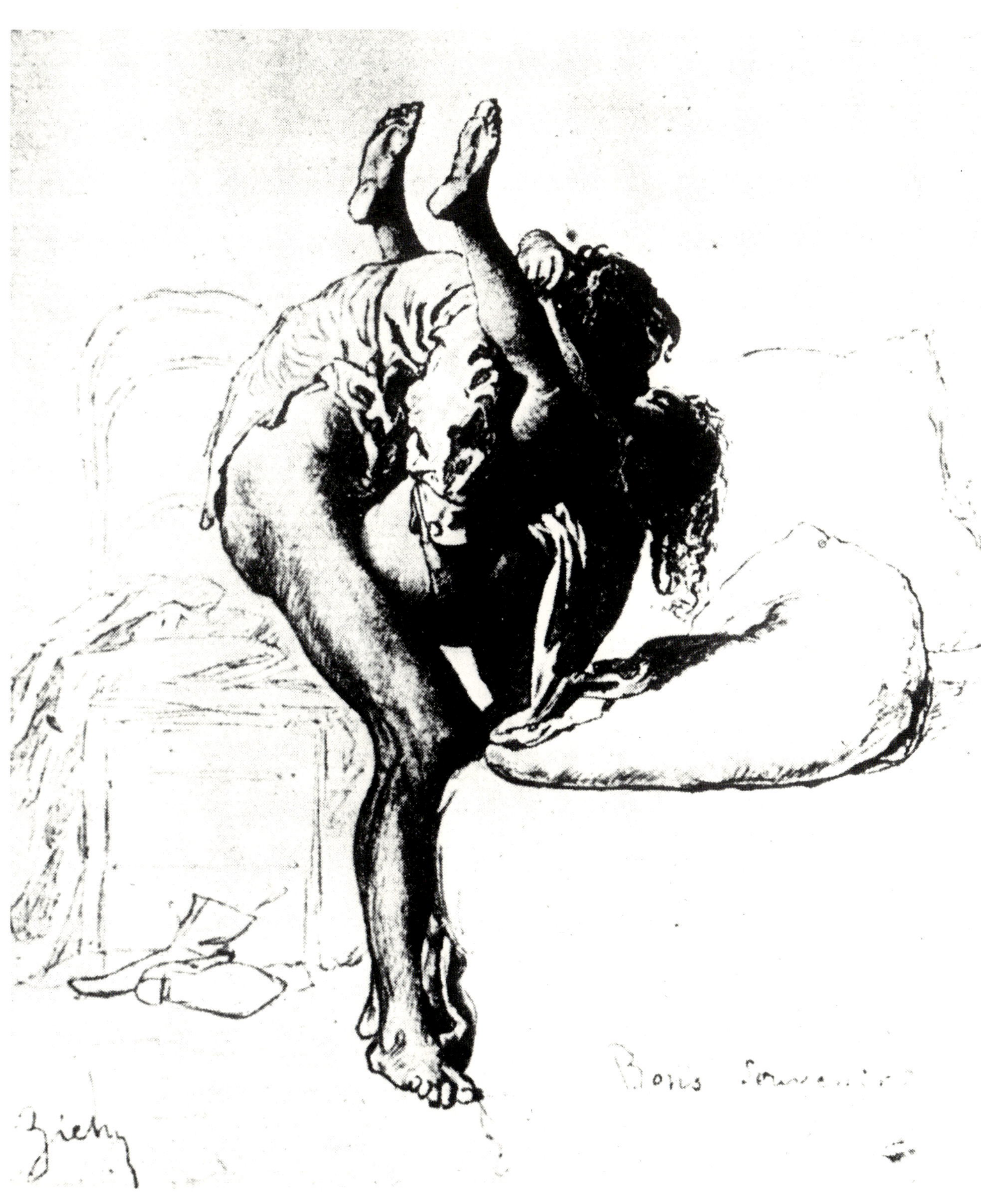

116 Zichy: *Bons souvenirs*, etching for *Love*, c. 1874-82

117 Zichy: untitled etching for *Love*, c.1874-82

twentieth were the years when perversion flourished. Men who had been taught at their mother's knee that babies were brought by storks, found under gooseberry bushes or brought in doctor's bags, and had been brought up to believe in the essential sinfulness of sex, grew up to find themselves affected by their natural sexual urges. The absolute segregation of the sexes and the complete covering of every part of the female form except the hands and face produced an obsessive fascination, for the male, for the sight of even an ankle, that it is hard to visualize today. Middle-aged gentlemen would quiver on seeing an actress in a corset; others became obsessed not only by parts of the naked female form but by all sorts of fetishes. Drinking the lady's toast in champagne from one of her shoes was one of the more innocent of fashionable gestures.

118 Zichy: *Hands*, pencil drawing. Coll. Lawrence E. Gichner, Washington DC

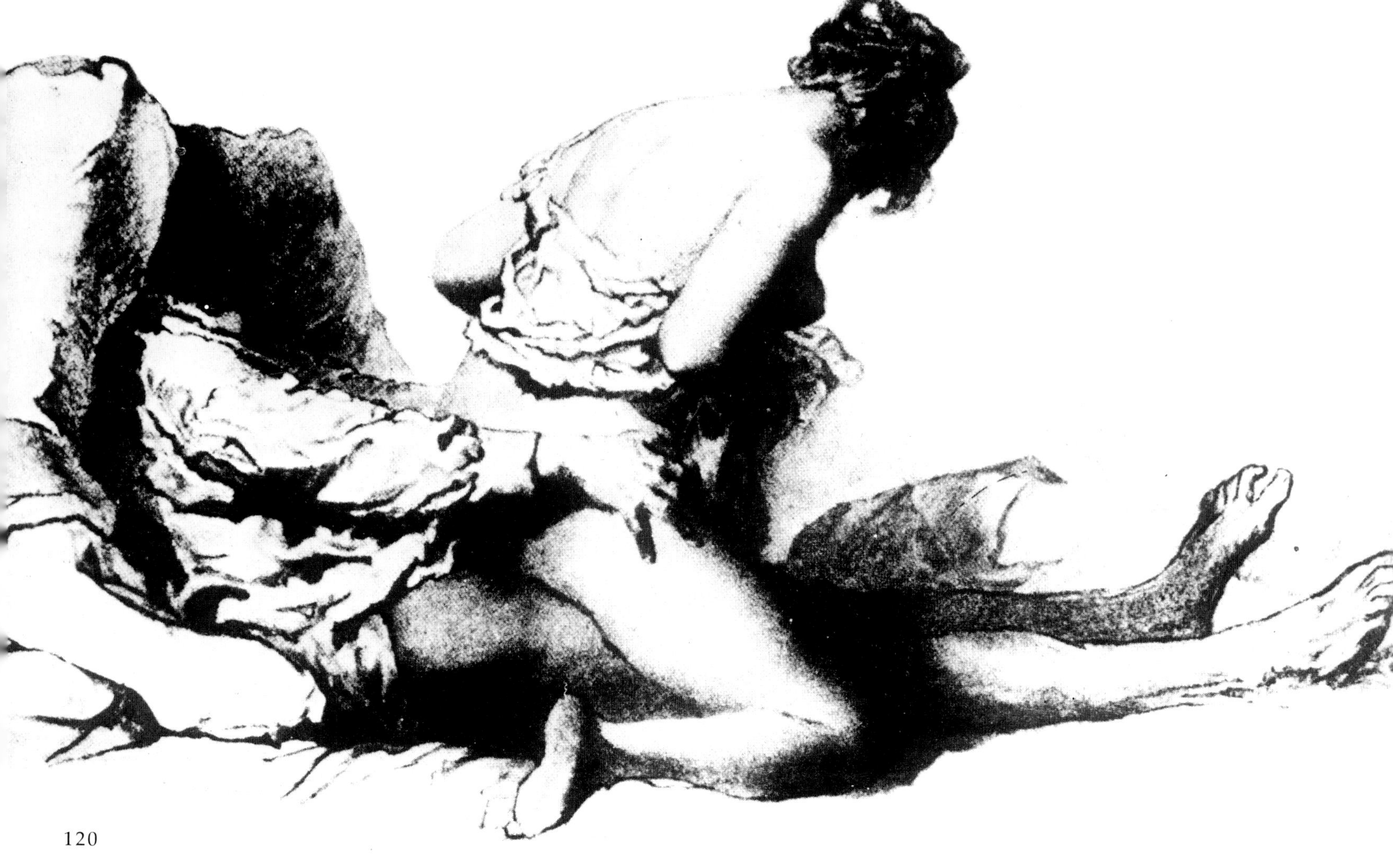

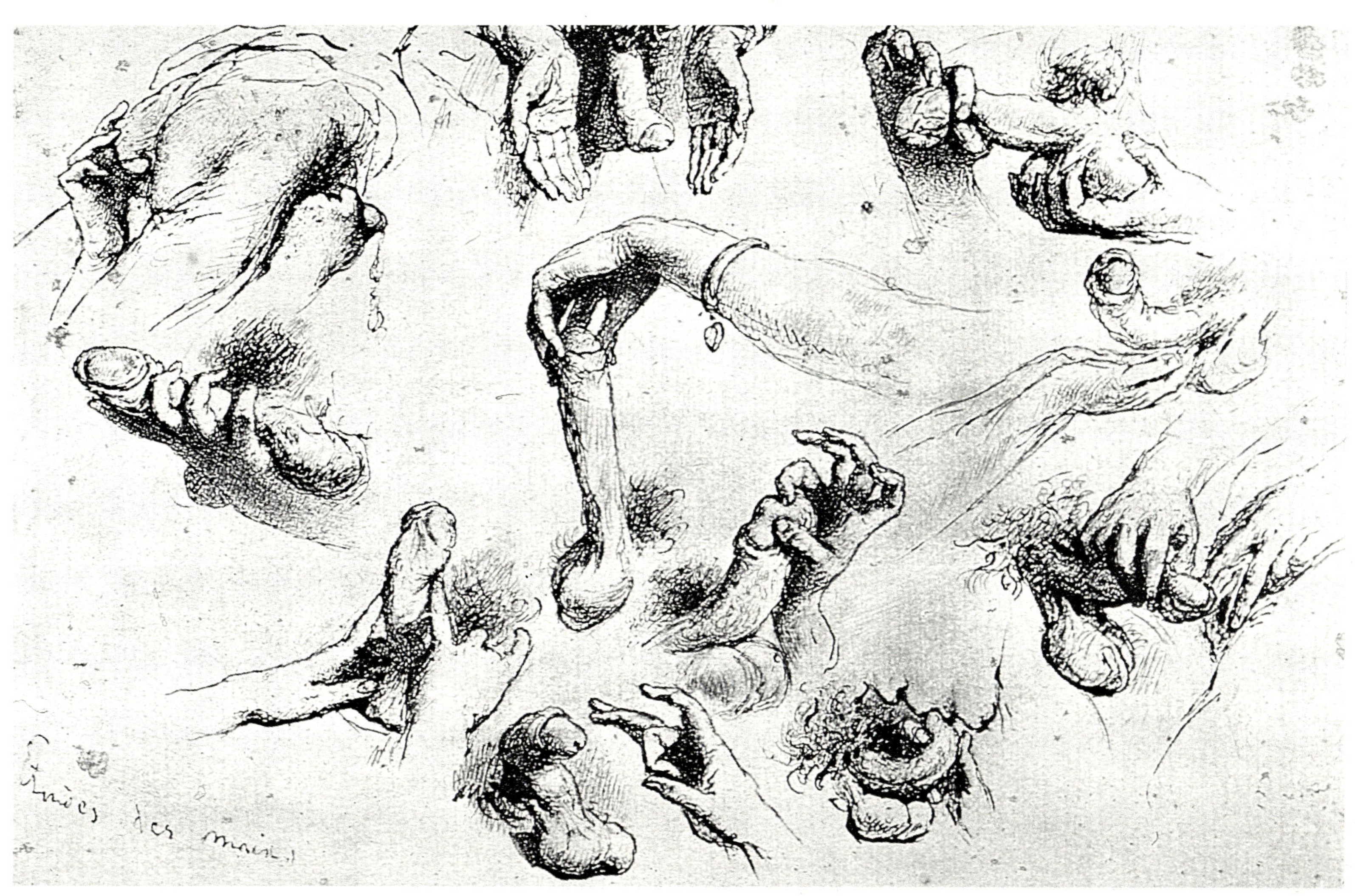

An artist who documented the attitudes of this era was the Belgian Félicien Rops (1833-98). After studying lithography he went to Paris in 1862 and became an etcher, with a talent for erotic illustration. He was fascinated by different aspects of sex and was equally attracted by the curvaceous Flemish girls of his homeland and the slim, chic, Parisian girls who formed a contrast. He became a member of the so-called 'Decadence', which included Baudelaire and the Goncourts. This group of artists and writers searched for freedom by denying religion and, realizing the power and attraction that women had over them, denounced the sex as devilish. Fascinated by these sexual attitudes, Rops adopted the role of an observer. Victor Arwas quotes Rops as

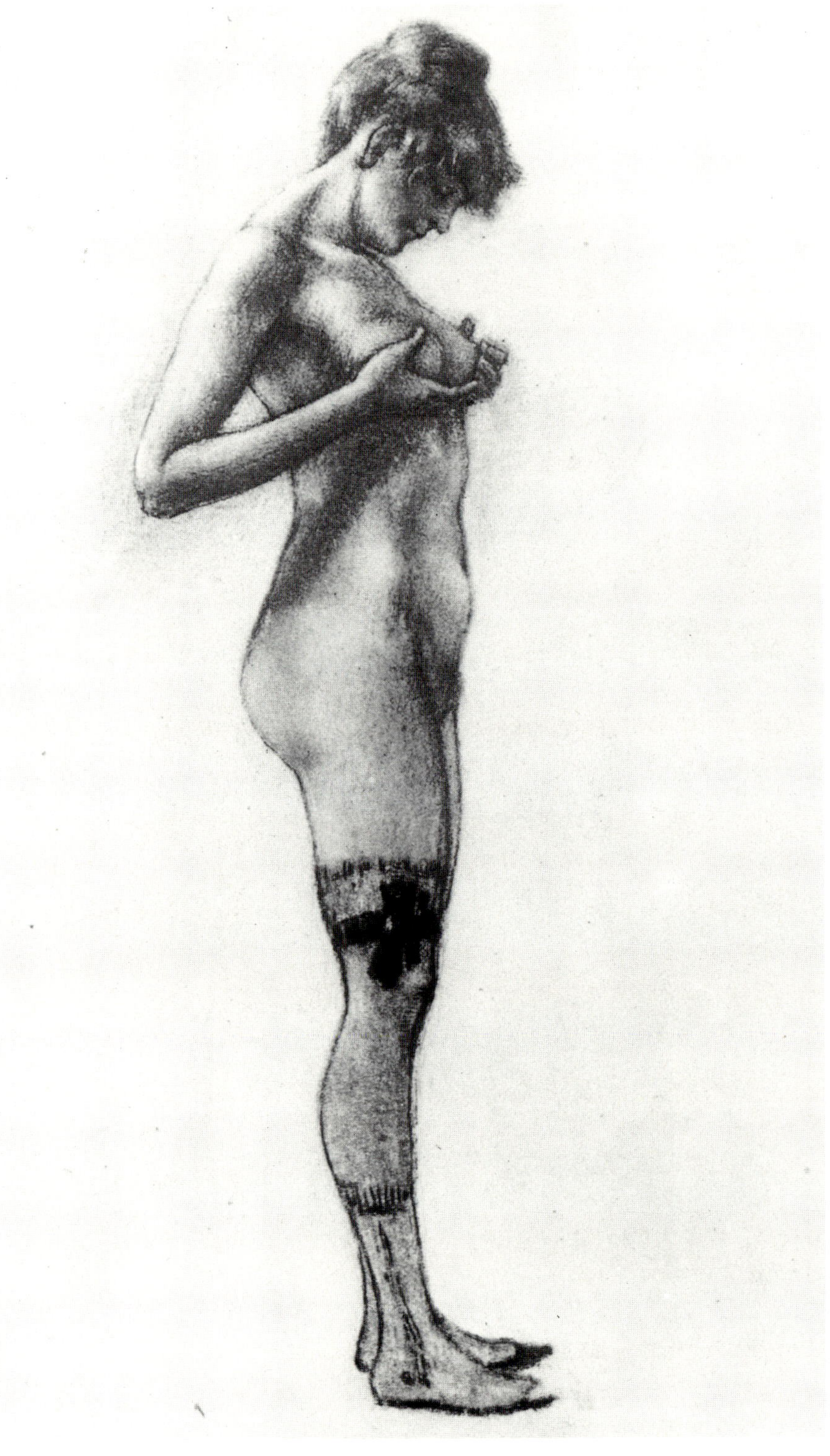

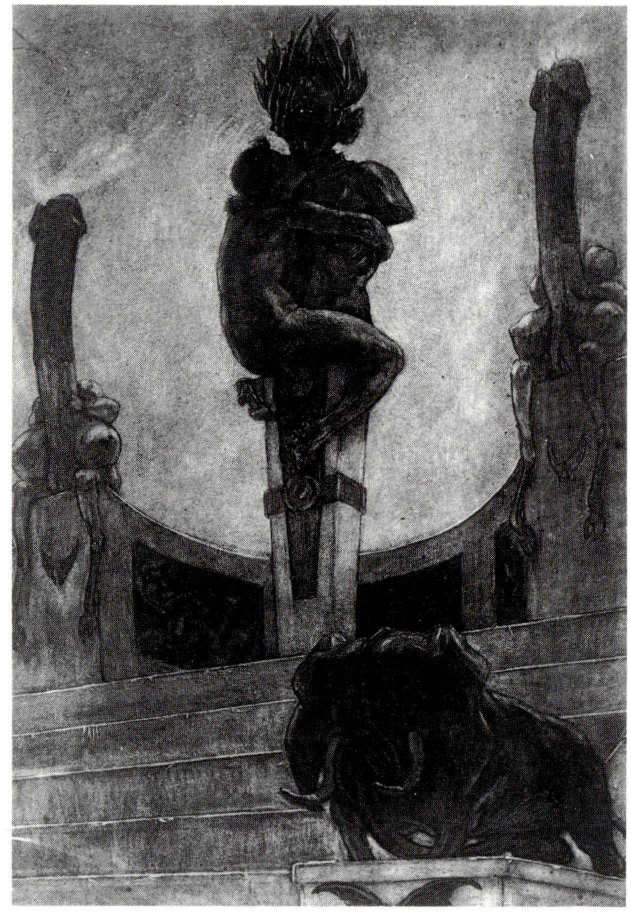

119 *(Left)* Félicien Rops: *Nubility,* softground etching. Editions Graphiques, London

120 *(Above)* Félicien Rops: *The Idol,* etching. Editions Graphiques, London

writing that his contemporaries had 'a sinister mask in which the perverse instinct mentioned by Edgar Allan Poe can be read in capital letters: all this seems to me sufficiently amusing and characteristic that well-meaning artists should attempt to render the look of their time.' Illustrated are some typical etchings of the kind which Rops knew would arouse his contemporaries. *The Idol* is an etching from the blasphemous series *Les Sataniques*, which shows a woman who

121 Félicien Rops: *The Little Cousin*, etching. Editions Graphiques, London

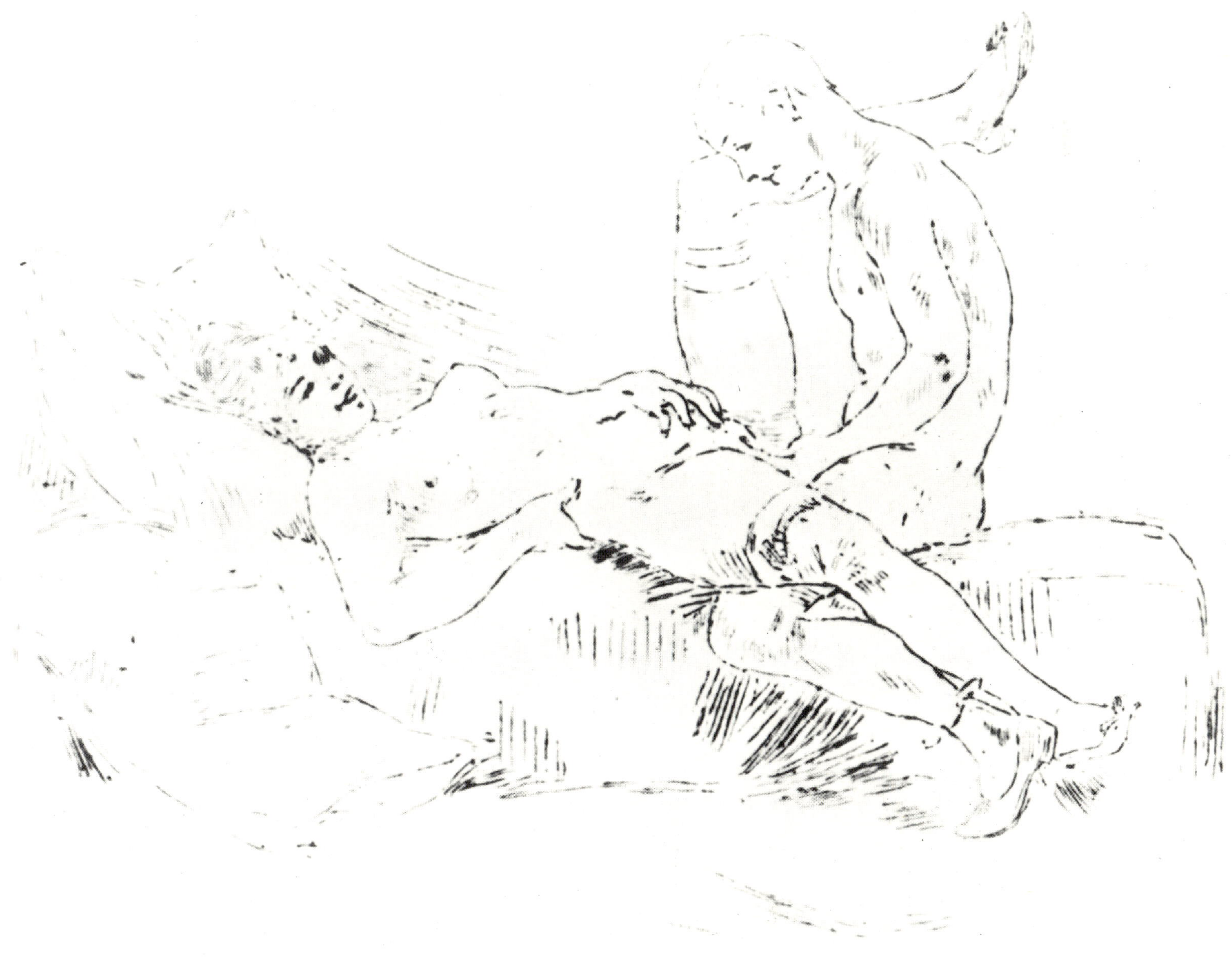

122 Beardsley: *Cinesias entreating Myrrhina to coition*. Plate from Aristophanes' *Lysistrata*, 1896. British Library

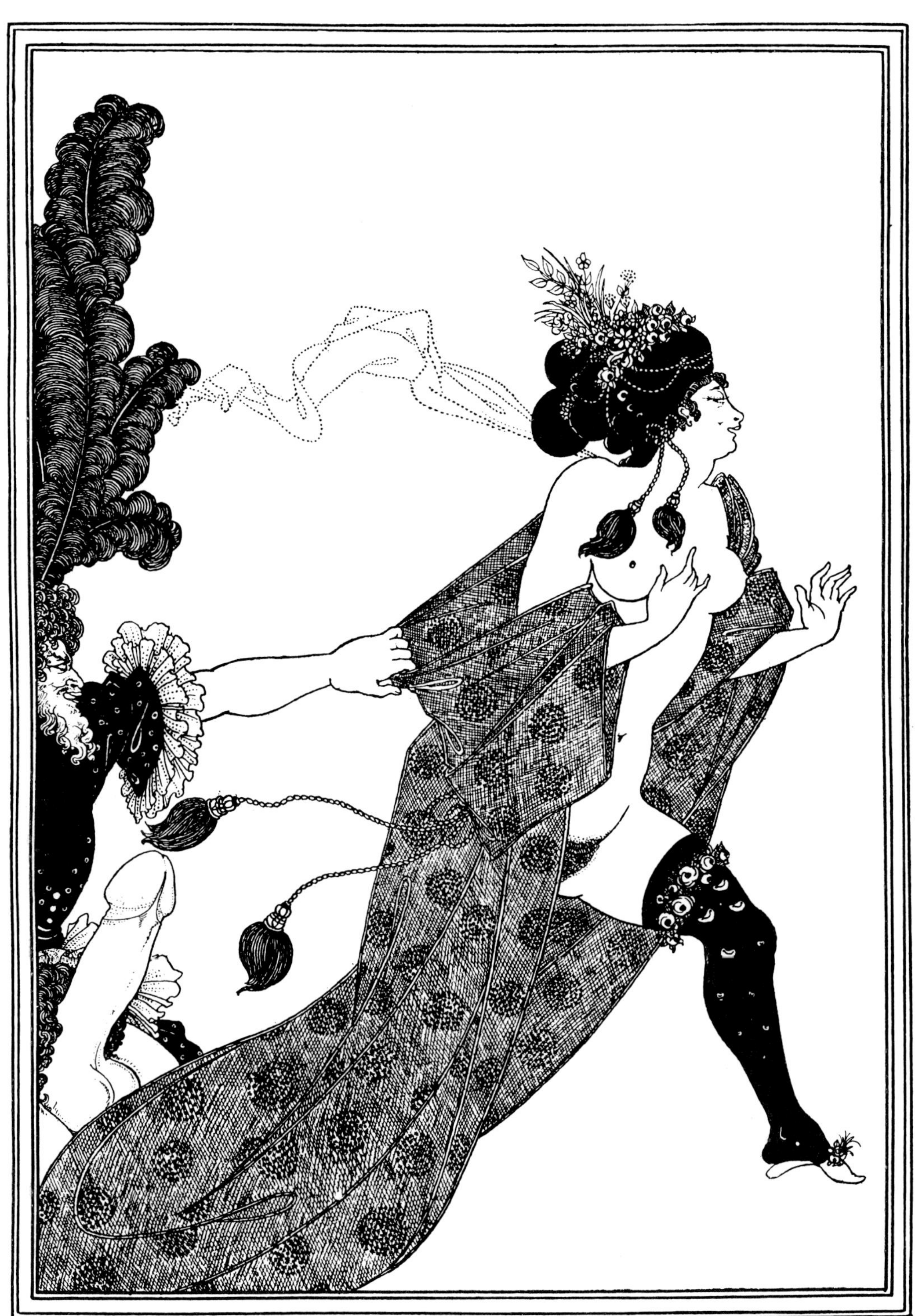

has sold her soul to the Devil. Rops himself seems to have been a genial man with a considerable sense of humour and a flair for producing ingenious sexual fantasies which pleased his generation.

The mother and sisters of the Norwegian artist Edvard Munch (1863-1944) died of tuberculosis when he was very young. Brought up by a strictly Protestant father, he seems to have lived all his life with a morbid fear of dying. He developed his own style of Expressionism, using exaggeration of outline and colour to produce striking effects. He was strongly attracted by women but always afraid of them, and he never married. He once fell in love with his best friend's wife and it was about this time, in 1895, that he made his drypoint and aquatint picture *The Kiss* (Plate 105), which was one of his very few erotic pictures. He was a neurotic man; he had painted his famous picture of *The Scream* two years earlier and he was probably in a state of intense jealousy when he made the picture. Having lived his life in fear of death he died at the age of over eighty, recognized as one of Norway's finest artists.

During the last ten years of the nineteenth century Aubrey Beardsley (1872-98) produced the drawings which were to bring him future renown, and which influenced many other artists. Tuberculous by the age of seven, a weakly child with a precocious talent for drawing, and mainly self-taught, at the age of twenty he took the art world by storm with his book illustrations. He was a member of a smart artistic set in London, a number of whom were homosexual, including Oscar Wilde. By producing frankly erotic drawings with an intent to shock, Beardsley became labelled 'decadent'. Some of his illustrations showed undoubted nuances of homosexual art, but heterosexual themes predominated and there is nothing in his history to give credence to public suspicions that he was himself a homosexual. Nevertheless his publishers, under pressure after Oscar Wilde's trial in 1895, terminated Beardsley's position as editor of the *Yellow Book*, an avant-garde journal. Alarmed at their imputations and the effect on his reputation, he ostentatiously went about in the company of women during the months that followed. His illness was advancing, but he continued to work intensively and his drawings for *The Lysistrata of Aristophanes* were published in 1896.

Lysistrata was a comedy in which the women of the warring states of Athens and Sparta persuaded their husbands to make peace by

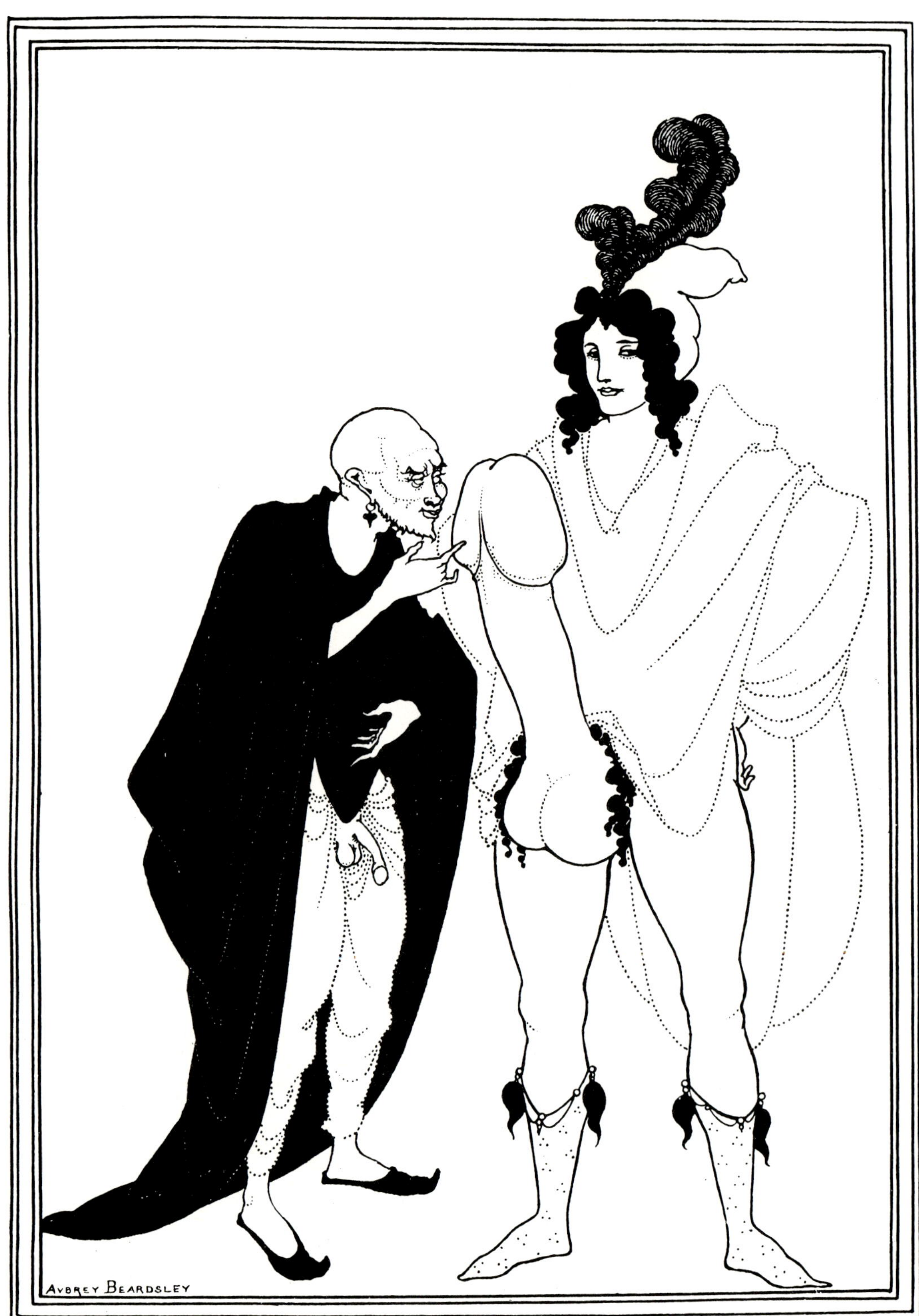

123 Beardsley: *The examination of the herald*. Plate from *Lysistrata*, 1896. British Library

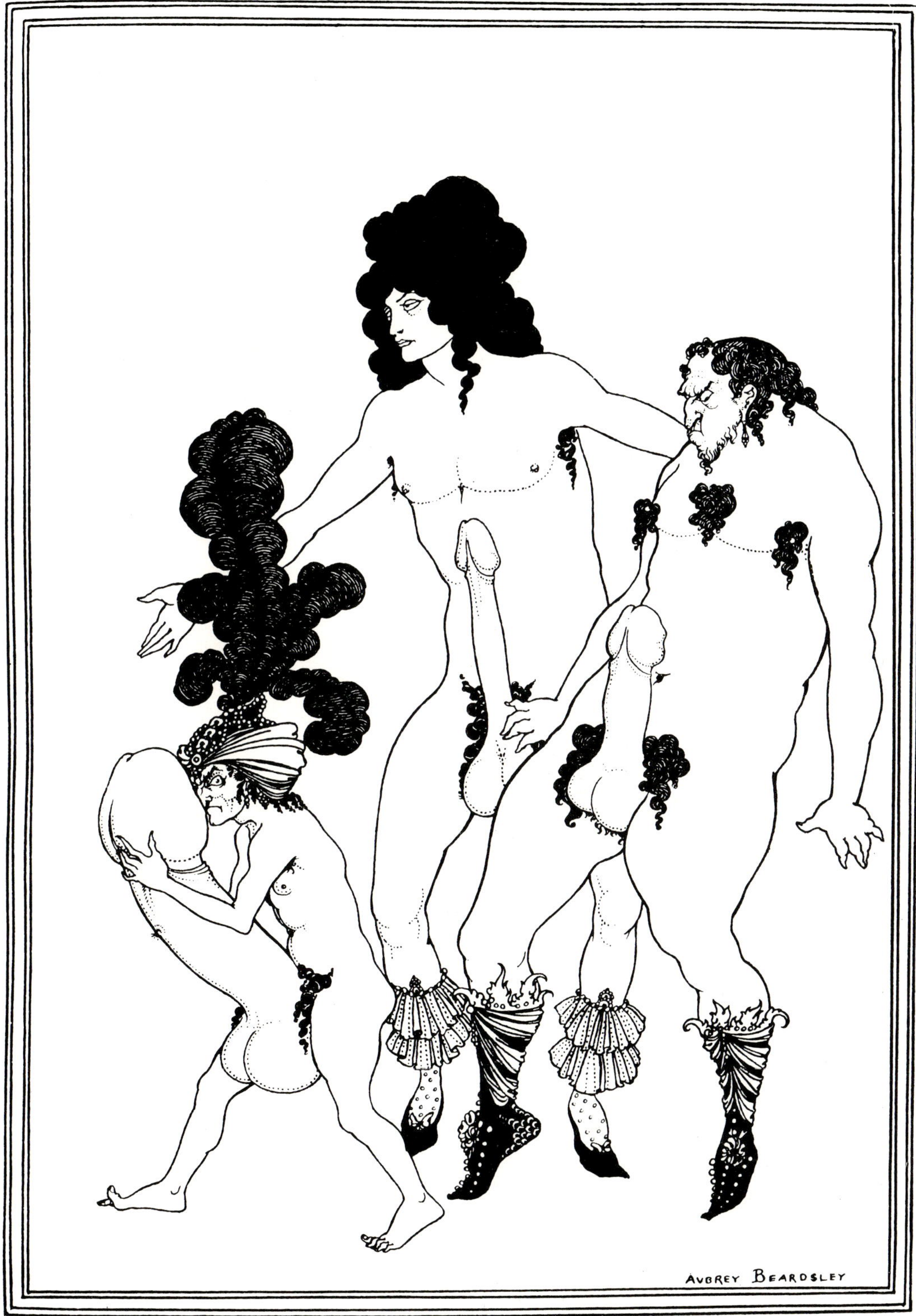

124 Beardsley: *The Lacedaemonian ambassadors*. Plate from *Lysistrata*, 1896. British Library

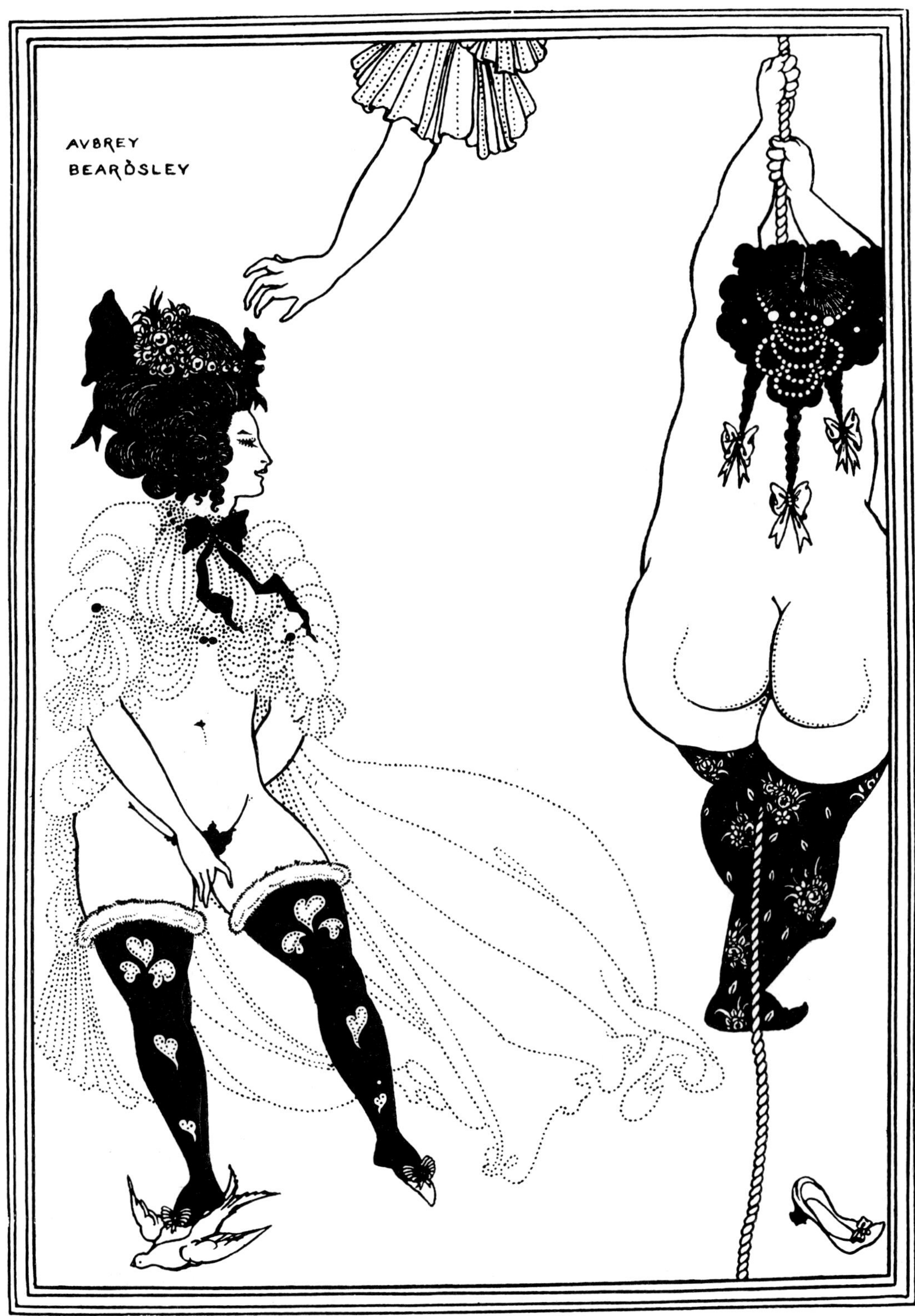

125 Beardsley: *Two Athenian women in distress*. Plate from *Lysistrata*, 1896. British Library

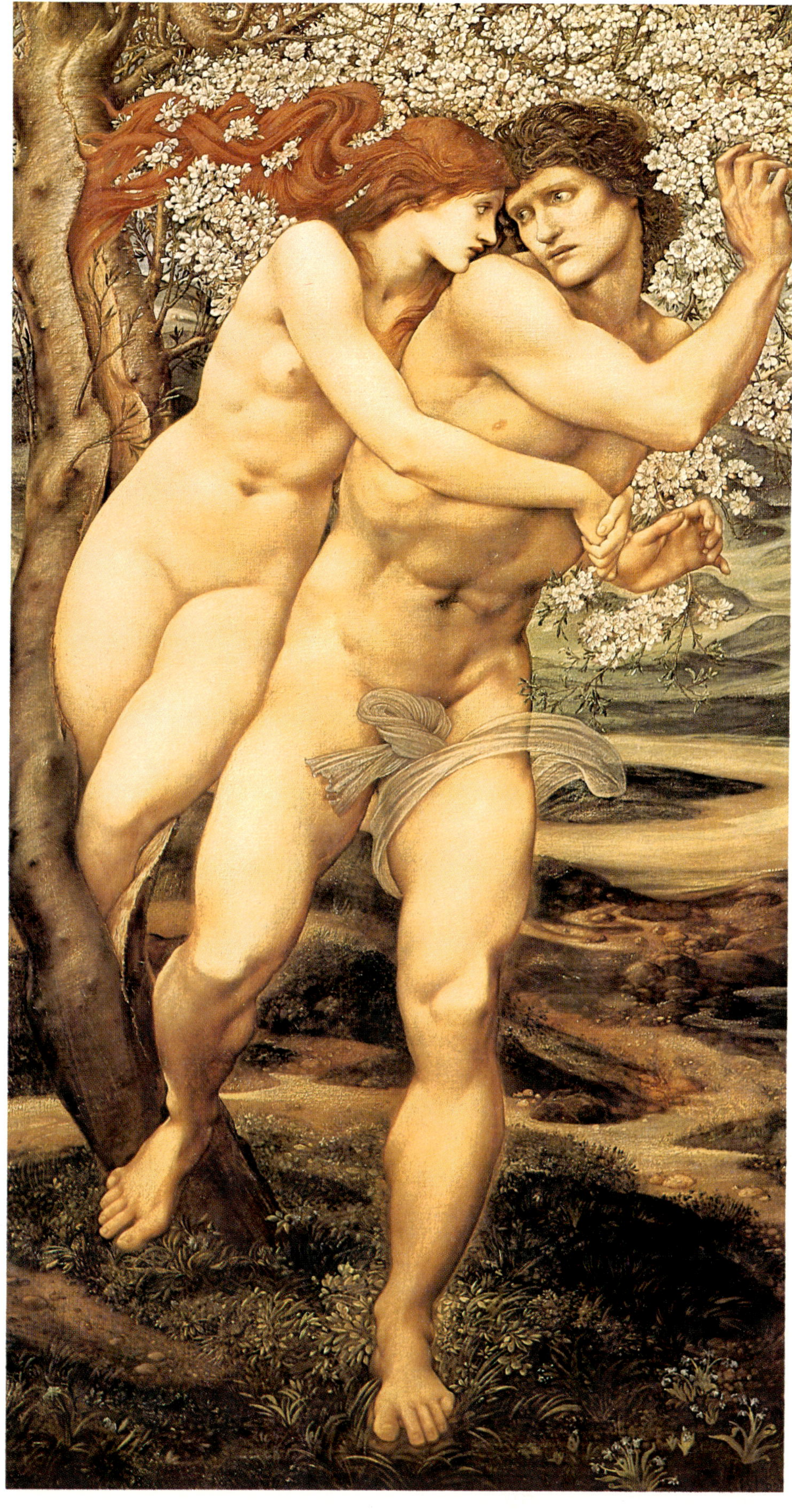

126 Edward Burne-Jones: *The Tree of Forgiveness*, 1882. 190.5×61cm. Lady Lever Art Gallery, Port Sunlight

127 Beardsley (attr.): unpublished drawing for Aristophanes' *Lysistrata*, c. 1896

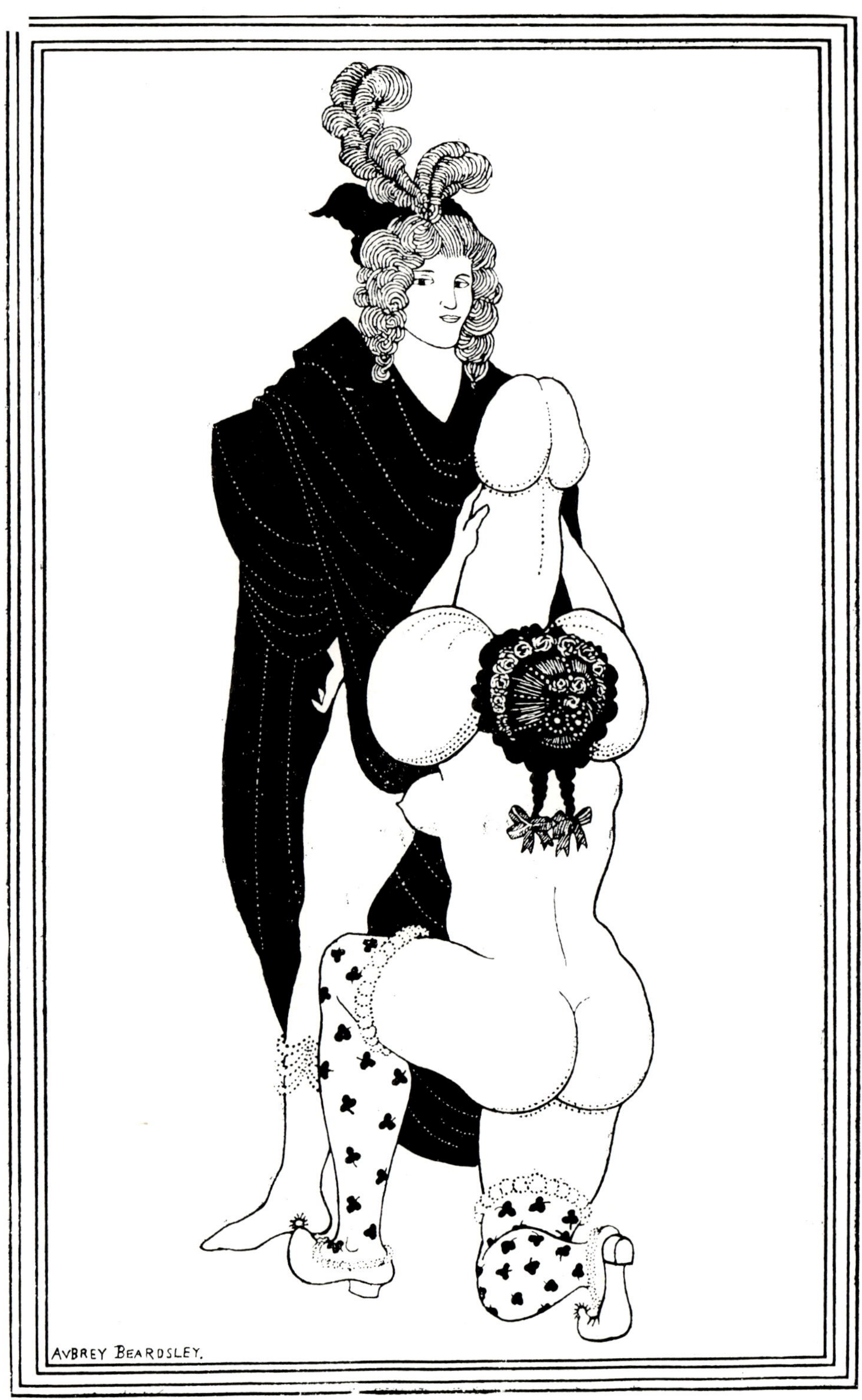

refusing them intercourse. In classical times it was played by actors with Rabelaisian gusto (see Chapter One). Beardsley, who had studied the art and the life of classical Greece, made his drawings a burlesque satire of the play's ancient humour. He would also have been aware of the ingenuity with which the playwright had prevented either sex from scoring too heavily over the other. Plate 127 was not among the eight drawings which were published in his book and he may have held it back to prevent it destroying the balance by suggesting a male victory. Shortly before his death, at the age of only 25, Beardsley was converted to Roman Catholicism and unavailingly pleaded with his agent to 'destroy all copies of *Lysistrata* and bad drawings'.

An erotic artist who was deeply influenced by nineteenth-century attitudes to sex was the Marquis Franz von Bayros (1866-1924). An Austrian who was trained at the Academy in Vienna, he married one of the daughters of the 'Waltz King', Johann Strauss, in 1896. The marriage was annulled one year later and he did not marry again until 1913. He became a successful book illustrator, with a style influenced by Beardsley but modified by a four-year study of the age of Louis XV which enabled him to make brilliant drawings of the elegant, cultured girls on which his mind seems to have dwelt. He began to produce erotic art in 1911 and had to leave Munich to escape prosecution. Back in Vienna, during the next few years he produced a number of portfolios of erotic drawings. It is notable that men seldom appear in these except as onlookers or as tormented victims of dominating women. *The Fetishist* from *Tales of the Dressing-Table* shows a pathetically subservient man in fancy dress. Most pictures show women who masturbate, use dildos, or are stimulated by a variety of animals or by each other. Frequently they whip one another and sometimes the victim is tied up. In some extraordinary pictures they play with the decapitated heads of men! The whole constitutes an exercise in superb draughtsmanship and elegant perversion.

Auguste Rodin (1840-1917) was one of the world's greatest sculptors and, at the same time, one of the most controversial. Largely self-taught, he was 37 before the Paris salon, rather doubtfully, accepted his famous statue *The Age of Bronze*, which is now represented by more than 150 replicas in museums and galleries all over the world. He had always been attracted by pretty women

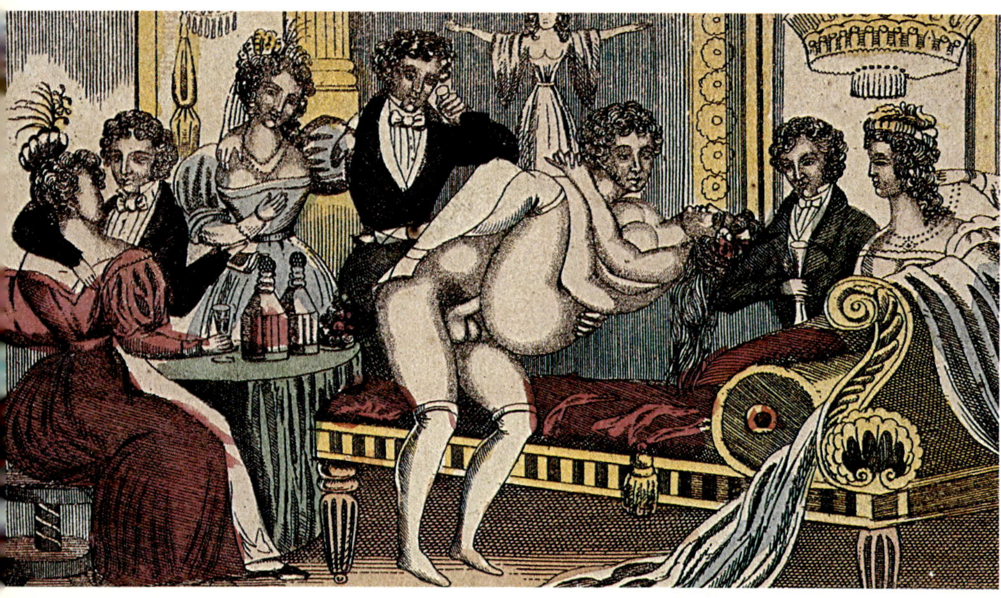

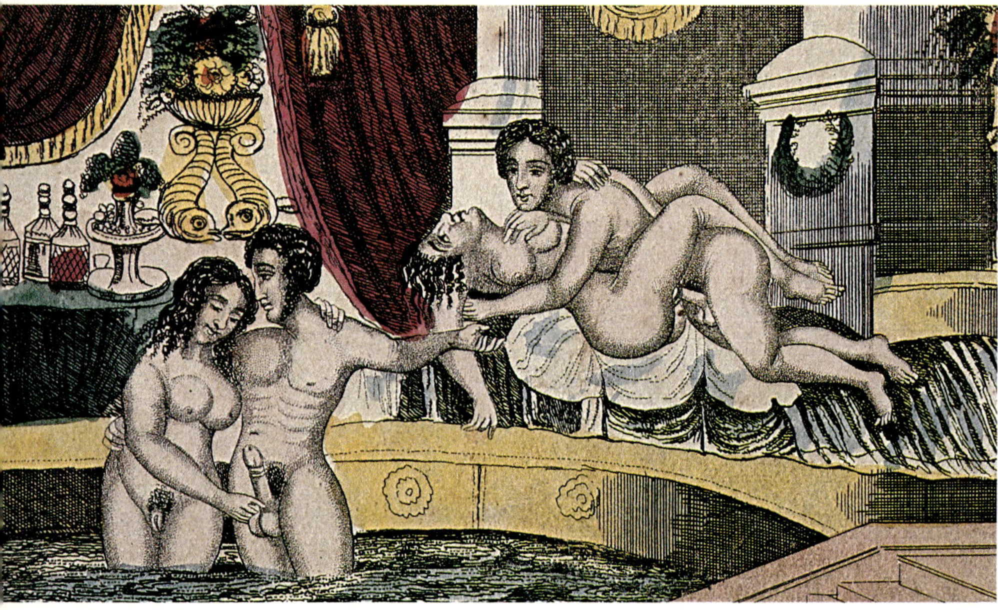

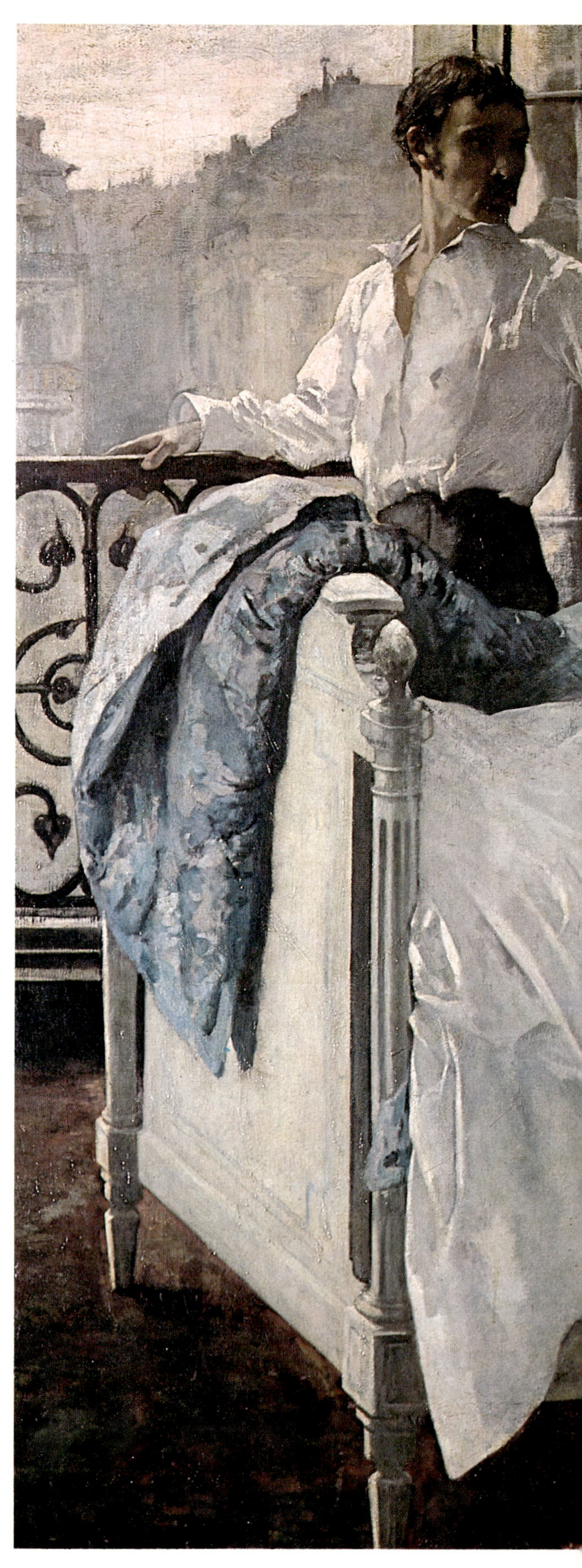

128 *(Top)* Anon: *Private sex exhibition*, illustration to *Fanny Hill*. Coloured engraving. Lawrence E. Gichner, Washington DC

129 *(Above)* Anon: *Sex and the swimming-bath*, illustration to *Fanny Hill*. Coloured engraving. Lawrence E. Gichner, Washington DC

130 *(Right)* Henri Gervex: *Rolla*, 1878. 175×220cm. Musée et Galerie des Beaux-Arts, Bordeaux

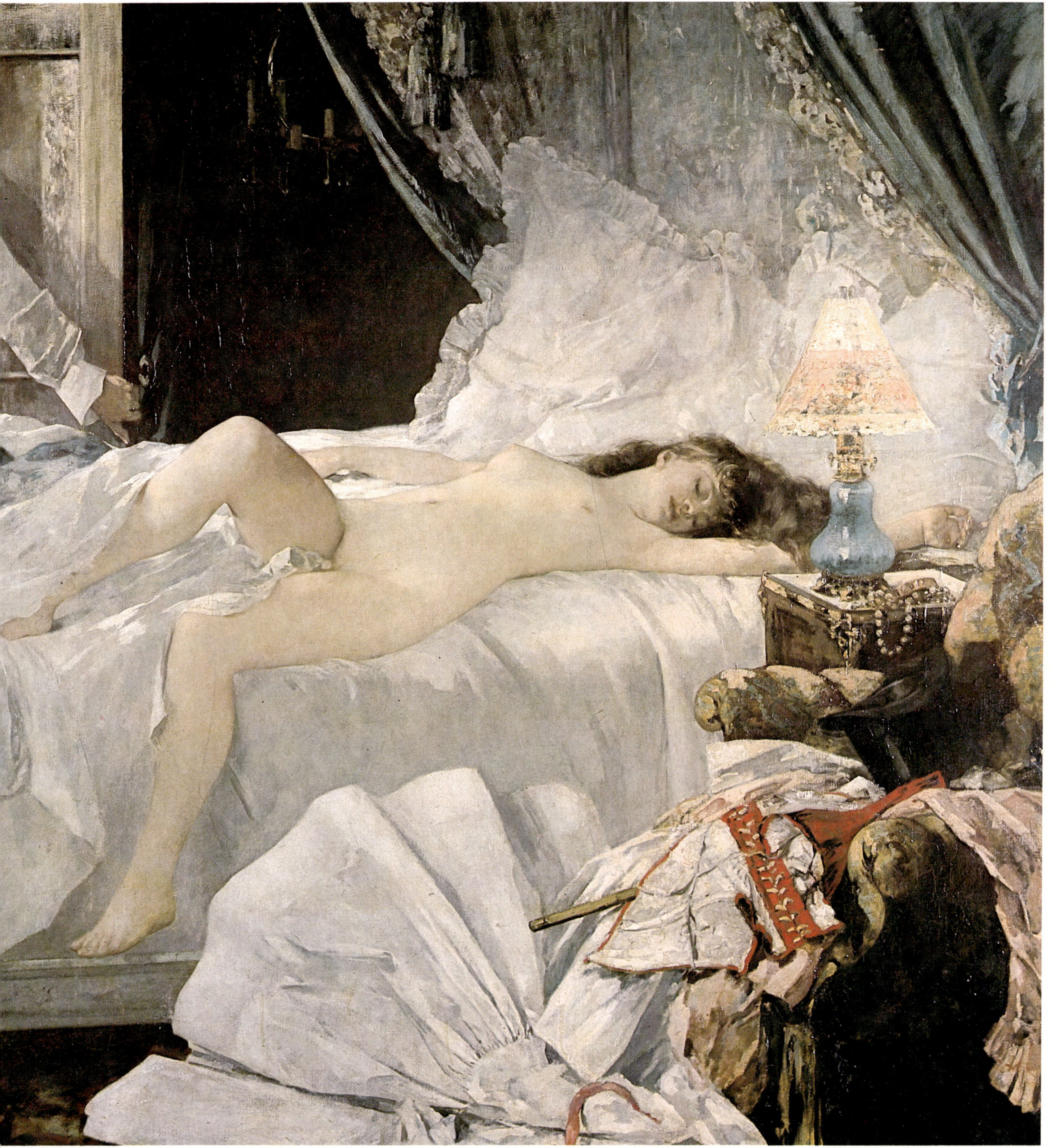

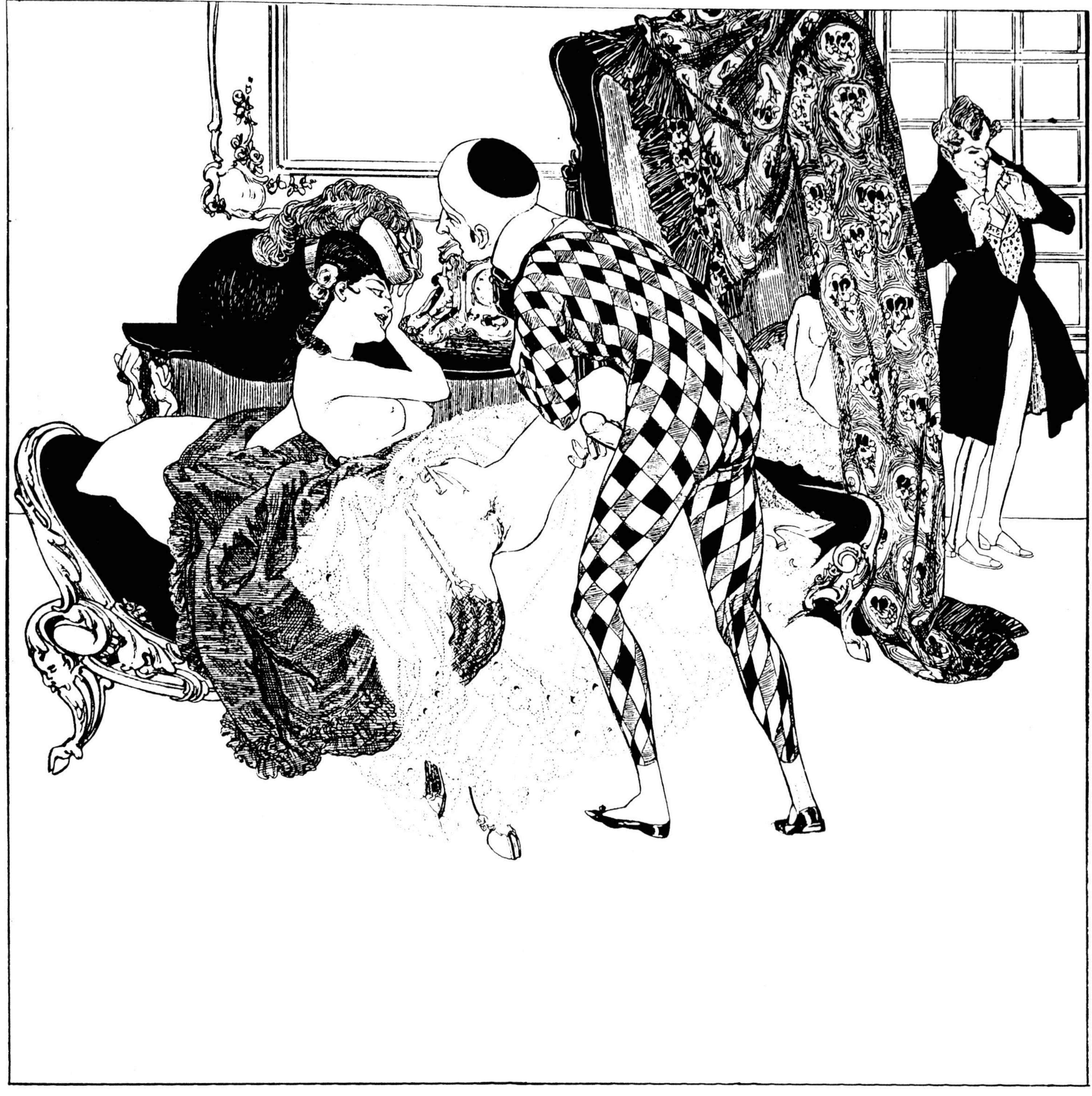

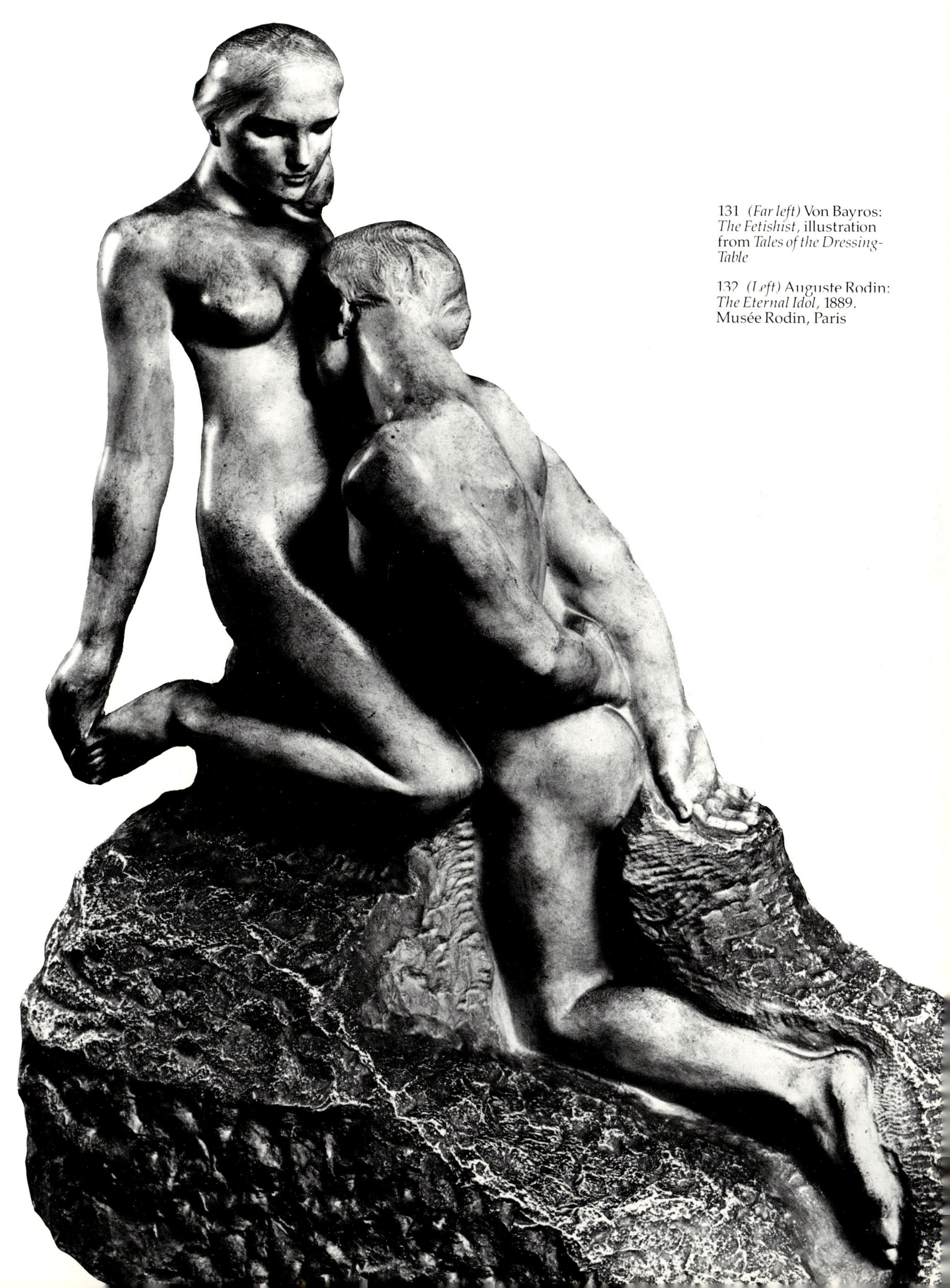

131 *(Far left)* Von Bayros: *The Fetishist*, illustration from *Tales of the Dressing-Table*

132 *(Left)* Auguste Rodin: *The Eternal Idol*, 1889. Musée Rodin, Paris

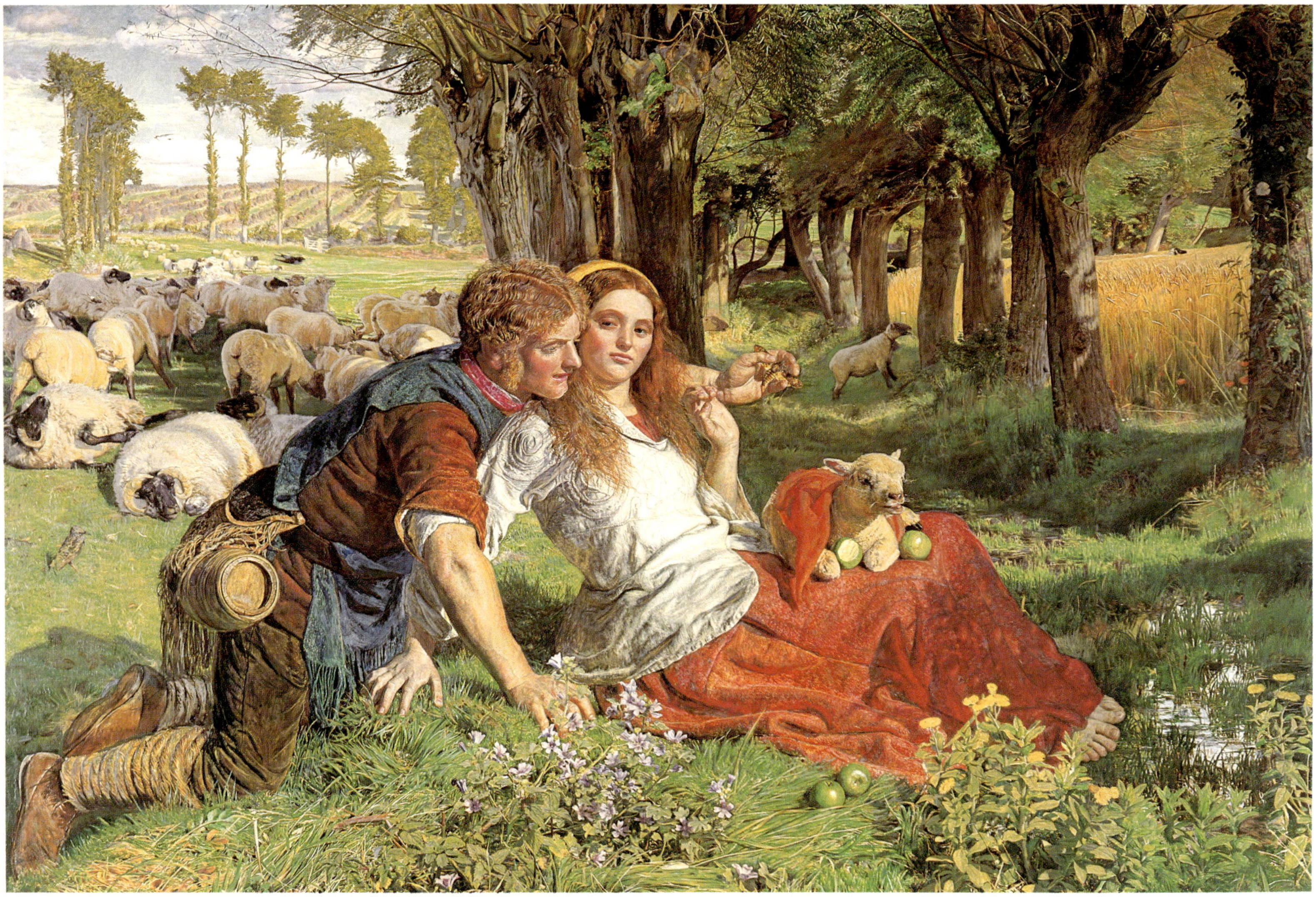

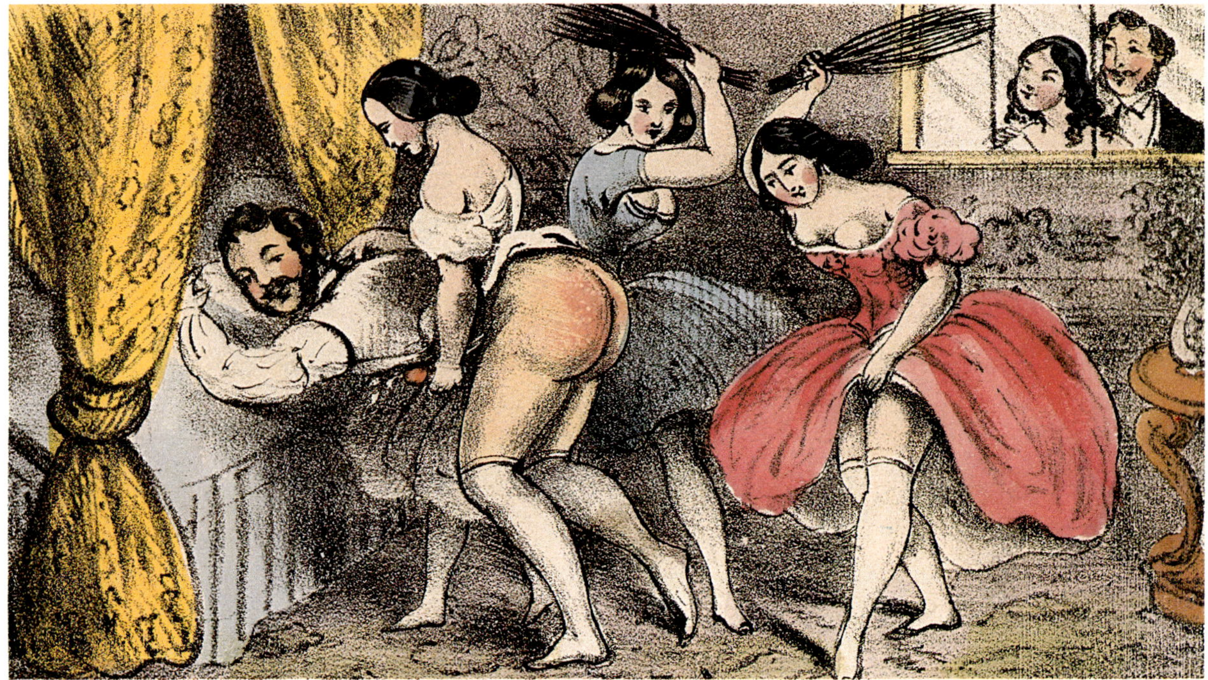

133 *(Above)* William Holman Hunt: *The Hireling Shepherd*, 1851. 76.4×109.5cm. City of Manchester Art Galleries

134 *(Left)* Anon: Plate from *The Exhibition of Female Flagellants*, 1860. Published by William Dugdale. British Library

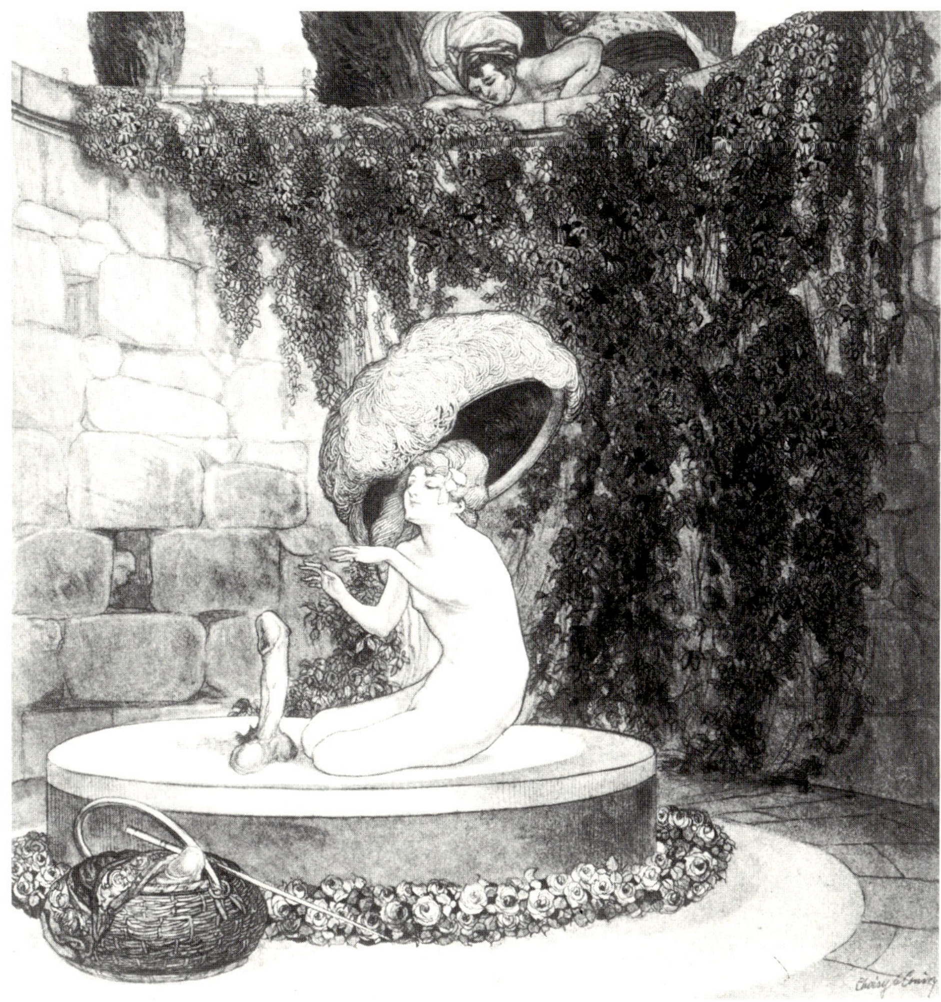

135 Von Bayros: illustration from *The Boudoir of Madame CC*, 1912

and as soon as he became fashionable as a portrait sculptor he gained the reputation of trying to seduce any attractive woman that he met. In 1883, however, when he was 43 years old, he met the 23-year-old Camille Claudel, who was herself a sculptress. She was to become the great love in his life. It was at this time that he began to make a series of erotic sculptures of which *The Eternal Idol* is a fine example. He is reported to have said that his attitude was one of homage to woman and her body, a woman no longer merely submitting to man, but matching him in ardour. The 'New Woman' was already on her way.

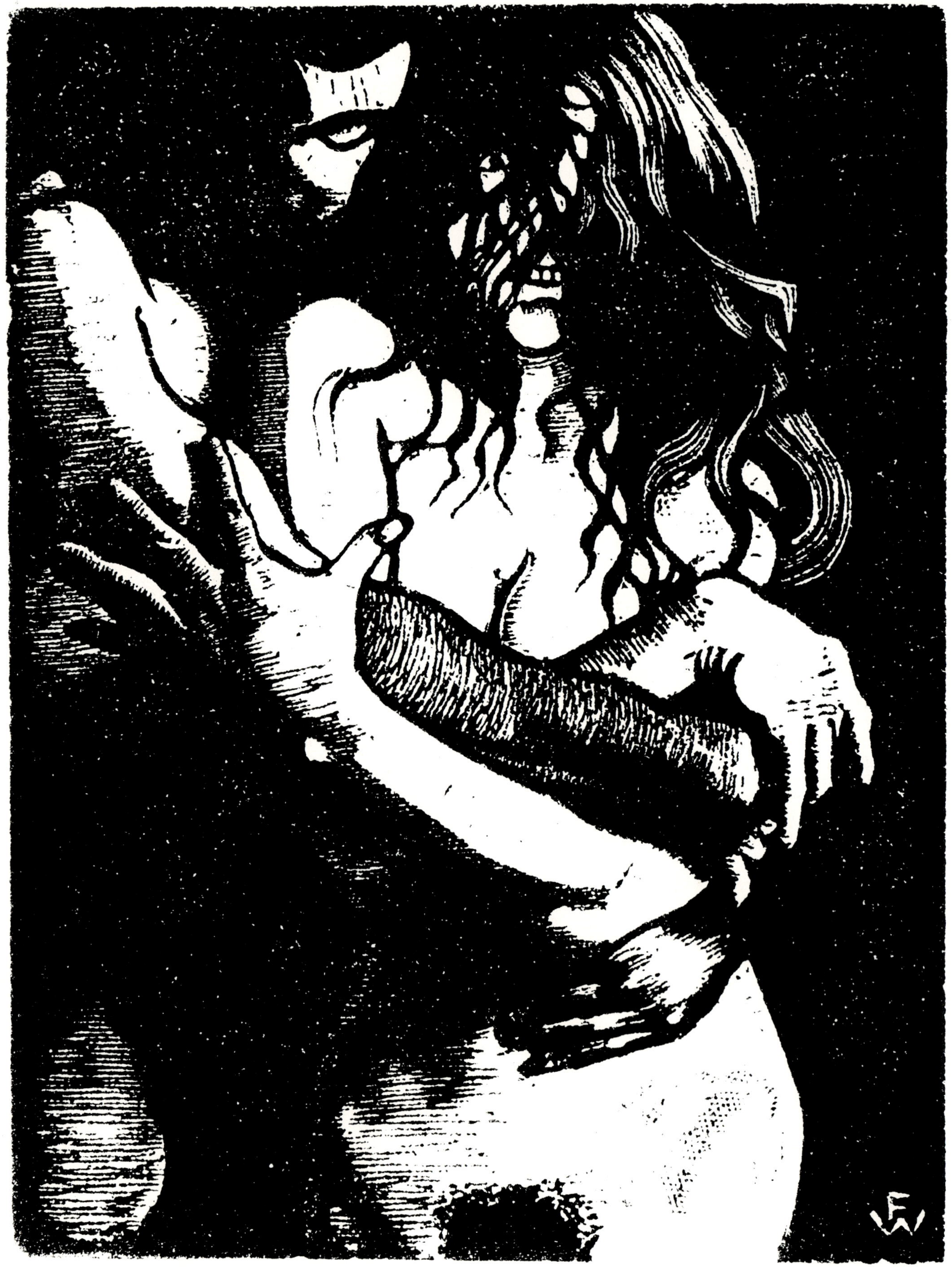

CHAPTER 7

The Last Hundred Years

As the nineteenth century moved towards its close, public life all over Europe was circumscribed by accepted rules of behaviour. Many intelligent people must have been aware that this rigid façade concealed much about which a discreet silence was observed, but it was generally held that this discretion was a protection for the community against disruption and immorality. People brought up behind this wall of hypocrisy came to place such importance upon it that any breach in accepted conduct filled them with genuine fear and shock. It was a time when, in some aspects, life had become very artificial: it was often assumed, for instance, that a husband would never see his own wife naked during the whole of their married life and that both wife and husband would have been upset if they did. The strain of trying to reconcile the actual facts of life with these unrealistic standards was great, and many good men came to believe themselves wicked because they could not live up to the code of behaviour they believed was right.

Realism in art had reached a peak and representational art had achieved a commonplace excellence which produced results almost akin to a colour photograph. Graphic illustration had reached a standard that enabled the *Illustrated London News* to flourish without the need for photography. It became accepted that every picture was usually expected to point a moral or express some sentimental theme that would be improving to the viewer.

Below the surface, however, there were artistic rebels. The restless spirits of independent young artists increasingly began to yearn for something new and for art which went beyond the staid limits of popular approval. Artists like Beardsley in England, the Impressionists in Paris, and Expressionists like Munch, had stimulated a series of artistic experiments. By the turn of the century, new ways of expression, involving the distortion of shape, colour and texture, each ephemeral and quickly superseded by some contrasting style, proceeded to undermine the foundations of orthodox realism.

Vienna was one of several European capitals where a community with a fundamental belief in law and order had established a very conservative social life. The small group of intellectuals, which included Freud, was ignored or ostracized. Sexuality was thought to be a disturbing and dangerously disruptive influence and sex, as a subject, was never talked about. But prostitution remained a tacitly

136 William Fulljames: *Bear Hug*, 1979. Wood-engraving, 12×7.5cm

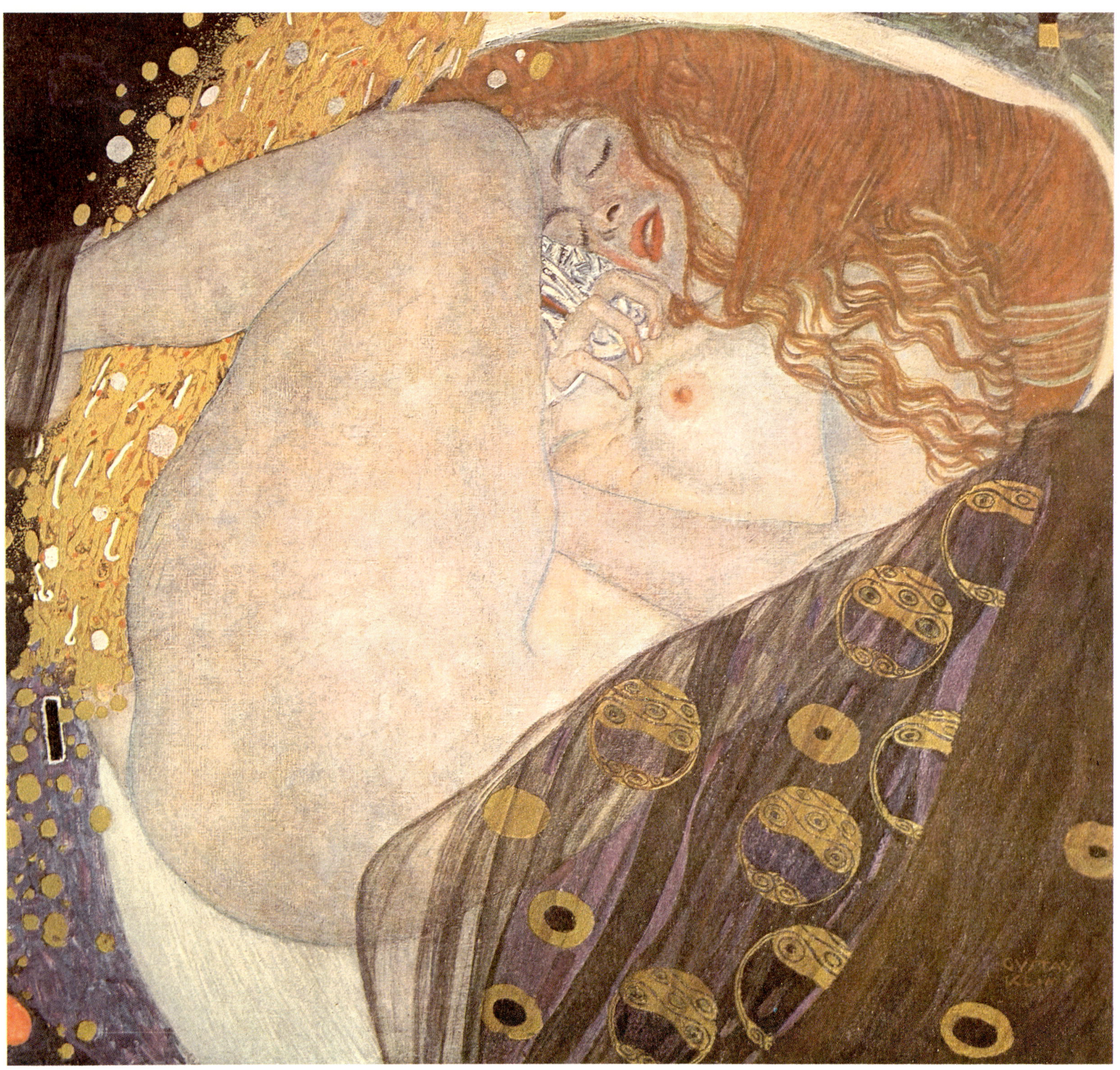

137 *(Left)* Gustav Klimt: *Danaë*, 1907-8. 77×83cm. Galerie Würthle, Vienna

138 *(Right)* Amedeo Modigliani: *Nude*, c.1917. 92×60cm. Courtauld Institute Galleries, University of London

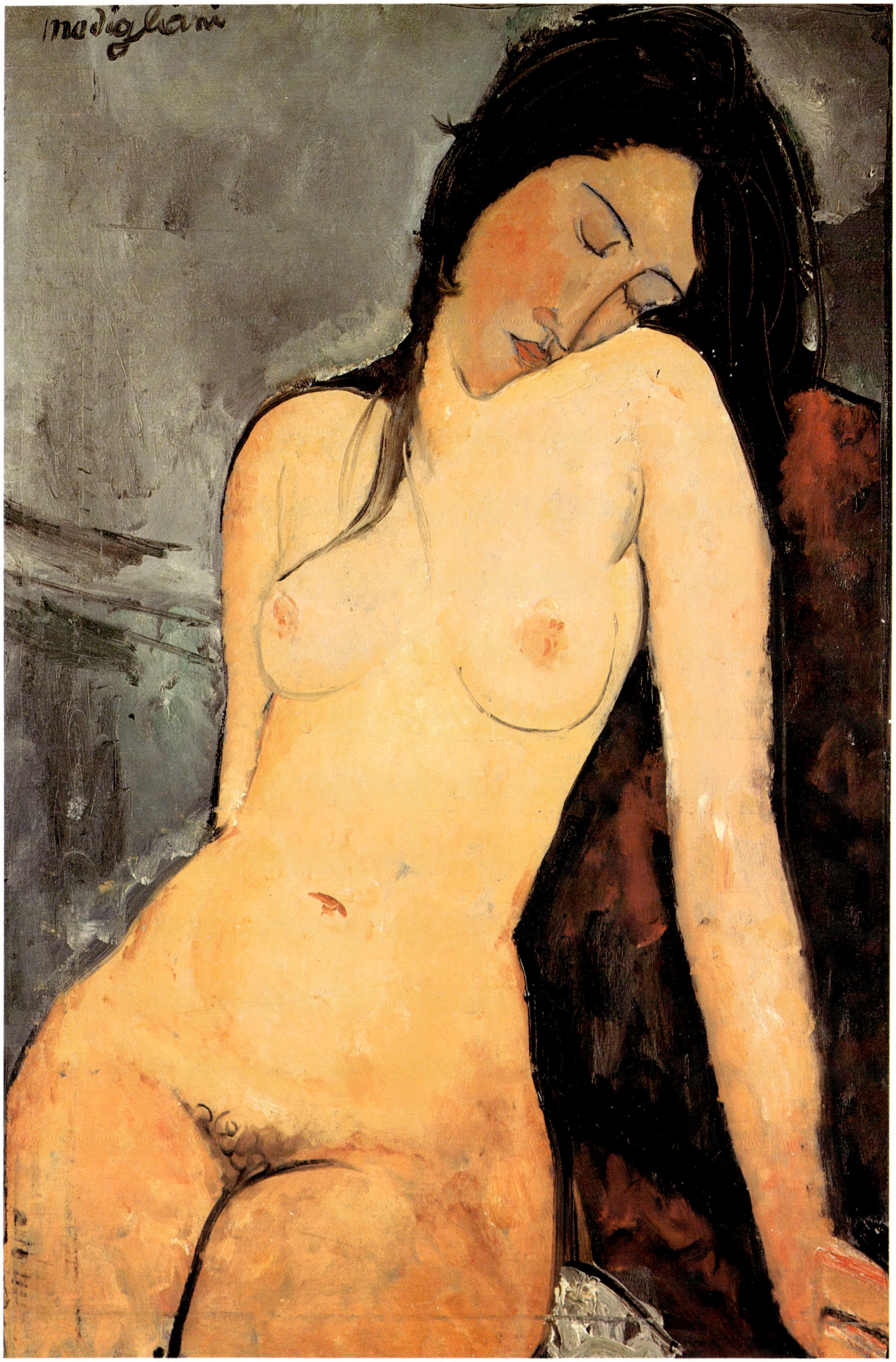

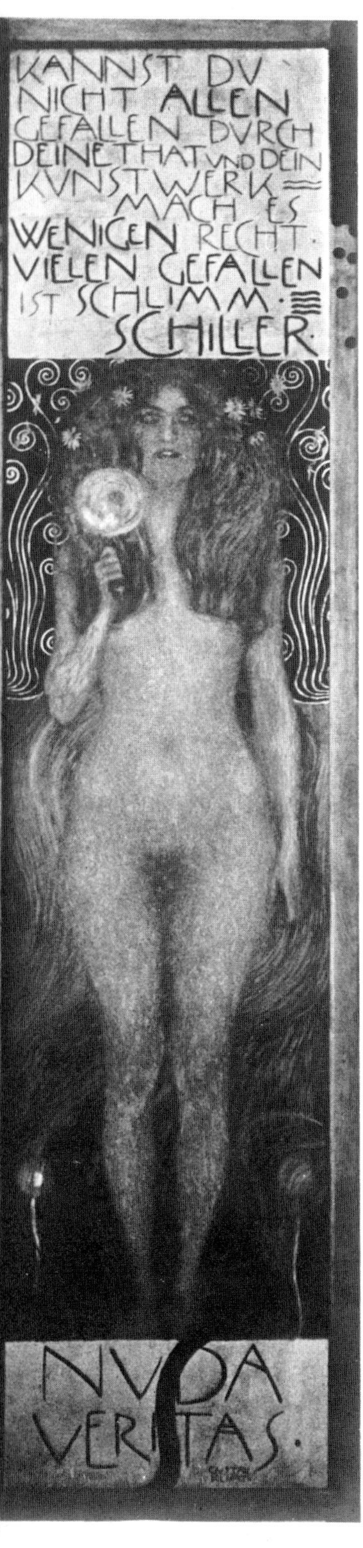

accepted institution, in complete contrast to the view of the sanctity of a modest woman. The arts were controlled by the Academy and one orthodox exhibiting society; seniority and conformity were deciding factors in an artist's progress. The whole system was ripe for revolt. After years of agitation by younger artists a new society, the Secession, was formed in 1897.

The first President of the Secession was Gustav Klimt (1862-1918), who was a technically superb realist. In the Second Secession Exhibition in 1898, he showed a picture in a new, bolder style, of *Pallas Athene*, wearing a strange helmet and golden armour, and holding in her right hand a miniature, frontal nude figure of a young girl. He was personally attracted by the female form and liked to have one or more nude models about in his studio while he was painting. Seemingly indifferent to public opinion, he began to shock orthodox Viennese taste by introducing naked female figures into his public pictures. In 1899 he painted a frontal nude figure, five feet high, *Nuda Veritas*, complete with pubic hair. It carried the inscription by Schiller, 'If thou canst not please all men by thine actions and by thine art, then please the few; it is bad to please the many.' Pubic hair is not erotic in a nudist camp but, in Vienna, false modesty had caused it to be regarded with horror. Criticism of the picture was intense, and it was confiscated by the police. In 1908 he painted his celebrated picture of *Danaë*, in which she shows obvious sensual appreciation of the shower of gold which flows over her. By now his paintings were known and admired throughout the art world. *Woman Masturbating* was one of the illustrations which he had drawn for an edition of *Lucian's Dialogues*, published in 1907, and after his death a series of previously unknown fine erotic drawings and etchings was found. *The Embrace* probably dates from about 1905. It shows how skilfully he could express erotic feeling with only a few fine pencil lines.

Egon Schiele (1890-1918) was a natural rebel, with a talent for drawing. His art suffered because he did not persist with formal training after he had obtained a place in the Vienna Academy. He boasted that he liked to live from hand to mouth, and this policy kept him, his mistress and his friends so poor that in many of his nude paintings the models seem pitifully thin because they were half-starved. Most of the women in the nude pictures which he liked to paint are in ungainly postures so that he could emphasize the

139 *(Left)* Gustav Klimt: *Nuda veritas*, 1899

140 *(Right)* Gustav Klimt: *The Embrace* (detail), c.1916. Pencil drawing, 54.9×34.9cm. Museum der Stadt Wien, Vienna

141 *(Below right)* Gustav Klimt: *Woman masturbating*, illustration from Lucian's *Dialogues*, 1907. British Museum

genitalia. In 1912 he was sentenced to twenty-four days in gaol for disseminating indecent material, after explicit sexual drawings were found in his lodgings. One picture was publicly burned in court. Three years later he married, and this radically changed his attitude to life. Simultaneously the quality of his art began to improve. His work, while still concentrating on the sexual area, showed improved composition, better use of colour and more skilful brushwork. In March 1918 Schiele had his first real public success. It was ironic and tragic that in October the same year both Schiele and his wife died within three days of each other during the influenza epidemic.

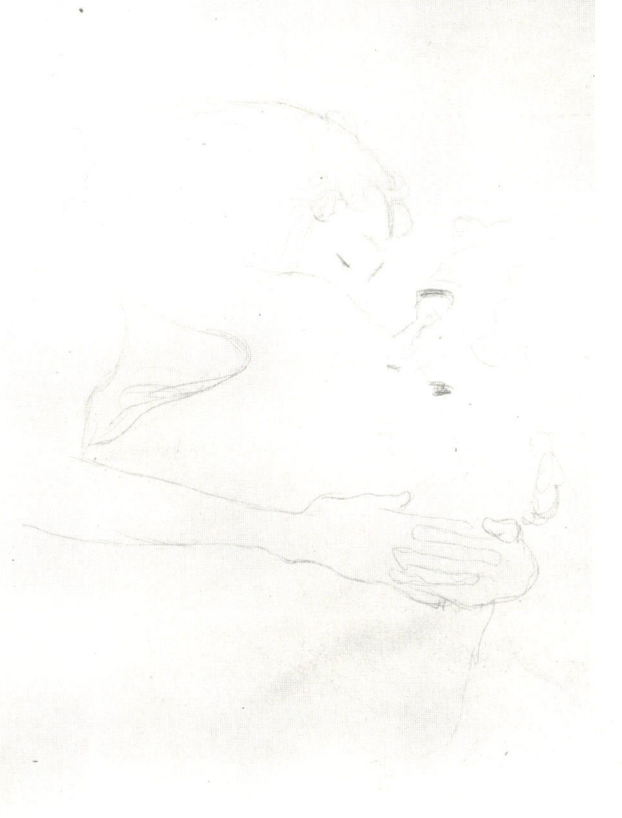

With the successive fashions in experimental art a realist artist was a figure of fun around the café tables of the Bohemian quarter in any of the European capitals. On the other hand fantastic shapes and colours were greeted with respectful applause and serious discussion of the psychological symbolism which could be read into them. All the traditional artistic standards were discarded, trampled underfoot by artists vying with one another to think of some new and exciting variant of artistic expression. Erotic art became relatively rare, since increasingly abstract pictures were unable to show any but the simplest erotic images. Moreover, many self-taught artists lacked the technical ability to produce sexually stimulating effects. There were great artists like Picasso (1881-1973), who could produce fine

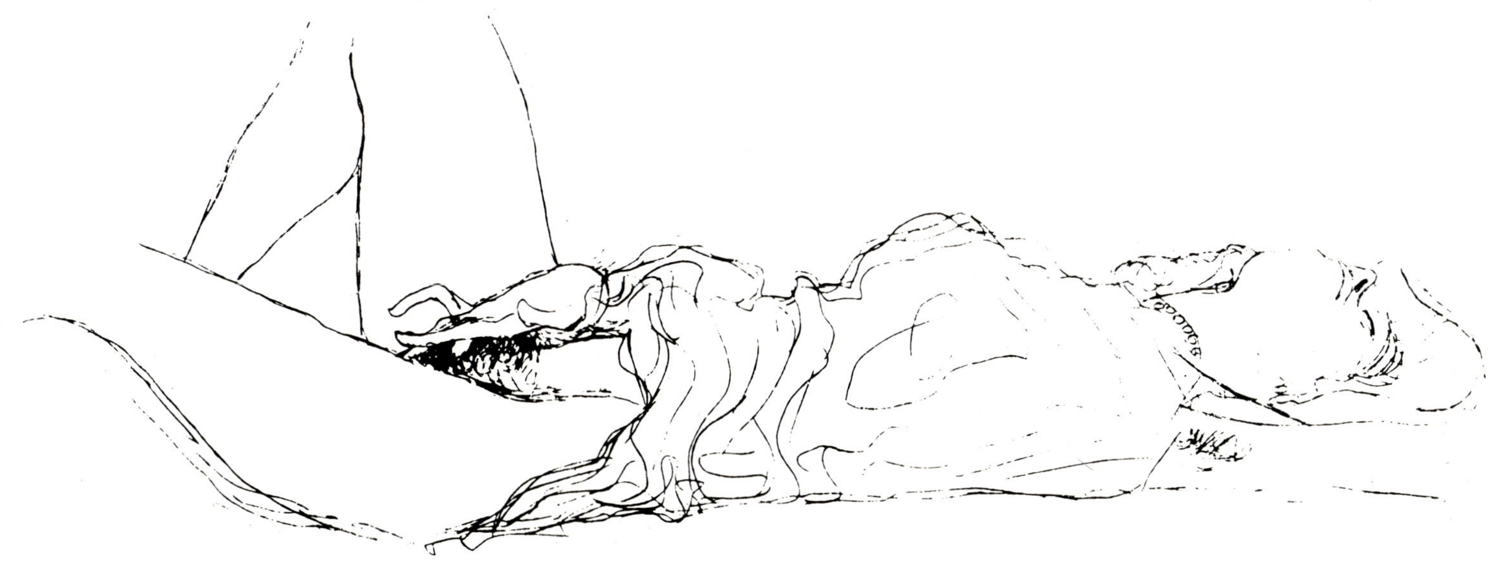

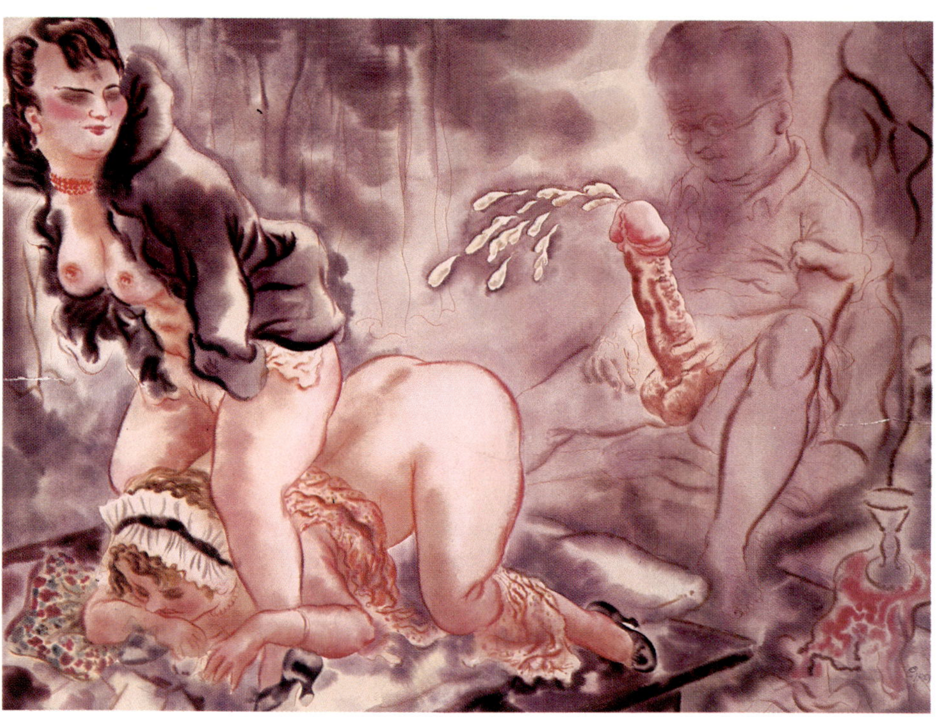

142 George Grosz: untitled watercolour including self-portrait, c.1925. Coll. Bradley Smith, La Jolla, California

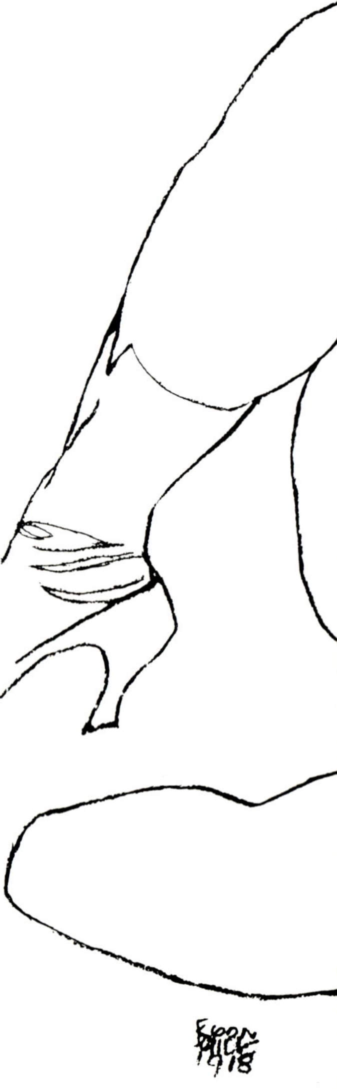

pictures in many of the experimental styles, but these did not always try to depict erotic ideas. Picasso himself, who during his long life was seldom without intimate women friends, frequently painted the female form. Usually, however, he showed it as an artistic shape rather than as a sexual object. *The Lovers and the Cat* (Plate 1) is an example of a frankly sexual picture which he painted in 1902, when he was twenty. Towards the end of his life, shortly before his 87th birthday in 1968, he made Plate 144, which was one of a large series of etchings. In it he is thought to have portrayed himself as the voyeur.

Modigliani (1884-1920), like Beardsley, was a tragic figure, crippled by and eventually dying of tuberculosis. As a young student in Italy he was entranced by the beautiful outlines of Botticelli and Raphael. Later, in Paris, he was influenced by Picasso, Lautrec and many others but formed his own, very individual style. In spite of his disease he was a handsome and very amorous young man, and with a total disregard for his health he indulged in alcohol, drugs and many love affairs. For years he had great difficulty in selling his pictures, but in 1917 he found a dealer who would pay him 40 francs and a bottle of brandy for each of his female nude pictures. By this

143 Egon Schiele: *Two Women*. Drawing, 1918. Coll. Victor A. Lownes

time his tuberculosis was rapidly advancing. In 1918 he had his first one-man exhibition, but this was closed by the police on the grounds of indecency. In January 1920 he died from alcoholism and tuberculosis before his talent had been recognized. Plate 138 is typical of his mature work, showing an amalgam of Cubism in the face, Expressionism in the figure, and the strong colours of the Fauves.

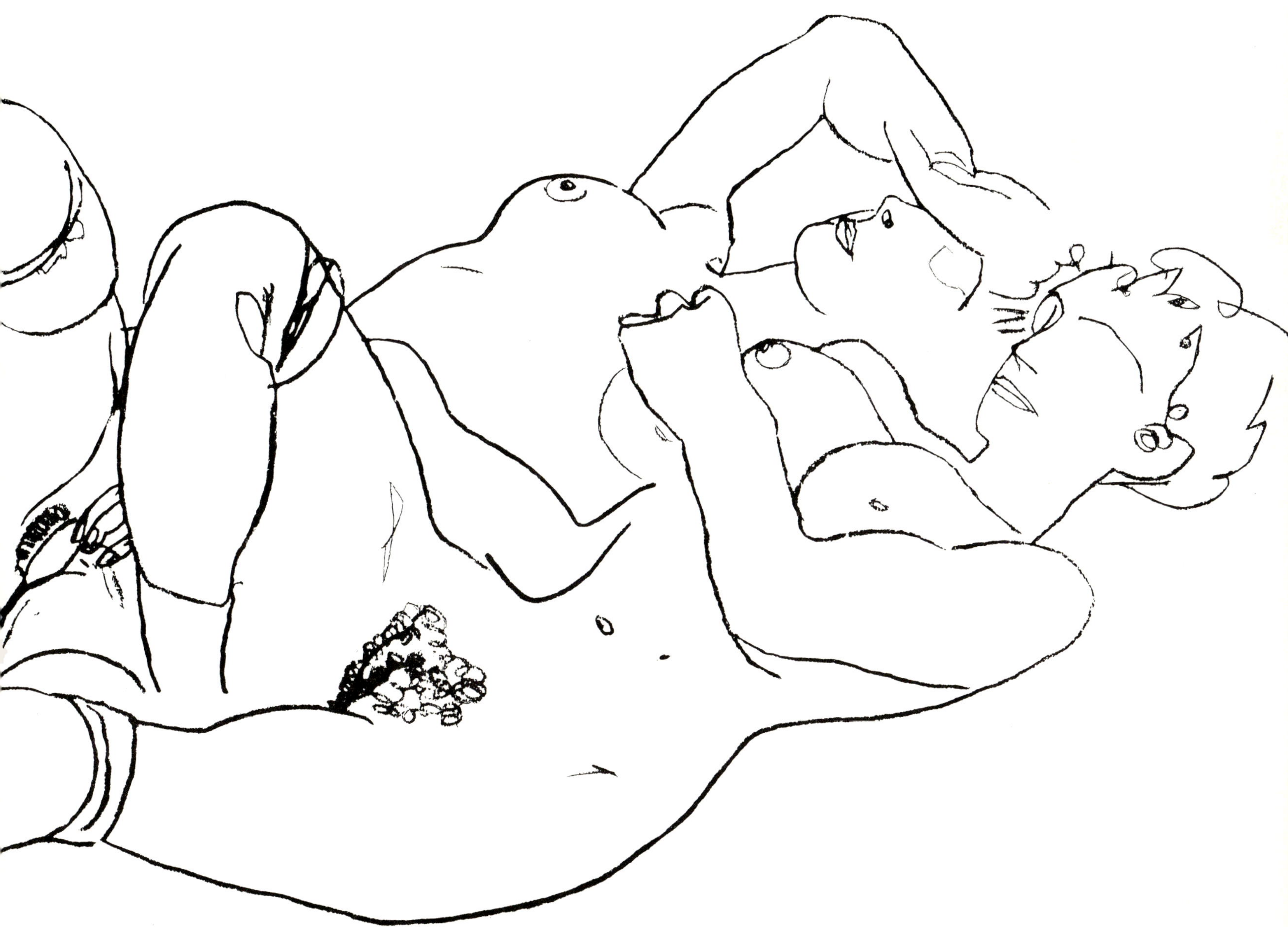

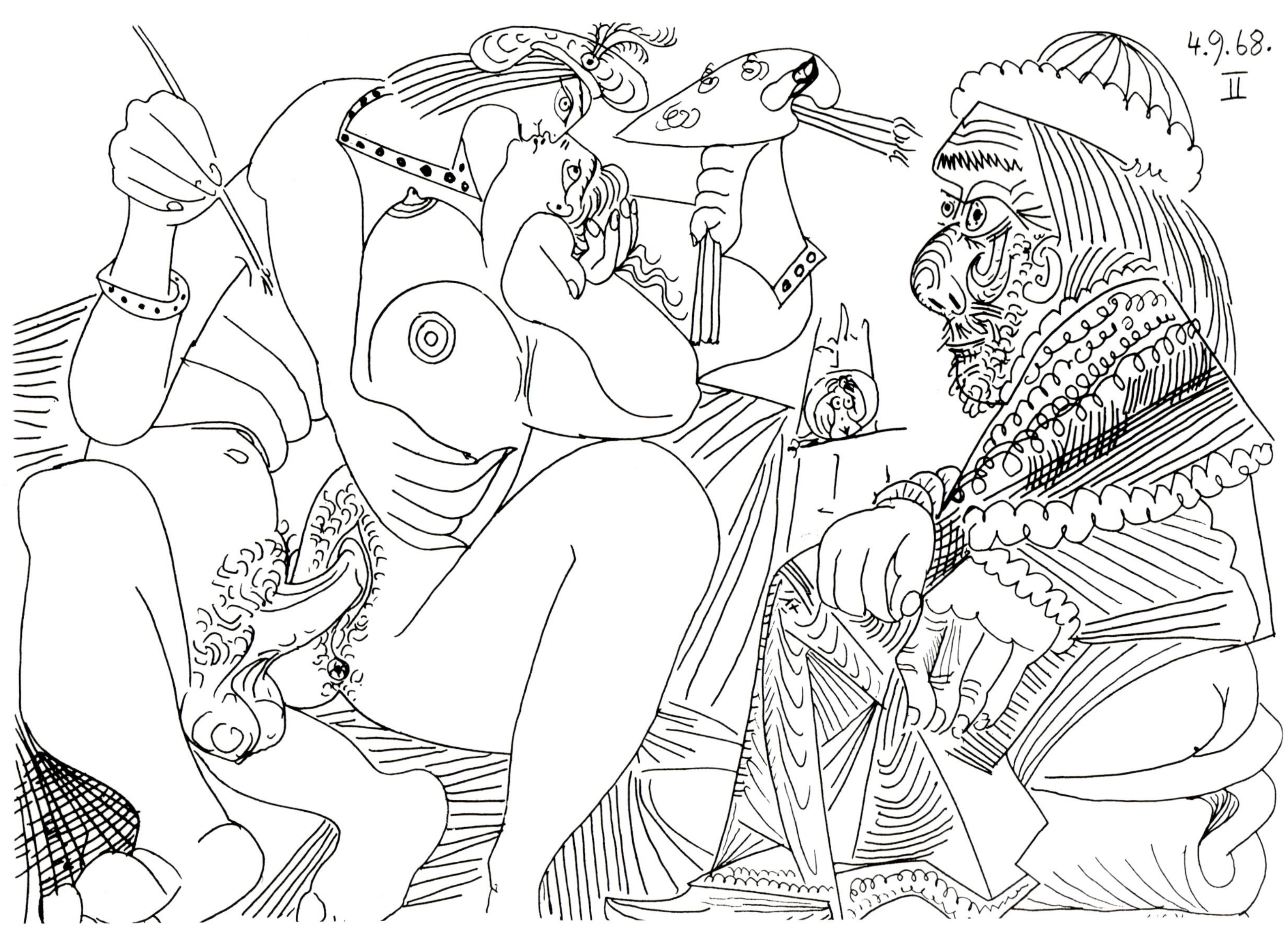

144 Picasso: untitled etching, 1968. 25×32.5cm. Galerie Louise Leiris, Paris

Wood-engraving was a recognized medium of artistic expression in Europe from the fifteenth and sixteenth centuries onwards, following the great works of Dürer (1471-1528), Altdorfer (1480-1538), Cranach (1475-1531) and many others. In the nineteenth century in Britain it was mainly used as a means of reproducing line-drawn illustrations for books, periodicals and newspapers. The method continued to be used extensively until about 1885 when it was superseded by newer methods of reproduction and by photography. At the beginning of the twentieth century a few artists began to

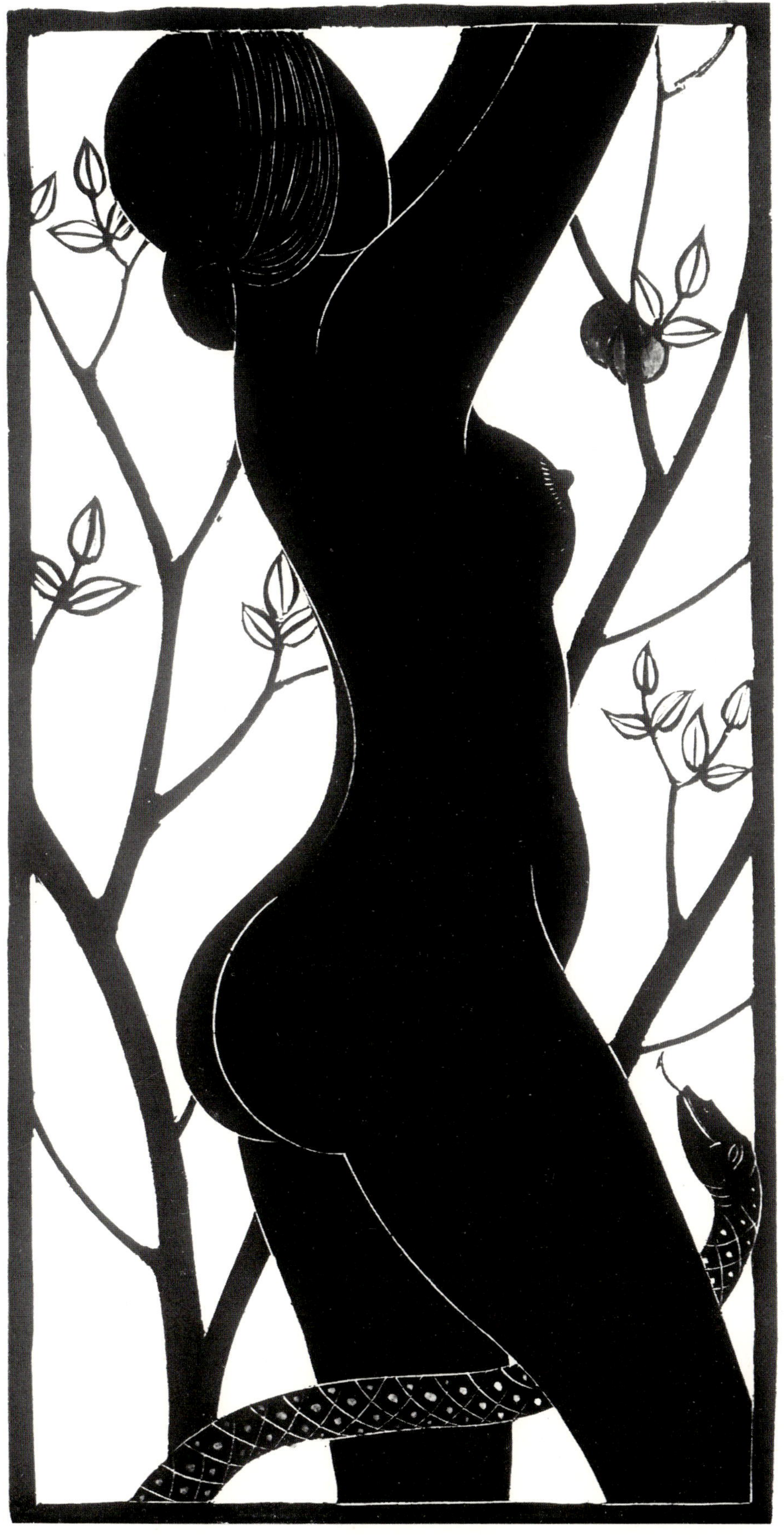

145 Eric Gill: *Eve*. Wood-engraving, 1926. Victoria and Albert Museum

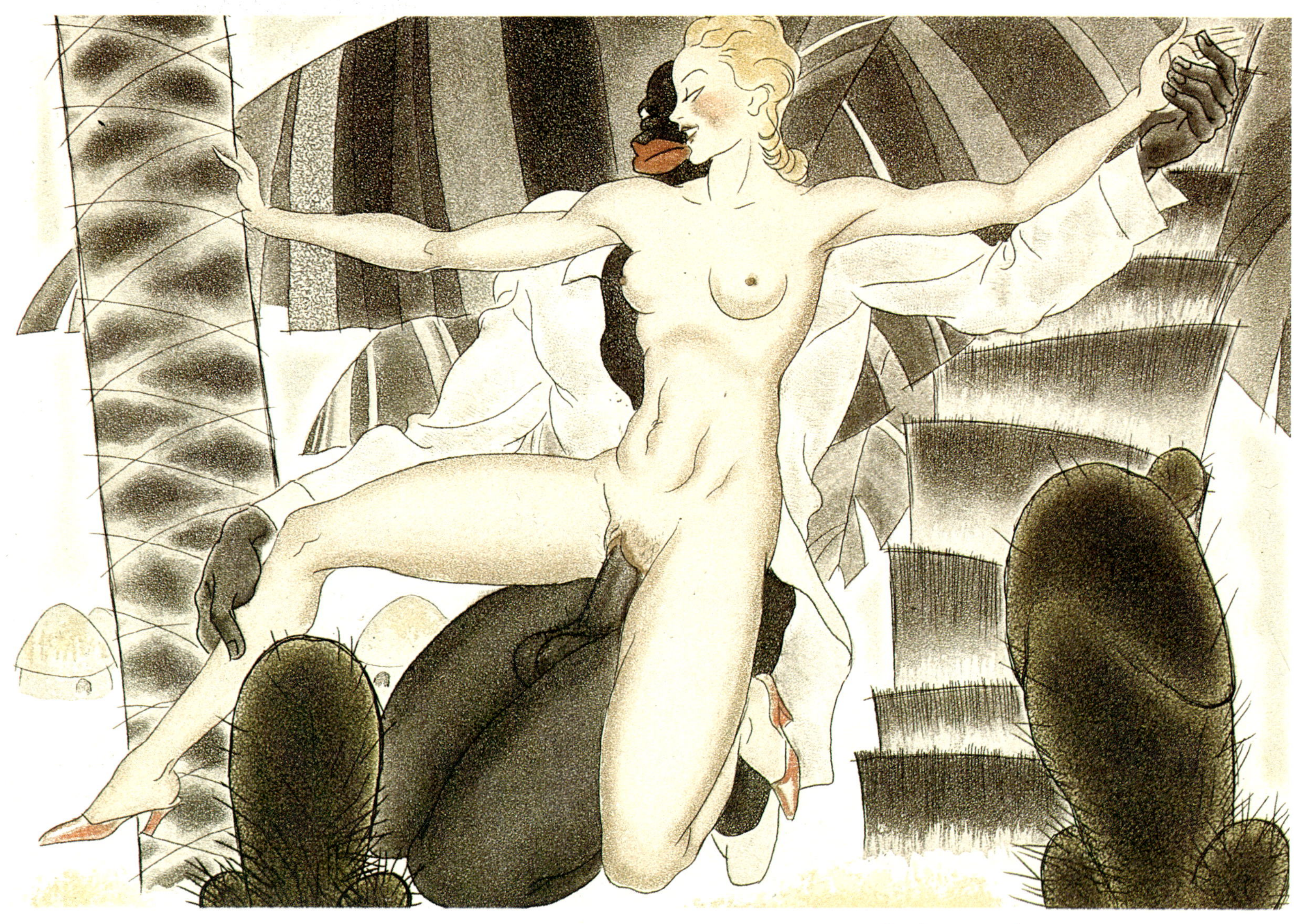

146 Anon: *Nègre en chemise,* illustration from the limited edition of *Menu Galant*

experiment with wood-engraving as a creative art form. Among these was Eric Gill (1882-1940), who first produced a few small engravings about 1908. From 1915 onwards he began to design a steady stream of wood-block illustrations, which were to make him one of the most outstanding wood-engravers of the century. He was a very religious man, who became an ardent Roman Catholic. He was also intensely interested in sexual matters and entranced by the female nude, which he repeatedly used as a subject. His wood-engraving of *Eve* (Plate 145) is one of the most powerfully erotic

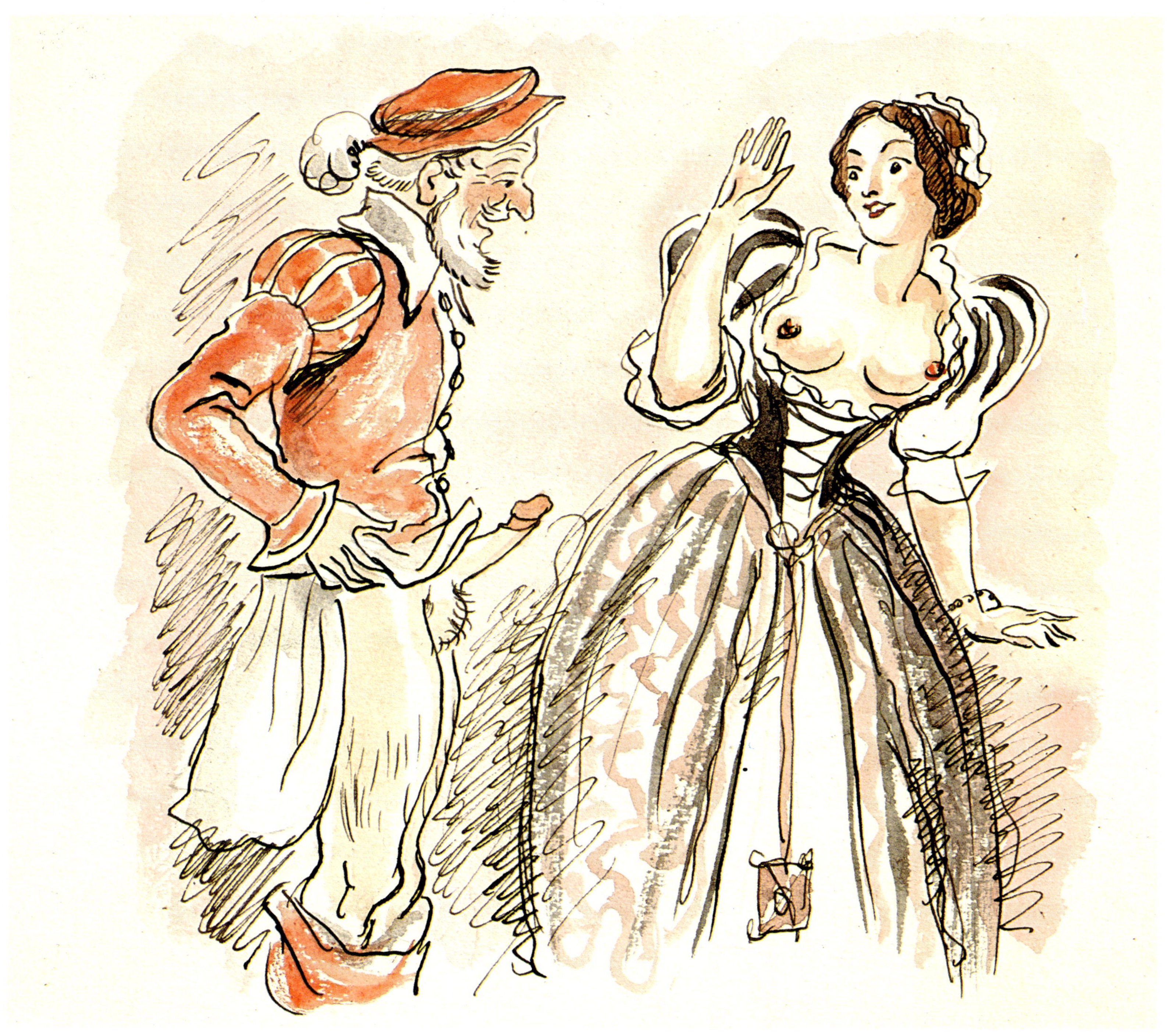

147 Collot (attr.): *Odelette*, pen and wash illustration from the unique copy of *Choix d'Oeuvres*, c.1930

depictions of this subject in art and is a fine example of his work. As he said in the introduction to his book *Drawings from Life*, which contained 36 drawings of nude girls, 'Our love of such drawings is neither of necessity sinful nor the occasion of sin . . . it seems best to draw whatever is natural and normal and trust to the good sense of people to see things in a reasonable manner.' That book together with another entitled *25 Nudes* and others are now collector's pieces. Besides his published art he left many drawings of an erotic nature: Plate 148 is an example of one of these.

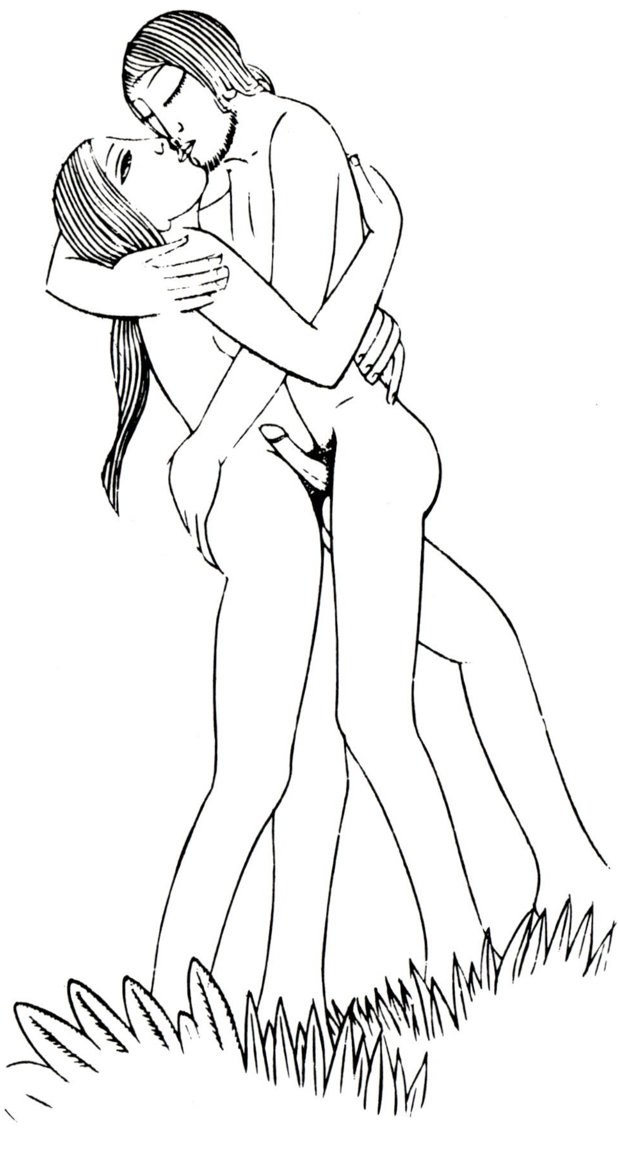

148 Eric Gill: *Man and Woman*. Pencil drawing, c.1930

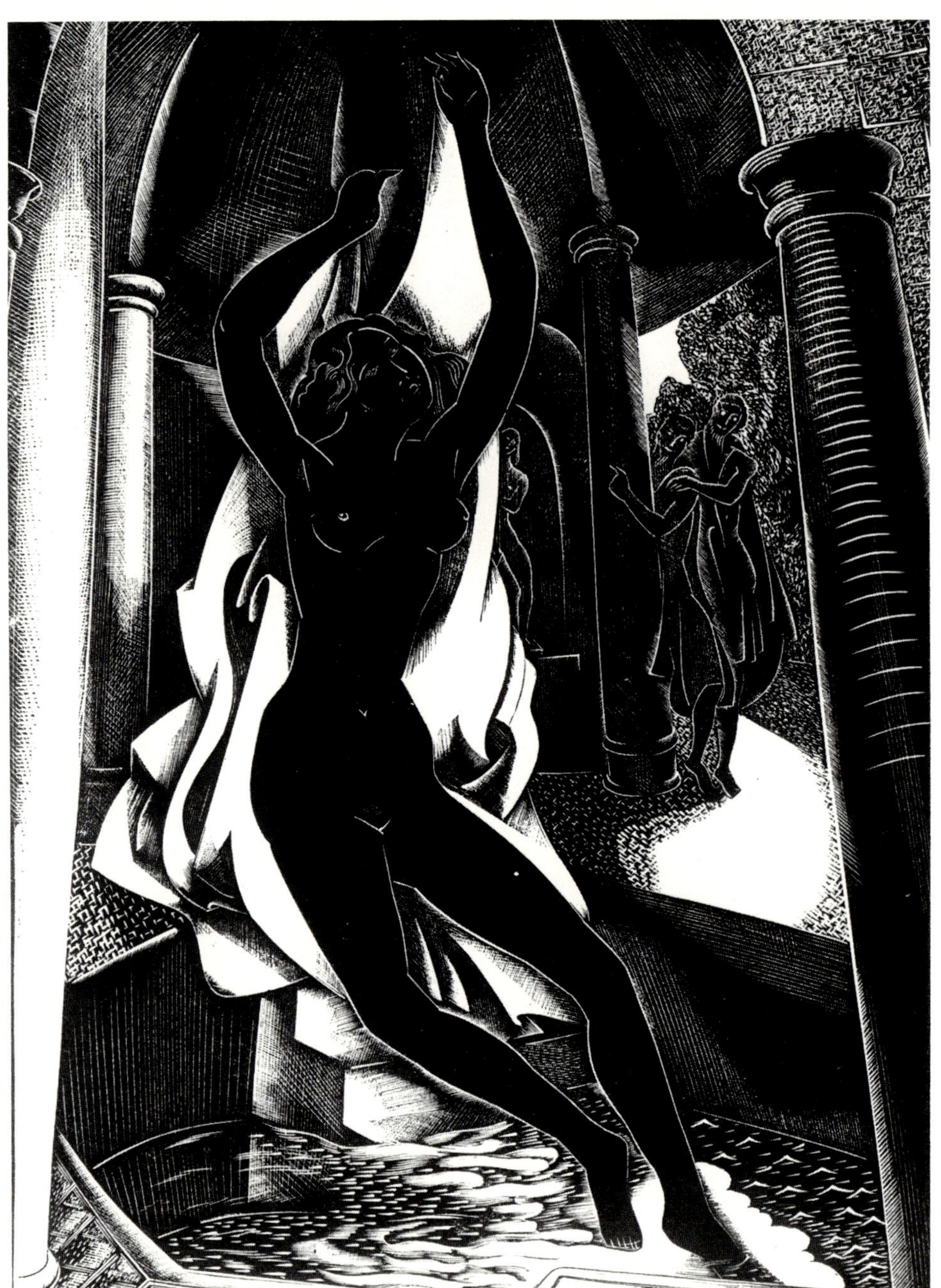

Karl Thylmann (1888-1916) was born in Darmstadt, trained in Germany and was influenced by the *Jugendstil*, the German form of *Art Nouveau*, and by other art movements which were breaking away from traditional realism. He worked as a book illustrator, using etching and lithography, and in 1912 became a wood-engraver. *Black Hair* is one of more than 60 woodcuts which he had produced by the outbreak of the First World War. Unfortunately he was mortally wounded at Verdun.

After the First World War a number of young artists realized afresh the possibilities of wood-engraving. When Robert Gibbings bought the Golden Cockerel Press in 1922 he found that he was able to call

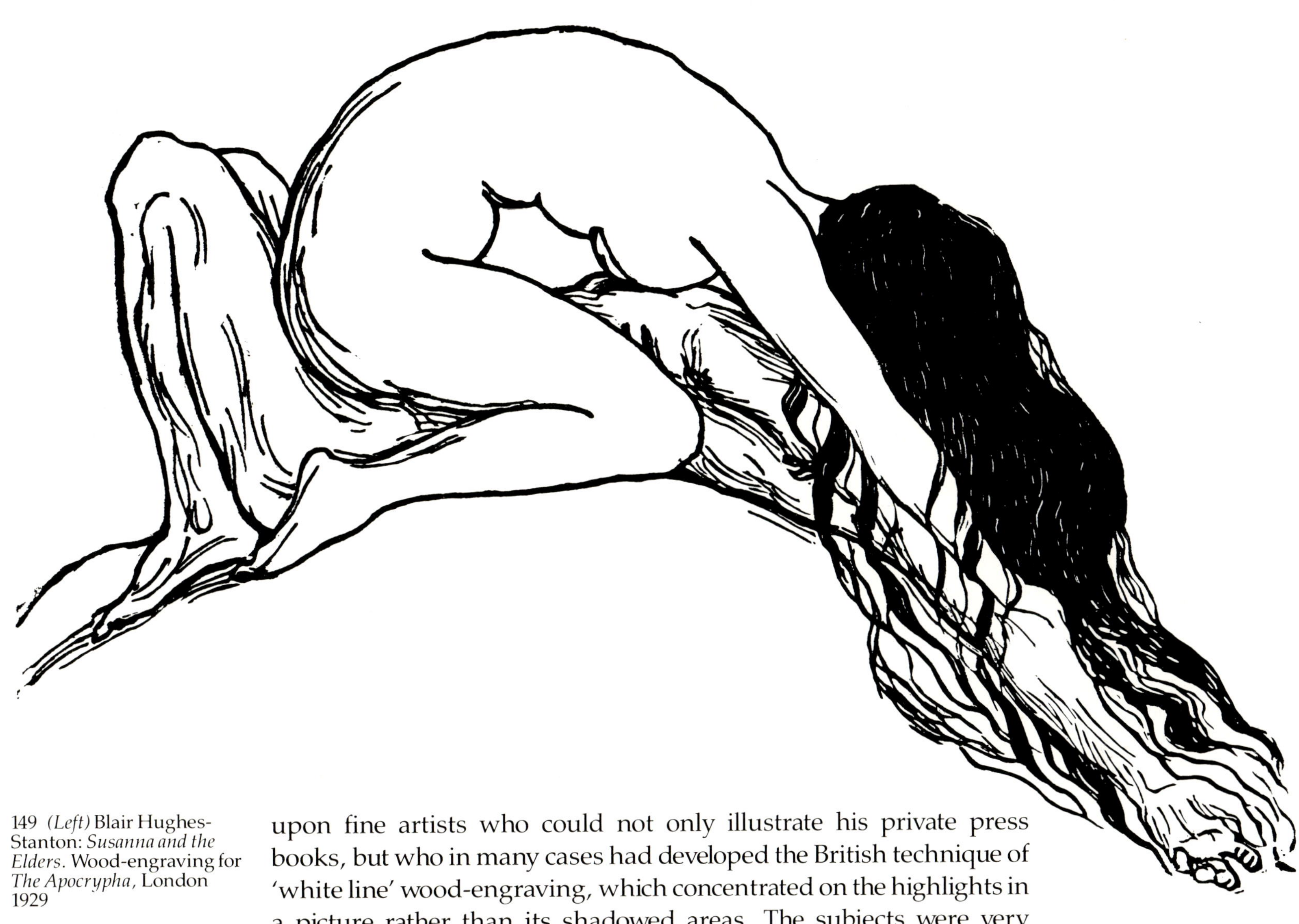

149 *(Left)* Blair Hughes-Stanton: *Susanna and the Elders.* Wood-engraving for *The Apocrypha,* London 1929

150 *(Above)* Karl Thylmann: *Black hair.* Woodcut, c.1913

upon fine artists who could not only illustrate his private press books, but who in many cases had developed the British technique of 'white line' wood-engraving, which concentrated on the highlights in a picture rather than its shadowed areas. The subjects were very varied but some had erotic aspects. *Susanna and the Elders* is a 'white line' wood-engraving by Blair Hughes-Stanton (b. 1902), a book illustration for *The Apocrypha*, published in 1929.

Another fine artist, with a great range of subject and style, was John Buckland-Wright (1897-1954). Born in New Zealand, educated in England, he lived for many years in France until he returned to England in 1939, with an international reputation. *Love Night* is a rare additional illustration to a limited edition by the Golden Cockerel Press in 1936 and demonstrates his unerring construction and draughtsmanship. He was also a skilled copper-plate engraver, and *Cupid's Pastime* is a sensitively erotic picture from the book of that name which he illustrated in 1935.

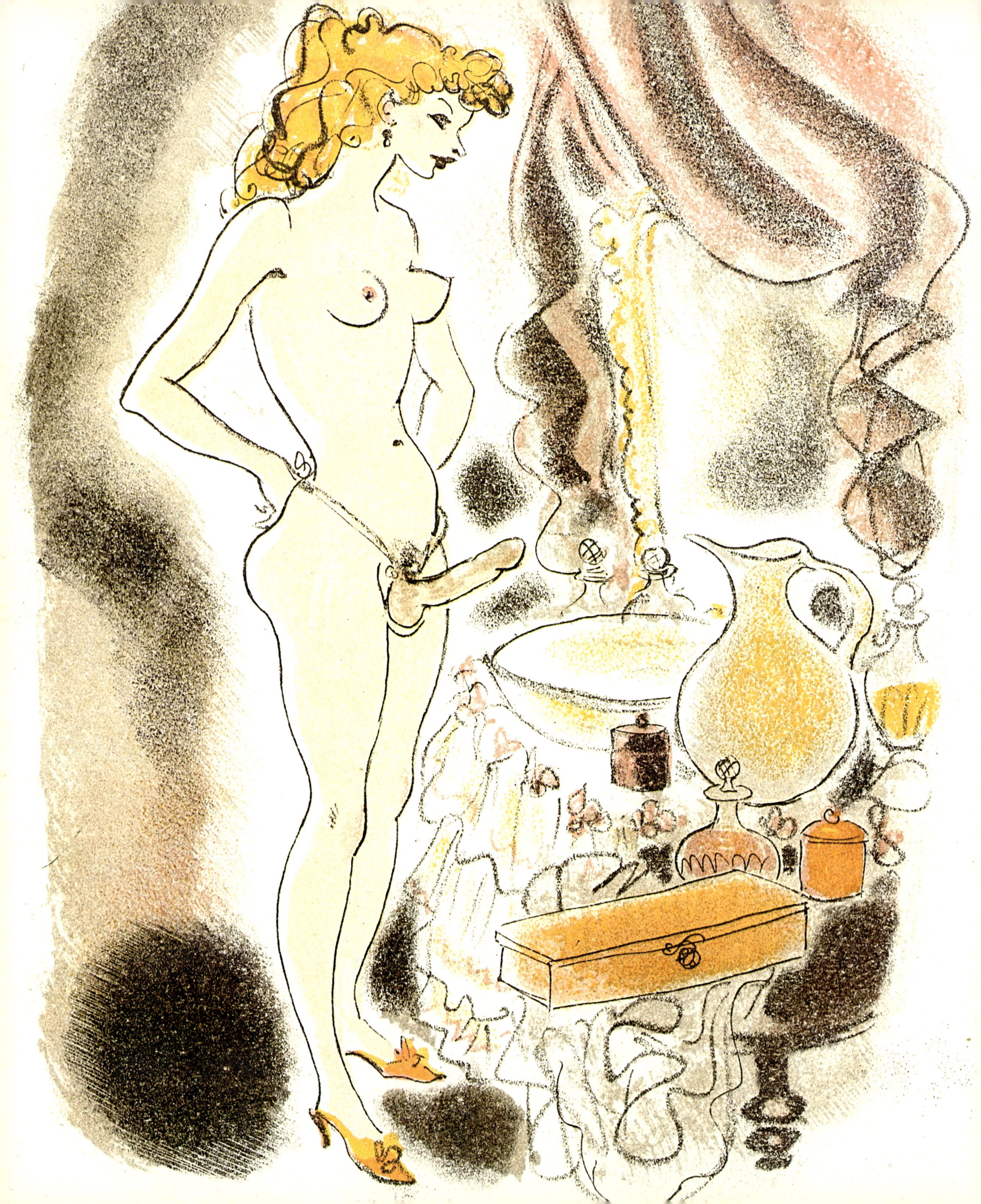

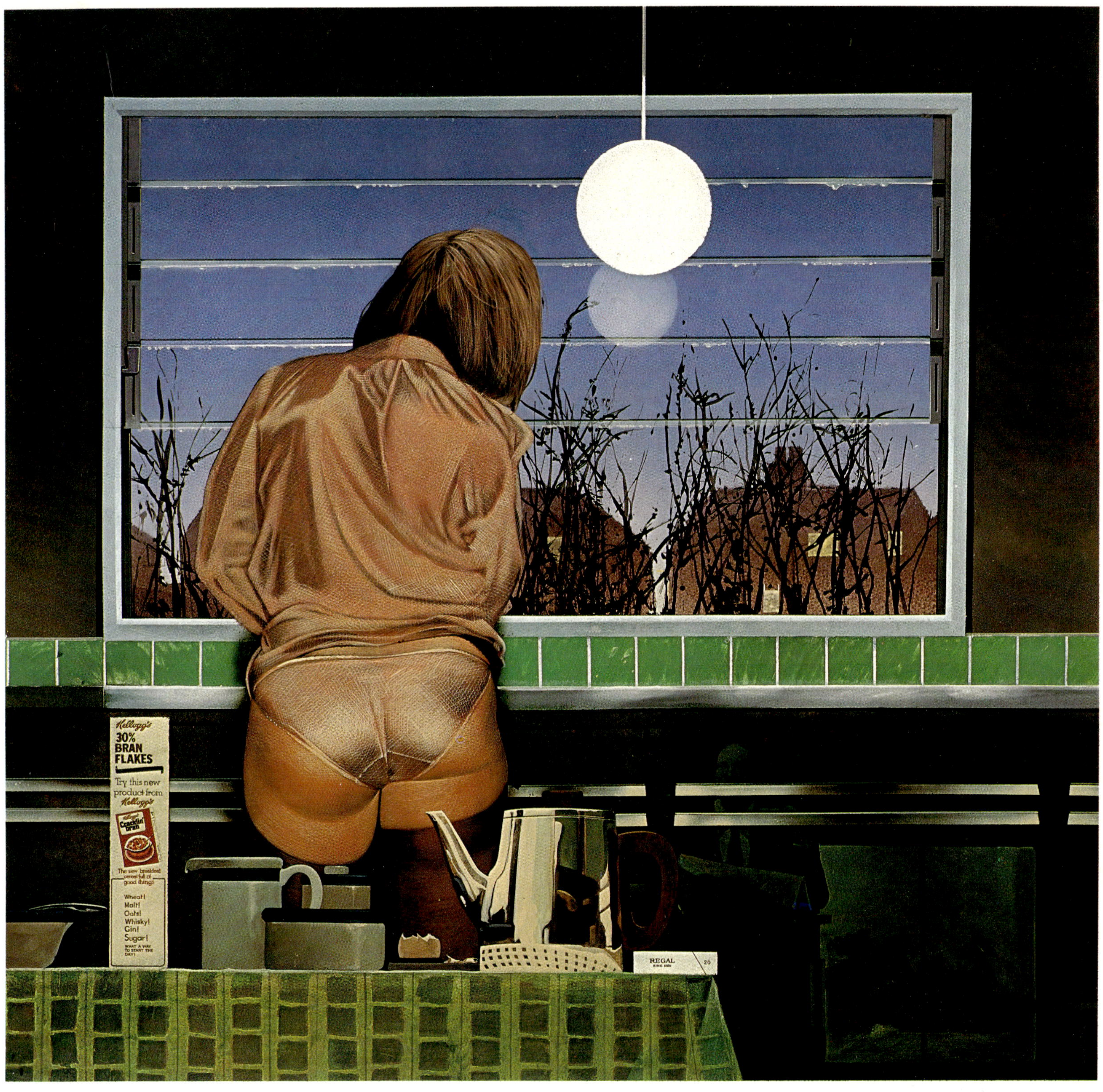

151 *(Left)* Anon: untitled illustration to *L'Ecole des Biches ou Moeurs des Petites Dames de ce temps*, Paris 1939. First published 1863

George Buday (b. 1907) was born in Transylvania and had been a wood-engraver for nine years before he began living in Britain in 1937. His talent was at once recognized both in England and in America, and he illustrated many books. Plate 155 is an illustration he produced for *The Vigil of Venus* in 1952 which illustrates the lines:

152 Mike Francis: *Early Morning Tease*, 1980. Acrylic and mixed media on board, 122×122cm. Nicholas Treadwell Galleries, London

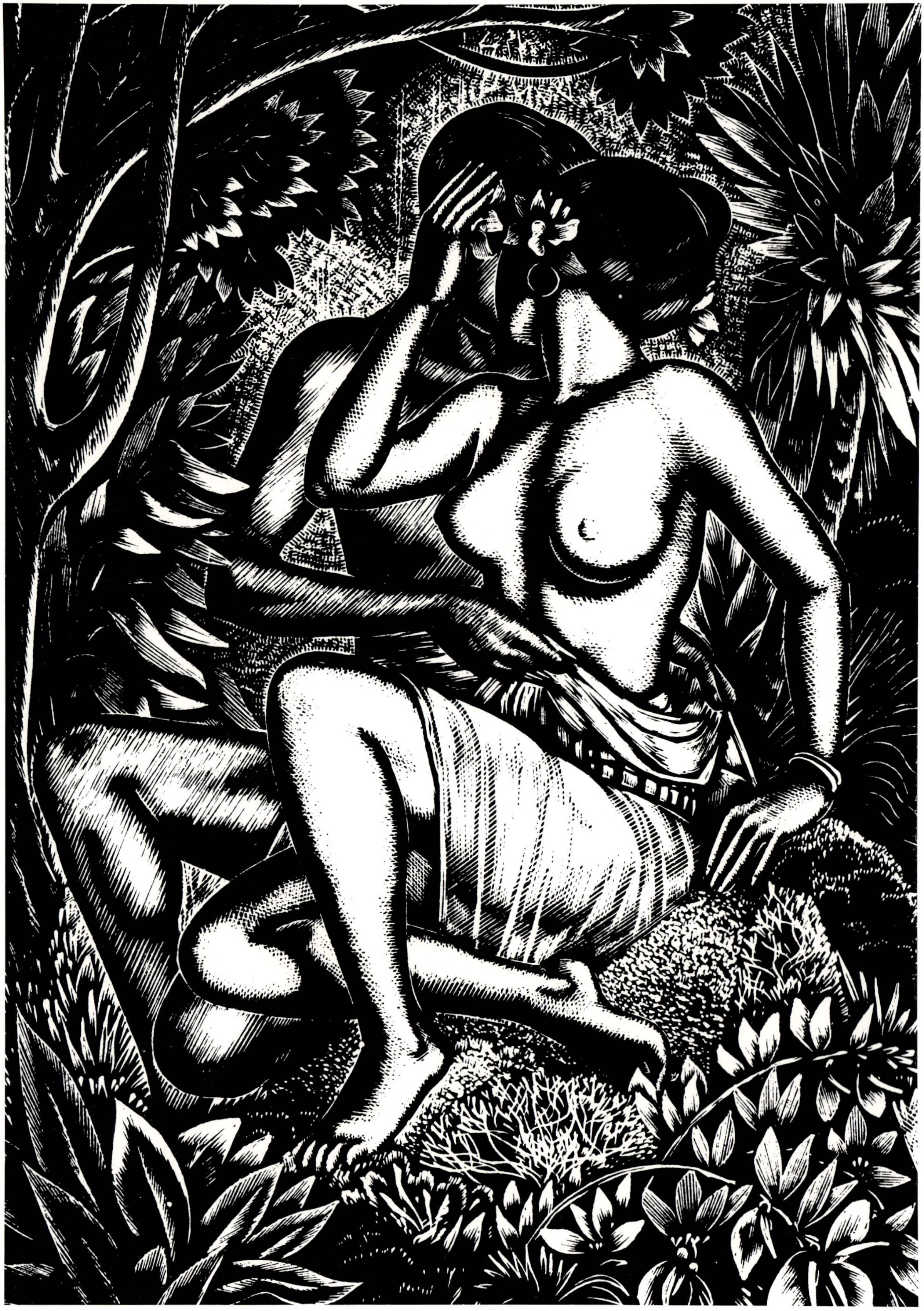

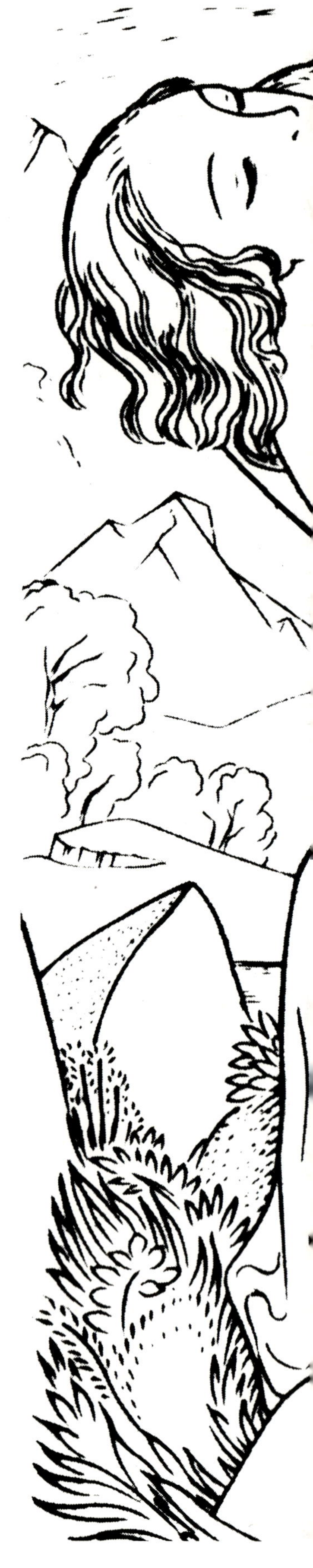

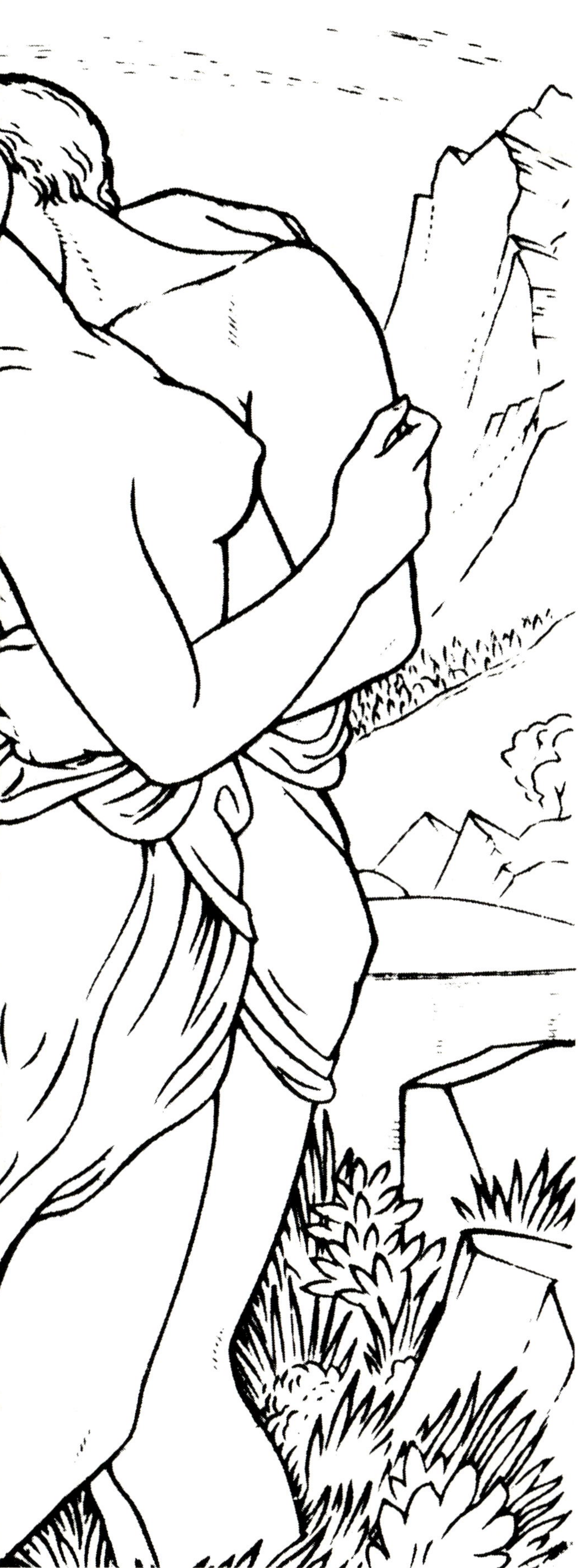

153 *(Far left)* John Buckland-Wright: wood-engraving, additional illustration to a limited edition of *Love Night*, 1936

154 *(Left)* John Buckland-Wright: copper-plate engraving from *Cupid's Pastime*, 1935

155 *(Below)* George Buday: *Venus*. Wood-engraving for *The Vigil of Venus* (tr. Lewis Gielgud), London 1952

156 *(Overleaf)* Eric Scott: *Adam and Eve*, 1980. 185×121cm. Nicholas Treadwell Galleries, London

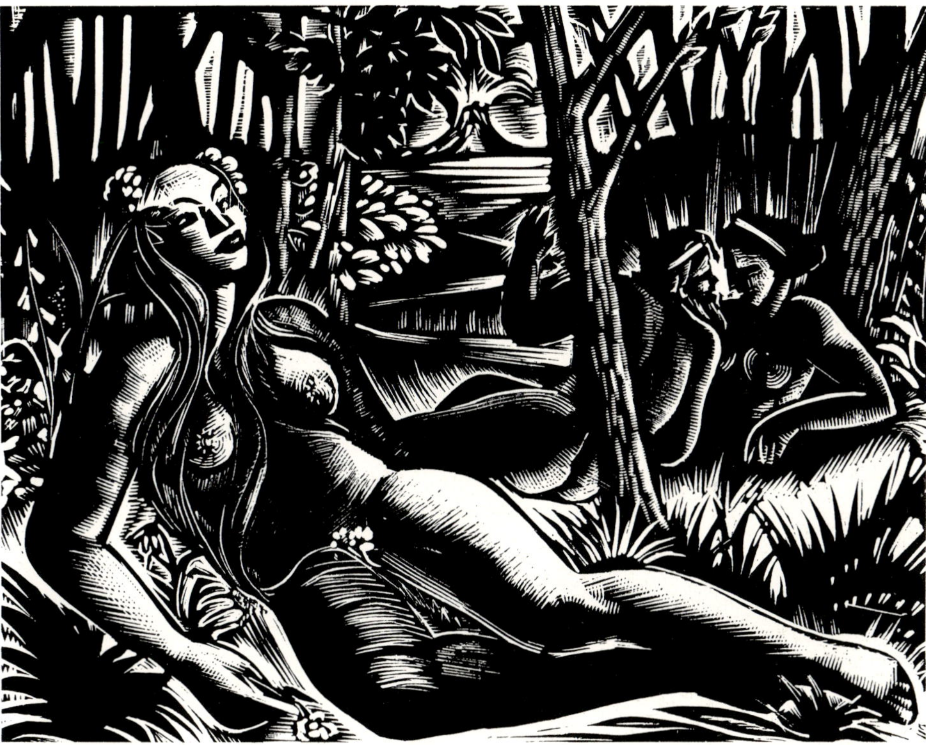

Our Lady has bidden the world go breeding
To learn love's pleasure and know love's pain,
Tomorrow be lovers who ever were lovers
And they that were lovers be lovers again.

William Fulljames (b. 1939) was a painter and sculptor for about ten years before he moved to Ibiza in 1972, and he has been a wood-engraver ever since. He has a penchant for depicting nude girls on Mediterranean beaches whom he frequently contrasts with old Spanish fishermen. *The Bite* and *Bear Hug* (Plates 157 and 136) are two powerfully erotic wood-engravings which demonstrate the dramatic power of the medium in a masterly way.

Hilary Paynter (b. 1943) is one of the notable group of wood-engravers who trained under Gerry Tucker at the Portsmouth College of Art, Hampshire. Her meticulously etched wood-engravings cover a wide variety of subjects from delicate flower pictures, landscapes or great trees to lovingly detailed pictures of old buildings. *In the Afternoon*, which is treated with the

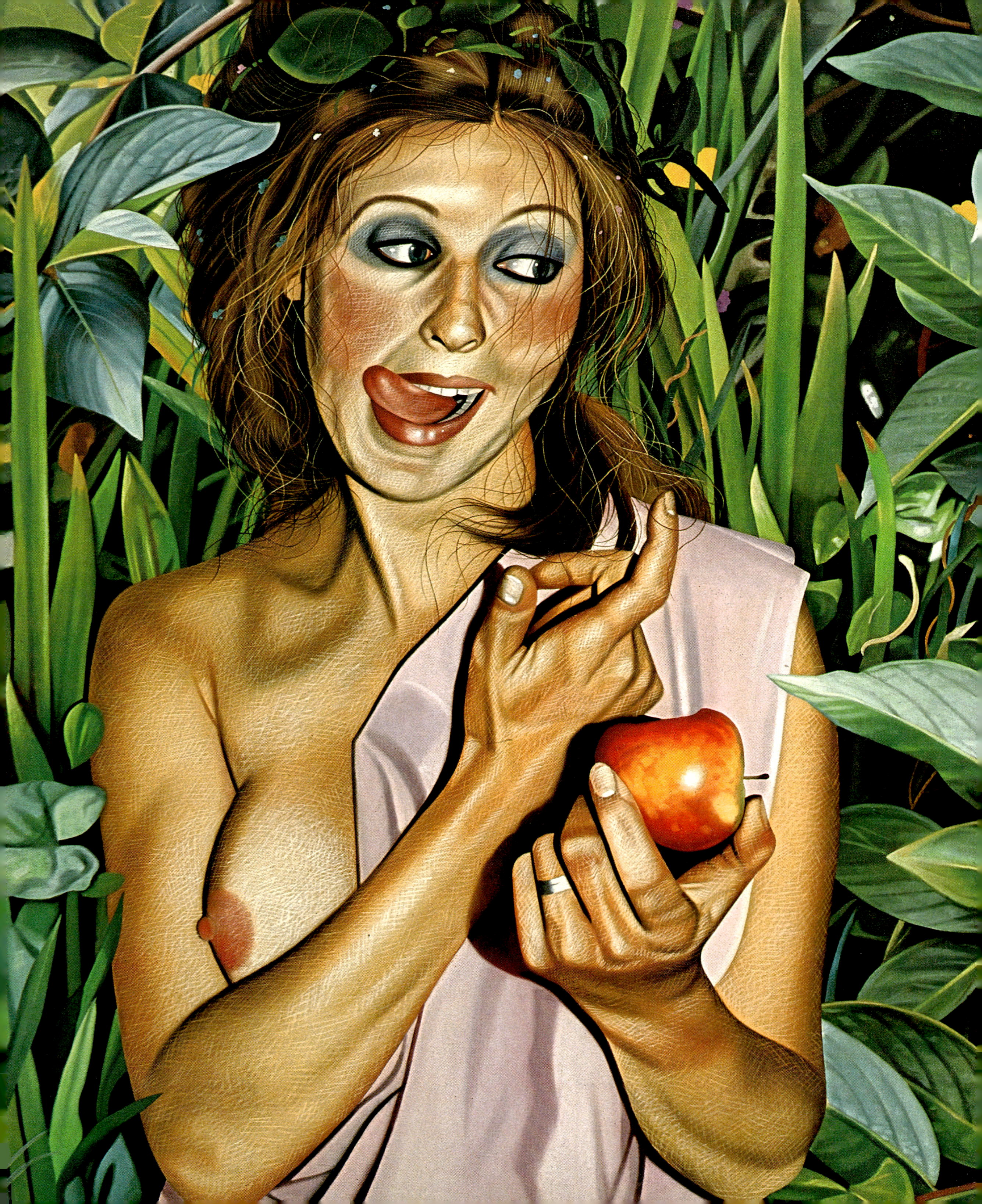

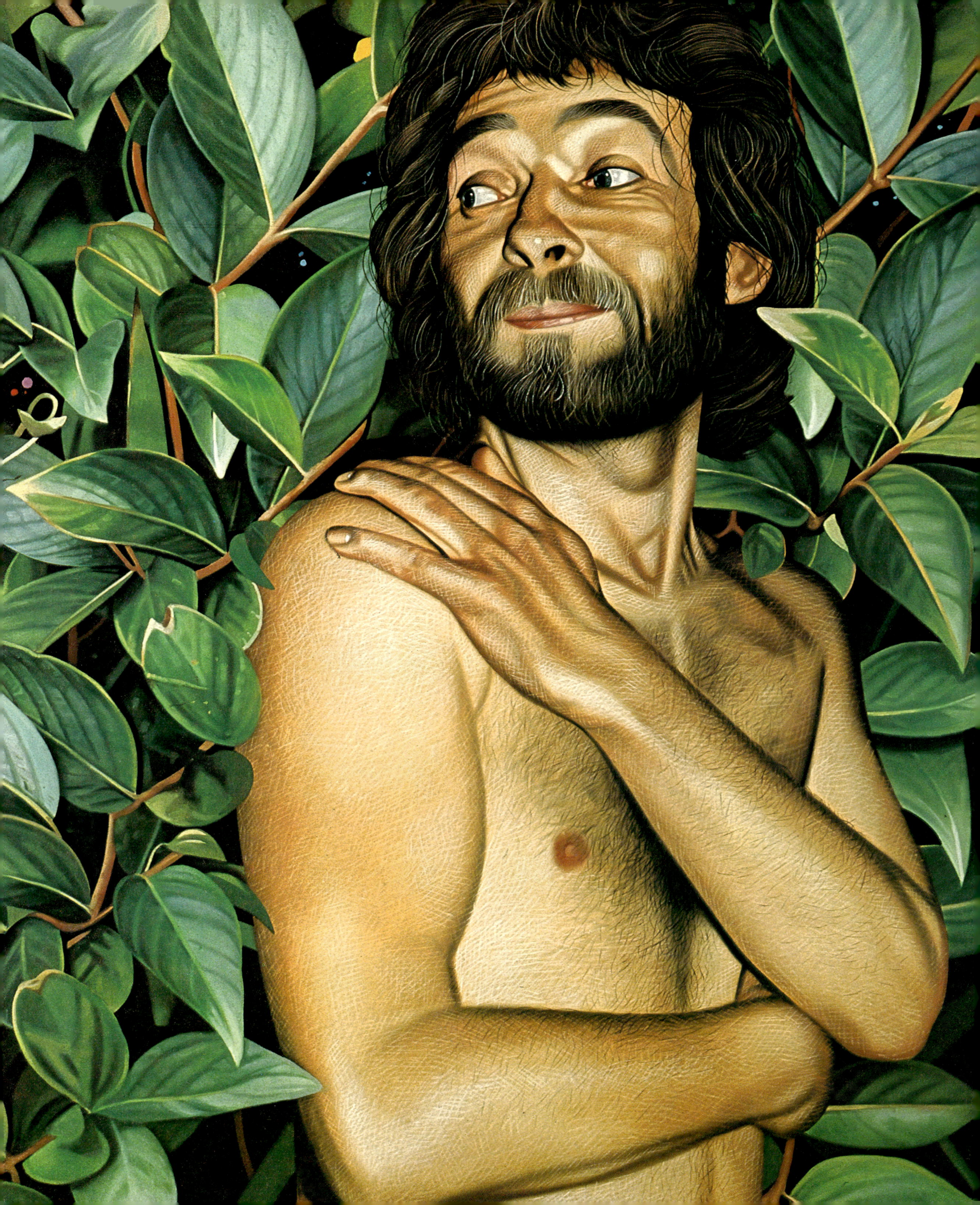

157 William Fulljames: *The Bite*, 1980. Wood-engraving, 16×11.5cm

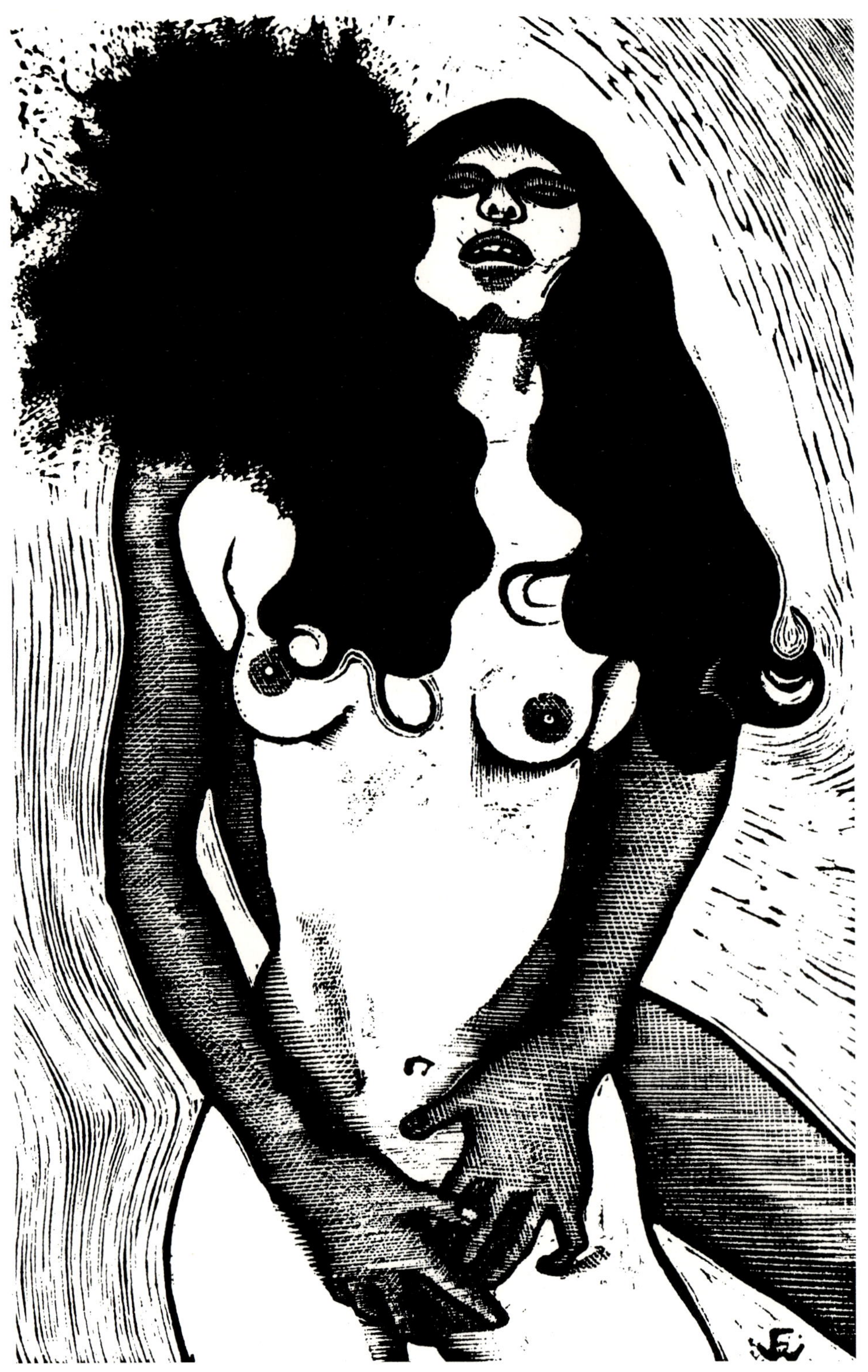

158 Hilary Paynter: *In the Afternoon*, 1981. Wood-engraving, 7.5×12cm

same meticulous detail, is a brilliantly contrived and explicitly erotic picture.

Salvador Dali (b. 1904) abandoned Cubism to become a Surrealist. He was a fine painter and draughtsman and often displayed an ingenious and imaginative sexual symbolism, but, while an ideal artist for those who could appreciate the subtlety of his works his pictures were generally too intellectual to be erotic for the ordinary viewer. However, an untitled drawing demonstrates his more obvious erotic talent, which showed itself in his informal pencil sketches.

Hans Bellmer (1902-75) was an artist who restricted himself entirely to erotic themes. In a lengthy interview, detailed by Peter Webb, he

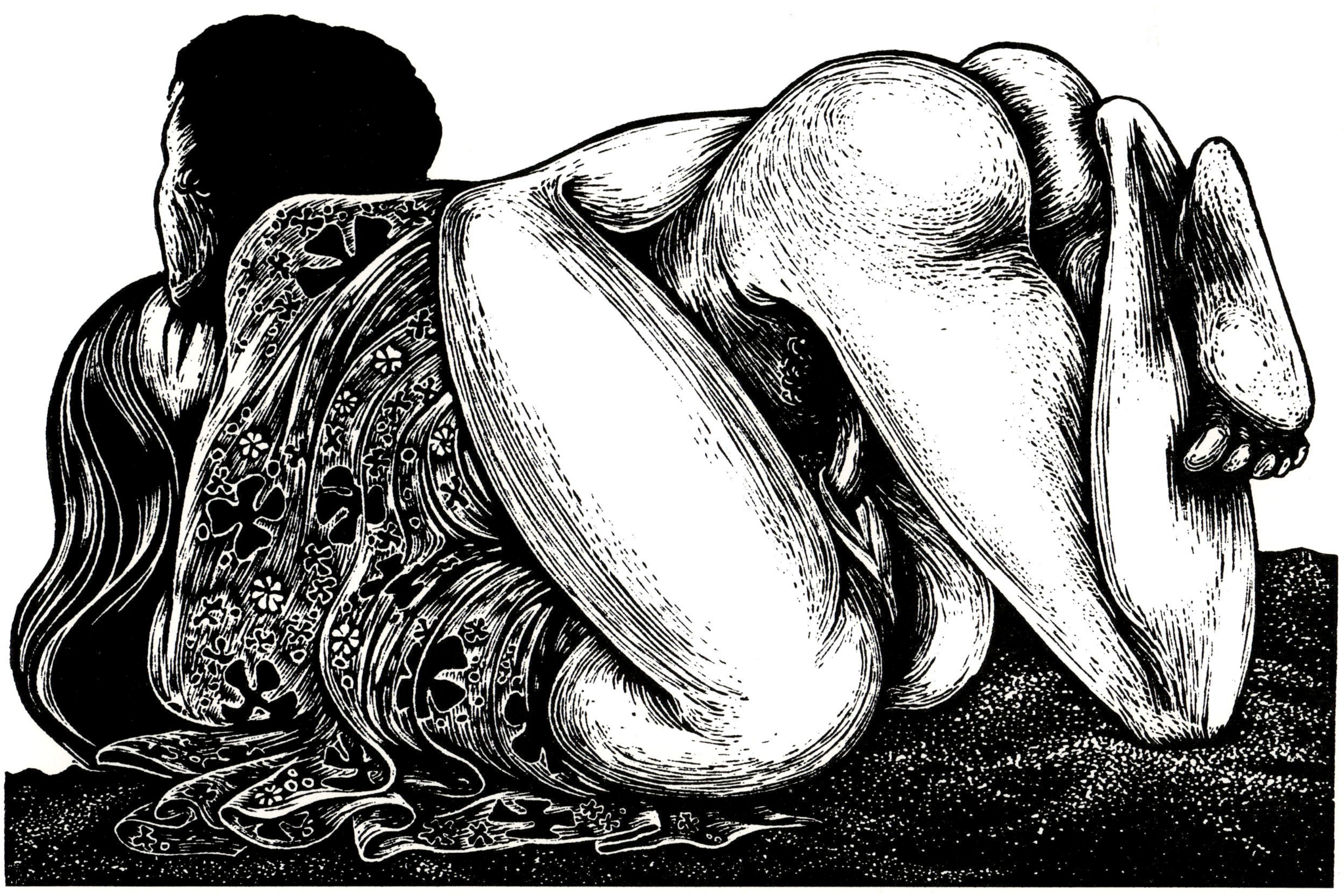

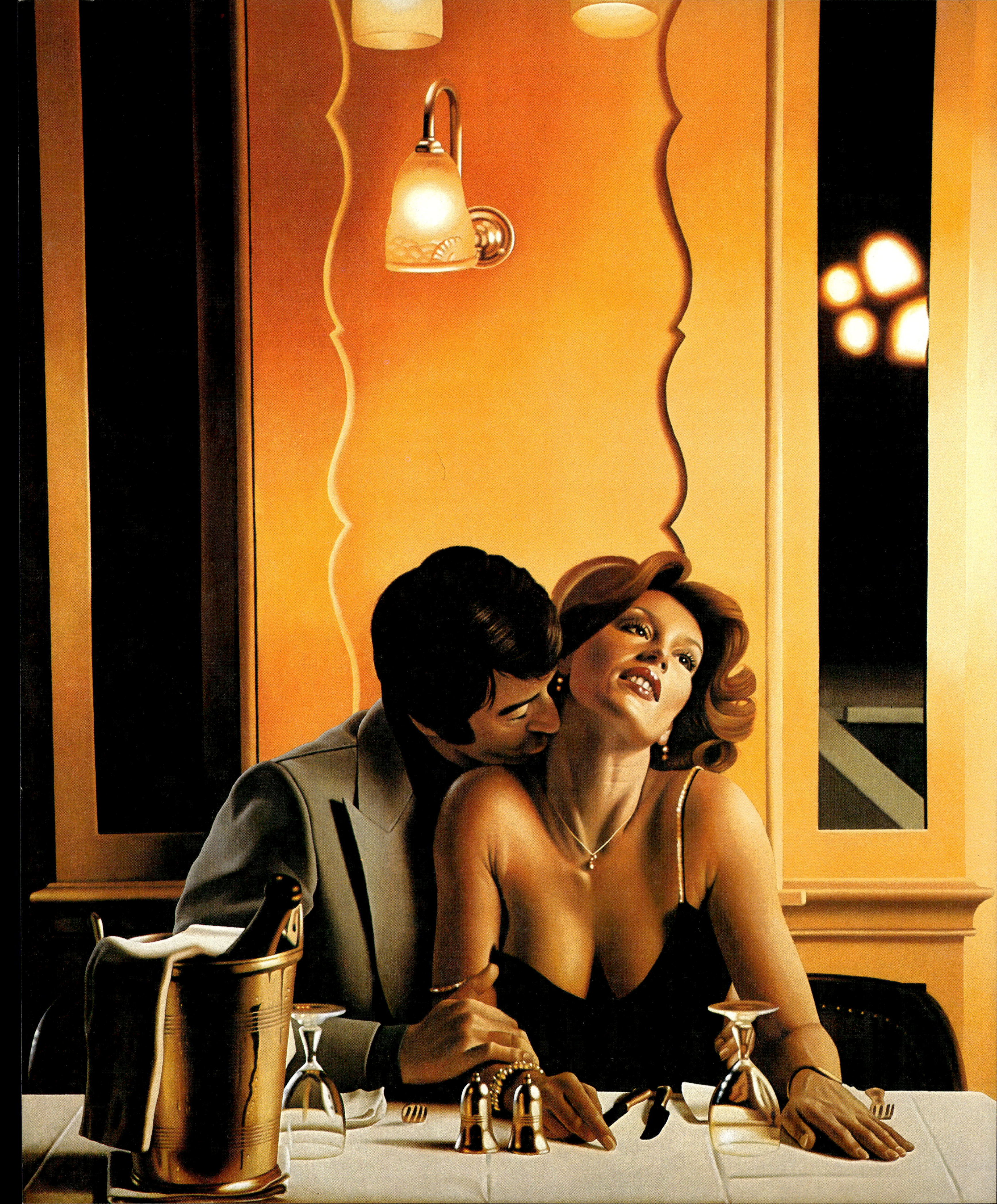

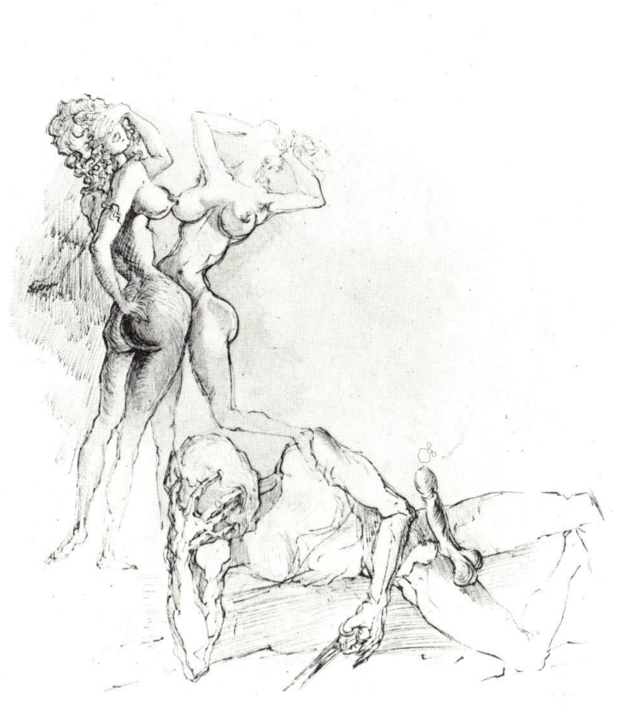

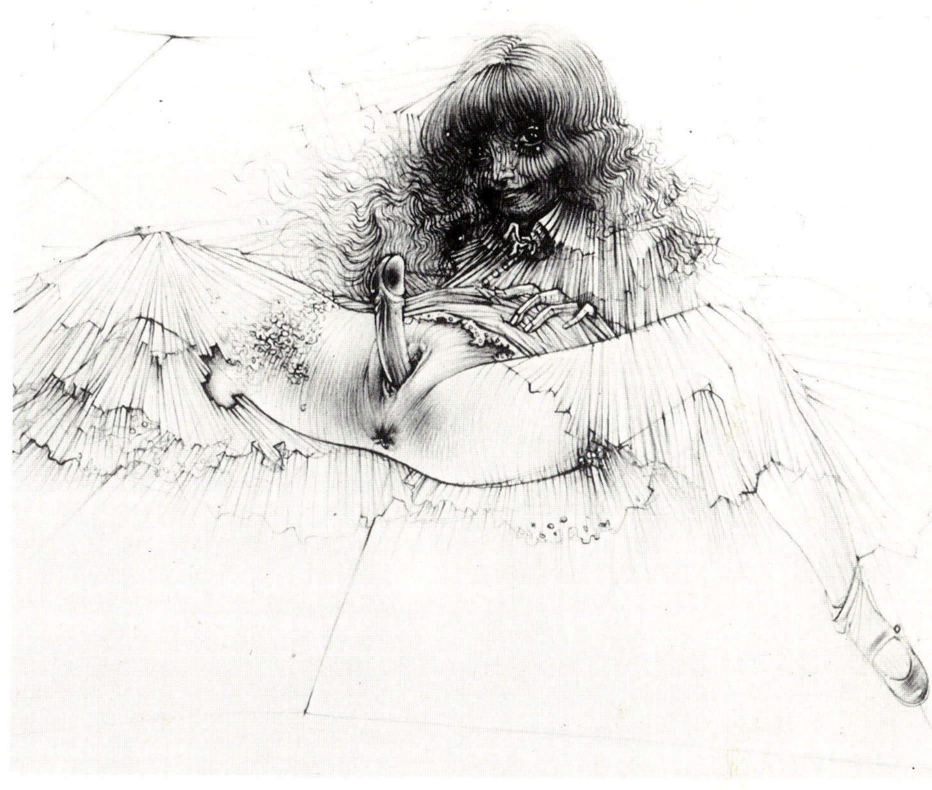

159 *(Left)* Paul Roberts: *Hors d'oeuvres*, 1977. 137×168cm. Nicholas Treadwell Galleries, London

160 *(Above)* Salvador Dali: untitled drawing. Pen and ink, 26×19cm

161 Hans Bellmer: untitled drawing. Private collection

stated, 'All my work is erotic – it always has been . . .' In the course of a long life he used a variety of means of expression. In the Sixties, however, he had developed a linear style with which he rearranged the anatomy of the female body and created semi-surrealist designs. An untitled drawing shows a typical, fantastic result. As with other surrealist works, however, the eroticism is diminished by the fact that the picture is so far divorced from reality.

George Grosz (1893-1959) had a naturally independent mind, and while serving in the German Army during the First World War was court-martialled for insubordination and came near to being shot. After the war he joined the German Dada group, who were politically motivated and strove to attack the social order they felt had been responsible for the war and its suffering. His satirical art resulted in fines for insulting the Army, for immorality and for blasphemy. In the 1920s Grosz shocked public opinion when he depicted the sexual underworld used by some of the staid middle classes. Many of his

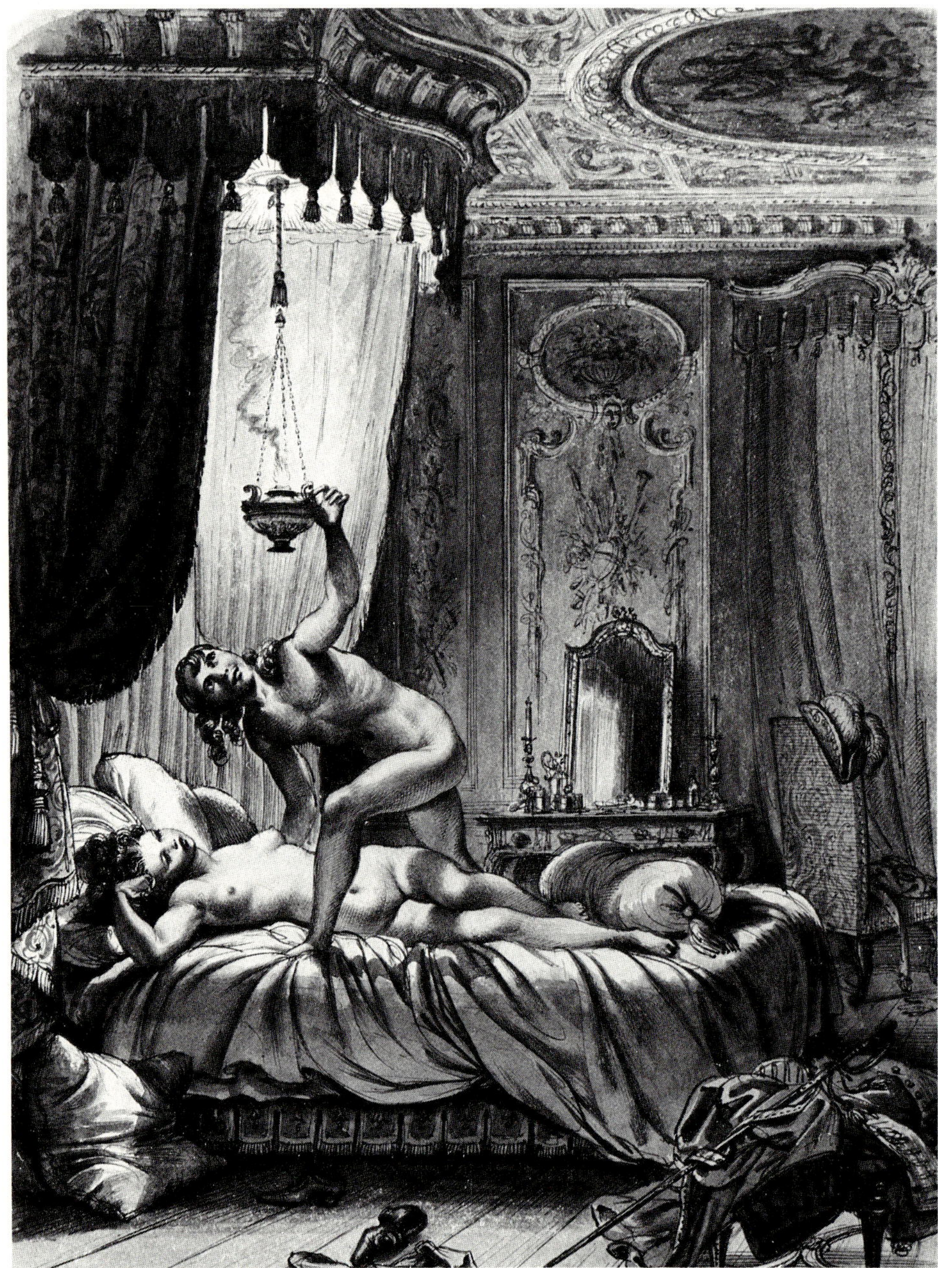

162 Rex Whistler: *Turning out the Light*, sepia illustration to A.E.W. Mason's *Königsmark*, 1940-1. 33.7×25.4cm. Tate Gallery, London

pictures had explicit sexual themes and Plate 142 is said to include a self-portrait of the artist.

Rex Whistler (1905-44) was well known for his illustrations to children's books, using a variety of techniques. Although he is not usually thought of as an erotic artist, this type of subject was well within his range. *Turning out the Light* is one of his illustrations to *Königsmark* by A.E.W. Mason.

Another skilled book illustrator was the Belgian artist Viset. The untitled etching is one of his boisterous and frequently humorous illustrations, reminiscent of Rops. It was produced in 1927 for a republished, limited edition of Théophile Gautier's Rabelaisian anecdotes, *Lettres à la Présidente*, which was originally published in

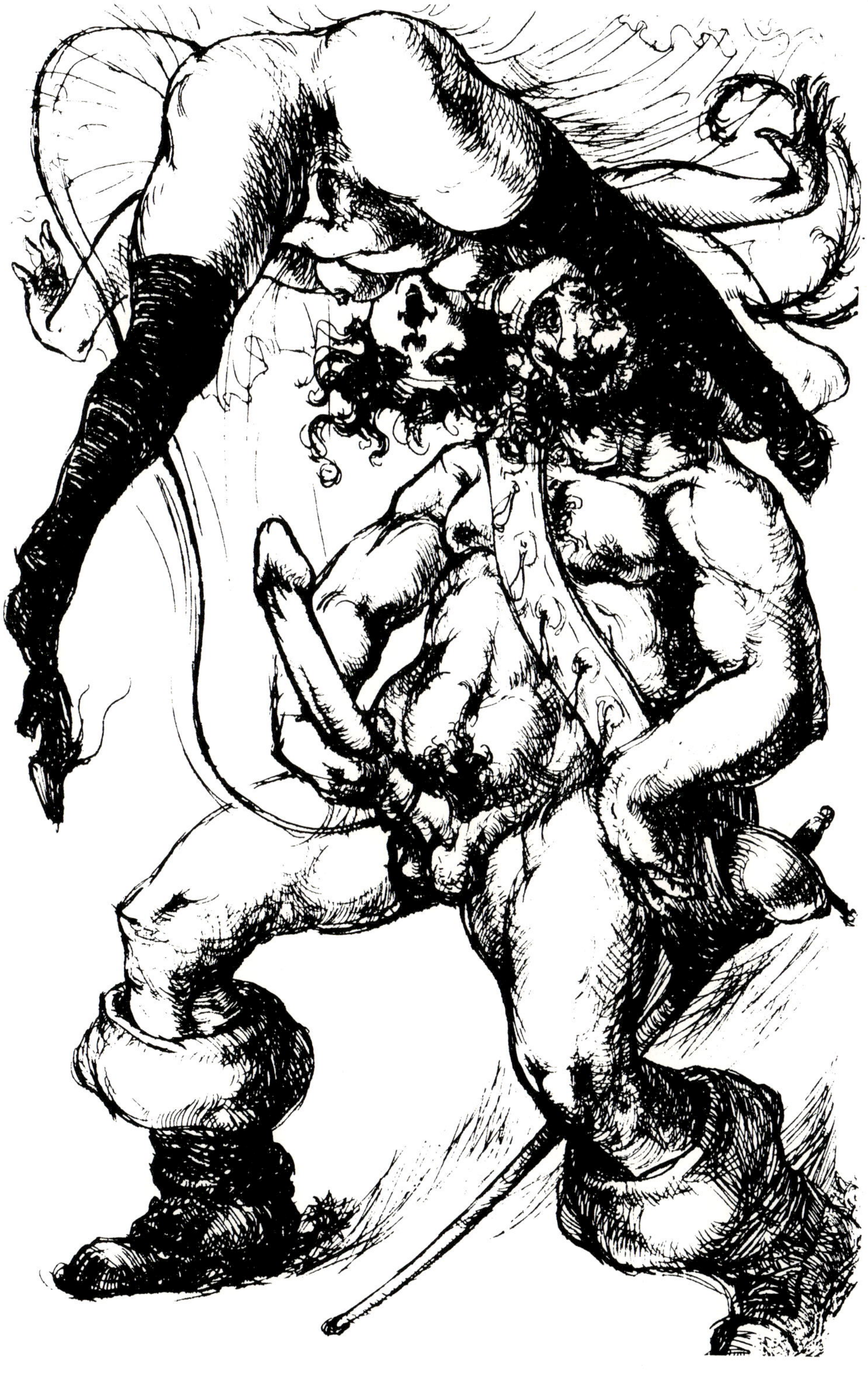

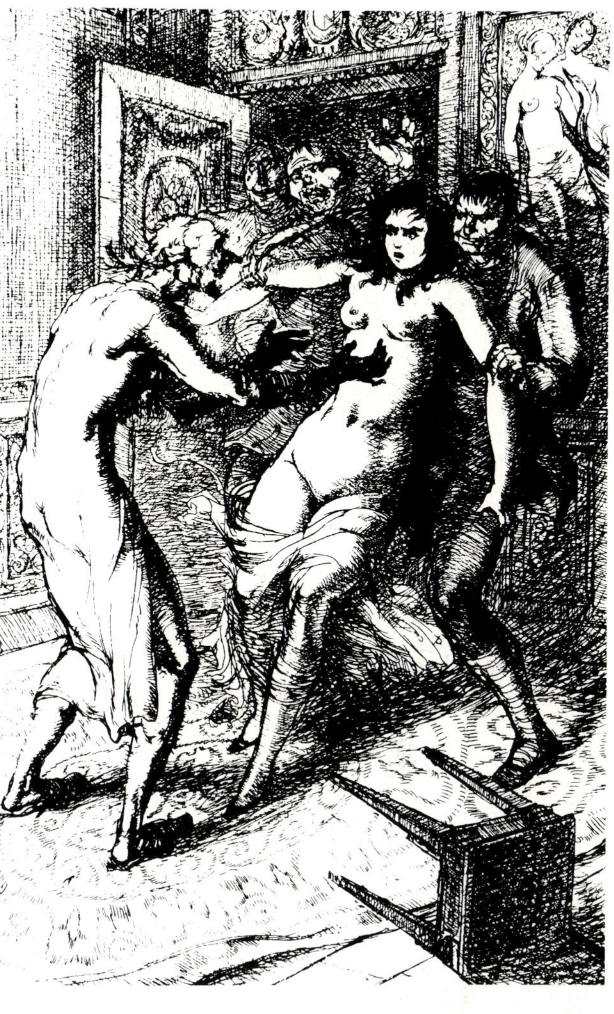

163 *(Left)* Viset: untitled etching for Théophile Gautier's *Lettres à la Présidente*, 1927

164 *(Above)* Viset: *Come hither, my dear.* Engraving for the Marquis de Sade's *Léonore et Clémentine ou les Tartuffes de l'Inquisition*, Paris 1930

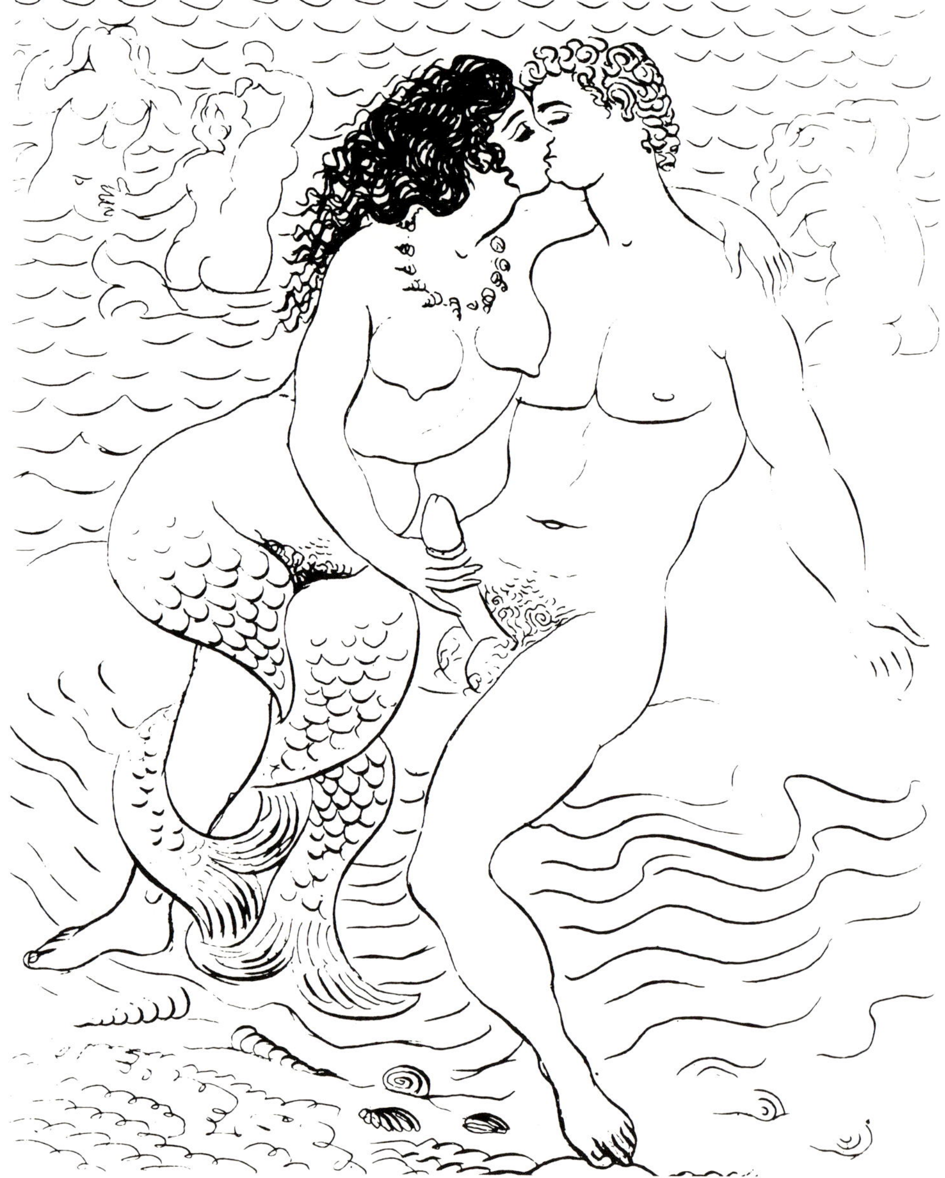

165 Demetrius Galanis: frontispiece for Alfred Jarry's *Les Silènes*. Engraving, c.1930

1850. Plates 36, 44 and 164 are from an edition of *Léonore et Clémentine* by de Sade, similarly republished in 1930. These demonstrate not only his skill but also the variety of drama which he imparted into each picture. Demetrius Galanis made a number of erotic prints and book illustrations in the Twenties and Thirties, including a frontispiece to *Les Silènes* by Alfred Jarry. The artist has wisely provided both participants with a leg as well as a tail.

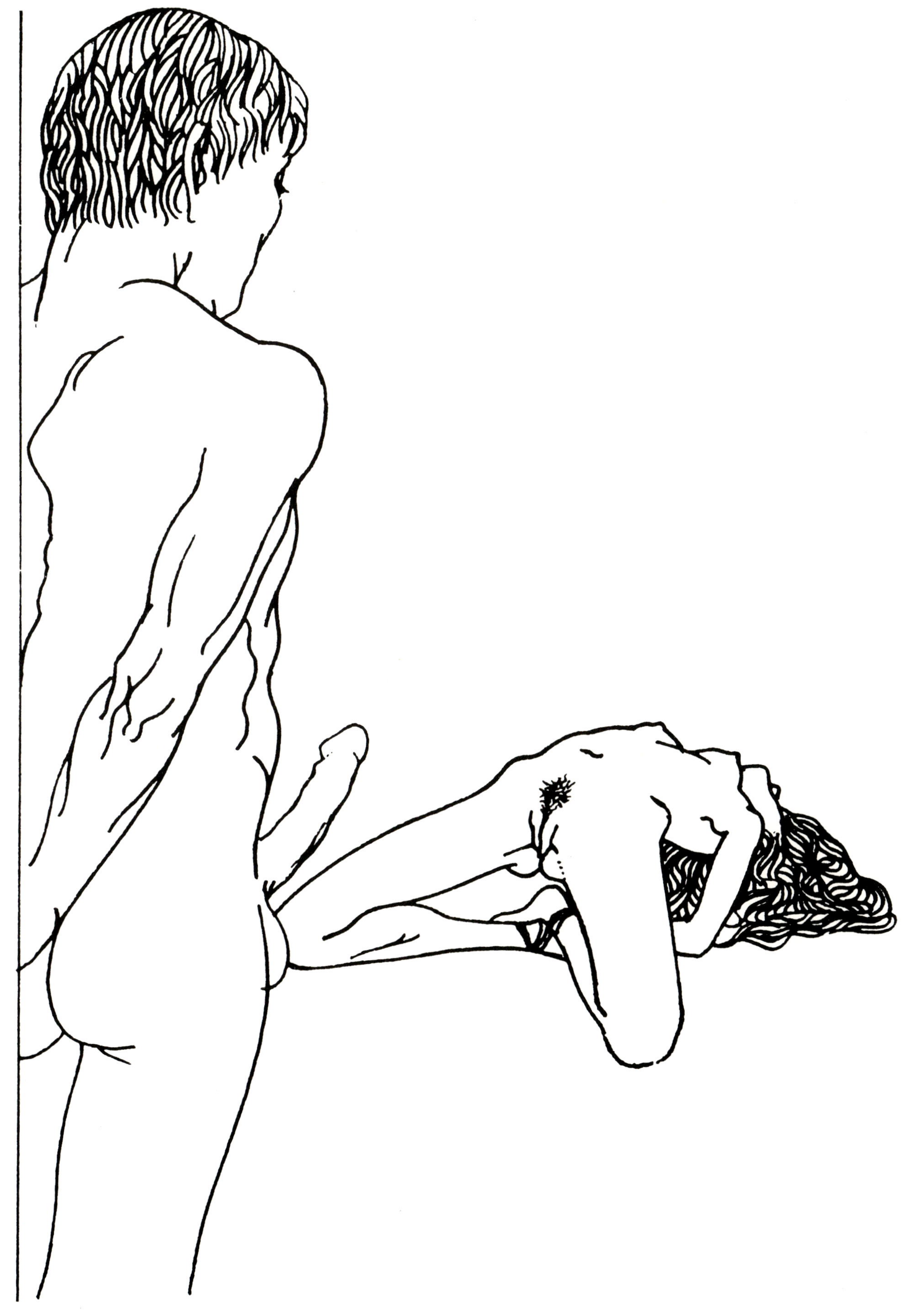

166 Krepinsky: untitled illustration to F. von Schiegel's *Erotische Sonette*, 1969

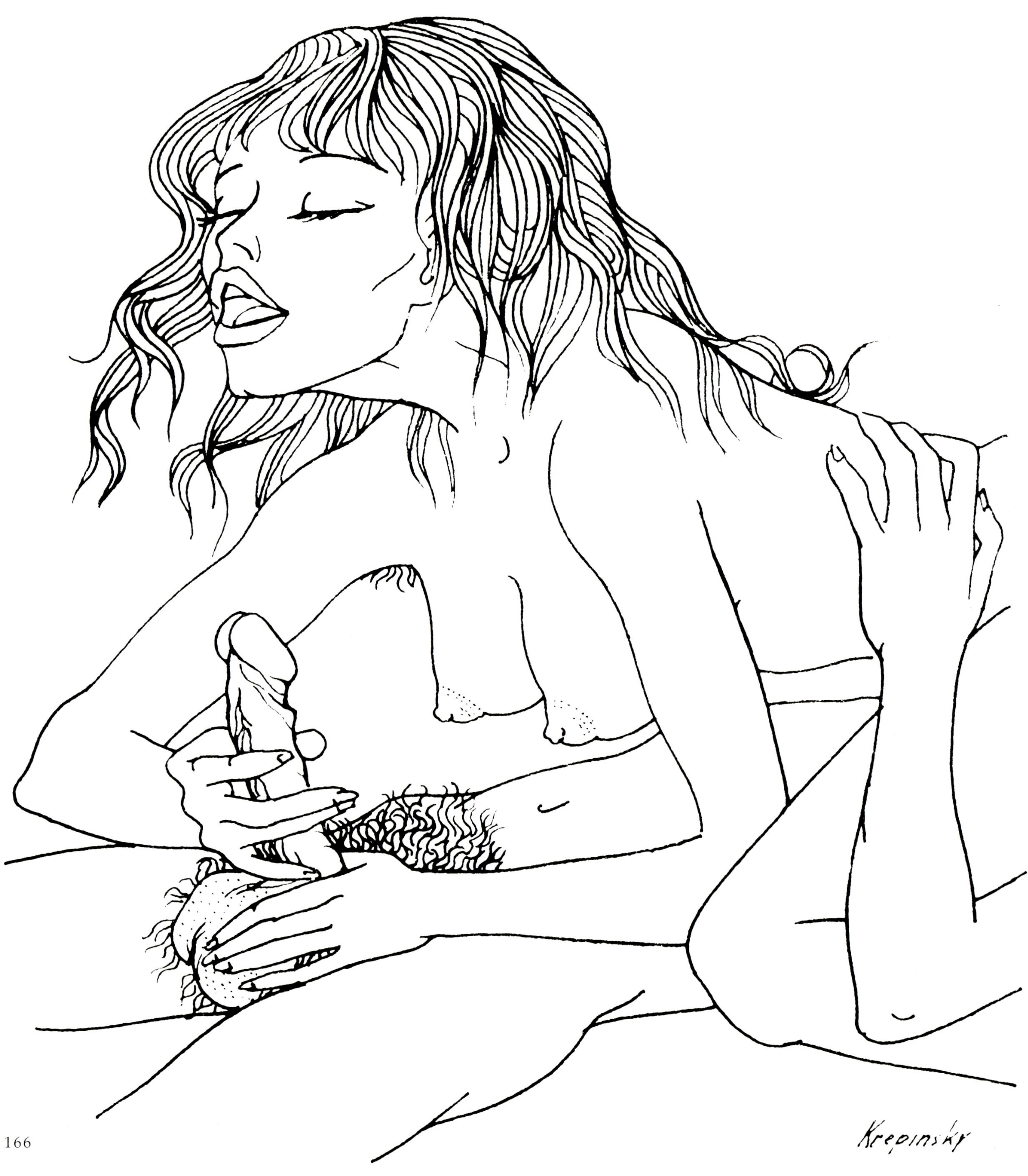
Krepinsky

167 Krepinsky: untitled illustration to F. von Schiegel's *Erotische Sonette*, 1969

During the Thirties France was the pre-eminent source of clandestine erotic books, usually anonymously illustrated. These were often produced in small editions. *Nègre en Chemise* (Plate 146), by an anonymous artist, is an example from the rare *Menu Galant*, limited to only one hundred copies. The name of each picture, with its accompanying text, was the title of a famous dish. *Odelette* (Plate 147), attributed to Collot, is from a unique book with pen and wash illustrations and a hand-written text which was produced about 1930. Titled *Choix d'Oeuvres*, it contains a series of erotic poems by famous authors. This one illustrates the poem *Odelette* by Ronsard:

Even though I may have a headpiece
As white as though crowned by lilies
While you have a clear, young complexion
Like the bud of a beautiful rose

One cannot escape the fact
That I have a head of white hair
But if I've signs of age at the top
Down below I've a stem that rises quite boldly!

Do not be taken aback and recoil
For to make something beautiful with flowers
– a delightful bouquet with a lily –
One should always surround it with roses!

Plate 151 is an illustration from the 1939 edition, of 99 copies, of *L'Ecole des Biches*. It was probably written by an Englishman, Frederick Hankey, and was originally published in Paris in 1863. It is written in dialogue form and concerns three heterosexual young women who decide, during the temporary absence of men friends, to experiment with a dildo which they can wear. While not unpleased by their experiment they conclude that they still prefer the real thing! A small edition of 16 of Aretino's *Sonnets Luxurieux (Sonetti lussoriosi*, see Chapter Three), illustrated by engravings, was published in 1948 (Plates 56 and 57).

Vladimar Krepinsky, born in Prague in 1917, is a modern artist well known for his portraits and other work in major cities all over Europe

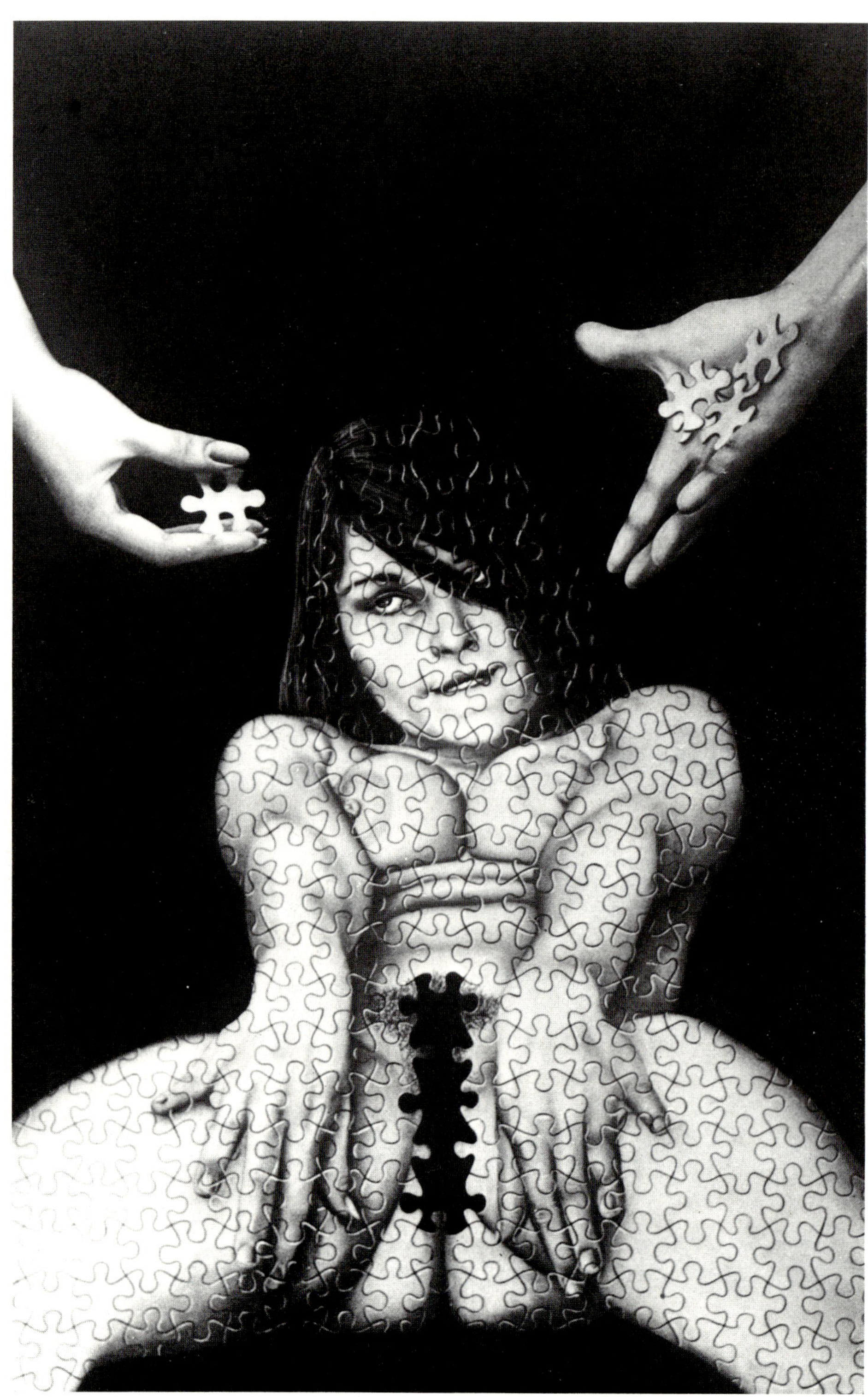

168 John Holmes: *Make me an offer.* Wax and crayon, 1971. Nicholas Treadwell Galleries, London

169 Betty Dodson: *Making Love,* pencil drawing. Private collection

and in North America. His power as an erotic artist is undeniable. He produced illustrations for the book *Erotische Sonette* by Friedrich von Schiegel, which was published in a limited edition at Hanau, Germany, in 1969.

The spread of knowledge about sexual matters and the corresponding changes in attitudes have occurred so quickly in the last half-century that the wisdom of how to make use of the new ideas has lagged behind. Many misconceptions of the past have been swept

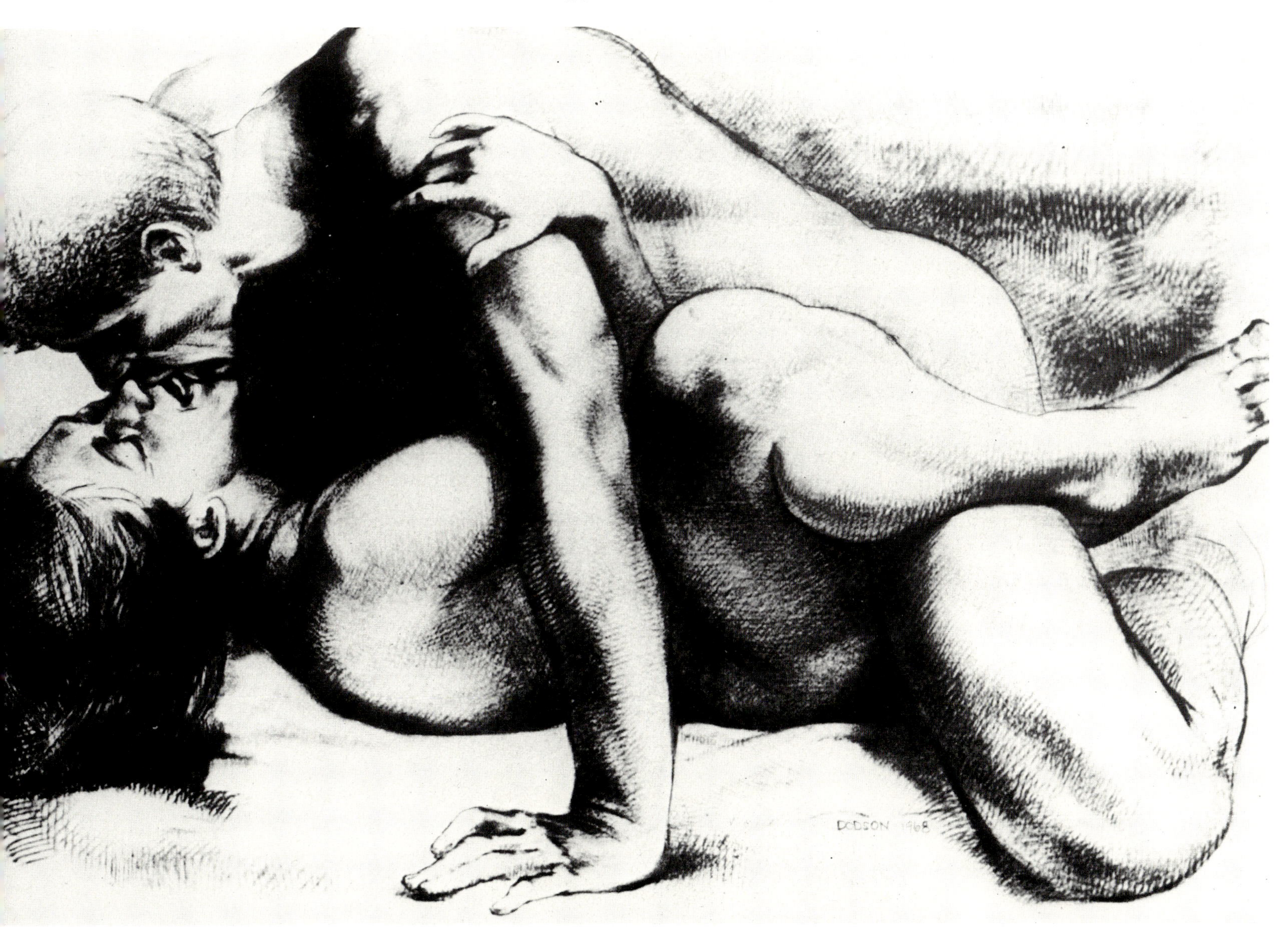

away, but while effective birth control, easy divorce, acceptance of the one-parent family and tolerance of the unmarried co-habiting couple have eased some problems, they have created others.

As censorship eased in the Sixties, artists responded by making more explicit pictures of sex organs, only to find that nudity can quickly pall and cease to be erotic. Others, like Betty Dodson in the United States, succeeded in making fine drawings of intercourse, such as *Making Love*. As time went on increasing ingenuity was displayed and, for example, John Holmes (b.1935) in *Make me an Offer* makes clever use of a jig-saw puzzle.

The last twenty years have seen artistic fashion turn full circle and realism is back again. *Woman Washing* by Celestino Valenti (b. 1943) uses sensitive pencil drawing to express the feel and texture of a woman's body. The development of skilled techniques enables today's artists to express the character and emotions of the people they depict, and this has allowed the development of a new humanism comparable with that of Cranach and Jan Steen.

Early Morning Tease (Plate 152) by Mike Francis (b.1938) uses detail and composition to produce subtle eroticism from a morning breakfast scene. *Hors d'Oeuvres* (Plate 159) by Paul Roberts (b. 1948) tells a story of two people, their relationship and their intentions, and *Adam and Eve* (Plate 156) by Eric Scott (b. 1938), in a relaxed style of light-hearted humour, may well be the most erotic picture of the subject ever painted.

With artists such as these, Western erotic art of today has nothing to fear from comparison with anything in the past and the signs augur well for the future.

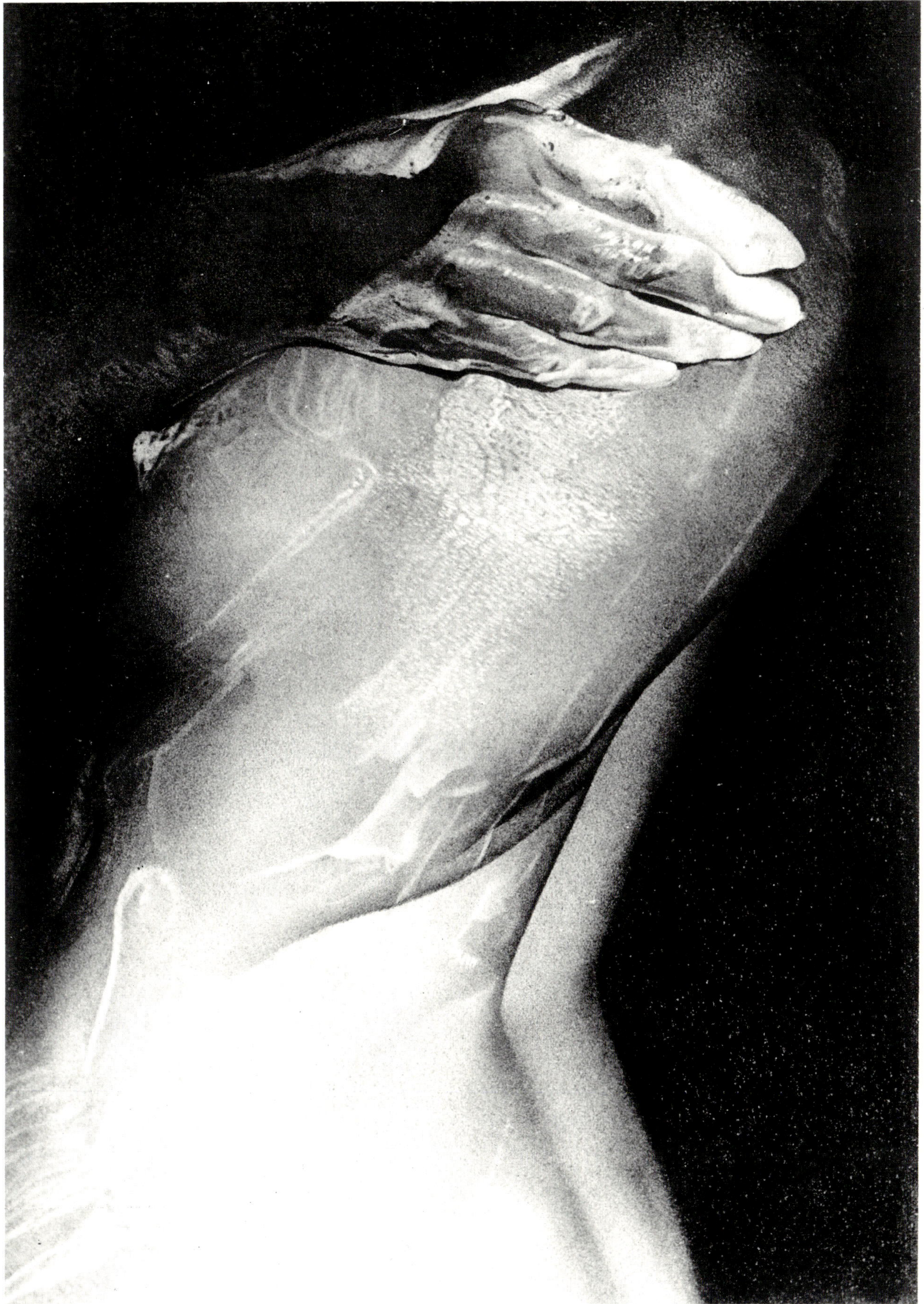

170 Celestino Valenti: *Woman Washing*, 1970. Pencil drawing, 14×29cm. Nicholas Treadwell Galleries, London

Bibliography

ADAMS, Henry, *Mont Saint Michel and Chartres*, London 1980
ARWAS, Victor, *Félicien Rops*, London 1972
BAYROS, Franz von, *The Amorous Drawings of the Marquis von Bayros*, USA 1968
BOGGS, Jean Sutherland, et al., *Picasso and Man*, exhibition, Toronto and Montreal 1964
BOUCHER, No.39 in *The Masters* series, Bristol 1966
BOWIE, Theodore (ed.), *Studies in Erotic Art*, USA 1970
BRIDGEMAN, Harriet, *Erotic Antiques*, Lyle 1974
BRIGGS, Asa, *A Social History of England*, London 1983
BRUSENDORFF, Ove and HENNINGSEN, Poul, *Love's Picture Book* (Vols. I, II, III), New York 1969
BRUYN, Lucy de, *Woman and the Devil in Sixteenth-Century Literature*, Wiltshire 1979
BURFORD, E.J., *Bawds and Lodgings*, London 1976
BURKE, Joseph and CALDWELL, Colin, *Hogarth*, London 1968
CARTLAND, Barbara, *Book of Love and Lovers*, London 1978
CLARK, Kenneth, *Feminine Beauty*, London 1980
CLARK, Kenneth, *The Nude*, London 1956
CLARK, Kenneth, *Rembrandt and the Italian Renaissance*, London 1966
CLARKE, Desmond, *Louison*, Belfast 1979
DANIEL, Howard, *Devils, Monsters and Nightmares*, London 1964
DURUY, Victor, *The World of Legendary Greece*, Geneva 1975
Eros in Antiquity, USA n.d.
FORD, Clellan S. and BEACH, Frank A., *Patterns of Sexual Behaviour*, London 1952
FUSELI, Tate Gallery Exhibition Catalogue, London 1975
GARRETT, A., *British Wood Engraving of the 20th Century*, London 1980
GERHARD, Poul, *Pornography or Art?*, London 1971
GILL, Eric, *The Engraved Work of Eric Gill*, Victoria and Albert Museum, London 1963
GOMBRICH, E.H., *The Story of Art*, London 1950 (13th edn 1978)
GOULD, Cecil, *Titian*, Feltham (Middx) 1969
GRAVES, Robert, *The Greek Myths*, Vols. 1 and 2, London 1955
HALL, William Harlan, *The World of Rodin 1840-1917*, USA 1969
HENDY, Philip, *The National Gallery of London*, 1955
HENRIQUES, Fernando, *Stews and Strumpets*, London 1961
HUNT, Morton M., *The Natural History of Love*, New York 1959

JOHNS, Catherine, *Sex or Symbol*, London 1982
JONG, Erica, *Witches*, London 1982
KEARNEY, Patrick J., *A History of Erotic Literature*, London 1982
KIEFER, Otto, *Sexual Life in Ancient Rome*, London 1934
KRONHAUSEN, Drs Phyllis and Eberhard, *Erotic Art* Vols. 1 and 2, New York 1978
LARKIN, David (ed.), *Temptation*, London 1975
LEVY, Mervyn, *The Moons of Paradise*, London 1962
LEWIS, John, *The Twentieth-Century Book*, London 1967
LEYMARIE, Jean, *Picasso, Metamorphoses et Unité*, Geneva 1971
LUCIE-SMITH, Edward, *Eroticism in Western Art*, London 1972
MARCADE, Jean, *Eros Kalos: Essay on Erotic Elements in Greek Art*, Geneva 1962
MARCADE, Jean, *Roma Amor: Essay on Erotic Elements in Etruscan and Roman Art*, Geneva 1965
MARTINEAU, J. and HOPE, C. (eds.), *The Genius of Venice 1500-1600*, London 1983
MASSA, Aldo, *The World of the Etruscans*, Geneva 1973
MATT, Leonard von, *Ancient Roman Sculpture*, London 1960
MAY, Geoffrey, *Social Control of Sex Expression*, London 1931
MEIER, Kurt von, *The Forbidden Erotica of Thomas Rowlandson, 1756-1827*, USA 1970
MELVILLE, Robert, *Erotic Art of the West*, New York 1973
MOUNTFIELD, David, *Greek and Roman Erotica*, Fribourg 1982
MURRAY, P. and L., *A Dictionary of Art and Artists*, London 1959
MYERS, Bernard L., *Goya*, London 1968
PEARSALL, Ronald, *The Worm in the Bud*, London 1969
Picasso's Erotic Pictures, New York 1969
RAGGHIANTI, Carlo R., *The National Gallery, London*, 'Great Museums of the World', London 1970
RAYNAL, Maurice, *Modern Painting*, Geneva 1960
READ, Herbert, *A Concise History of Modern Painting*, London 1959
READE, Brian, *Beardsley*, London 1967
SMITH, Bradley, *Erotic Art of the Masters*, USA n.d.
STRONG, Donald E., *The Classical World*, London 1965
VERGO, Peter, *Art in Vienna 1898-1918*, London 1975
YOUNG, Wayland, *Eros Denied*, London 1964
ZIGROSSER, Carl, *Prints and their Creators*, USA 1937

Acknowledgements

The author and John Calmann and Cooper Ltd would like to thank those who have supplied photographic material. The following is a list of photographic credits for material not obtained directly from museums and collectors. Some collectors wish to remain anonymous.

HARRY N. ABRAMS INC., New York: 43
AEROFILMS LTD, Boreham Wood: 29
BILDARCHIV PREUSSISCHER KULTURBESITZ, Berlin: 14; 33
BY COURTESY OF BOSWORTH BOOKS, Leicestershire, England: 41; 56; 57; 107; 135; 146; 147; 151; 163; 166; 167
BRADLEY SMITH, GEMINI SMITH INC., La Jolla, California: 111; 142
THE BRIDGEMAN ART LIBRARY, London: 114
BY PERMISSION OF THE TRUSTEES OF THE BRITISH LIBRARY, London: 84; 85; 86; 115; 122; 123; 124; 125; 134
BY PERMISSION OF THE TRUSTEES OF THE BRITISH MUSEUM, London: 8; 15; 35; 40; 48; 49; 50; 51; 52; 53; 54; 55; 58; 59; 64; 92; 102; 141
J.E. BULLOZ, Paris: 70
MAURICE CHUZEVILLE, Hauts de Seine: 3
ALAIN DANVERS, Bordeaux: 130
C.M. DIXON, PHOTORESOURCES, Canterbury: 5
GIRAUDON, Paris: 38; 83
ARCHIVIO FOTOGRAFICO I.G.D.A., Milan: 61
HARTWIG KOPPERMAN, Munich: 17
ANTONIA MULAS, Milan: 7; 10; 11; 16; 18; 26; 27
MUSÉES NATIONAUX, Paris: 12; 21; 25; 97; 112
OREGON PRESS, London: 165
PHAIDON PRESS LTD, Oxford: 139
SCALA, Florence: 1; 13; 20; 31; 34; 45; 65; 67; 72; 79; 96; 103
S.P.A.D.E.M., 1984: 1; 144
WIM SWAAN, London: 37
LEONARD VON MATT, Buochs, Switzerland: 23
REPRODUCED BY PERMISSION OF THE TRUSTEES, THE WALLACE COLLECTION, London: 98
PUBLICATIONS DEPARTMENT, WALKER ART GALLERY, Liverpool: 113; 126
WEIDENFELD AND NICOLSON ARCHIVES, London: 60; 62; 71; 80; 127; 160; 161
GALERIE WELZ, Salzburg: 137

Index